Service Business Model Innovation in Healthcare and Hospital Management

Mario A. Pfannstiel • Christoph Rasche
Editors

Service Business Model Innovation in Healthcare and Hospital Management

Models, Strategies, Tools

Springer

Editors
Mario A. Pfannstiel
Hochschule Neu-Ulm
University of Applied Sciences
Neu-Ulm, Germany

Christoph Rasche
University of Potsdam
Potsdam, Germany

ISBN 978-3-319-46411-4 ISBN 978-3-319-46412-1 (eBook)
DOI 10.1007/978-3-319-46412-1

Library of Congress Control Number: 2016960759

Printed on acid-free paper

This Springer imprint is published by Springer Nature
The registered company is Springer International Publishing AG
The registered company address is: Gewerbestrasse 11, 6330 Cham, Switzerland

Preface

The articles in this anthology provide examples of service-oriented business models in health and hospital management. They enlarge upon the drivers, strategies and tools to seize opportunities for analysing, modelling and implementing groundbreaking business models. In turn, they act as a basis for our classification while ensuring the success of and safeguarding the existence of service organisations in the health market. In the final analysis, the only guarantee of sustainable success is achieved in the case of co-aligning the interests of customers, business partners and one's own organisation. Value creating healthcare ecosystems decisively depend on the coordination of multiple internal and external stakeholders by means of a network governance.

On the one hand, it is not only necessary to revise already existing business models and foster the emergence of new ones, which can be either complementary and supportive or disruptive. Critically reflecting the entrenched orthodoxies in health care prevents the incumbents from becoming self-complacent and path dependent with respect to legacy models to be replaced by service model innovations.

On the other hand, service organisations can only survive in increasingly disruptive health markets if they deliberately let patients and cases evolve into customers and clients displaying desires, needs and preferences.

Furthermore, to keep the competition at bay, it is important to create truly distinctive products, services and benefit bundles to gain a sustainable competitive advantage over competitors by means of being cheaper, better, different or disruptive.

One way to do so is combining the components of one business model in new and different ways or through designing new business model modules. That means that differentiation can be accomplished by creating and establishing unique business model components (such as services) to enhance overall value from the viewpoint of the customer, client or patient.

Of course, it is necessary to keep customers aware of the uniqueness of a service, which is somehow difficult in the case of trust-based healthcare services, since they resist clear-cut validation and measurement with respect to process qualities or outcomes. Nevertheless, successful business models in health care boost customer loyalty, enhance customer benefit and may contribute to a competitive cost structure of service organisations with respect to the automations and digitalisation options.

This is why decision-makers in service organisations need a strategy to systematically come up with business models for profitably positioning themselves on the market while augmenting the value of their service organisations in the healthcare industry. Hospitals compete on efficiency and effectiveness on the one hand and are challenged to pre-empt the future by means of business model innovation and disruptive services.

They have to place a good amount of their bets on disruptive models to be braced for prospective customer, technology and therapy challenges, which may endanger the status quo of rejected or neglected. Confirming and continuing established healthcare doctrines contributes to unproductive path dependencies in health care that forestall the opportunities of radical paradigm shifts towards 4.0 applications.

Adopting the perspective of radical business model innovation, groundbreaking business models serve as the stepping stones for next-generation innovations challenging hitherto accepted wisdoms of doing business in health care. The art of business model management lies in change leadership to master the present efficiently while pre-empting the future by means of innovation, creativity and disruptive initiatives.

In order to be poised for the future, service organisations should address the following questions, which in sum resemble a 'stress test' to assure the organisational resilience and agility:

- Which (disruptive) combinations of services can be offered as outstanding customer solutions beyond standard operation procedures or best practices?
- How can healthcare organisations and hospital add substantial value to their core business or augment the latter by means of business development, portfolio restructuring or competence-based diversification?
- How can expert organisations be transformed into patient-centred service organisation for the purpose of perceived end user satisfaction?
- How can hospitals manage the transition from functional professional organisations to integrated healthcare providers resembling a hub with outgoing service spokes?
- How to design and implement user-driven service value chains considering the patient as a cornerstone of co-value creation?
- What are the appropriate steps to overcome hospital legacies, core rigidities and constraints by means of entrepreneurial zest and service model redesign?

Hospitals and healthcare providers increasingly compete for overarching business models instead of narrowing their lenses to single end services, therapies or dedicated outcomes. Additionally, many service organisations prefer the exploration of 'blue oceans' to defending 'red oceans'.

Rule-breaking breakthrough ideas have to be analysed against the state-of-the-art service-oriented businesses incorporating past commitment and legacies. We make the point that conventional management wisdom clings to a methodology which performs greatly when it comes to rationalisation, rationing and prioritisation. But business model innovation goes far beyond the 'lean and mean' debate because it challenges the architecture of value generation in the healthcare sector. Interdependencies, interfaces and interacting value partners are the ingredients of service model innovation, which could either harness the power of scale economies, automation and uncompromising lean imperatives or emphasise elite positioning by means of rocket science innovation. No frills as well as many frills can be options for business models to gain and sustain competitive advantages.

Radical business models should cast an open eye on the overall risk which can be dissected into sub-risk dimensions such as market risks, technology, risks, social risks or financial risks. A risk-taking attitude is endemic for front runners that want to stand out from the crowd through exceptional market offers and benefit bundles. Business model coherence amounts to a dynamic balance between a flurry of internal and external destabilising factors which may cause derailment of service delivery.

Service-oriented business models are anything but blueprints, since they must incorporate a governance model having concrete objectives, steps and customer benefit in its track. In the final case of implementation, they represent lived realities and powerhouses of value creation.

In any event, there is one thing that pioneering business models can achieve: they can reach new target groups. After all, it is only by meshing efforts with the customer that constitutes the key to successfully developing progressive business models. It is not the resources but the strategy that decides on the success of cutting-edge business models. This is the reason why no service organisation taps the full potential of innovative business models. The changing environment of organisations has an impact on existing business models, which is why it contributes an element of innovative business models (refer to Fig. 1).

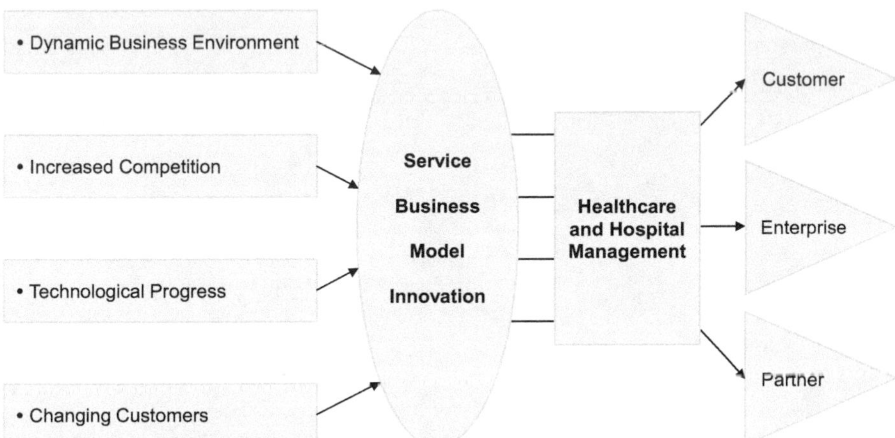

Fig. 1 Service business model innovation in healthcare and hospital management. Source: Own illustration (2016)

The contributions of the authors in this anthology are structured in the following fashion: contribution title, summary, introduction, main part, conclusion, bibliography and biography. Furthermore, each author sums up his or her explanations and insights in the article for a summary at the end of the article.

We would like to thank the numerous authors of this anthology who brought a wide array of fascinating issues from practical experience and engrossing science topics into our anthology. Finally, we want to extend our warmest gratitude to Ms. Balaraman, Mr. Naren and Dr. Glaeser at this point who contributed his ideas to support us in compiling the layout of this anthology and put the whole book with the chapter together.

Neu-Ulm, Germany
Potsdam, Germany
2016

Mario A. Pfannstiel
Christoph Rasche

Contents

Editors

About the Editors

Mario A. Pfannstiel is a researcher and lecturer in the field of hospital and healthcare management and Assistant to the Dean at the University of Applied Sciences Neu-Ulm. He holds a diploma from the University of Applied Sciences Nordhausen in the field of social management with the major subject finance management, an MSc degree from the Dresden International University in patient management and an MA degree from the Technical University of Kaiserslautern and the University of Witten/Herdecke in health care and social facilities management. He worked as executive assistant to the medical director in the Heart Centre Leipzig in Germany. At the University of Bayreuth, he worked as Research Associate at the Department of Strategic Management and Organization in the Joint Research Project 'Service4Health'. His current research interests focus on Service Management, Digitalisation of Services and Service Business Model Innovation.

Christoph Rasche heads the chair of professional and corporate services at the University of Potsdam. He adopted visiting professorships at the Universities of Innsbruck, Alcalá de Henares as well as the Hochschule Osnabrück. He teaches strategic and general management in national and international MBA programmes with special respect to subjects connected with the healthcare and hospital industry. Formerly, he consulted with Droege International AG and was co-founder of Stratvanguard and the General Management Institute Potsdam. Prof. Rasche's research subjects circle around the field of strategic and general management in the healthcare and hospital sector, which witnesses an era of professional value creation by means of a strong management and leadership focus. Practically, he consults with healthcare players and is actively involved in executive trainings—ranging from corporate universities to MBA and PhD programmes for healthcare professionals.

Contributors

Patricia E. Alafaireet University of Missouri, Columbia, MO, USA

Niowi Amgwerd Hirslanden AG, Zürich, Switzerland

Andrea Appolloni Department of Management and Law, University Tor Vergata, Rome, Rome, Italy

Daniele Binci Department of Management and Law, University Tor Vergata, Rome, Rome, Italy

Steve Boßelmann Department of Computer Science, TU Dortmund, Dortmund, Germany

Jennifer Bohn Arlington, VA, USA

Lesley A. Clack Armstrong State University, Savannah, GA, USA

Mark Compton St Luke's Care, Potts Point, NSW, Australia

Giacomo Copani National Research Council of Italy (CNR), Institute of Industrial Technologies and Automation (ITIA), Milan, Italy

Leonel Corona-Treviño Facultad de Economía UNAM, CEPCyT, Mexico City, Mexico

Martin Dietrich Faculty of Law and Economics, Saarland University, Saarbrücken, Germany

Sören Eichhorst McKinsey & Co., Cologne, Germany

Austin English RCF Associates, Charlottesville, VA, USA

Barry D. Floyd Orfalea College of Business, California Polytechnic State University, San Luis Obispo, CA, USA

Guy Ford Management Education, The University of Sydney, Darlington, NSW, Australia

Brenda Gleason Arlington, VA, USA

Harri Haapasalo Industrial Engineering and Management, University of Oulu, Oulu, Finland

Florian Hilfinger Faculty of Law and Economics, Saarland University, Saarbrücken, Germany

Howard Houghton Department of Psychiatry, University of Missouri, Columbia, MO, USA

Sean Jackson University of Virginia, Charlottesville, VA, USA

Seppo Kuula Industrial Engineering and Management, Siili Solutions Oyj, University of Oulu, Helsinki, Finland

Anna-Lena Lamprecht CSIS and Lero, The Irish Software Research Centre, University of Limerick, Limerick, Ireland

Daniel Liedtke Hirslanden AG, Zürich, Switzerland

Karl Liese McKinsey & Co., Cologne, Germany

Constanza Márquez-Aguilar Facultad de Economía UNAM, CEPCyT, Mexico City, Mexico

Manuel Möller McKinsey & Co., Frankfurt, Germany

Tiziana Margaria CSIS and Lero, The Irish Software Research Centre, University of Limerick (Ireland), Limerick, Ireland

Dietmar Mauer Hirslanden AG, Zürich, Switzerland

Graham Millett MGSM, North Ryde, NSW, Australia

Stefan Moder McKinsey & Co., Munich, Germany

Stephan Pahls Hirslanden AG, Zürich, Switzerland

Gabriele Palozzi Department of Management and Law, University Tor Vergata, Rome, Rome, Italy

Golboo Pourabdollahian National Research Council of Italy (CNR), Institute of Industrial Technologies and Automation (ITIA), Milan, Italy

Christoph Rasche Universität Potsdam, Humanwissenschaftliche, Potsdam, Germany

Donald Stevenson Gist Learning, Charlottesville, VA, USA

Alex Tzortzis Johnson & Johnson Medical, North Ryde, NSW, Australia

Elliott N. Weiss The Darden School, University of Virginia, Charlottesville, VA, USA

Christian Westerhoff Hirslanden AG, Zürich, Switzerland

Alexander Wickert Institute for Computer Science, University of Potsdam, Potsdam, Germany

Ole Wiesinger Hirslanden AG, Zürich, Switzerland

Service Model Innovation in Hospitals: Beyond Expert Organizations

Christoph Rasche, Tiziana Margaria, and Barry D. Floyd

Abstract

Service model innovations take on added significance in the hospital sector, facing disruptive shifts and sweeping changes. While in the past decades hospital management focused on rationalization, rationing and prioritization efforts from the viewpoint of expert organizations, the latter are challenged to become patient centered service organizations. Clinics must go beyond cost dumping and operational excellence (lean, mean, clean) to be braced for the age of digital convergence. In this article we sketch-out, why hospitals should also define service from the patient's perspective and why smart and client focused hospitals might get in trouble with safety, security, surveillance and supervision imperatives, since zero risk sometimes comes at the cost of zero convenience. Service model innovations serve as means to make both ends meet.

C. Rasche (✉)
Universität Potsdam, Humanwissenschaftliche, Sportökonomie, Weinbergstraße 38, 14469 Potsdam, Germany
e-mail: rasche@stratvanguard.de

T. Margaria
CSIS and Lero, The Irish Software Research Centre, University of Limerick (Ireland), Tierney Building, Limerick V94 T9PX, Ireland
e-mail: tiziana.margaria@lero.ie

B.D. Floyd
Orfalea College of Business, California Polytechnic State University, San Luis Obispo, CA 93405, USA
e-mail: bfloyd@calpoly.edu

M.A. Pfannstiel, C. Rasche (eds.), *Service Business Model Innovation in Healthcare and Hospital Management*, DOI 10.1007/978-3-319-46412-1_1

1 The Next Competitive Battle in Healthcare: The Innovation Imperative

Hospitals increasingly evolve into economic entities facing severe competition alongside multiple dimensions. While in the past two decades efficiency and cost reduction ranked high on the management agenda, hospital leaders increasingly acknowledge that they cannot shrink to greatness and strategic prosperity (Rasche and Braun von Reinersdorff 2015, 2016). Moreover, value generation in the healthcare and hospital sector stems from an outcome and a cost dimension (Porter 2010). The latter can be measured easily in contrast to the value dimension which incorporates many issues and provides leeway for interpretation. Costs and investments underlie a concrete monetary logic and thus serves as the bedrock for radical red-alert turnaround decisions. Cost dumping, law dumping and tax dumping are crucial management steps when it comes to the short-term achievement of measurable results in the hospital sector. Statistics illustrate that a vast number of German hospitals will face bankruptcy in due course, if no fundamental restructuring takes place (Braun von Reinersdorff and Rasche 2014).

Unfortunately many hospital managers confuse restructuring with myopic cost slashing and piecemeal efficiency gains through intramural process improvements or the digitalization of standard operation procedures. In a similar vein, overhead costs, redundant activities and slack resources are popular targets of hospital reorganization consultants for the sake of value creation. Adopting an overarching portfolio perspective, the managerial eagerness for cost savings allows hospitals to enter the sphere of mergers and acquisitions since many hospital managers sell, close, or merge value destroying departments or clinics. If turnaround strategies fail, board members often resort to M & A deals or watch-out for private equity stakes for the purpose of better results by means of asset exploitation and better HR-productivity. While competition for lowest costs, highest efficiency, perceived quality and accelerated processes may lead to 'lean and mean' hospitals, many clinic managers only focus on speeding up the same treadmill. But 'more of the same' or 'try harder' imperatives cannot substitute for disruptive business model innovations (Osterwalder and Pigneur 2011; Hogan et al. 2012; Christensen et al. 2013; Williamson 2010). These managers reject entrenched healthcare wisdoms and path dependent routines which may forestall mind boggling perspectives on how to create value in a truly sustainable way—beyond lean and mean (see also Porter and Kramer 2011). So let's envision a hospital scenario that is not only cost, but also outcome focused, because value creation relates to costs as well as performance items (Rasche et al. 2010).

The vast bulk of the hospitals perform on the well-known key success factors which reflect the perspective of healthcare specialists, instead of adopting the viewpoint of the patient. These professionals feel deeply committed to the key success factors of their 'community of interest' and are thus inclined to treat patients as cases, rather than as clients or customers to be served. Until now most of the hospitals are good at expert treatment while neglecting the sphere of patient centeredness (Hogan et al. 2011). To turn full circle, expert centeredness revolves around the 'black box' of healing, treating, and prescribing from the point of view of a patient who often lacks critical insight into the complex therapy mix. Most of the 'hospital business models' reflect an inside-out value chain which is hierarchical as well as specialty focused. Doctors, nurses, support staff, and clinic management may perform well as stand-alone experts, but often do not form inter-professional centers of treatment excellence—let alone service and patient centeredness. To make things worse, a main cause of value destruction lies in hospital governance systems which honor technical innovations, but do not challenge the options and opportunities for business model innovations (see also Rasche et al. 2010). Given IT led revolutions such as virtual service dispatch, telemedicine, big data and artificial intelligence, combined with inflating patients' wants and the demographic shift—altogether defining a new competitive landscape—hospitals will have to choose between 'leaner and meaner', 'better', 'different', or 'disruptive'. For sure, the four options are not mutually exclusive but call for different capability sets (Rasche 2013; Frey and Osborne 2013).

We should plea for a balanced paradigm shift from 'lean and mean' to 'different or disruptive', because lessons learned from other industries convey a vivid picture of rule breaking companies which resist solid benchmarking against the 'best of breed'. It is their strategic intent not only to design the products and services of tomorrow, but to create unique and disruptive business models (Müller and Rasche 2013; Schmidt 2015). Business examples abound where entrenched players such as Kodak Eastman or Nokia fell into oblivion because they competed on technologies and platforms and not on user driven business models to serve market desires. It goes without saying that hospital business model innovators cannot be compared with business model innovators from the airline or the Technology, Information, Media and Electronics (TIME) industries, but this is no excuse for protecting and buffering the orthodoxies of caregiving and medical treatment. Despite the regulative straightjacket of political healthcare administrations, hospitals are challenged to rethink the relevance of service innovation as well as the role of experts when celebrating their skills and experiences. The latter will only unfold their usefulness within the context of holistic service models. Hospitals as typical expert organizations (Rasche and Braun von Reinersdorff 2016) are required to watch out for innovative ways of value creation by means of becoming:

Lean and mean: This option includes all activities related to resource and competence exploitation to avoid idle capacities and unproductive assets. Hospitals undergo a process of liposuction through fat cutting as a means of last resort. Lean and mean can only be an ad-hoc ultima ratio option in face of bankruptcy.

Better: Solid mainstream hospitals are eager to become better through benchmarking, continuous improvement and quality assurance systems, since undue risks, defects and hampered patient safety cannot be tolerated. "Better" often means commitment to high safety and commitment to operative excellence.

Different: Beyond lean, mean and better, hospitals will have to strive for uniqueness and sustainable competitive advantages to stand out from the crowd. Hospitals compete for the brightest talents as well as patients, payers and political spheres of interest. Outstanding therapies, top-notch equipment, interdisciplinary emergency departments or empathy and courtesy can be cornerstones of differentiation.

Disruptive: Many hospitals cling to orthodox caregiving service models that are deeply rooted in an expert dominated hemisphere of preordaining, prescribing and proceeding. Disruptive means different in a path breaking way when leaving the established ecosystem. In the case of hospitals, they must seize anticipatorily the opportunities of cross-over digitalization when getting 'online' with multiple stakeholders for the purpose of real-time big data sharing, knowledge collectivization and lateral expert harvesting, and patient centered decision making. Distance based telemedicine is only one pillar of a healthcare 4.0 concept which bridges the gap between professionals and patients by means of wearable diagnostic devices, smartphones and other interlinked micro-devices. Mindful patients progressively take care of their health to enhance quality of life, assure lifetime employability and last, but not least, capitalize on own and others' human capital. Instead of calculating the losses due to illness one should control for the returns of well managed health on the individual and the collective level. For this reason hospitals must redefine their core competencies, their value propositions and the relevant markets they service to avoid the pitfalls of strategic myopia. Disruptive business models in healthcare step outside the established ecosystem and define a new one in which other institutional species will survive (Christensen et al. 2013).

2 Ten Tenets: Overcoming the RRP-Paradigm

Rationing, rationalization and prioritization (RRP) is an operational paradigm promoting 'lean and mean' as well as 'better'. RRP identifies value based steps concerning asset utilization and effective resource deployment by means of coordination, networking and IT employment. Unfortunately, RRP misses on addressing the innovation imperative since hospitals cannot thrive on operational excellence forever. Moreover, innovation issues must complement the dominant logic of zero risk, zero defects and zero standard deviation. Hospitals will not move from 'zero to hero' through clear-cut RRP measures because these measures only help to master the present. Preempting the future requires hospitals to think and act differently and disruptively to overcome legacies of age and core rigidities. In the short run RRP perfectly fits with performance improvement while in the long run transformation processes might be forestalled (Braun von Reinersdorff and Rasche 2014; Rasche and Braun von Reinersdorff 2016). Figure 1 pushes the RRP logic towards innovation by means of ten tenets, which question conventional healthcare wisdoms.

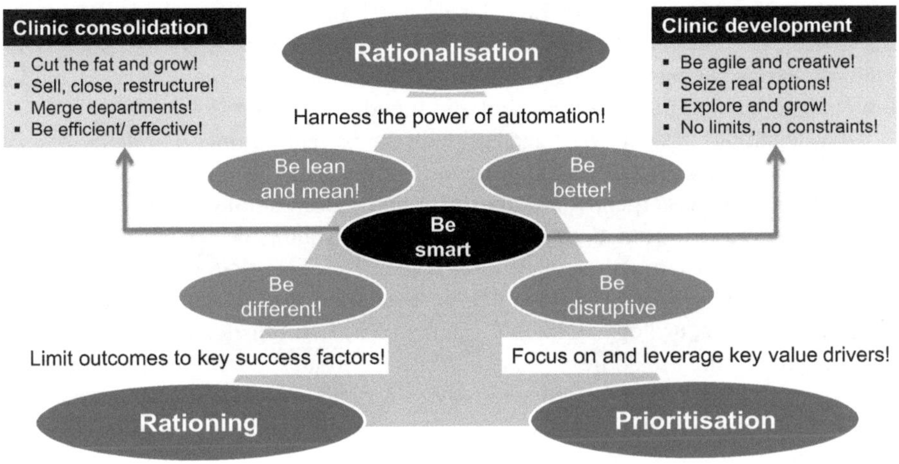

Fig. 1 Beyond the RRP-paradigm. Source: Author's own illustration (2016)

Smart hospitals are ambidextrous organizations, able to enter the red ocean arena of business consolidations as well as the blue ocean arena of business development. Performing smartly on key success factors means on the one hand professionally managing the RRP-framework, which is often straightjacketing strategic options due to economic, political, and legal imperatives. On the other hand, even hospitals underlying a tight regime of rules, regulations, and restrictions are challenged to strike the smart four options to either defend their territory (be lean and mean, be better) or to enter and occupy attractive arenas beyond the core business. Clinic development implies the exploration of new customers, therapies, services, sales channels, benefit bundles or technologies by means of business model innovation and non-trivial strategies.

The innovation imperative challenges the mindset of many expert organizations underlying rigid formal regulations and mental constraints. Physicians, accountants, professors or architects are normally intrinsically motivated and often highly committed to their expert status, which also parallels their reputational status. Highest salaries, prestigious infrastructures and generously awarded fringe benefits do not only have a material meaning, but are expressions of social climbing and hierarchy rank among ambitious professionals (Hänel et al. 2011a, b). While on the one hand expert organizations can count on their competitive professionals to pave the way towards high performance organizations, they run on the other hand the danger of emerging as 'nerd and freak organizations'. The latter organizations are internally profession and aspiration focused by resorting to a 'raising the bar policy' (i.e., up or out, grow or go) which can foster alienation from customers, colleagues, patients, competitors, and market expectations. In this context, declared innovations rather meet the criteria of inventions since experts are often beset by the 'not invented here' syndrome. Ideas, concepts or brainstorms must be reflections and outcomes of the expert's world to be accepted. Innovative impulse from outside the closed expert system are often devaluated, ignored or simply shunted aside. This kind of expert arrogance might hinder hospitals to implement service model innovations beyond medical treatment and functional nursery jobs.

Service should not only start and end with the patient but incorporate aspects of internal customer orientation. Think here of supportive medical activities such as those provided by emergency, anesthesia, radiology or pathology departments that should be assessed from a service rather than a treatment perspective (Hogan et al. 2012). Taken together, they define an internal market on which to offer services and competencies recruited from 'customer' disciplines such as cardiology, surgery, or urology. Notably managerial, administrative infrastructural services are required to address safety and security issues in a professional manner, because a hospital cannot be reduced only to functions of caregiving and medical treatment. These visible outcomes are the peaks of a service ice rock which is mostly hidden below the waterline.

In Germany, the hospital landscape witnesses sweeping changes by means of networked healthcare powerhouses which invest in market opportunities outreaching the classic clinic approach. Parenthetically, outsiders from the TIME industries such as Apple, Google, Microsoft, Cisco or Intel enter attractive healthcare segments such as the quantified-self market space or wireless, 24/7-healthcare services. What does this mean for the healthcare and hospital sector? Global ICT firms analyze, define and forecast the healthcare and hospital market in a different or even disruptive way (see also Taylor et al. 2014; Huber et al. 2015):

First, they consider patients not only as cases, but also customers who want to be smart, fit and attractive. Beyond healing, prevention, and rehabilitation, generation Y patients define themselves as well surrounded personalities displaying a lifestyle of heath and sustainability, which makes them eligible for all kinds of products and services fitting with well-being and life quality. Wearables, digital health assistants, and the quantified-self movement fall under the overall category of real time life tracking in a dawning big data era.

Second, 'healthstyles' emerge as the cornerstones of postmodern lifestyles which lead patients to pay for fitness, vitality, and well-being. Many ICT and internet giants no longer inspect the health market with respect to mobile app-solutions, but move the productivity line towards the cusp of disruptive services and underlying business models. The latter address the trend of mindfulness which incorporates the desire for a dedicated life which is under full control of the individual.

Third, opposite newcomers and disruptive healthcare innovators, municipal hospitals adopt the role of incumbents suffering from legacies of age, organizational constraints, and dysfunctional commitments. Proclaimed hospital visions often morph into piecemeal micro-changes because of political, legal, infrastructural, or mental constraints. Thus hospitals are 'healing' experts whilst 'freewheeling' innovation capacities evolve as core competence in healthcare markets. Firms like Apple and Google think the unthinkable and design cross-over service models counting on converging technologies, benefits, expectations, and lifestyles.

Fourth, blurring sectoral demarcation lines give rise to holistic, interfacing, and networked healthcare solutions that capitalize on many business constellations, such as hospital-2-patient, hospital-2-customer, hospital-2-payer or patient-2-patient, amounting to a flurry of unforeseen business opportunities. Real healthcare worlds converge with virtual big data worlds, since the next competitive battleground will be the one of tracing, profiling, inference, and prediction. Beyond business intelligence and business analytics, prospective patient treatment increasingly hinges on big data competence in pursuit of 'customized' and genetically focused therapies. The future will evidence if this is either the new domain of hospitals or for disruptive game changers exploring healthcare markets from outside.

Fifth, although not yet recognized, healthcare markets are at the verge of disruption because winds of change evolve into competitive hurricanes when it comes to cross-over innovations. The often cited Kondratieff cycles of breakthrough innovations gain insofar additional momentum as digitalization and healthcare are not only converging, but pave the way towards new service models with respect to sports, fitness and vitality. Augmented realities in sports, EMS-training as well as the myriad of animated tracking apps foreshadow a virtual, augmented, distance-based, user-driven, personalized, and somehow gamified era of health-styles.

Sixth, bear in mind that the hospital market is not foredoomed to be a local or regional one. At the moment a sweeping wave of mergers and acquisitions takes place in Germany. This process of massive industry consolidation not only pertains to hospitals, but also to outpatient care, retirement homes, and health insurance companies. On the one hand, big is beautiful with respect to scale economies and pooling effects. On the other hand, specialization is also beautiful when it comes to elective patient customers who are interested in plastic surgery, eye surgery, or orthopedic interventions. Moreover, diversification and cross-over business development is a matter of fact in healthcare. The mantra of integrated and networked healthcare can be seen as a call for converging sectoral value systems displaying hub-and-spokes logics. Mega ecosystems of healthcare might evolve in which not only players and payers play the dominant role, but also many other stakeholders—having managed care solutions or healthcare franchising in its track.

Seventh, orthodox healthcare interpretations command the patient to be become a compliant and subservient part of an evidence based treatment and therapy procedure to be endured without moaning and groaning. Bitter pills are prescribed, processes are preordained and cases and case-mix indexes have to be controlled for within the diagnostic related grouping (DRG) paradigm. But convenience and courtesy as well as touch and feel aspects should not be sniffed at or discarded, since they emerge as key success factors from the patient's point of view. Sweeping demographic changes towards geriatric societies and healthcare involved silver agers let us think of 'slow care' and process deceleration. High-speed and fast track interventions appropriate to the age span of 18–25 years may fail when dogmatically applied to the causes and symptoms of poly-morbidity. Age-related chronic diseases require holistic care-giving and service models transcending the old mechanistic Plan-Do-Check-Act (PDCA) cycle which is still underlying many therapy concepts.

Eighth, when McKinsey coined the 'war for talent' slogan many hospitals were prospering in well-established comfort zones of over-supply and abundant human resources. At the moment the pendulum is swinging in the other direction, because hospitals are fully committed to employer branding, employee marketing, demographic management, and talent search. Not only finding and binding high potentials seems to be a problem, but also the management of demographic changes with respect to the established workforce is an energy absorbing process of labor redefinition. Many hospital positions will have to be readjusted in a tripartite way: Patients and personnel are aging rapidly, calling for redesigned HR models to be braced for the challenges of tomorrow. Additionally, feminization of the medical profession calls for more normal and bearable HR management in hospitals and care professions, and minorities become more prominent both on the caregiver side (doctors and nurses and elderly care from Eastern Europe) and on the patient side (migrants, minorities, international and interracial mix in the population).

Ninth, complexity, multi-tasking and condensed processes let hospitals involve into high performance organizations which have to cope professionally with multiple constraints: legal, economic, technological, cultural, procedural, organizational, strategic and so forth. Striking the right balance between these bottlenecks is anything but trivial, because top healthcare executives must excel in leadership services instead of clinging to a mainstream managerial logic as taught in many healthcare MBA courses. Expert organizations such as hospitals often display the features of high reliability and integrity organizations because safety, security, risk, and quality issues are paramount to survival and institutional legitimacy. Many experts lack professional status from a patient's point of view, because real professionals always anticipate the deficits and skill gaps of the patient to assure a high degree of compliance. Opposite 'functional' expert professionals are dedicated to the patient's sphere of thinking and acting, whereby compensating for all hindrances of desired outcomes.

Tenth, the rationing, rationalization and prioritization mantra challenges established comfort zones because the policy and public impose an unforgiving 'value for money' doctrine on hospitals. In face of restricted resources hospitals are inclined to ration their services, to leverage their assets and to focus on top decision categories which have a strong bearing on medical and economic outcomes. The RRP-paradigm reflects economic realities because of raising expectations, exploding therapy costs, an aging population, and a huge influx of uninsured immigrants who want to take full advantage of advanced healthcare systems in the first world. Third world tsunamis can no longer be effectively buffered and fenced off by means of border control regimes, since the Schengen treaty outlived its usefulness. To put it into a nutshell, innovation must go beyond the effective resource exploitation in order to sufficiently meet inflating expectations. It is about the exploration of competences, services and business models to leapfrog the RRP-logic. Replacing current RRP management thinking is an important issue to address in order to fix current healthcare problems.

The healthcare and hospital industry is strongly regulated and 'suffers' from political interference, over-administration, and institutional burdens. Referring to Porter's five forces logic and the underlying industrial organization paradigm, many hospital managers act as law abiding rule takers in a rather clerk-like manner. But competitive forces and the regulation framework are at the verge of transition. Disruptive or at least differentiating business models and modernized governance regimes question the dominant hospital and healthcare logic of safeguarding equilibrium stasis through a shortsighted range of piecemeal market adaptations. Expert organizations, although committing to excellence, often miss on transformational excellence and strategic resilience because functional specialists tend to resist any change that might endanger their core domains. Paradoxically, many expert organizations such as consultancies proclaim innovations and mental shifts, but are themselves only inclined to 'welcome' innovation as long as fits with their weltanschauung or mental gravitation model. Likewise, healthcare pundits command high-tech utilization such as Da Vinci devices, whilst resorting to pre-industrial craftsmanship instead of employing integrated and patient-centered value chain management. Encapsulated innovations are mostly constrained to functional areas. For this reason the remainder of this chapter addresses the pitfalls and fallacies of expert organizations in healthcare and foreshadows viable avenues of hospital transformation to challenge the status quo.

3 Overcoming the Pitfalls of Expert Organizations

3.1 Determinants of Expert Organizations

In the past decade professional expert organizations sprang into prominence because competence based services contributed significantly to high value generation. These organizations competed solely on the outcomes of their professionals, who can command the highest salaries due the scarcity and the uniqueness of their talents and competencies. While expert organizations primarily competed on competencies, sophisticated procedures and complex outcomes, they were vulnerable to opaque assessments and interpretations. Competing on outcomes—as often proclaimed in healthcare—does not always correspond with service competition. While outcomes reflect the inside-out viewpoint of experts, services incorporate an outside-in viewpoint of the patient, client, user, or buyer. Lacking patient empathy—irrespective of highest quality of outcomes—is a main cause of perceived dissatisfaction (Rasche and Braun von Reinersdorff 2016).

Proceeding with Porter's value logic relating outcomes to costs we should like to augment this train of thought by means of holistic problem solving. Experts are obliged to comply with therapy gold standards for liability reasons. By the way, an experts' job satisfaction hinges on the accumulated respect and reputation within their professional society. Intrinsic motivation and a zest for performance and perfection culminate in a meritocratic system of belief which disparages mediocre performance and honors 'progression of profession'. Up or out careers as well as peer reviews and performance measurement are widespread to protect the uniqueness of expert status. Job markets for experts are characterized by high entry barriers; elite consultancies such as McKinsey burst with the enormous rejection quota of applicants assuring that its recruited talent stands out from the crowd.

In Germany, many ambitious youngsters are often programmed to become medical consultants since excellent exams results trigger a self-fulfilling prophecy. Being eligible to access highly prestigious professional markets such as medicine creates a distorted selection process in which top scores at high school substitute for passion, compassion, commitment, and competence. For this reason, it is useful to differentiate between high potentials and right potentials, since formal qualifications often do not account for social intelligence, empathy, and on the job performance. Expert organizations, such as research driven university hospitals, often acclaim nerd competencies because scientific careers follow publish or perish trajectories and prestigious invited conference presentations. Career paths are thus a function of specialization and focused knowledge application rather than built along the ability to take care of integrated healthcare solutions.

Hospitals and healthcare institutions do not lack competition, but cooperation among experts. Egotistic and sometimes autistic organizational behavior in expert organizations can be traced to the cat herding phenomenon which alludes to the fact that many experts resist coordination, steering, and interfacing (Hogan et al. 2012). Many experts think of functions, specialties, and disciplines instead of clients, processes and over-arching problem solutions. Many healthcare problems are not solved but fixed, because they pinned down to the closed shop mind-set of expert A, B or C when coming up with dissected stand-alone procedures. The latter approaches reflect the hemisphere of the expert, while processes should be patient centered and problem driven. All too often procedures, tools or employed technologies are not the means, but the ends of expert driven healthcare. Incentive and compensation systems favor technologies instead of customized patient therapies. Referring to institutional economics, experts tend to capitalize on information asymmetries and selfish behavior, opportunistically. Altruistic helping and healing motives are spoiled with hidden agendas to add value to the expert instead of contributing to patient value. The latter is achieved by means of cooperation, communication, coordination, clearing, consensus, controlling, and compliance. Many expert organizations are weakly performing on these key success factors (Hogan et al. 2012).

3.2 Being Braced for the Digital Era: Establishing the 6-S-Concept in Hospitals

Right now hospitals are facing multiple challenges which can be predominantly inferred from turbulent, volatile, and unforgiving competitive forces such as hyper-competition and a flurry of risks to be handled in a professional manner.

Prospectively, hospitals will have to cope with financial, medical, political, legal, societal or technological shifts exposing them to uncomfortable risk positions. The latter shall be addressed by the 6-S-Concept, not to be confused with the well-known 7-S-paradigm of former McKinsey consultants Peters and Waterman (1982). Risks entering the clinic arena call for corresponding management approaches that enable organizations to control for them proactively. The 6-S-concept is designed on the premise that security, safety, surveillance, supervision, smartness, and service issues lie at the heart of operational risk management. It goes without saying that the vision of zero risk hospitals will not be accomplished since monitoring and control costs would explode. Zero risk comes at the cost of hysteria effects, decelerated processes, and a culture of mistrust. We defend the point of view that professional risk-adjustments focus on the curve-linear relation between improved risk positions and enforcement efforts. Paradoxically a zest for zero tolerance, zero defects and zero risks may even hamper the aspired overall risk status due to lost innovation opportunities, since every outlier or maverick phenomenon resembles a deviation from enforced best practice regimes. Progress, innovation, change, and serendipity as well as creative momentum hinge on freedom of choice conflicting with 'zero everything clinics' approach. Myopic risk shrinking fails at the strategic rather than the operational level because industry foresight suffers. To some extent we must acknowledge a trade-off between juxtaposing risk categories to be balanced. The 6-S concept strikes a balance between them (Fig. 2).

Security: This key requirement connotes that hospitals resemble high risk areas of service dispatch which are exposed to violence, attacks, and terrorism. As weak targets, they are not only vulnerable to physical assaults but may also suffer from cybercrime. Security issues address the 'criminal minds' in the hospital sphere unfolding their negative energy in neuralgic contexts that should be safeguarded from any offensive or destructive behavior. For this reason security based service models will take on added significance in the hospital sector. Emergency departments, for instance, absorb a flurry of critical incidents, thus calling for dedicated security architectures to fence off spontaneous violence on the one hand and intended assaults on the other hand. Security can be enforced by means of employed technologies (i.e., access cards, cameras, face recognition) and staff induced interventions. We defend the standpoint that hardware, software, brainware, and peopleware should undergo a joint and coordinated security stress test to make sure that the overall system meets security requirements. Robust and agile hospital architectures which incorporate human capital, structures, systems, processes, and technologies should not emerge as an evolutionary process of trial and error learning, but call for a tight clinic governance and compliance regime. The latter defines the guiding principles of corporate security policies and ensuing codes of conduct when it comes to concrete security steps.

Safety: While security issues are closely linked with prevention and handling of human related misbehavior, safety means compliance with provisions, standards,

Fig. 2 Digital healthcare imperatives. Source: Author's own illustration (2016)

and prescribed codes of conduct to assure expected fulfillment of desired outcomes. Products, processes and people may fulfill security requirements but they can nevertheless underperform on safety aspects. Safety is not a matter of criminal minds but a matter of professionalism and conformance to rules and regimes which are established for the sake of harm avoidance and patient inconvenience. Holistic quality management, critical incident reporting systems and hygienic training efforts intend to protect healthcare involved professionals and patients, since infections are all-pervading and many errors of diagnosis and treatment happen due to unawareness, over-routine, lacking commitment or self-complacency. Technologies, therapies and treatments must be safe, but the degree of safety is a function of professionals in charge of conducting processes. Big data applications in the healthcare and hospital sector also challenge entrenched safety and security wisdoms, since deep access to fine granular patient data displays opportunities and risks. The flipside of better, faster, and cheaper patient treatment due to data profiling and prediction can be seen in possible IT breakdowns, software and systems fragility or uncontrolled data leakages.

Surveillance: It goes without saying that restrictive command and control regimes relying on observing, spying, and inspecting paradoxically can aggravate the achieved risk status because clinic professionals are intimidated, thus may abstain from deciding and acting due to fear of sanctions or legal suits. Professional organizations such as hospitals cannot control for everything but can enable and empower people to mobilize resources, overcome bottlenecks, and handle outlying incidents with agile decision making processes. Surveillance as a service differs from the aforementioned command and control regimes because advanced technology employment such as face and noise recognition devices, therapy monitoring or

ED observation systems provide professionals with relevant information to anticipate risky constellations by means of pattern recognition. Smart surveillance systems must be convenient and comfortable, because professionals and patients should not endure an 'under armor' atmosphere. Attitudes towards public infrastructure surveillance have dramatically changed since obvious and perceived security and safety are longer seen as a harm, but as a service.

Supervision: Opposite to surveillance systems, supervising activities often resist automation and computerization. Efficient and effective supervision hinges on serendipity, acumen, and experience based pattern recognition. Master professionals and hospital executives show a high degree of mindfulness when supporting and coaching each other. Apparent skill gaps can be filled and problems be fixed flexibly in the case of mutual supervision. The latter is not only a domain of hierarchy and formal power status, but also a productive outcome of practiced interprofessionalism. Supervision means support and service rather than mistrust or detection of malpractices. Mutual mindfulness leads to a different interpretation of supervision—one which prefers coaching to control by means of either technology or human interference.

Smartness: How to bridge security, safety and surveillance requirements with a strong desire for smart hospitals conveying a feeling of comfort, convenience and competence? Smart hospitals are patient centered (and not only professional driven), they employ contemporary information technologies on behalf of patients and physicians and try to emulate the hoteling business model. Severely injured patients are first and foremost interested in excellent outcome delivery that is a category of its own and not to be meshed-up with service gimmicks and gadgets (i.e., free high speed wlan). Smart hospital systems should not be reduced to digital convenience store services, but represent a kernel of interconnected, user-driven, and self-explaining designs that overcome monolithic legacy solutions or overcomplex systems of systems architectures. In a broader sense, smartness amounts to clever resource utilization since scarce assets must be deployed according to their highest benefit. Smart hospital management is a matter of 'tech and touch' to convince professionals and patients that technology employment is anything but inhumane or competence debasing. Thanks to virtualization options, hub and spokes solutions, internet of things and shared services, hospitals may become smart and clever while not compromising on courtesy, empathy, and patient centeredness. The latter items can only be addressed when standard operation procedures and daily routines are smartly handled. This means a relief to the humans, because scarce competencies are no longer occupied by tasks and jobs eligible for computerization.

Service: Smart hospitals excel in service centeredness. Smart technologies are a means to the end for desired outcomes, patient satisfaction, and a high therapy impact. A precondition for an external service focus is internal and interprofessional appreciation of complementary and supporting units. Integrated and cross-sectional workflows resemble the masterpiece of shared competencies, activities, technologies and mindsets by means of coordination, cooperation and communication. For this reason, secondary and tertiary support activities should not be degraded to cost centers, but instead regarded as pre-conditional services within an integrated value system. Service and smartness are those critical factors to success which obviously mirror perceived expectations. While to some extent security, safety, surveillance, and supervision issues—although closely linked to aspired overall risk reduction—can cause 'psychological pain' to the patient, smart processes and convenient services make them easier to endure. Product, service, and business model design should also envision the users' aspiration level, since experts see patients' problems through a professional lens not always incorporating the viewpoint of 'therapy amateurs'. Healthcare and hospital marketing prioritizes service and smartness to make sure that patients get what they want. Trust based healthcare service endemically resist direct quality and outcome assessment. For this reason a smart service and infrastructure appearance resembles a proxy measure for deeply ingrained security, safety, surveillance, and supervision requirements.

The overall model acknowledges that on one hand security, safety, surveillance and supervision issues may thwart personal freedom due to perceived infringements, but on the other hand smartness and service can alleviate those negative necessities towards an excellent risk status. The latter is a final lead performance indicator for high risk organizations commanding themselves to commit to zero tolerance policies.

4 Smart Service Organizations in Healthcare

4.1 Applying SMART to Hospitals

Hospitals are anything but smart service organizations because experts and professionals are inclined to let patients emerge as evidence based cases rather than treat them as clients or customers. Smart service organizations as hospitals are expected to be are often high risk organizations with respect to the 6-S-model: the legal and moral system is unforgiving when it comes to avoidable patient damage due to malpractice, law infringement or SOP deviation. Thus smartness cannot substitute for those critical factors. Nevertheless, expert status and professionalism alone are only necessary but insufficient factors of overall clinic success. The acronym SMART stands for specific, measurable, attainable, realistic and time focused, to denote that organizational objectives will only contribute to sustainable competitive advantages if they pass this combined test (see also Rasche and Braun von Reinersdorff 2013).

Smart hospital services must be specific for the purpose of desired outcomes and impacts on patients' perceived well-being. Individualized therapies aim at targeting personal traits and genetic expressions instead of recurring to shot gun approaches.

Telemedicine and digital assistants give rise to the vision of personalized healthcare due to real time information access. Big data technologies employing the PPTT logic (tracing, tracking, profiling and prognosis) represent the kernel of medical micro data analysis. The latter provide professionals and patients to take advantage of specific rather generic information about health, fitness and vitality.

Hospitals are paid for achievement of key performance indicators such as quality, outcome or patient satisfaction, being subject to measurement problems because of complexity of healthcare services. Medical progress and compliance issues are highly dependent on reliable, valid and objective metrics to indicate fulfillment level. Until now, privileged data access was deemed to be an expert prerogative. Today and tomorrow the quantified-self movement enables and empowers patients to measure their own health and well-being. The growing lifestyle of health and sustainability (LOHAS) is propelled by a zest for metrics and measures about life status of mindful target groups. They are committed to benefit bundles which serve the goal of a mindful, valuable, and appreciable life.

Patients comply with attainable therapy objectives which should not be out of reach. So called stretch goals do not fit with present resource endowments but are intended to raise the bar for continuous improvements. Patients are forced to go to moderate pains to accumulate the required skills for therapy success. Fitness, mental, or cardio apps—underlying 'gamified health'—are the bedrock of attainable goals which must be somehow motivating and challenging. The phenomenon of digital natives can be measurably characterized by a dashboard of goals to be checked by means of interconnected devices.

While unrealistic goals are demotivating, realistic goals may challenge entrenched routines and health habits. Digitally assisted therapies and sports programs must rely on solid individual data to define skill and status adjusted objectives. Wearables and implantables are those digital devices that produce real-time data for advanced algorithms, with which to decide and re-calibrate goals. Constant goal recalibration is constitutional to fine-tuned disease management and professional training. Sport 4.0 applies the PDCA-logic to fitness and training when it comes to online-monitoring of master athletes. Trainers and athletes can take great advantage of big data access because evidence based high performance coaching complements experience and intuition-driven rules of thumb. Evidence and experience approaches should encompass a balanced mix instead of competing against each other.

According to the SMART approach goals must fit into a timeframe to be pursued efficiently step by step. Abstract long-term goals often lack concreteness resulting in poor results. Moreover, they are simply shunted aside or miss on efficient and effective achievement, because means end relations fall prey to causal ambiguity. Digital dashboard management systems follow the logic of objective cascading breaking: rather generic master visions are broken down to milestones and ensuing activities which can be optimally scheduled with respect to individual resources, responsibilities, and deadlines. Advanced ERP systems feeding balanced scorecards and the like resemble not only decision support systems but also effective monitoring tools to get visions translated into action. But health-aware natives may not wish to be ERP-ed in their behavior calling for a 'balanced' big data approach that does not incorporate a 'big brother' logic.

The mantra of user driven and agile design in software engineering is a plea for more smartness and more service. Applied to the orthodox business model of hospitals this implies that they should harness digitalization as a means to transform themselves into smart service organizations. It goes without saying that this disruptive change—although technologically induced—is first and foremost a matter of soft facts such as culture, people and path dependencies.

4.2 Roadmap for Smart Service Organizations

Smart service organizations represent the culmination point of institutional evolution towards high performance organizations. In contrast to many other organizational formats, smart service organizations bridge the professional's point of view with the perspective of the user, client or patient. The latter are parts of an ecosystem to be handled with care due to different spheres of interest, power, and expectations. We scrutinize five organizational formats widespread in the healthcare and hospital sector and conclude with an outlook on the not yet fully implemented smart service organization (see also Rasche and Braun von Reinersdorff 2011; Rasche et al. 2012).

High reliability organizations place emphasis on compliance with rules and standards. These machine-like service organizations capitalize on economies of scale and routine execution according to best practices. They must guarantee achievement of pre-defined outcomes, similar to airlines that perform on punctuality, safety, price, service, and destination coverage. Many baseline hospitals focus on deviation and gap control by means of monitoring, supervision, and surveillance. But reliability is just a call for duty, not for excellence of exceptional performance, since consumers are conditioned to expect fulfillment of promised outcomes.

Expert organizations differ from the aforementioned category through the delivered services, outcomes, and employed human capital. In contrast to security firms which must be reliable, expert organizations resort to highly specialized competencies in terms of idiosyncratic learning trajectories. The latter can be traced to an academic and on the job skill development process that culminates in an experienced senior status, as can be observed in accounting firms, law factories, partnerships, hospitals or universities. Experts accumulate a portfolio of formal and tacit qualifications which empower them to solve specific problems painstakingly and creatively. Unfortunately, experts of these organizations emerge as nerds or freaks such as top scientists in healthcare—preferring problem solving to patient satisfaction. Patients simply expect hospital to be reliable.

Professional organizations exploit deeply rooted expertise but do not want to be classified as expert organizations because professionalism embodies client or customer focused expertise to create value on behalf of the user Medical professionals altruistically proclaim to follow the clear-cut order "Patients first, hospital second, and staff third!" to denote that they are 'driven' by a superior ethic or morale. These values include respect for needy patients, humbleness, and a commitment to procedural justice. Although many professional organizations are client, case, patient or outcome focused, they are not impact centered. Patients are often patronized in a truly empathetic and convenient way, but they are not involved as co-value creators into the therapy value chain. Modern compliance acknowledges that high performance is not only a matter of professionalism, but a matter of social ecosystem management. Success of disease management programs is highly dependent on the symbiosis of professionals and patients.

High performance organizations stress impact, not aseptic outcome. Evidence based outcomes reflect the science driven hemisphere of the professional while the (perceived) impact resembles the hemisphere of the amateur. In some fortunate instances the latter achieves professional status, if they are given the opportunity to master the problem on their own. High performance organizations discretely replace themselves because self-empowered patients are no longer dependent on them. High performance organizations are competence development and teaching engines since they endow their clients with a professional skill set to renounce any patronizing support. All too often patients are deskilled by classic full-service support including surgery and rehabilitation while not providing them with a progressive prevention toolkit. To put it in a nutshell, high performance organizations do not celebrate their own professionals and competencies, but are willing to imbue their clients with professionalism by means of learning, training, coaching, and educating.

Smart service organizations offer an ideal mix of the discussed organizational modes when striking an optimal balance between the ambitions of experts, professionals, clients, and other involved stakeholders, bearing in mind that high performance is a matter of viewpoint and perception.

We concede that the portrayed service organizations are simplified stereotypes, not mutually exclusive, and may be observable as subtypes in one overarching service holding. Smart service organizations are still in the infancy and incorporate many real options for business model transformation. It is safe to say that healthcare organizations must be smart to attract smart professionals (and patients), since they contribute to the vast proportion of value creation.

5 Conclusion

Service model innovation transcends the myopic end user logic because it is about value creating organizational formats, and not only about service delivery according to pre-defined performance criteria. We sketched the dimensions of strategic service positioning, ranging from being efficient and lean to being different and disruptive. We made the point that to overcome resource bottlenecks innovative hospital management cannot be reduced to the rationing, rationalization and prioritization (RRP) paradigm. Certainly an RRP kind of constraint management may contribute to short-term and mid-term success improvements on the operational level, but one should consider that operational excellence cannot compensate for a lack of inspiration, innovation, and disruptive energy. Many expert organizations show classic signs of age since they excel in standard operation procedures and best practices while all too often denying the fact that complying with rules, standards, and mainstream requirements is anything but smart or path-breaking. Thus we described the paradigm of smart service organizations, with the ensuing 6-S-model to delineate the cornerstones of a digital era hexagon comprising security, safety, surveillance, supervision, service and smartness as key success factors. Smartness resonates with the progressive attitude towards service design displayed by smart service organizations. We coined this term to challenge four types of widespread organizations in the service sector that have not yet outlived its usefulness in general, but provoke criticism concerning their premises and genetic code. High reliability organizations, expert organizations, professional organizations, and high-performance organizations follow an evolutionary logic. In face of the all-pervading debate over the disruptive effects of digitalization on industries and service sectors alike, hospitals can no longer evade the TIME induced imperatives. Converging telecommunication, information, media, and even entertainment applications may have a great bearing on business model innovation in healthcare.

Digital natives and social media users are the ingredients and participants of the big data community welcoming smart healthcare solutions to overcome the legacies and core rigidities of 'paper and pencil' clinics. For the time being, we are deeply concerned about the preponderance of healthcare administration in face of an era of disruptive business transformation that calls for new management, leadership and entrepreneurial competences.

References

Braun von Reinersdorff, A., & Rasche, C. (2014). Mobilisierung strategische und operativer Leistungsreserven im Krankenhaus – Gestaltungsfelder und Grenzen der Service-Industrialisierung, erscheint. In R. Bouncken, M. A. Pfannstiel, & A. J. Reuschl (Hrsg.) Dienstleistungsmanagement im Krankenhaus (Band II) (S. 76–S. 85). Berlin.

Christensen, C. M., Wang, D., & van Bever, D. (2013). Consulting on the cusp of disruption. *Harvard Business Review, 91*(5), 106–114.

Frey, C. B., & Osborne, M. A. (2013). *The future of employment: How susceptible are jobs to computerisation*. Oxford: University of Oxford.

Hänel, P., Rasche, C., & Tiberius, V. (2011a). Ärzte im Zwiespalt von Geld und Autonomie. Auswirkungen finanzieller Anreize auf ärztliche Arbeitsmoral und -qualität. *f&w führen und wirtschaften im Krankenhaus*, Nr. 3, S. 248–252.

Hänel, P., Rasche, C., & Tiberius, V. (2011b). Autonomie von Ärzten – Chancen und Grenzen bei angestellten Ärzten. *Das Krankenhaus*, Jg. 103, Nr. 11, S. 1100–1106.

Hogan, B., Singh, M., & Rasche, C. (2011). Patientenzufriedenheit und Wartezeiten. In W. Von Eiff, C. Dodt, M. Brachmann, & T. Fleischmann (Hrsg.), *Management der Notaufnahme – Patientenorientierung und optimale Ressourcennutzung als strategischer Erfolgsfaktor* (Vol. 1, No. 3, S. 298–307). Stuttgart.

Hogan, B., Braun von Reinersdorff, A., & Rasche, C. (2012). Value creation in emergency departments: In search of sustainable management paradigms for medicine. *Italian Journal of Emergency Medicine* (Kohlhammer Verlag), 136–139.

Huber, J., Kirig, A., Rauch, C., & Ehret, J. (2015). *Gesundheitsstudie – Wie Vertrauen zum Treiber einer neunen Gesundheitskultur wird 2015, Die Philips Gesundheitsstudie 2015*. Frankfurt: Zukunftsinstitut GmbH.

Müller, H.-E., & Rasche, C. (2013). Innovative Geschäftsmodelle. *WISU, 42*(6), 805–809.

Osterwalder, A., & Pigneur, Y. (2011). Aligning profit and purpose through business model innovation. In G. Palazzo, & M. Wentland (Hrsg.), *Responsible management practices for the 21st century* (pp. 61–75). Pearson: Paris.

Porter, M. E. (2010). What is value in health care? *New England Journal of Medicine, 26*, S.2477–S.2481.

Peters, T. J., & Waterman, R. H. (1982). *In search of excellence: Lessons from America's best-run companies*. New York: Harper & Row.

Porter, M. E., & Kramer, M. R. (2011). The big idea: Creating shared value, rethinking capitalism. *Harvard Business Review, 89*(1–2), 62–77.

Rasche, C. (2013). Big data – Herausforderung für das Management. *WISU, 42*(8–9), 1076–1083.

Rasche, C., & Braun von Reinersdorff, A. (2011). Krankenhäuser im Spannungsfeld von Markt- und Versorgungsauftrag: Von der Medizinmanufaktur zur Hochleistungsorganisation. In G. Rüter, P. Da-Cruz, & P. Schwegel (Eds.), *Gesundheitsökonomie und Wirtschaftspolitik. Festschrift zum 70. Geburtstag von Prof. Dr. Dr. h.c. Peter Oberender* (pp. 473–502). Stuttgart: Lucius & Lucius Verlag.

Rasche, C., & von Reinersdorff, B. (2013). Zielorientiertes Klinikmanagement: Meilensteine, Methoden und Maßnahmen. In J. F. Debatin, A. Ekkernkamp, & B. Schulte (Eds.), *Krankenhausmanagement: Strategien, Konzepte, Methoden, 2*. Berlin: Aktualisierte und erweiterte Auflage.

Rasche, C., & Braun von Reinersdorff, A. (2015). Gesundheitsmanagement. *WISU, 44*(8–9), 279–286.

Rasche, C., & Braun von Reinersdorff, A. (2016). Krankenhäuser als Expertenorganisationen – Wertschaffung und Produktivitätssteigerung durch innovative Geschäftsmodelle. In M. A. Pfannstiel, C. Rasche, & H. Mehling (Eds.), *Dienstleistungsmanagement im Krankenhaus - Nachhaltige Wertgenerierung jenseits der operativen Exzellent* (pp. 1–24). Wiesbaden: Springer-Gabler-Verlag.

Rasche, C., Braun von Reinersdorff, A., & Tiberius, V. (2012). Führung und Steuerung relationaler Expertenorganisationen – Strategien, Geschäftsmodelle und Positionierungsoptionen. In A. Seisreiner & S. Armutat (Eds.), *Differentielles Management: Individualisierung und Organisation in systemischer Kongruenz* (pp. 215–240). Wiesbaden: Springer Verlag.

Rasche, C., Margaria, T., & Braun von Reinersdorff, A. (2010). Value delivery through IT-based healthcare architectures: Towards a competence-based view of services. In M. Stephan, W. Kerber, T. Kessler, & M. Lingenfelder (Eds.), *25 ressourcen- und kompetenzorientierte Forschung: Der Kompetenzbasierte Ansatz auf dem Weg zum Schlüsselparadigma in der Managementforschung* (pp. 417–443). Wiesbaden: Gabler-Verlag.

Schmidt, A. (2015). *Überlegene Geschäftsmodelle – Wertgenese und Wertabschöpfung in turbulenten Umwelten*. Wiesbaden: Springer-Gabler-Verlag.

Taylor, K., Ronte, H., & Hammett, S. (2014). *Healthcare and Life Sciences Predictions 2020 – A bold future?* London: Deloitte.

Williamson, P. J. (2010). Cost innovation: Preparing for a 'value for money' revolution. *Long Range Planning, 43*(2–3), 343–353.

Christoph Rasche, born 1965 in Münster, heads the chair of professional & corporate services at the University of Potsdam. Prof. Rasche adopted visiting professorships at the Universities of Innsbruck, Alcalá de Henares as well as the Hochschule Osnabrück. He teaches strategic and general management in national and international MBA-Programs with special respect to the healthcare and hospital industry. Formerly he consulted with Droege International AG and was co-founder of Stratvanguard and the General Management Institute Potsdam. Prof. Rasche's research subjects circle around the field of strategic and general management in the healthcare & hospital sector, which witnesses an era of professional value creation by means of a strong management and leadership focus. Practically, he consults with healthcare players and is actively involved in executive trainings—ranging from corporate universities to MBA- and PhD-programs for healthcare professionals.

Tiziana Margaria is Chair of Software Engineering and Head of Department at the Dept. of Computer Science and Information Systems at the University of Limerick (Ireland). She is also a Principal Investigator of Lero, The Irish Software Research Center, where she is heads the Committee on International Relations Development. In Lero, she heads research projects on Scientific Workflow and model-driven HW/SW Cybersecurity. She received a Laurea in Electrical Engineering and a PhD degree in Computer and Systems Engineering from the Politecnico di Torino, Italy. She has broad experience in the use of formal methods for high assurance systems, in particular concerning functional verification, reliability, and compliance of complex heterogeneous systems, through major industrial projects (where she won the European IT Award in 1996, and a start-up competition in 2001) and consulting, as well as through her activities as founder and CEO of startup companies, holding two USPTO patents, one of which with NASA. She is currently Vicepresident of the European Association of Software Science and Technology (EASST), President of FMICS (the ERCIM Working Group on Formal Methods for Industrial Critical Systems), and steering committee member of ETAPS, the European joint Conferences on Theory and Practice of Software, member of the Board of EF-ICST, the European Forum on Information and Computation Science and Technology.

Barry D. Floyd is Full Professor of Information Systems and Management and Coordinator of Information Systems at the Orfalea College of Business, California Polytechnic State University. He received his BS in Mathematics and MS in Systems Science from Michigan State University and his MBA and PhD in Information Systems from The University of Michigan. He has worked both domestically and internationally developing and implementing IT solutions for industry and government. He has taught internationally in numerous countries been a visiting professor in numerous countries including Finland, Ireland, Spain, England, China, Mexico, Italy, Thailand, Vietnam, and Germany where he received a DAAD Fellowship. His research interests include Simplicity in IT, Hospital Information Systems, ERP, and HCI. He has won numerous teaching awards during his 30 years as an educator.

Strategies with Service Business Model Innovation

Lesley A. Clack

Abstract

Due to the complex and fragmented nature of health care, innovative business models are needed to increase efficiency and improve quality of care. There are a vast array of barriers to innovation in health care. An understanding of the elements of a good business model design is essential to overcoming those barriers in order to implement innovative business models in healthcare. Using an innovative business model can help organizations gain competitive advantage. Knowledge of the driving factors in competition and how to build and sustain competitive advantage in health care is vital. With the understanding of the elements of a good business model design and the strategies essential to business model innovation, organizations can then understand how to integrate a business model with strategy to protect competitive advantage.

1 Business Model Design

Service business model innovation is essential for hospitals and other healthcare organizations to create and form a new healthcare market and to achieve competitive advantage. Most service business model innovations focus on sources and components of value creation. It is important for managers to know how to use service business models and how to achieve service business model innovation. After reading this chapter, you will be able to:

- Understand the elements of a good business model design.
- Describe approaches for creating innovative business models.
- Understand innovative ways to create value for customers.

L.A. Clack (✉)
Armstrong State University, 11935 Abercorn St., Savannah, GA 31419, USA
e-mail: lesley.clack@armstrong.edu

M.A. Pfannstiel, C. Rasche (eds.), *Service Business Model Innovation in Healthcare and Hospital Management*, DOI 10.1007/978-3-319-46412-1_2

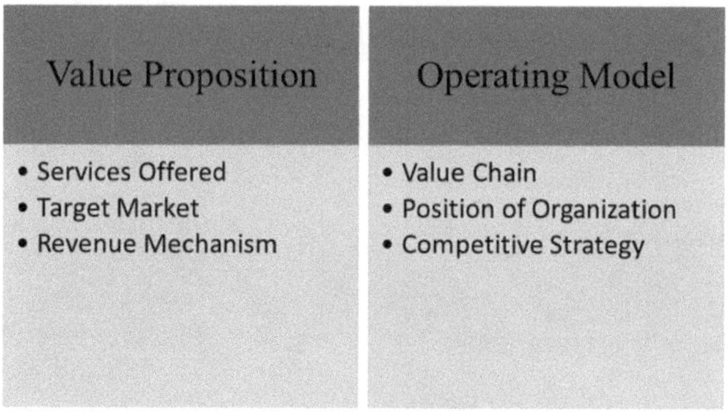

Fig. 1 Components and elements of a business model

- Identify barriers to innovation in health care.
- Describe strategies essential to business model innovation.
- Describe how to integrate a business model with strategy to protect competitive advantage.

The term business model is used to describe an organization's "unique value proposition, how the firm uses its sustainable competitive advantage to perform better than its rivals over time, and whether, as well as how, the firm can make money now and in the future" (Morris et al. 2006). In simpler terms, "a business model consists of what a business does and how it makes money doing those things" (Ranck et al. 2007).

A good service business model consists of two critical components (Fig. 1):

- Value proposition, which consists of the target market, services offered, and the revenue mechanism.
- Operating model, which consists of the value chain, position of the organization, and the competitive strategy (Lindgardt et al. 2009).

Within these two essential components, the core elements of a business model are (Chesbrough 2007; Lindgardt et al. 2009):

Within the Value Proposition

1. Articulate the value created for users. Organizations do this through the unique services offered.
2. Identify the target market. Target customers are those who pay for value.
3. State the revenue generation mechanism. The revenue generation mechanism refers to the means by which organizations make money.

Within the Operating Model

1. Define the value chain structure. The value chain structure refers to how organizations arrange activities and resources to create value.

2. Specify the position of the organization within the value network. The position refers to the ways in which the organization and customers interact, and the networks of relationships the organization forms to maximize value.
3. Articulate the competitive strategy. Describe how the organization will differentiate themselves from the competition (Chesbrough 2007).

2 Business Model Innovation

Innovation is defined as "the intentional introduction and application within a role, group or organization of ideas, processes, products or procedures, new to the relevant unit of adoption, designed to significantly benefit the individual, the group, the organization or the wider society" (West 1990). Innovation is the key to improved access, earlier diagnosis and treatment, and better outcomes (Plsek 2014).

Business model innovation is about "delivering existing products that are produced by existing technologies to existing markets" (Girotra and Netessine 2014). Or simply, "doing something differently to generate significantly more value" (Beckham 2015).

There are two principal dimensions of healthcare innovation: environmental and operational. The operational dimension involves improvement of clinical outcomes, efficiency, effectiveness, provider shortages, patient satisfaction, patient safety, profitability, improved quality, and cost containment. The environmental dimension involves physician acceptance, organizational culture, regulatory acceptance, partnerships, and collaborations (Omachonu and Einspruch 2010).

Utilizing innovative models in healthcare can be beneficial in balancing quality and cost containment. Innovation is critical to survival (Omachonu and Einspruch 2010). Innovation in healthcare is more difficult than in other industries, mostly because of the unique nature of the business, and the complexity involving legal and regulatory matters (Meyers 2014). Health care is ailing and in need of help, and such problems beg for innovative solutions in every aspect of health care, including its delivery to consumers, its technology, and its business models (Herzlinger 2006).

Historically, innovation required organizations to invest in expensive technology, and research and development. Today, costs are too exorbitant for that to be a viable option. Innovation must start with the business model (Chesbrough 2007). Thus, organizations must rely on their own employees for new innovative ideas (Grajewski 2016).

A New Method for Innovating Business Models (de Jong and van Dijk 2015)

1. Identify the Dominant Business Model in the Industry
2. Separate the Most Important Belief into Supporting Ideas
3. Turn a Supporting Idea into a New Approach
4. Test Your New Approach
5. Transform the New Approach into the Industry's New Business Model

Identify the Dominant Business Model. Determine the main belief in the industry regarding how to create value.

Separate the Most Important Belief into Supporting Ideas. Examine the underlying beliefs regarding customer needs and interactions, technology, regulation, business economics, and ways of operating in the industry.

Turn a Supporting Idea into a New Approach. Articulate a new proposition that is radically different from the current approaches used in the industry.

Test Your New Approach. Use an approach that has already been proven successful in another industry.

Transform the New Approach into the Industry's New Business Model. Transition from the existing business model to the new approach, and evaluate how the new approach creates value (de Jong and van Dijk 2015).

2.1 Additional Avenues for Innovation

Customer Relationships. Businesses have always placed significant value on customer loyalty. But, technology has made pursuing customer loyalty more complex. Instead, organizations should focus on empowerment of customers. Customers now have access to all of the information needed to make sound decisions (de Jong and van Dijk 2015).

Activities and Resources. A common belief in the industry is that improving efficiency is the best way to increase profits. In a rapidly changing healthcare market, this may not be a viable option. Using technology to enhance performance has proven to be a smarter alternative (de Jong and van Dijk 2015).

3 Service Business Model Innovation

"Service innovations seek to improve or transform an offering for an entire service or pathway of care for a specific group of patients" (Bevan 2013).

Service innovation involves new services using new methods and technologies. Service innovations are higher risk than process innovations because they are more complex (Bevan 2013). Service innovation in healthcare is complicated by staff shortages, technology, patient characteristics, and the size of the organization (Changkaew et al. 2012). Health service innovation is more difficult than innovation in other service industries due to the complexities involved, such as regulatory, financial, social, clinical, and ethical risks (Changkaew et al. 2012). Service innovation in healthcare is often motivated by new market opportunities or new technology (Banaszak-Hall et al. 1996).

Service innovations in healthcare can be categorized as embodied or disembodied innovations. Embodied innovations are tangible, such as medical devices and pharmaceutical products. Disembodied innovations are intangible and constructed from new knowledge, such as advanced surgical techniques and new care protocols. Disembodied innovations includes innovations in healthcare processes, operations, and healthcare organizations (Bower 2003).

4 Creating Value

"Value is the customer defined difference between the tangible and intangible benefits of a particular product offering less, or divided by, the tangible and intangible costs" (Meyers 2014). In other words, in healthcare value can be defined as "better outcomes for each dollar spent" (Castano 2014). Organizations are constantly seeking to produce services that customers value (Walston 2014).

4.1 Decision Making in the Value Chain

Organizations are often able to improve decision making in the value chain by changing the individuals who are responsible for making decisions. A few things organizations can do:

1. Assign an individual who possesses the knowledge necessary to make good decisions. Empower employees by giving them the information they need to make a well-informed decision.
2. Decision risk should lie with individuals that can best manage the consequences. If no party has more information than any other, shift the risk of decision making to the party best able to handle the risk.
3. Choose the appropriate decision maker. Decision makers should be those in the chain with the most to gain (Girotra and Netessine 2014).

Another significant factor is in examining why key decision makers make the choices that they do. Business model innovation often stems from adjusting the motivations of key decision makers. There are three ways that this can be done:

1. Modify the revenue stream. The revenue stream should align to the interests of the stakeholders of the decision.
2. Coordinate the timeline. If your organization relies on outsourcing, ensure that schedules are coordinated to create long-term value.
3. Incorporate incentives. Use an agreed upon incentive to maximize the desired outcome (Girotra and Netessine 2014).

5 Barriers to Innovation

To move forward in terms of innovation, organizations must confront the following barriers:

Lack of employee engagement due to already high workloads. Organizations can overcome this by establishing a protective environment, creating teams of innovators, and allocating work time for innovating thinking (Grajewski 2016).

Varying ideas about what is considered innovation. Misconceptions can occur when organizations use engineers, technical experts, or other non-clinicians for innovation. Organizations should utilize individuals that are actually doing the work to come up with new innovative ideas (Grajewski 2016).

Oversight of regulations. Regulations can make innovation a time-consuming process. Organizations can reduce the barrier placed by regulations by discussing and brainstorming with other providers to determine what works (Grajewski 2016).

Business Model Value Analysis. Organizations may have difficulty determining the exact value of an innovation. Instead, organizations should focus on whether there is a market for the service, and the cost involved in providing the service (Grajewski 2016).

Outdated technology. Outdated technology inhibits innovation. Organizations should utilize the latest technology to optimize innovation (Grajewski 2016).

Varying support and shortage of continuous investment. For innovation to work, all stakeholders must get behind it (Pennic 2015).

6 Strategies for Innovation

In order to thrive, one of the driving factors for innovation in an organization should be physicians as leaders. Physicians must have an entrepreneurial mindset with a goal of creating value for patients through the use of innovation (Meyers 2014). "Physician leaders need to embrace innovation and entrepreneurship as the major tool to drive change in the health care system" (Meyers 2014).

Sustainability is another driving force of innovation. Sustainability in healthcare involves a tremendous amount of organizational and technological innovations that yield significant returns. Striving towards innovation is changing the competitive landscape by forcing organizations to change the way they think about technologies, processes, and business models. By making sustainability a priority, organizations can gain competitive advantage (Nidumolu et al. 2009).

According to Herzlinger (2006), there are Six Forces that drive innovation in health care (Fig. 2):

1. Players. The individuals in the health care system that can improve an innovation's chance of success.
2. Funding. The methods used for revenue generation.
3. Policy. Industry regulations that drive innovation.
4. Technology. The foundation for innovations that can make health care delivery more efficient and effective.
5. Customers. The individuals that consume health care services.
6. Accountability. The responsibility for innovations being safe and effective (Herzlinger 2006).

Fig. 2 Six forces that drive innovation in healthcare

Being innovative requires cultural and behavioral changes. Several Opportunities exist to create a Culture of Healthcare Innovation (Pennic 2015):

1. Give employees the opportunity to experiment. Encourage employees to spend time developing innovations.
2. Support innovation, rather than inhibiting it. Management should review and direct innovation activity to ensure it is pursued correctly and focused on the right goals.
3. Gain buy-in from stakeholders. The largest reason for failure is a lack of resources. Organizations should involve stakeholders in innovation from the beginning.
4. Apply lessons from other industries. Organizations should learn from innovations in other industries in order to be able to innovate faster.
5. Leaders should establish high expectations. The entire organization must be engaged from top to the bottom, starting with leadership (Pennic 2015).

7 Integration of Business Model with Strategy to Protect Competitive Advantage

Competitive advantage involves an organization developing a distinct characteristic that cannot be easily imitated by competitors (Ginter et al. 2013). "The ability to innovate is considered a major competitive advantage in organizations, enhancing their effectiveness, efficiency, and thus their potential for long term sustainability"

(Barnett et al. 2011). A strategic goal of the organization should be to achieve and maintain competitive advantage (Ginter et al. 2013).

An organization can use their core values to gain competitive advantage. Every hospital or healthcare organization should have a statement of values that describes who they are and what they stand for. These core values create competitive differentiation for organizations (Tye 2013).

Historically, there were two dominant business models (Trimble 2016):

1. The Equality Model. The belief that everyone can be an innovator, and anyone can come up with new ideas and take initiative to implement them at any time.
2. The Champion Model. The idea that if you invest in people who are capable of being an innovator, you can simply sit back and wait for them to produce results.

Over time, we have learned that the answer lies somewhere in between the two. Innovation in healthcare requires a culture, leadership and infrastructure that supports innovation (Ezziane 2012). Strategies should involve changing the payment model, investing in teams that can redesign care, and using physician leaders as innovators (Trimble 2016).

Several activities are particularly important when establishing a capability for Business Model Innovation:

- Discovering New Opportunities. Organizations should understand their current choices before looking for new opportunities. Once an organization understands its current model, it will be better positioned to brainstorm for new innovations.
- Applying the New Business Model. Organizations must decide whether to integrate the new model in the core business or to establish it separately.
- Constructing the Platform and Developing Abilities. Organizations must build a platform and develop the skills needed for managing the business model innovation process (Lindgardt et al. 2009).

8 Conclusion

Innovative business models have proven to be a successful way to gain competitive advantage. Thus organizations should focus on how to implement new models, rather than how to invent new technologies. Leaders should be at the forefront and should do everything necessary to help their organizations adopt innovative business models in order to maximize the probability of success (Ehrbeck et al. 2010). With the ever changing landscape in healthcare, using innovative service business models is key to success for hospitals and healthcare organizations.

References

Banaszak-Hall, J., Zinn, J. S., & Mor, V. (1996). The impact of market and organizational characteristics on nursing care facility service innovation: A resource dependency perspective. *Health Services Research, 31*(1), 97–117.

Barnett, J., Vasileiou, K., Djemil, F., Brooks, L., & Young, T. (2011). Understanding innovators' experiences of barriers and facilitators in implementation and diffusion of healthcare service innovations: A qualitative study. *BMC Health Services Research, 11*(342), 1–12.

Beckham, D. (2015). How to foster innovation in health care delivery. *Hospitals & Health Networks Magazine*. Accessed April 29, 2016, from http://www.hhnmag.com/articles/6638-how-to-foster-innovation-in-health-care-delivery

Bevan, H. (2013). Three steps to a new innovation strategy. *Health Service Journal*. Accessed April 29, 2016, from http://innoquest-id.blogspot.com/2013/11/helen-bevan-three-steps-to-new.html

Bower, D. J. (2003). Innovation in healthcare delivery. In J. Tidd (Ed.), *Service innovation: Organizational responses to technical opportunities and market imperatives*. London: Imperial College Press.

Castano, R. (2014). Towards a framework for business model innovation in health care delivery in developing countries. *BMC Medicine, 12*(233), 1–7.

Changkaew, L., Vadhanasindhu, P., Taweesangsakulthai, D., & Chandrachai, A. (2012). Three dimensions model: Stage for service innovation in hospitals. *Interdisciplinary Journal of Contemporary Research in Business, 4*(2), 806–814.

Chesbrough, H. (2007). Business model innovation: It's not just about technology anymore. *Strategy and Leadership, 35*(6), 12–17.

de Jong, M., & van Dijk, M. (2015). Disrupting beliefs: A new approach to business-model innovation. *McKinsey Quarterly*, 1–13. Accessed April 17, 2016, from http://www.mckinsey.com/business-functions/strategy-and-corporate-finance/our-insights/disrupting-beliefs-a-new-approach-to-business-model-innovation

Ehrbeck, T., Henke, N., & Kibasi, T. (2010). The emerging market in health care innovation. *McKinsey Quarterly*, 1–6. Accessed April 29, 2016, from http://www.mckinsey.com/industries/healthcare-systems-and-services/our-insights/the-emerging-market-in-health-care-innovation

Ezziane, Z. (2012). Pathways and complexity of innovation in health care. *RISAI, 3*(1), 1–11.

Ginter, P. M., Duncan, W. J., & Swayne, L. E. (2013). *Strategic management of health care organizations* (7th ed.). Westford, MA: Jossey-Bass.

Girotra, K., & Netessine, S. (2014). Four paths to business model innovation. *Harvard Business Review*. Accessed April 30, 2016, from https://hbr.org/2014/07/four-paths-to-business-model-innovation

Grajewski, B. (2016). The barriers healthcare providers must overcome to move medical innovation forward. *Executive Insight: Advance Healthcare Executive Magazine*. Accessed April 29, 2016, from http://healthcare-executive-insight.advanceweb.com/Features/Articles/Top-Barriers-to-Hospital-Innovation.aspx

Herzlinger, R. E. (2006). Why innovation in health care is so hard. *Harvard Business Review*. Accessed April 29, 2016, from https://hbr.org/2006/05/why-innovation-in-health-care-is-so-hard

Lindgardt, Z., Reeves, M., Stalk, G., & Deimler, M. S. (2009). Business model innovation: When the game gets tough, change the game. *The Boston Consulting Group*, pp. 1–8. Accessed April 17, 2016, from https://www.bcg.com/documents/file36456.pdf

Meyers, A. (2014). 10 major barriers to health care innovation. *LeadDoc-The Online Journal for Emerging Physician Leaders*. Accessed April 29, 2016, from https://www.linkedin.com/pulse/10-major-barriers-health-care-innovation-arlen-meyers-md-mba

Morris, M., Schindehutte, M., Richardson, J., & Allen, J. (2006). Is the business model a useful strategic concept? Conceptual, theoretical, and empirical insights. *Journal of Small Business Strategy, 17*(1), 27–50.

Nidumolu, R., Prahalad, C. K., & Rangaswami, M. R. (2009). Why sustainability is now the key driver of innovation. *Harvard Business Review*, 57–64. Accessed April 17, 2016, from https://hbr.org/2009/09/why-sustainability-is-now-the-key-driver-of-innovation

Omachonu, V. K., & Einspruch, N. G. (2010). Innovation in healthcare delivery systems: A conceptual framework. *The Innovation Journal: The Public Sector Innovation Journal, 15* (1), 1–20.

Pennic, J. (2015). Report: 5 ways to create a culture of innovation in healthcare. *HIT Consultant*. Accessed April 29, 2016, from http://hitconsultant.net/2015/09/17/4-key-challenges-to-healthcare-innovation/

Plsek, P. (2014). Recognizing the importance of innovation in health service delivery. *AHRQ Healthcare Innovations Exchange*. Accessed April 29, 2016, from https://innovations.ahrq.gov/article/recognizing-importance-innovation-health-service-delivery

Ranck, J., Falcon, R., & Kaisel, D. (2007). Rethinking business models in the global health economy: a toolkit for innovation. *Institute for the Future*, 1–46.

Trimble, C. (2016). Breaking barriers to innovation in healthcare delivery. *Physicians Practice*. Accessed April 29, 2016, from http://www.physicianspractice.com/blog/breaking-barriers-innovation-healthcare-delivery

Tye, J. (2013). Using values to gain competitive advantage. *Hospitals & Health Networks Daily*. Accessed April 29, 2016, from http://www.hhnmag.com/articles/6460-using-values-to-gain-competitive-advantage

Walston, S. L. (2014). Business models and common strategies. In *Strategic healthcare management: Planning and execution*. Chicago: Health Administration Press.

West, M. A. (1990). The social psychology of innovation in groups. In M. A. West & J. L. Farr (Eds.), *Innovation and creativity at work: Psychological and organizational strategies* (pp. 309–334). Chichester: Wiley.

Lesley A. Clack is an Assistant Professor of Health Services Administration and Coordinator of the Health Informatics Program at Armstrong State University in Savannah, GA. She teaches undergraduate and graduate courses, and specializes in the areas of Organizational Theory and Behavior, Strategic Management of Health Care Organizations, and Health Informatics. She has 11 years of teaching experience, in addition to clinical and administrative experience in healthcare. Dr. Clack earned her Doctor of Science degree in Health Systems Management from Tulane University School of Public Health and Tropical Medicine.

The Integrated-Physician-Model: Business Model Innovation in Hospital Management

Daniel Liedtke, Niowi Amgwerd, Ole Wiesinger, Dietmar Mauer, Christian Westerhoff, and Stephan Pahls

Abstract

This chapter describes the integrated-physician-model as an innovative hospital business model within the context of the Swiss health system. Its defining elements are (1) a specific model of organization and cooperation of medical doctors which allocates tasks and defines roles differently for basic medical services (Medical Service Units) and for specialized medical services (Medical Specialist Units) within the hospital; (2) a centralized Performance Management Unit executing the core functions of patient advocacy, quality management and productivity management; as well as (3) Medical Coordination Units which coordinate the delivery of specialized medical care along clinical pathways and perform administrative tasks for the Medical Service Units and Medical Specialist Units. Our business model aims to improve collaboration between competing medical teams within the same hospital (i.e. on firm-level) and between competing hospitals (i.e. on industry-level) by creating a framework for innovative "coopetition". By achieving this, the integrated-physician-model does not only create value for doctors and hospitals, but also for patients. We are convinced that only those physicians and hospital providers who focus primarily on the patient will emerge strengthened from the increasing competition in the health care sector. Patient orientation will be key for success. Our innovative business model provides a framework for a successful alignment of the different care providers in our hospitals with each other and with the needs of our target customers, our patients.

D. Liedtke (✉) • N. Amgwerd • O. Wiesinger • D. Mauer • C. Westerhoff • S. Pahls
Hirslanden AG, Corporate Office, Seefeldstrasse 214, 8008 Zürich, Switzerland
e-mail: daniel.liedtke@hirslanden.ch; niowi.amgwerd@hirslanden.ch; ole.wiesinger@hirslanden.ch; dietmar.mauer@hirslanden.ch; christian.westerhoff@hirslanden.ch; stephan.pahls@hirslanden.ch

M.A. Pfannstiel, C. Rasche (eds.), *Service Business Model Innovation in Healthcare and Hospital Management*, DOI 10.1007/978-3-319-46412-1_3

1 Introduction

The Swiss hospital landscape is undergoing profound changes as a result of new hospital planning and financing laws introduced in 2012. The new system creates an intricate mix of planning and competition. In some areas the cantons regulate much more tightly and stipulate in detail the services to be provided by each hospital, the quality requirements and minimum case numbers to be fulfilled, the amount of personnel to be trained and costs deemed to be acceptable. At the same time, subsidies to public hospitals were reduced and competition between public and private hospitals has increased. Today, all hospitals are competing with each other for patients, nursing staff and the best doctors, while having limited scope for strategic development due to a shortage of specialist staff, cost pressure and governmental regulations.

However, these regulatory changes are only the tip of the iceberg for the Swiss hospital industry. The business environment for the health care industry is changing profoundly due to various demographic, economic and societal factors. This poses specific challenges to the stakeholders of the Swiss hospital industry—especially the patients, the doctors and the hospital operators:

The patients' needs towards healthcare services have become more complex: Today patients place very high claims on quality and on the transparency about quality of medical services. But although they have rapidly expanding access to medical information, we perceive widespread disorientation of the patients about the use and the value of the information in practice. In addition, our society's understanding of illness and health and what being healthy means is changing. Lack of strength and beauty is increasingly seen as a form of disease in affluent societies. Even though universal comprehensive medical treatment is promised form all sides, health and beauty at all costs is not affordable for the individual patient or the society as a whole (Sigrist et al. 2015).

The doctors' profession is changing as well: non-clinical, administrative duties are steadily increasing, while the reputation of the profession in general has declined during the last decades. Even though patients are much better informed, doctors struggle to satisfy the specific, personalized information needs of ever more demanding patients. Furthermore, structural alterations are challenging the composition of the medical workforce: younger female doctors are increasingly replacing older male doctors. The feminization of the physician workforce prompts us to rethink the existing structures. In order to be attractive for female doctors, part-time work and job-sharing possibilities must be facilitated.

Along with these developments come vast challenges for the hospital providers: Traditionally, hospitals used to focus on their core medical business while neglecting the service needs of the patients, thereby disregarding the core concept of customer orientation as known in other service industries. Today, medical care processes and clinical pathways must be tailored to the patient's needs in all dimensions, not only in a narrow clinical sense.

In order to overcome the above-mentioned challenges, we innovated our business model. We aimed to improve value for our patients, our doctors and the hospital in general. The defining elements of our business model are (1) a specific model of organization and cooperation of medical doctors which allocates tasks and defines roles differently for basic medical services (Medical Service Units) and for specialized medical services (Medical Specialist Units) within the hospital; (2) a centralized Performance Management Unit executing the core functions of patient advocacy, quality management and productivity management; as well as (3) Medical Coordination Units which coordinate the delivery of specialized medical care along clinical pathways and perform administrative tasks for the Medical Service Units and Medical Specialist Units.

Our article is organized as follows: After providing a theoretical background of business models in general, the concept is applied to the health care industry. We develop a differentiated description of the hospital business model at industry-level (macro perspective) and at firm level (micro perspective). Thereafter we describe our business model, the integrated-physician-model, while comparing it with traditional hospital business models in Switzerland. The St. Gallen Business Model Navigator provides a useful framework for the description of our hospital business model on firm level.

The configuration of our business model followed a clearly practice-oriented approach. The typology of the traditional business models, as they will be described, builds on our own experience, expert interviews and discussions with senior executives in the hospital industry. Thus, we make no claim to a thorough academic approach and validity.

2 Hospital Business Models and Business Model Innovation

In the business model literature, business model innovation has become a stream of increasing relevance. Business models themselves are seen as the prime substance of innovation in order to create added value (Mitchell and Coles 2003). Before describing the business model innovation that was implemented at Klinik Hirslanden, we describe the basic principles of business models and business model innovation as theoretical concepts.

During the last two decades, business models have become a buzzword in academic literature and among practitioners (Zott et al. 2011). Despite its prominence, very few managers are able to define their company's business model or are capable of describing its theoretical aspects. So far, numerous scholars have outlined their definition of a business model, however, no general consensus on the term has been found yet. One of the most cited definitions put forward by Amit and Zott (2001) describes a business model as "the design of transaction content, structure and governance so as to create value though the exploitation of business opportunities". In more recent works, Zott and Amit (2010) conceptualize business models as „the set of activities from raw materials through to the final consumers with value being added throughout the various activities." Thereby, they describe the activity system as a set of interdependent organizational activities centered

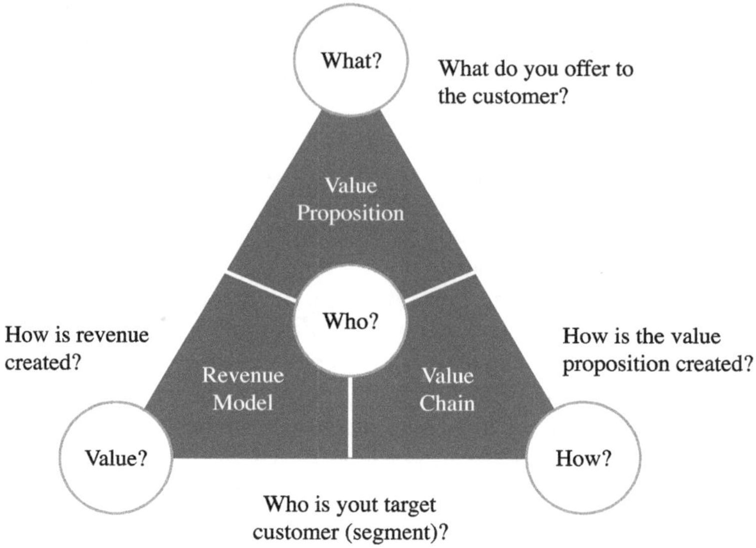

Fig. 1 Business model definition—the magic triangle. Source: Own illustration based on Gassmann et al. (2013)

around the main firm, and refer to activities that are either conducted by that main firm itself, or by its partners, customers or vendors (Zott and Amit 2010). As such, content, structure and governance make up the design characteristics that symbolize the activity system.

For the description of the integrated-physician-model, we decided to employ a conceptualization of business models that uses classifications based on a meta-analysis of the most recent literature as proposed by Gassmann et al. (2013). This approach understands business models as a holistic concept covering all relevant aspects of a business. According to the authors, a business model consists of four central dimensions: A company's target customer, the value chain behind the creation of this value, its value proposition towards the customer, and the revenue model that captures the value. When innovation happens in at least two of these four dimensions, business model innovation happens. Figure 1 depicts the business model concept as described above.

Based on this theoretical approach, we apply the concept of business model innovation on the case setting, i.e. the Swiss health care industry. Since our experience during the development process revealed that industry-level innovations highly influence firm-level innovations (and vice versa), we will show what hospital business model innovation might look like on industry-level (macro perspective) before proceeding to the firm level (micro perspective).

2.1 Hospital Business Models on Industry-Level (Macro Perspective)

As described, business models are a description of a firm's set-up and organization of its system of activities. They can be analyzed as a construct with four main dimensions. Traditionally, scholars and practitioners applied the construct on firm level, taking a micro perspective within the relevant firm. However, there are attempts to shift the focus from dyadic relationships to an industry-wide perspective, analyzing how firm-boundary spanning business models revolutionize a whole industry (Jacobides et al. 2006). For that purpose a connected set of principles and constructs has been established, which explains how an industry itself is set up for competition and how firms shape their business models within the sector.

We follow Jacobides et al.'s (2006) suggestion and use the term "industry architecture" to describe the setting of an industry. The construct of industry architecture combines, first, the features and degree of specialization of the competitors, or "organizational boundaries", and, secondly, the structure of the relationships between those players. The individual players can benefit from innovation by organizing their business models in a manner as to become the holdup in the industry's architecture and occupy the segments where there is limited flexibility and weakened competition (Jacobides et al. 2006). The industry's structural design provides a macro perspective on business models within an industry. This perspective allows insights on how healthcare providers position their business model within the health care industry as well as how their business model innovations shape the industry's structural developments (Tersago and Visnjic 2011).

Our research on the topic, applied to the health care industry, shows that only few scholars have dealt with business model innovations on industry architecture level, i.e. the macro perspective. However, one practice-oriented case study on Belgian health care providers described three main archetypes of business model innovations on industry architecture level, all of which represent a liaising or coupling between firms (Tersago and Visnjic 2011): within-discipline grouping, across-discipline grouping and competitor-grouping.

- Within-discipline grouping is mainly undertaken through mergers between hospitals. This is observed frequently, but in our opinion it is the least innovative type of business model innovation.
- Across-discipline grouping is also common in the hospital industry. Hospitals are mature examples of this type of business model innovation on the firm level, as they normally group different medical disciplines at one location and make it possible for different specialists to work together and share patients in order to provide patients with a holistic care solution. Increasingly these multi-disciplinary specialist groups or networks include specialists from different hospitals, which constitutes business model innovation on industry architecture level.

- The third archetype, competitor-grouping, can be considered the most pioneering type of liaising. It is also known as 'coopetition' (Tersago and Visnjic 2011). In Switzerland this type of business model innovation on the industry-level is rarely seen so far.

The choice of the appropriate type of business model innovation depends on the goals and the drivers for that innovation. According to Tersago and Visnjic (2011) incremental innovations, such as within-discipline grouping, aim to achieve rather conventional forms of value increases such as cost reductions, efficiency and quality gains. Contrarily, more radical business model innovations like competitor-groupings aim to enhance value drivers like "uniqueness" and "origination potential". These innovations are usually implemented through looser governance mechanisms.

There is a great need for further research. Among other topics the transferability and validity of Tersago and Visnjic's (2011) findings for the Swiss health care industry ask for verification. We believe that the Swiss health care industry provides interesting potential for scholars of industry-wide business models and respective innovations. Furthermore, our experience with business model innovation shows that industry-level business innovations highly influence firm-level innovations, which will be described in the next chapters.

2.2 Hospital Business Models on Firm-Level (Micro Perspective)

Before discussing the integrated-physician-model as an innovative form of hospital management, we briefly explain what we consider to be the traditional business models of hospital management in Switzerland. The scope of this article does not allow for an in-depth analysis of the competing business models, nonetheless, providing the basics is key for a thorough understanding of the improvements we made. It needs to be mentioned, however, that this description is based on experience and personal opinions of hospital managers and makes no claims to academic validity. The different business models are described in a stylized manner in order to facilitate understanding for the general reader.

2.2.1 Traditional Business Models

Traditionally, two main business models for hospitals are employed in the Swiss healthcare industry: The chief-physician-model in public hospitals leading to a "disciplines factory" and the attending-physician-model in hospitals that function mainly as "infrastructure provider"; as depicted in Fig. 2.

The Chief-Physician-Model

The traditional chief-physician-model is applied in the great majority of Switzerland's public hospitals. In the chief-physician-model, comprehensive silo-organizations are established for individual medical disciplines under one chief physician (e.g. department of cardiology). Within these disciplines or departments,

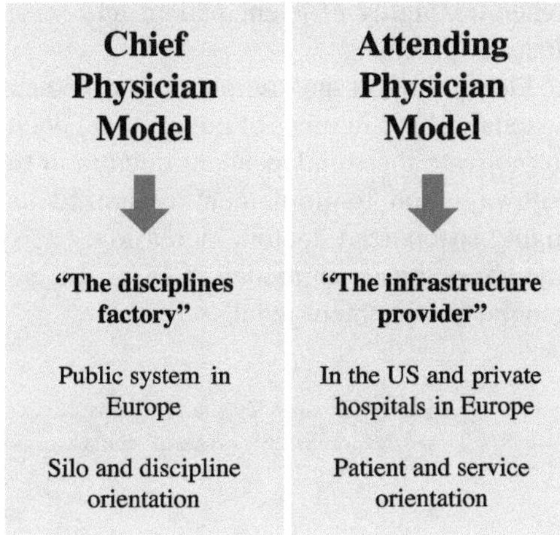

Fig. 2 Traditional business models. Source: Own illustration (2016)

the various stakeholders like employed physicians, nursing staff, therapists and administrators tend to develop into a self-sustaining silo-organization. This model is characterized by a consistent medical discipline orientation with a strict hierarchical organization, driven by a demanding chief physician position.

Depending on the medical services provided by the hospital, multiple silos emerge within the hospital. The challenge is to integrate and consolidate these independent silos on hospital management level. As this organizational model develops it requires steadily increasing levels of planning and control within and between the different silos of the hospital. Therefore, this business model is not only demanding in regards to administrative and management tasks on chief physician level, but bears high risks of conflict on general hospital management level too.

> „The overabundance of administrative duties as a chief physician is certainly one of the most negative points compared with the model of attending physicians."
> (Statement of a chief physician)

The Attending-Physician-Model

Counterpart to the chief-physician-model, we define an organizational model around self-employed attending physicians. In this model the hospital acts as a mere infrastructure provider. The attending physicians run their practices within the walls or in the vicinity of the hospital and carry out their services in an independent manner. Formally, they are entrepreneurs and have limited liability towards the hospital. In this "shop-in-shop" model independent physicians provide outpatient services in their practices and inpatient treatments in the hospital. The model generates highly efficient patient and service orientation within the independent doctors' practices.

Depending on the complexity of medical services provided and the size of the hospital, a high number of independent doctors has to be managed. The challenge is to motivate these independent doctors to treat their patients along unified clinical pathways and to implement organized teamwork. Especially the younger and highly specialized doctors increasingly need a teamwork approach. Generally, the attending-physician model requires an enormously high coordination effort on general management level.

„The all-rounder attending physician will cease to exist; we must learn to increasingly work in teams around defined patient pathways."
(Statement of an attending physician)

2.2.2 Critiques of the Traditional Business Models

From our perspective, the life cycles of both business models have passed their peaks. We see a strong need for an innovative business model that is able to overcome the main weaknesses of the previously described models, which are as follows:

- Rigid thinking in medical-disciplines in both models
- Rigid silo-thinking in the chief-physician-model
- Rigid single-doctor-thinking in the attending-physician-model

Rigid Thinking in Medical-Disciplines in Both Models

Both business models are predominantly supply oriented. Since the medical disciplines define the way how and what kind of the medical services are to be provided, they also define the organizational structures and the processes of care provision. We all know, however, that curing illness requires a multidisciplinary approach. Any model that fails to foster and achieve multidisciplinary interaction (i.e. effectively crossing borders between departmental silos and between individual doctors) sooner or later leads to under-treatment or over-treatment of patients as well as inefficient processes. In our experience, both traditional business models struggle to achieve holistic treatment for patients, because they dependent highly on individual medical disciplines, which define care provision based on discipline-intrinsic rules instead of rules that take into account the whole care setting.

Especially within the hierarchically organized chief-physician-model, it remains a challenge to guide patients efficiently along the patient's treatment path, irrespective of the deeply-rooted vertical structures. As a consequence, patients feel unsafe and at the mercy of that one highly specialized but isolated discipline. A good example is spine therapy after a slipped disk: instead of orthopedists, neurosurgeons, rheumatologists and chiropractors following a team approach and interdisciplinarily taking care of the disorder, in many hospitals these professions operate in an unnecessarily competitive manner according to their discipline-oriented organizational structure, which may not be in the interest of the patient.

Rigid Silo-Thinking in the Chief-Physician-Model

The chief-physician-model not only promotes rigid disciplinary thinking in silos but also leads to corresponding actions. Within the established silos, we perceive low levels of sectorial (i.e. in- and outpatient) and departmental (medical and non-medical) interaction between the individual stakeholders. The chief-physician-model often lacks openness and flexibility towards innovative changes. Usually medical services are supplied within a hospital's silo of one discipline. There is insufficient cooperative integration of external resources or know-how, e.g. through external doctors or medical staff in order to acquire new patients and increase the hospital's efficiency, as well as patient centered innovations. All in all, this business model lacks short-term agility, efficiency and the possibility to recognize the urge of innovation towards patient centered care. From the perspective of the hospital provider, the chief-physician-model bears the risk of being too dependent on the hierarchically oriented chief physician. The predominance of hierarchical thinking tends to curb innovations rather than spurring them.

Rigid Single-Doctor-Thinking in the Attending-Physician-Model

In the attending-physician-model comprehensive planning and steering of the various hospital activities is a great challenge for the hospital management. Due to the high number of stakeholders that are often acting independently on their own behalf, effective and efficient resource allocation becomes highly complex and at times nearly impossible. One of the biggest challenges is interdisciplinary cooperation between the self employed medical units or physicians, which is a decisive prerequisite for building structures that permit maximum patient safety and efficiency. From the perspective of the hospital provider, the main risk of the attending-physician-model is lack of influence of hospital management regarding patient safety and quality requirements.

2.2.3 Potential for Hospital Business Model Innovation

Many hospitals respond to the current regulatory and political challenges in Switzerland as described above by changing their legal form, streamlining management, modernizing the hospital infrastructure, forming centers of expertise and strengthening collaboration with other hospitals. However, we are convinced that this is not sufficient. We promote a re-engineering of the existing business explicitly through the eyes of the patients and doctors. What needs to be done is creating an efficient model of medical care provision for the patient that merges the pros of the two traditional business models while eliminating their cons.

Patients must offered care not only according to the medical disciplines, but truly tailored to their health needs. The ultimate goal must be to provide an all-round carefree package of medical treatment, which enables the patient to focus fully on the healing process. The patient should be enabled to devote his/her full energy on recovery and increased well-being—physically, mentally and emotionally—while the hospital operator should be enabled to take final responsibility for the best outcome of treatment at appropriate costs.

To achieve this, rigid thinking in medical disciplines, rigid silo-thinking and rigid single-doctor thinking need to make way for specific cooperative involvement of all specialized actors within and outside the hospital in a more open business model, which employs nevertheless clear rules for all.

Our goal was to create such a business model that allows for "coopetition" between independently working medical teams (1) within the same hospital and (2) between competing hospitals. Through this model the hospital operator and the involved physicians are truly able to create value for the patient, doctors and hospital alike.

3 The Integrated-Physician-Model: Business Model Innovation in Swiss Health Care

As already touched upon, Klinik Hirslanden in Zurich reconfigured its business model from the traditional attending-physician-model in which the hospital acts as a mere infrastructure provider to a unique and innovative business model merging the chief-physician-model and the attending-physician-model. Klinik Hirslanden, one of the most prominent private hospitals in Switzerland, was founded in 1932 and is now part of the Hirslanden Private Hospital Group, which was formed in 1990 by the merger of several private hospitals. In 2007, the group has become a subsidiary of the South African Medi-Clinic Corporation Hospital Group.

In its 50 medical competence centers and institutes, Klinik Hirslanden offers a broad range of medical services covering most procedures and custom tailored treatments, applying the highest professional standards of medical and nursing care. The main focus areas are cardiology, cardiac and visceral surgery, neuroscience, orthopedics, gynecology, obstetrics and a 24-7 emergency unit (Fig. 3).

By applying the St. Gallen Business Model Navigator as outlined above, we will now describe in detail the integrated-physician-model—a true business model innovation in the Swiss health care industry.

3.1 Target Customers

Every business model appeals to a certain customer group (Chesbrough and Rosenbloom 2002; Hamel 2000) and needs to answer the question "Who is the customer?" (Magretta 2002). Following Morris et al. (2005, p. 730) argumentation line—i.e. the "failure to adequately define the market is a key factor associated with venture failure"—defining our target customer groups is the first dimension in the configuration of our business model. In order to be successful, we need to address the needs of our individual customer groups separately, using the language they can

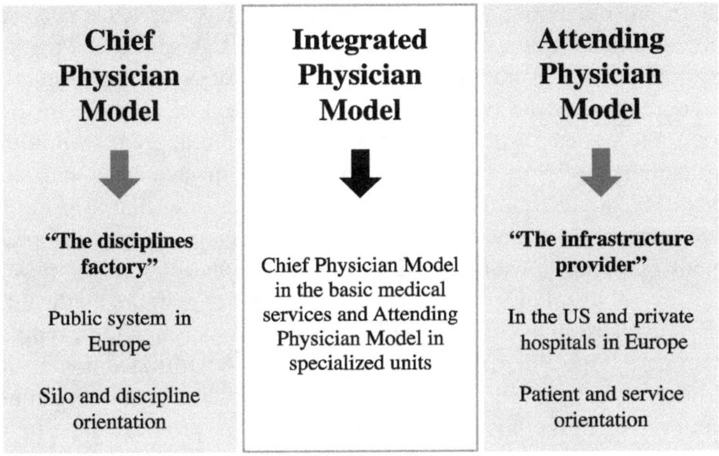

Fig. 3 The integrated-physician-model model as a merger. Source: Own illustration (2016)

identify with and the channels they can access. In our business model, we have defined four categories of target customers:

Our main customer group is our patients. We have deeply incorporated our patient-orientation in our core values. "Patients first" marks one of three main pillars in the strategy Hirslanden 2020, focusing intensively on patient safety and patient value in all aspects of our daily business. However, recent developments have clearly shown that not all patients have the same needs or value the same services equally, which is why we aim to align our services more concretely with the diverse demands of our patients.

Our business model's target customer A is the privately insured or self-paying patient. Besides excellent medical treatment, private patients ask for high levels of personalized care, extra time devoted to them by doctors and nurses, high standards of room and gastronomy services, as well superior infrastructure and interior design. In order to comply with the needs of our A customers, our hospitals need to provide far more than just industry-standard medical treatment. A customers have higher demands on individualized medicine, higher expectations on comfort levels and additional services, for which they are willing to pay higher insurance fees, which in turn provide higher profit margins for the care providers (i.e. mainly the hospital and the doctors).

Our business model's target customer B is the patient with basic health insurance, which is compulsory in Switzerland and covers all aspects of medical care that are deemed necessary to treat illness according to international best practice. However, basic insurance does not cover free choice of the treating doctor and no extras in terms of patient service, room standard, gastronomy, and other amenities.

B customers are either not willing or not able to pay for extra services. Their expectation and their right as a patient is to receive state-of-the-art medical treatment without "frills". From our perspective, the focus of the hospital for this customer segment must be on effective, appropriate, and efficient medicine. We like to point out that any hospital business model, including our own, must ensure maximum patient safety for all patients, irrespective of their insurance status.

Our business model's target customer C is the doctor affiliated with our hospital—either working in a stand-alone practice or organized in group practices or centers made up of multiple doctors. Since independent affiliated doctors are free to practice in several hospitals they are not only our partners in the medical treatment process, but also customers of the hospital's services. Through their reputation and by maintaining a large network of referring doctors the affiliated doctors act as the main recruiters of patients for our hospitals. However, they can only maintain their high reputation when the hospital they are working in provides superior levels of care too. Hence, the hospital and the attending physicians operate in a form of symbiosis based on mutual dependence. This is why we consider the relationships with our attending physicians as one of highest importance. However the fact that the doctors are both partner and customer makes the relationship complex and at times fragile, requiring high levels of management attention from the side of the hospital.

Our business model's target customers D are the funding agencies (insurance companies and cantons). In the Swiss health care system, a hospital strongly depends on this subgroup of customers as they prescribe in detail which services the hospital may provide as well as the prices and conditions of service provision.

3.2 Value Chain

Following the St. Gallen Business Model Navigator this chapter provides the answer for the question: How does the integrated-physician-model create its value proposition? A firm has to master and orchestrate several processes and activities, resources and capabilities in its internal value chain to build and distribute the value proposition. This constitutes the second dimension within the design of a new business model. By applying this framework it will become clear that the main focus and prime innovation of the integrated-physician-model lies in the area of orchestration of the other factors.

3.2.1 Processes and Activities

We assume that all activities concerned with the hospital's core value creating process, i.e. the medical care of patients (diagnosis, treatment, nursing care, rehabilitation, prevention, counseling) as well as auxiliary patient services (accommodation, food & beverages, patient administration) are deployed in accordance with applicable medico-legal regulation, scientific evidence and best practice, independent of the hospital's specific business model. This principle also holds for the core processes of providing medical and auxiliary patient care. The clinical pathway (integrated care process) of a patient with a specific condition is to a large part mandated by best practice and medical evidence. It is therefore fairly independent of a hospital's business model.

3.2.2 Resources

We also assume that the resources (competent staff, infrastructure, technology, etc.) needed to carry out the core activities (medical and auxiliary patient services) of any hospital are available as needed. Hirslanden provides a very high standard of care by investing in its resources at levels above average of the Swiss hospital industry. However, this was equally true before the introduction of our new integrated-physician-model.

3.2.3 Capabilities

We also assume that the capabilities (know-how and skills) required to carry out the activities of the core value-creating processes in the hospital are available as needed. Medico-legal regulations stipulate in detail the level of skill and training necessary for the different activities constituting medical care. Every hospital needs doctors, nurses and technical staff with defined capabilities to provide medical care. Hirslanden provides a very high standard of care, e.g. by employing and partnering with the best doctors in the market. However, this was also the case before the introduction of our new integrated-physician-model.

3.2.4 Orchestration

Applying the framework of the St. Gallen Business Model Navigator reveals that the integrated-physician-model creates added value mainly through innovative orchestration of the core activities and processes, resources and capabilities. The integrated-physician-model is basically a management system, with focus on better orchestration (i.e. defining roles, tasks and organizational structure) of the main value-creating actors in the hospital. Because the integrated-physician-model is fairly independent of processes, resources and capabilities, it becomes attractive for other hospitals and the hospital industry as a whole. From a theoretical perspective, any hospital, independent of its ownership structure, market environment, service portfolio and its state of processes, resources and capabilities, should be able to create added value for its core clients (patients and doctors) by implementing the integrated-physician-model.

Main Principles of the Integrated-Physician-Model

The integrated-physician-model is built on five main principles:

- Give hospital doctors more time for their core duties. By this we mean clinical work with patients, training of doctors, clinical research and innovation. Consistent focus on these core duties has an immediate positive effect on the outcome and the satisfaction of patients, employees and referrers; however, it also means that not every chief physician must be represented in the hospital management board any longer.

- Provide structures for stronger division of labor between professions and operating units, as well as function-specific internal organization of the operating units and the medical management.
- Create a differentiated organization of doctors, which represents a merger of the chief-physician-model and attending-physician-model, which defines the role and organization of doctors differently for basic medical services and for specialized services.
- Manage the core processes tightly through centralized Performance Management Units, which are organizationally independent from the care providers (Medical Service Units and Medical Specialist Units).
- Support the Medical Service Units and Medical Specialist Units with administrative tasks and in the provision of multidisciplinary care along integrated clinical pathways through Medical Coordination Units.

The Main Building Blocks of the Integrated-Physician-Model

In accordance with the principles described above, the integrated-physician-model is characterized by two types of service provision units and two corresponding units for managing their specific activities, as depicted in the following graph (Fig. 4):

The main characteristics of these units are depicted in Table 1.

Medical Service Units

The Medical Service Units are the primary care providers within the hospital and service providers for patients and specialists. They include medical (anesthesia, intensive medicine, radiology, emergency medicine, etc.) and Non-Medical Service Units (nursing, therapy, etc.) and report to a common management. They operate the central medical infrastructure of the hospital such as the emergency department, the operating rooms, intensive care unit and the wards. Their primary goal is high interdisciplinary integration of all inpatient treatment processes, patient safety and 24/7 readiness of the hospital for primary patient care. The Service Units are involved in all process steps of patient treatment from admission to discharge in close consultation with the Specialist Units.

In order to achieve a high level of commitment and a common service culture, all doctors of the Medical Service Units are listed in a chief-physician-model. These chief physicians, as well as the managers of the non-physician Service Units (e.g. nursing, therapies) report to one central manager of the Service Units, who should be a member of the hospital's highest executive management level.

The managerial responsibility of the heads of the Services Units includes in particular the subjects of service quality, process integration and patient safety. Possible conflicts of interest between the heads of the Service Units can be solved by the impartial central manager function with regard to the common objectives of patient safety, patient satisfaction and process efficiency. This focus on common objectives in the sense of a "corporate culture" provides a recognized standard to solve conflicts within the Service Units and vis-à-vis the Specialist Units.

The significance of the Service Units for the recruitment of medical specialists also deserves mention. High levels of expertise, service quality and process

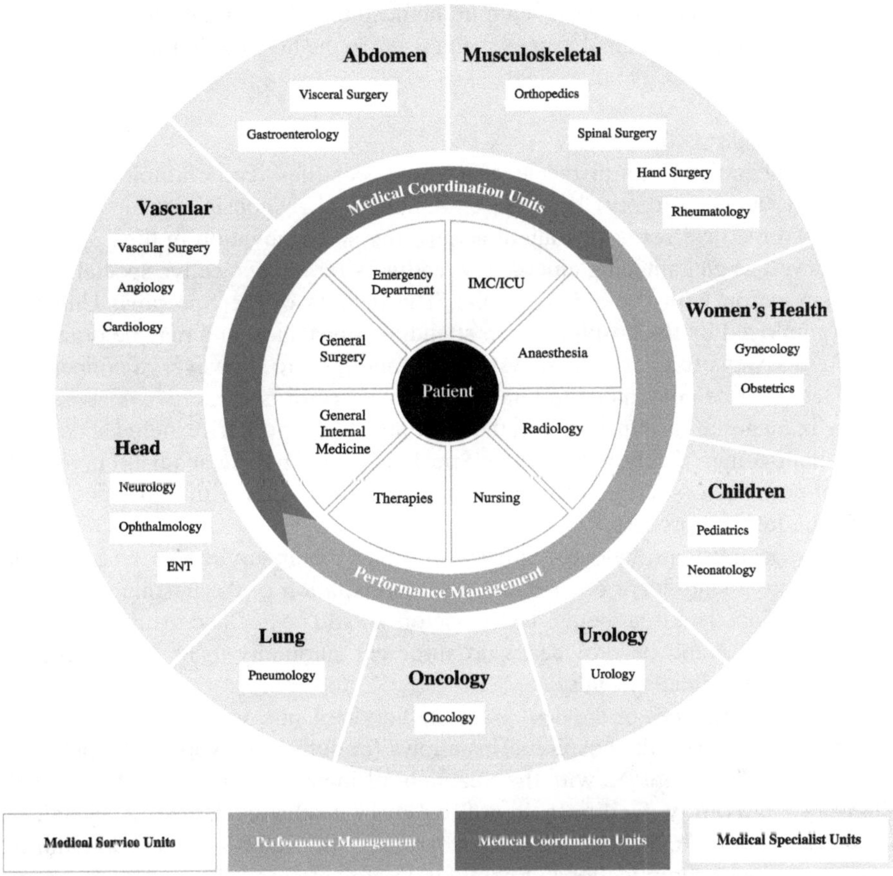

Fig. 4 Organization of the main building blocks in the integrated-physician-model. Source: Own illustration (2016)

Table 1 Characterizations of the units

Organizational Unit	Medical Service Unit	Medical Specialist Unit
Type of service	Basic hospital services	Specialties and sub-specialties
Goal	Patient safety, integration	Specialization, innovation
Leadership	Single head, chief physician	Partnership
Contract status	Employed or in close contractual relationship	Attending or employed
Unit with steering function	Centralized Performance Management Medical Coordination Units	

Source: Own illustration (2016)

efficiency of the integrated basic care in the hospital are often decisive criteria for successfully binding medical “super specialists” to the hospital in times of increasing competition.

Medical Specialist Units

Medical Specialist Units at the level of sub-specialties (e.g. cardiology, gastroenterology, spinal surgery) bear the entrepreneurial responsibility for providing specialized medical services, patient acquisition and innovation in their specialist area, as well as guaranteeing emergency readiness for the respective specialist area in collaboration with the Service Units. The doctors of the Specialist Units are either employed by the hospital or are attending physicians, and may be organized in different ways (e.g. chairman system, partner system), however, a cooperative approach must be guaranteed to retain attractiveness for doctors.

The managerial responsibility in the Specialist Units primarily includes creation of a patient-centered culture within the Specialist Units, patient acquisition, recruitment of new doctors to the team and continuing innovation within the specialized medical treatment process.

Many specialists provide a significant portion of their services in the outpatient sector, make a significant contribution to the reputation of the hospital, and refer patients for inpatient treatments. These doctors should be enabled to concentrate on their core duties and be provided with sufficient autonomy to be able to further develop their medical specialty.

Ideally the practices of the doctors of the Service Units are located in a “doctor house” within or near the hospital. This allows for outpatient work in the practices to be seamlessly combined with the treatment of inpatient patients in the hospital. The close proximity facilitates interdisciplinary exchange between specialists, simplifies patient transfers, and is a condition for timely intervention during emergencies and complications in complex treatment cases. The hospital benefits from a wide availability of sub-specialties without having to employ all the specialists itself and generates opportunities to offer “super-specialists” of high reputation flexible employment solutions (employment or attending physician status, full- or part-time, etc.) according to their personal preference. The “doctor house” bundles the resources of the specialists and makes part-time work easier, which again mitigates the lack of specialist doctors.

Performance Management

A centralized Performance Management Unit ensures hospital-wide productivity management, clinical quality management, as well as information management, ultimately seeking maximum patient safety, patient satisfaction and efficiency. By doing this the Performance Management Unit relieves the Service Units and Specialist Units from a score of administrative and other duties which do not constitute core tasks of medical doctors. Performance management holds a key position in the integrated-physician-model and should report directly to the executive board or the director of the hospital in order to guarantee an effective level of managerial authority vis-à-vis Service Units and Specialist Units in their area of expertise. It is preferable that a medical specialist with an additional managerial qualification holds the function. To ensure effective division of power that is not tied to the interests of a particular group, this unit should not be managed by a chief physician of the Service Units nor an affiliated physician of the Specialist Units.

Patient's Advocate as a Single Point of Access

As the need for reconcilement between the Specialist Units and Service Units as well as between the patients, their relatives and the referrers is increasing, the importance of a single point of access, through which all critical information relevant to patient's treatment is managed, becomes evident. In the integrated-physician-model this manager of information and processes for the patients, their relatives, referring doctors, the involved physicians and other hospital units is best described as a "Patient Advocate". Especially for complex cases an inter- and multi-disciplinary circle of care is key, but requires specific management. The Patient Advocate is a kind of case manager who coordinates the care process of selected patients according to their needs, irrespective of individual sensitivities of the involved physicians. She/He coordinates all the involved medical and non-medical participants along the patient's clinical pathway in the hospital, while bearing highest possible patient orientation in mind. The Patient Advocate takes full responsibility for the case management as the warrantor for maximum patient benefit. Thereby, the Patient Advocate involves and guides the relevant medical and non-medical participants in the care process in accordance with the performance criteria of patient experience, quality and efficiency.

Medical Quality Management

Practically all Swiss hospitals have institutionalized "general quality management" at the level of the firm and employ qualified quality managers who relieve doctors of a considerable amount of work, e.g. with process documentation, implementation of quality systems, with hospital hygiene and with quality measurements. However, many important quality management tasks at the level of the medical disciplines (treatment standards, indication boards, morbidity & mortality conferences, register management, etc.) continue to be fragmented. Every medical discipline manages its own standards and boards and the interdisciplinary collaboration is complex. There is a striking discrepancy in many hospitals between the centralized, usually well-staffed "general quality management" and the wide variety of decentralized, often under-staffed solutions in "discipline-level" clinical quality management. However, it becomes increasingly unsustainable to rely on physicians who should be focused on their patients, or on under-qualified secretariats or assistant doctors for this important task of clinical quality management. By centralizing clinical quality management and staffing it with qualified specialists, it will become much more professional and efficient. Communication of the results will be more objective and more transparent and there is an increased likelihood that measures to improve quality are consistently implemented.

Defining the discipline-specific treatment and quality standards remains the responsibility of the heads of the Service Units or Specialist Units. However, the central clinical quality management can request that standards be so aligned that the clinical pathways are guaranteed as a whole in accordance with "best practice". While the autonomy of the specialists over the treatment and quality standards remains guaranteed, the central clinical quality management will greatly improve management of the standards and increase commitment by all to adhere to them.

Productivity Management

An important premise of the integrated-physician-model is the departure from the concept that surgeons carry the responsibility of capacity planning of operation theatres and patient beds. A high degree of capacity utilization is decisive for the economic success of a hospital and can only be achieved through centralized and flexible planning. This will be difficult to achieve if the beds or operation theatres are fixed to particular disciplines (silos within the hospital) with chief physicians controlling the occupancy.

In the integrated-physician-model, the capacities (e.g. beds, operation theatres) of the Service Units are made available to the specialists and their patients based on demand. The centralized scheduling ensures that the patients are taken care of in the most suitable infrastructure by the specialist with the required competence, while achieving high occupancy at the same time. This allows patients of several Specialist Units to be treated in a particular operation theatre or in a particular ward without conflicts of competency on the side of the physicians. This concept of "case management" instead of "bed management" constitutes a fundamental cultural change for many chief physicians with historically accrued privileges in hospitals applying the traditional chief-physician-model.

Medical Coordination Units

Medical Coordination Units take on coordination and administration duties such as duty roster planning, reporting, organizing medical training, coordinating treatment standards between specialist areas, etc. for a group of closely-related Service Units and Specialist Units. In this way, they make use of synergies and generate efficiency gains in non-clinical services, which in return generate more time for core medical duties.

The management of the coordination units should always be cooperative/coordinative in nature, however, could be realized in a variety of ways. In smaller hospitals, for example, the chief physician of a Service Unit can adopt this role; however, he/she should not interpret the duties as the role of a classic hospital director but rather as a service provider for the associated Service Units and Specialist Units. In larger hospitals, the function can be fulfilled e.g. by a specialist who reports directly to the executive board of the hospital. A rotating chairman system represents another fruitful option. Close collegial cooperation with the Specialist Units is decisive for the acceptance of the coordination units here.

3.3 Revenue Model

According to the St. Gallen Business Model Navigator the third dimension explains why the business model is financially viable, thus it relates to the revenue model. In essence, it unifies aspects such as, for example, the cost structure and the applied revenue mechanisms, and points to an elementary question of any firm, namely how to make money in the business (Gassmann et al. 2013).

In Switzerland payment of hospitals for inpatient care is divided into (1) payment for a basic package of services through the basic health insurance system, which is obligatory for every permanent resident in the country and (2) payment for additional services through private health insurance, which is at present bought by around one quarter of the population as an add-on to the obligatory basic insurance. (De Pietro et al. 2015).

Included in the basic package are all medical treatments, while private insurance covers extras like free choice of doctors and better hotel services. Payment for the basic package is defined by the system of diagnosis-related groups (DRGs) combined with regulated prices, while the tariffs for additional services within the private care package can be negotiated freely between hospitals and insurance companies (De Pietro et al. 2015).

Hospital infrastructure, medical technology, as well as nursing care and hotel services must provide tangible added value to the private patient. This service offering is comparable to the luxury-goods industry. Branding, marketing and packaging of add-on private health care services create added value to the patient, and, thus, generate competitive advantage for a hospital.

When Switzerland introduced the DRG system relatively late in 2012, the financial room for maneuver for hospitals declined. The costs of infrastructure are included into an all-inclusive reimbursement rate (base rate) and the cost weight assigned to an individual DRG by the system is adapted every year to the actual costs, which the Swiss hospitals incur. Hence, efficiency gains achieved by some or all hospital in 1 year are immediately translated into lower tariffs in the following years. In addition, subsidies that have earlier been granted by the cantons to many public hospitals, were reduced significantly and deficit guaranties abolished. The highly regulated DRG tariffs are only just covering the costs for the majority of hospitals with average efficiency, while inefficient hospitals incur deficits and only very efficient hospitals make a small profit. Since many hospitals generate more than 80 % of overall inpatient revenue from obligatory insurance, which just covers the costs, the focus on efficiency and productivity has become one of the foremost concerns of hospital managers (De Pietro et al. 2015).

With its strong focus on division of responsibilities, assignment of clear roles to Specialist Units and Service Units, as well as management of the production process by a centralized Performance Management Unit, our business model significantly improves transparency of the production process and provides the tools to increase efficiency and productivity on a permanent basis. Our business model thus increases the ability of the hospital management to achieve profits in the tightly regulated segment of the basic service package governed by the

DRG-system and funded by obligatory health insurance—an area where most hospitals actually lose money today.

Since the profit margins are generally low in the basic package, it is of paramount importance for hospitals to attract patients with additional private insurance, where profit margins are higher. As a matter of fact, many hospitals are forced to subsidize their production of basic services with revenues generated from private services. This is the reason why most hospitals have invested significant resources in high-standard care facilities for private patients (e.g. private wards, guest relation services etc.). However, the market potential is limited and hospitals are competing heavily for the privately insured patients. The integrated-physician-model enables hospitals to attract doctors of high reputation who are able to recruit a higher-than-average ratio of private patients.

In summary our business model strengthens revenues and profits through efficiency gains in the segment of obligatory insurance (customer B) and through increased volumes in the segment of private insurance (customer A).

3.4 Value Proposition

The value proposition expresses the business model's offerings to its customers and can thus be seen as a holistic view of a company's combination of products and services that are of value to the customer (Osterwalder 2004). Our value proposition addresses all four of our target customer groups, however, at this point we subsume the basic and privately insured patients in one group. Furthermore, we point out the value proposition for the doctors working in our hospitals and, last but not least, the funding agencies (cantons and insurance companies).

3.4.1 Value for Patients

The integrated-physician-model differentiates service provision in terms of content and price for treating diseases and providing additional comfort services in order to increase the patient's individual, physical, psychological and emotional capability beyond the pure treatment. Hence, we define the patient's value proposition along the three dimensions quality, patient satisfaction and costs.

Medical Quality

The quality of a service can be defined by its degree of fulfillment of the patients' expectations. One central issue for hospitals is the quality of the doctors as perceived by the patients. In order to improve quality and guarantee objectivity, hospitals measure outcomes and benchmark them with medical guidelines. However, in today's highly complex health care environment the patient is often unable to objectively judge medical quality. Therefore patients rely a lot on the reputation of providers, on advice from relatives, friends and other health care providers and on media reports.

Our business model creates value for the patient in the area of medical quality by working with the best doctors, allowing these doctors to concentrate on their core duties, and by managing outcome parameters, treatment processes, patient safety and medical risk tightly through centralized and specialized structures of Performance Management, while also transparently publishing the relevant performance indicators.

Patient Satisfaction and Patient Experience

Due to its high level of subjectivity, patient satisfaction is difficult to influence. We define satisfaction as the patients' expectations as opposed to their perceived experience. To keep patient satisfaction high, our ambition in the first place is to offer the best possible experience, and secondly, we try to manage our patients' expectations. We aim for highest possible transparency in our service as well as differentiating service offerings for our different customer groups, by primarily curing diseases for our target customers B, as well as providing additional services to cater to the individual's physical, mental and emotional needs that go beyond basic medical treatment—as is our promise for our target customers A. These private patients are demanding more than just nice rooms and better room services. The possibility of access to and choice of the best doctors, short waiting times, high level of personalized care given by these doctors, integration of doctors in multidisciplinary teams have become more important than ever for private patients. Today, the majority of hospitals—no matter whether they employ the hierarchical chief-physician-model or the attending-physician-model—organize their most important workforce, the doctors, in a way that hinders them to respond at their best to these demands of private patients.

Our business model increases the ability of doctors to cater to the individual needs of private patients. Combined with superior services (luxury-goods segment) our specific assignment of roles among the doctors (which for example allows specialist in the Specialist Units to focus uniquely on patient care and innovation) our business model greatly increases the competitive advantage of our hospitals to attract private patients, and the best doctors to treat them.

All in all, we face several factors that influence our patients' expectations and we have chosen to transparently communicate what patients can expect from a stay at our hospital. This transparency in service differentiation between general and privately insured patients not only improves patient satisfaction but also allows for purposeful investments and economic case costs management.

Price and Costs

The value for patients regarding this dimension is perceived differently, depending on the county's health care system (Sigrist et al. 2015) and the patient's price sensitivity or willingness to pay for superior medical treatment and additional services. The main source of funding in the Swiss health care system are the citizens themselves, approximately two thirds of the health services are paid by private households through their insurance fees or private health expenditures (Sigrist et al. 2015). Therefore, the burden of private households in Switzerland is comparatively high: Around a quarter of total healthcare costs are paid privately, i.e. through cost investments in insured benefits or directly out of pocket. In our business model, we do not make a claim for producing or providing our services at lower costs than our competitors. Despite our constant attempts of reducing costs and attaining higher productivity levels, our business model is configured to achieve highest possible quality standards at lowest possible costs.

3.4.2 Value for Doctors

Our business model creates specific values for the doctors. In the integrated-physician-model all physicians experience gains in job satisfaction, since they are relieved of non-clinical administrative tasks and have more time for their core clinical work. This also translates into efficiency, quality and revenue gains, since doctors get time that can be invested in improving relationships to their patients or acquiring new patients. In addition, since the integrated-physician-model not only facilitates integration of attending physicians into all sub-specialties but also bridges the distance between hospital doctors working primarily in the inpatient sector and attending physicians who work primarily in the outpatient sector, the model provides a timely solution to manage the shift of inpatient services into the outpatient sector. The main value for specialist doctors in the Specialist Units, however, originates in the fact that the integrated-physician-model allows them to put into effect their entrepreneurial potential. The self-employed specialists in our Specialist Units are intrinsically motivated to deliver the best possible services as they are directly influenced by their patients' perception of the service, which increases their standing with patients and fills their practices.

3.4.3 Value for the Funding Agencies

In the segment of the tightly regulated obligatory basic insurance (see also Sect. 3.3) the concern of the funding agencies is to buy services of the quality-level defined by regulation at the lowest possible price. This price, i.e. the base rate, is negotiated between the hospital and the health insurance companies; however the upper price limit is heavily influenced and effectively capped by the regulator, i.e. the cantons. However, the focus on productivity and efficiency in our business model allows us to produce high quality care at the given low prices in the segment of obligatory basic insurance. Because of our ability to manage productivity by a centralized performance management, we do not need to internally subsidize basic care provision through private care provision, which would blur the line between basic and private insurance within the hospital and towards patients, doctors and funding agencies. As such, our business model can achieve this better than the majority of our competitors with the hierarchical chief-physician-model or the attending-physician-model.

In the segment of private health insurance, our business model creates value for the funding agencies (health insurance companies) by more clearly differentiating the value of the private care package ("luxury goods" plus personalized doctor's care) for the patient. The hospital and the insurance company both share the private patient as their customer and can expect attractive profit margins from this private insurance segment. In order to acquire and keep customers, the insurance companies heavily depend on the ability of the hospitals to provide private care at the best possible quality and visibly differentiate for their customers. Our business model is able to achieve this better than the majority of hospitals with the hierarchical chief-physician-model.

4 Conclusion

The Swiss health care industry is currently being transformed by extensive regulatory changes as well as various demographic, economic and societal factors. These create immense challenges for hospital operators and other stakeholders in the Swiss health care industry. In order to overcome these challenges and to successfully compete in the current business environment, hospitals operators are busy reconfiguring their business models either by re-engineering their business models on industry-level (i.e. strengthening collaboration with other participants in the market) or by adapting their business models on firm-level (e.g. streamlining management).

However, in our opinion the recent attempts are not sufficient. On firm-level many hospitals implement concepts adapted from other industries (e.g. lean management, just-in-time delivery), which certainly have their place in health care. But few efforts have been made so far in Switzerland to re-model the most defining factors of hospital care: the allocation of tasks and the organization of doctors in the core medical care process as well as steering of the core medical processes.

After realizing the importance of these factors Klinik Hirslanden re-engineered its business model accordingly, aiming to create value for patients, doctors and the hospital alike. We transformed our traditional attending-physician-model to an innovative business model that merges the chief-physician-model and the attending-physician-model into a model we call the "integrated-physician-model".

For the description of the integrated-physician-model we employed Gassmann et al.'s (2013) holistic conceptualization of business models, which suggests four central dimensions: The company's target customers, the value chain behind the creation value, its value proposition towards the customer, and the revenue model that captures the value. Application of the framework of the St. Gallen Business Model Navigator, reveals that our main focus of innovation in the value chain stems from the area of orchestration of our core activities and processes, resources and capabilities. Our model constitutes a management system that allows for better focusing on orchestration of the various production factors specific to hospital providers.

The integrated-physician-model allocates tasks and defines roles differently for basic medical services (Medical Service Units) and for specialized medical services (Medical Specialist Units) within the hospital. Furthermore, improved central performance management executing the core functions of patient advocacy, quality management and productivity management has an immediate positive effect on the medical outcome, the satisfaction of patients, employees and referrers as well as the financial output of the hospital. The integrated-physician-model provides structures for stronger division of labor between professions and operating units as well as function-specific, tailored internal organization of the operating units and the medical management. The core processes are tightly managed through a centralized Performance Management Unit, which is organizationally independent from the care providers (Service Units and Specialist Units). Medical Coordination Units coordinate the delivery of specialized medical care along clinical pathways and perform administrative tasks for the Service Units and the Specialist Units.

All these factors lead to a comparatively higher value proposition for our target customers. Through introducing the integrated-physician-model, we aimed at achieving the highest possible patient value and value for the doctors. In order to keep patient satisfaction high, it is important to manage the patients' expectations regarding the expected medical outcome, added services and resulting costs. We are convinced that only those physicians and hospital providers who focus primarily on the patient will emerge strengthened from the increasing competition in the health care sector. Patient orientation will be key for success. Our innovative business model provides a framework for a successful alignment of the different care providers in our hospitals with each other and with the needs of our target customers, i.e. our patients.

Further research is needed to understand the potential of our business model for adaptation to the industry-level (e.g. for realizing benefits of "coopetition" between hospitals). However, we are strongly convinced that our business model offers benefits to patients, doctors and hospitals on firm-level independent of the size, service portfolio, current management system and ownership structure of the hospitals.

References

Amit, R., & Zott, C. (2001). Value creation in e-business. *Strategic Management Journal, 22*, 493–520.

Chesbrough, H. W., & Rosenbloom, R. S. (2002). The role of the business model in capturing value from innovation: Evidence from Xerox Corporation's technology spinoff companies. *Industrial and Corporate Change, 11*, 533–534.

De Pietro, C., Camenzind, P., Sturny, I., Crivelli, L., Edwards-Garavoglia, S., Spranger, A., Wittenbecher, F., & Quentin, W. (2015). Switzerland: Health system review. *Health Systems in Transition, 17*(4), 1–288.

Gassmann, O., Frankenberger, K., & Csik, M. (2013). *Geschäftsmodelle entwickeln. 55 innovative Konzepte mit dem St. Galler Business Model Navigator*. München: Carl Hanser Verlag.

Hamel, G. (2000). *Leading the revolution*. Boston: Harvard Business School Press.

Jacobides, M. G., Knudsen, T., & Augier, M. (2006). Benefiting from innovation: Value creation, value appropriation and the role of industry architectures. *Research Policy, 35*, 1200–1221.

Magretta, J. (2002). Why business models matter. *Harvard Business Review, 80*(5), 86–92.

Mitchell, D., & Coles, C. (2003). The ultimate competitive advantage of continuing business model innovation. *Journal of Business Strategy, 24*, 15–21.

Morris, M., Schindehutte, M., & Allen, J. (2005). The entrepreneur's business model: Toward a unified perspective. *Journal of Business Research, 58*(6), 726–735.

Osterwalder, A. (2004). *The business model ontology – A proposition in a design science approach*. Lausanne: Universite de Lausanne.

Sigrist, S., Bornstein, N., Lesmono, K., Dür, A., & Folkers, G. (2015). Hacking healthcare – Das Gesundheitssystem verstehen und weiterdenken. *Verlag Neue Zürcher Zeitung*.

Tersago, S., & Visnjic, I. (2011). *Business model innovation in health care*. Academic Working Paper, University of Cambridge.

Zott, C., & Amit, R. (2010). Designing your future business model: An activity system perspective. *Long Range Planning, 43*, 216–226.

Zott, C., Amit, R., & Massa, L. (2011). The business model: Recent developments and future research. *Journal of Management, 37*(4), 1019–1042.

Daniel Liedtke is Chief Operating Officer of the Hirslanden Private Hospital Group. For more than 15 years he has held various senior medical, management and board functions, including the Directorship of Klinik Hirslanden, the largest hospital in the Group. Dr. Liedtke studied osteopathic medicine and holds a Doctorate in Business Administration.

Niowi Amgwerd is a staff member of the Business Development Unit of the Hirslanden Private Hospital Group. She holds a Master in Business Management and is a PhD Candidate in Management at the University of St. Gallen (Switzerland). Her research focuses on hospital business models and innovation.

Ole Wiesinger is Chief Executive Officer of the Hirslanden Private Hospital Group and Member of the Executive Committee of Mediclinic International Ltd, the parent company of Hirslanden. He has held various senior management and board functions in hospital and health care management in Germany and Switzerland including the Membership of the board Committee of Mediclinic International Ltd and the Directorship of Klinik Hirslanden, the largest hospital in the Group. Dr. Wiesinger is a medical doctor, a biologist and holds a Master in Health Economics.

Dietmar Mauer is the Head of Medical Services of Klinik Hirslanden, the largest hospital in the Hirslanden Private Hospital Group. He has held various senior medical and management functions in hospital and health care management in Germany and Switzerland. Dr. Mauer is a habilitated medical doctor, studied Health Care Management and is teaching anesthesiology at the University of Saarland, Homburg.

Christian Westerhoff is Chief Clinical Officer of the Hirslanden Private Hospital Group. He has held various senior management functions in hospital and health care management in Germany and Switzerland. Dr. Westerhoff is a medical doctor and holds a Master of Business Administration.

Stephan Pahls is Head of Business Development of the Hirslanden Private Hospital Group. He has held various management positions at Klinik Hirslanden and served on the Board of a cantonal hospital. For more than 10 years he worked as a consultant for health systems development with international organizations in the Middle East and with private and Governmental organizations in Switzerland. Dr. Pahls is a medical doctor and holds a Master of Business Administration.

The Hirslanden Private Hospital Group is the leading private hospital group and the largest medical network in Switzerland. It consists of 16 hospitals in 11 cantons, many of which have an integrated outpatient centre and emergency department, treating almost 100,000 inpatients in 2015. The Group also operates 4 outpatient clinics, 13 radiology institutes and 4 radiotherapy institutes. It has 2000 employed and affiliated doctors as well as 8500 members of staff. In the 2015/2016 financial year the Group generated a turnover of 1667 million Swiss francs. Hirslanden Private Hospital Group stands for first class medical quality, made possible with highly qualified, experienced doctors. In medical terms, Hirslanden stands out in the market as a system provider. Interdisciplinary medical competence centres and specialist institutes enable optimal and individual treatment of cases, whatever their level of medical complexity. The private hospital group was formed in 1990 out of the merger of a number of private hospitals, and became part of the South African hospital group Mediclinic International Limited in 2007.

The Role of Digital Disruption in Healthcare Service Innovation

Guy Ford, Mark Compton, Graham Millett, and Alex Tzortzis

Abstract

This chapter examines and explores the role of digital disruption in healthcare service innovation. We begin by reviewing extant and emerging technologies within the context of innovation in the provision of healthcare services. We then draw on the insights of key opinion leaders across industry, consulting and clinical practice as to how digitisation can be expected to impact on key aspects of the healthcare value chain, including stakeholder relationships, service activities, resource requirements and healthcare economic models.

1 Introduction

In this chapter we examine and explore the role of digital disruption in healthcare service innovation. We analyse the different ways in which various manifestations of digital technology have the potential to transform healthcare delivery, and draw on the insights of key opinion leaders across industry, consulting and clinical

G. Ford (✉)
Management Education, The University of Sydney, Room 4226, Business School H70, Darlington, NSW 2006, Australia
e-mail: Guy.Ford@sydney.edu.au

M. Compton
St Luke's Care, 18 Roslyn St, Potts Point, NSW 2011, Australia
e-mail: mcompton@slc.org.au

G. Millett
MGSM, 99 Talavera Rd, North Ryde, NSW 2113, Australia
e-mail: Graham.Millett@mgsm.edu.au

A. Tzortzis
Johnson & Johnson Medical, 1-5 Khartoum Rd, North Ryde, NSW 2113, Australia
e-mail: Alex.Tzortzis@hotmail.com

M.A. Pfannstiel, C. Rasche (eds.), *Service Business Model Innovation in Healthcare and Hospital Management*, DOI 10.1007/978-3-319-46412-1_4

practice on how digital disruption can be expected to impact on healthcare stakeholders, service activities, resources and economic models of healthcare.

Healthcare systems in most countries are experiencing significant challenges posed by population increases, ageing populations, increasing rates of chronic disease, the need to improve access to services for patients in remote areas, and ever-higher consumer expectations—all of which lead to the increasing cost of healthcare delivery and consequent pressures on public and private sector budgets. The rising cost of technology is also a challenge but, paradoxically, technology may contribute to solutions that transform the traditional structure of the healthcare industry and its operating model. It is anticipated that such transformation will enable more efficient and effective ways of delivering care and prevention programs which in turn may lead to improved health outcomes. Although there are three types of technology disrupting the industry, viz genomics, nanotechnology, and digitisation, the latter, combining software and hardware, is the focus of this chapter.

Digital disruption is a phenomenon of the twenty-first century that has transformed, and continues to transform, traditional industries. Broadcasting, publishing, retailing, financial services, music and film distribution have witnessed the introduction of new business models by new yet small and agile firms that employ new technologies to offer a more compelling value proposition than that offered by the incumbents. This is consistent with the broader concept of disruptive innovation which explains "how complicated, expensive products and services are converted into simpler, affordable ones" with the additional advantage of greater accessibility (Hwang and Christensen 2007).

Similarly, each part of the healthcare industry value chain, whether in the public or private sector, is beginning to be affected to varying degrees by digitisation. Hospitals, clinicians, pharmaceutical companies, pharmacies, medical device manufacturers, diagnostic firms, insurers, etc. must adapt their business models to the new environment in order to survive and prosper. These adaptations should be accompanied by complementary changes to policy to deliver an environment that meets the evolving needs of healthcare consumers.

To anticipate the impact of digital disruption on the healthcare industry it is necessary to consider how various sources of technological disruption will either independently manifest or converge to alter the composition and organisation of critical activities in the healthcare value chain. Healthcare is an information rich industry; even so, information asymmetry had typified traditional healthcare models. True disruption should represent a deviation from convention and for healthcare this could be borne by rebalancing this asymmetry through the capture and analysis of data as enabled by technology. To the extent that digitisation does not require regulatory approvals, with relatively inexpensive new technologies, the barriers to entry for new entrants are being lowered and this means that whilst opportunities and threats remain common to industry players, incumbents need to pay particular attention to agile new entrants willing and ready to disrupt because of lower levels of business model risk.

Since inception, healthcare practices have focused on treating disease and illness in patients. This largely reactive model of care has remained essentially unchanged for centuries characterised by a fragmented value chain but with numerous interdependencies that contributes to unnecessary duplication and potentially avoidable clinical errors. However, the advent and rapid advancement of information and communication technologies (ICT) since the mid-twentieth century is profoundly affecting the healthcare industry in terms of improved research, better delivery of care, better access to both broad and specific information by consumers, therefore driving informed choice and more efficient administration.

Further, ICT is also changing the traditional model by facilitating a much greater emphasis on the prevention of disease and illness. Indications are that the shift has already commenced from a provider-centric institutionally driven mass market healthcare model. Increasingly, consumers will be enabled by the technology to take the current sickness model to a more customer-centric and individually driven, personalised wellness/prevention model providing greater control of their own health as a complement to professional advice provided by clinicians. Significant benefits in the form of reduced episodes of institutional care (such as hospitalisation for acute exacerbations of chronic illnesses) will likely lead to a reduction in direct and indirect costs.

There are differing views as to precisely how digitisation in particular, and technology more broadly, will drive the evolution of the industry. This uncertainty is exacerbated by the rapid rate at which technological advances continue to occur. According to Christensen et al. (2009) one way that digitisation may cause disruption is in the form of decentralization. It will consist of taking the most recent or even inferior versions of technology that exist in hospitals and moving it outward—to clinics, retail clinics, and, eventually, to the home. Christensen suggests that medical experience will become more commoditized.

Advances in technology parallel advances in the body of research and evidence available to clinicians. Doctors have already made a shift from intuitive care to evidence-based medicine and subsequent evolution of personalised medicine. Payors, especially in Europe—most notably the UK, France and Germany—have led the way and are increasingly basing reimbursement on evidence based outcomes. With the exception of some orphan pharmaceuticals, incremental reimbursement is becoming more difficult for products that cannot prove they are more effective. Specific gene-based therapies are an example of targeted evidence-based medicine enabling treatment algorithms to become more explicit and therefore easier to teach with each gradation. This trend could potentially allow more parts of care to scale out from physician specialists to nurse practitioners to patients and families; one could perhaps contemplate a future where the next phase of evidence-based care allows medical decisions to be made upon phenotypes rather than genotypes.

With the swelling of available data, the ultimate impact of digital disruption could mean the creation of more certainty through timeliness, standardisation and evidence-based reasoning. This becomes particularly important in enabling a more discrete definition of healthcare outcomes and subsequent changes to payment and reimbursement models. This shift is significant for healthcare, an industry where fee for service payments represents convention, because traditional business models have been shaped by this dynamic.

Healthcare in Australia has an interesting B2C model because insurers (national and private) pay for products and services, and up until now this has rendered little accountability by both providers (who make purchase decisions and 'push' demand) and patients (who make consumption decisions and 'pull' demand). The potential to redefine value according to outcomes rather than discrete service is significant because it provides more granularity and clarity to stakeholder expectations across the chain, fundamentally altering the conversation between providers, payers and patients in the process. This change in the definition of value will force the value proposition of healthcare providers, and associated measures of success, to change.

In a developed economy, the sum of consumer demand for timeliness and transparency, data to effect evidence-based reasoning rather than intuitive decision-making, and payment for outcomes rather than service, may result in a more liberalized market exposed to natural regulation in supply and demand efficiencies, with minimal need for government intervention except where necessary to manage population-based risk.

2 Definitions

Digitisation has given rise to the introduction of new terminology to the healthcare industry. The most widely used of these is the term "telehealth", which encompasses the concepts of "telemedicine" and "telecare". Although there is no universally accepted definition for each of these terms, the following definitions are indicative of usage by healthcare practitioners in different countries.

Telehealth is defined by the United States Health Resources Services Administration as "the use of electronic information and telecommunications technologies to support long distance clinical health care, patient and professional health-related education, public health and health administration." Telehealth includes clinical services provided by telemedicine and non-clinical services in remote areas including provider training, administrative meetings and ongoing professional development (Healthit 2014).

Telemedicine is referred to by the Frontier Communications Corporation as "the provision of clinical services to patients in other locations". Examples include patient consultations via video link with clinical specialists; remote monitoring of patient vital signs, remote medical assessments and diagnoses based upon medical imaging digitally transmitted, and the prescription of treatment.

Telecare refers to the use of technology that enables patients to be cared for at home thereby avoiding the need for admission to an institutional setting. The patient maintains their independence in a familiar environment whilst reducing cost and pressure on the healthcare system.

3 Information Technology (IT)

Due to the disparate, complex and interdependent nature of digital information and communication technologies, an analysis of each technology and its potential contribution to transforming healthcare is warranted.

3.1 Apps

An "app" is a software application downloaded to a mobile device that is developed to enable a specific activity to be performed. The number of healthcare apps developed for clinicians and consumers has increased substantially since 2007, driven primarily by the growth in mobile digital devices such as smartphones, tablets and smartwatches.

Examples include apps that are designed to:

- monitor sleep patterns to assist in optimizing circadian rhythm;
- provide information to improve nutrition and diet;
- track individual physical activity against recommended benchmarks;
- monitor chronic conditions and alert of unexpected changes;
- test and improve cognitive abilities;
- enable remote diagnosis;
- analyze basic health data; and
- transmit anomalous data to healthcare professionals for more detailed analysis.

The overall objectives of such apps are to prevent illness from developing, improve the timeliness of clinical intervention, increase consumer convenience, and collect, collate and analyze vast amounts of disparate data to significantly enhance the diagnostic abilities of clinicians.

3.2 High Speed Broadband

Communications technology is a key enabler of digital disruption by providing the network infrastructure that transmits data in the form of text, voice and video between individuals, between groups, and between systems. High speed broadband is the most recent type of communications technology that comprises a network of optical fibre, coaxial cables, and/or wireless connections for the rapid transmission of large quantities of data in a reliable, timely and secure fashion across geographic locations. Data transfer speeds of up to 1 Gb/s are possible. Recent technological advances also permit broadband to function at relatively high speeds of up to 100 Mb/s over standard copper telephone lines and via satellite.

The technology is a platform for transmitting electronic patient records and diagnostic images. Additionally, by enabling greater data mobility through monitoring using wireless devices the accessibility and cost-effectiveness of patient care is improved.

Accordingly, high speed broadband is transforming where and how healthcare training, diagnosis and treatment are delivered. As an example, high speed broadband in conjunction with high resolution video and advanced robotics can enable an experienced surgeon or a trainee located in a major city to operate on a patient located in a regional hospital.

The implications for participants in the healthcare industry are that data networks and data services must be reliable and secure. This necessitates the allocation of appropriate amounts of capital investment and operational expenditure to ensure that IT infrastructure remains capable of supporting high speed transfer rates whilst ensuring that the most appropriate and sophisticated safeguards are in place to protect data transfer.

3.3 Wi-Fi

Wi-Fi is a network-dependent communications technology that provides mobile connectivity between enabled devices, thereby improving the flexibility and efficiency of clinical services. By providing wireless access to patient data in real time, clinical workflows are also improved. The technology already has a large installed base in most industries and provides good data transfer rates, high levels of interoperability and robust security characteristics. Constant advancements in Wi-Fi technology enhance the user experience by increasing capacity and data throughput, improving coverage and reducing latency.

Many of the devices and applications developed over recent years for use by healthcare practitioners incorporate Wi-Fi capability and include infusion pumps, smart beds, wireless EKGs and oxygen monitoring devices. These, and other devices, operate in conjunction with mission-critical information applications such as access to electronic medical records (eMRs) and real-time access to X-rays and MRI scans. The delivery of medical telepresence via Wi-Fi assists to scale the availability of quality health care in remote areas (Wi-Fi Alliance 2016).

3.4 Electronic Medical Records (eMRs)

Traditionally, patient records are kept in a hard copy format by individual healthcare providers. The discrete nature of storage of theses records prevents a connected, holistic and longitudinal perspective of the patient's medical history. In contrast, eMRs are kept in a digital format that makes real-time patient data available immediately and securely to relevant providers. These digital records can provide a patient's entire medical history, diagnoses of conditions, prescribed medications, treatment plans, allergies, details of immunization, and radiology and laboratory test results.

Unlike hard copy records, eMRs can enable better patient outcomes by offering benefits that include:

- A more holistic view of a patient's care resulting in improved decision-making by providers.
- The facility to easily and quickly share information with multiple providers involved in a patient's care.
- More accurate diagnoses and more effective treatment.
- Automated workflows and streamlined processes along the length of the healthcare value chain, resulting in improved efficiencies and greater cost reductions.

Apart from patient-specific benefits, access to electronic versions of grouped patient information also facilitates the aggregate analysis of patient populations at a provider level to enable comparative assessment of outcomes. Such information is therefore useful to derive value and subsequent reimbursement by payers. There is, however, a good deal of privacy legislation that needs to be dealt with to fully reach the potential of this idea. Additionally, national laws make a cloud computing approach to storage difficult and many jurisdictions will not allow their citizen's data to be stored off shore.

3.5 Big Data and Data Analytics

Clifford (2008) and Feldman et al. (2012) identify five interdependent dimensions of big data:

1. Volume refers to the amount of the data in terms of its management and storage.
2. Variety concerns the structure and different types of data.
3. Velocity is the frequency with which data are produced, processed and analyzed.
4. Veracity concerns the data's quality, relevance, predictive ability, and meaning.
5. Value is the benefit derived by those using the data.

It is critical that data integrity be maintained via management of data sources, content, consistency, access and security, stewardship, and user training. In the absence of effective management, issues associated with data unreliability, inaccessibility, inaccuracy or omission may occur (Shaw 2013).

Data analytics is the analysis of large volumes of data originating from multiple sources and the ease/speed with which the analysis can be performed. Big data and its analysis are inextricably linked with the content of electronic health records.

There is a wide range of applications for which big data and data analytics can be utilized in healthcare. Groves et al. (2013) suggests four broad categories of utilization:

1. Administration and delivery: the management of healthcare delivery and the associated costs.
2. Clinical decision support: to assist in the decision-making process.
3. Clinical information: comprises the data sets that are specifically available for data analytics.
4. Behaviour/consumer: demographic analysis including the behaviours and lifestyles of individuals and groups.

3.6 Cognitive Computing and Artificial Intelligence

Cognitive computing refers to a machine's ability to incorporate learning into its programming. It is a form of artificial intelligence that attempts to mimic how humans think in terms of perception, recognition, and reasoning. By accessing big data the objective is to solve complex problems that contain many ambiguous variables.

The software that is the foundation for cognitive computing and artificial intelligence typically requires computer hardware that possesses powerful data processing capability. Examples of applications to-date include weather forecasting and predicting stock market behavior. In healthcare, the use of the technology's modelling and simulation capabilities has wide application for improving patient outcomes. Oncology in particular is a field of application whereby the development paths of different cancers can be more accurately predicted using accelerated modelling techniques. This is already resulting in improved detection and treatment by clinicians but further significant improvements will occur in the short-term as the software becomes more sophisticated and the hardware becomes ever more powerful.

4 Perspectives

Since the industry is both fragmented yet highly integrated through interdependencies, the subsequent complexity means that those most appropriately positioned to understand the magnitude and scale of such disruption are those at the helm of decision-making for healthcare institutions, or those with a vested interest in the business of healthcare. Insights were gleaned from discussion with key thought leaders including the CEO of a global private hospital group consisting of over 200 hospitals across five countries, a senior executive from a global healthcare consulting practice, and a senior medical executive who has held clinical and leadership positions in university, healthcare and consulting organisations, including the Harvard Medical School. Collectively, these insights have been framed within four key contexts: (1) stakeholders (primarily patient outcomes), (2) service activities, (3) resources and (4) healthcare economic models.

4.1 Stakeholders

For stakeholders, the main source of disruption will be to the way care is delivered, with a greater focus on the customer experience.

There is an increasing consumer expectation that health systems and social care systems will respond more effectively to the needs of individuals. Rather than being treated as a number within a system, consumers expect to have their sovereign right to play a role in the determination of their care respected. One example is choosing what to eat and when to eat as a patient in a hospital. Since care institutions such as hospitals are tightly integrated ecosystems where connectivity between nodes creates inertia rather than agility, acceding to patient preferences even for seemingly simple requests cannot always be guaranteed. This is due to links with other standardised processes and procedures such as, but not limited to, availability of nursing staff to assist with feeding, mass production of meals and logistics working to tight timeframes to service large numbers patients. It can be said that whilst technology has enabled increased flexibility in meal preferences (and not without additional cost), such adaptability is likely to be more prevalent in private hospitals because choice goes to the core of private healthcare's value proposition.

The value of realising the demand for increased transparency and access to data in healthcare brings a more informed consumer and payer. Even though the technological infrastructure exists to support data capture and transparency, relevant and scaled reporting processes are not yet in place. For example, it is hard to find information that influences choice of surgeon, such as average length of stay for a particular procedure, unplanned readmission rate, and infection rate. In order to satisfy stakeholder demand for this information, further discourse on policy and regulatory changes, and legal considerations required to effect this dynamic is warranted.

Despite the promise of next generation technologies such as nanotechnology, targeted therapies and genetic screening, stepwise increases in progress are not being seen. At a macro level, incremental improvements in life expectancy and the fact that a cure for cancer remains elusive provide examples of this. So, whilst the entire human genome has been sequenced the impact to healthcare in terms of fundamental disruption to healthcare trends has yet not manifested.

4.2 Activities

The stepwise changes that have revolutionised healthcare over history include the discovery of penicillin; discovery of antipsychotics; advances in surgical techniques facilitating open heart surgery, joint replacement and kidney transplantation; and the discovery of bacteria as the etiology of peptic ulceration. Despite the exponential ascent of technology, manifesting through mass digitisation, there are some characteristics of the healthcare industry that may limit impacts of the same magnitude.

Regulation has a protective effect on industry providers and this provides some degree of buffering against wide-scale disruption and regulatory pressures seem to increase in complexity every year in line with the expectation that risk will be managed to zero were possible. For the most part, the question of how and where to deliver coordinated care safely is ultimately a function of the complexity of care. For example, substitutes for hospital procedures at the lower end of complexity such as gastroenterological interventions, do exist and day surgeries perform these functions at scale. Even so, extrapolation of this trend to settings beyond day surgeries is unlikely because of the regulatory pressures that exist within healthcare generally and the expectation that safety is a priority that cannot be compromised.

4.3 Resources

When screening for disruptive impacts to institutional care, it is difficult to anticipate a technology-based alternative to the services delivered by people, the major resource composition. Currently, no viable substitutes for the subtleties of human interaction and empathy exist and because the vast majority of services provided by all hospitals are delivered through people, the core business of all hospitals should remain unaffected for the foreseeable future. Unless Artificial Intelligence makes rapid advances such that a robot can effectively replace the subtleties of human understanding and interaction, the resource base should act to insulate healthcare from role substitution and fundamental service disruption.

In other resource areas, technological progress does not yet necessarily correlate to progress in general in healthcare. The rejection of digitization in the area of electronic medical records (eMRs) in some hospitals makes sense from both economic and risk management perspectives. Although electronic records are espoused to increase accuracy and reduce error, they are not without risk. With respect to cyber security concerns, paper based records are intrinsically protected from the "perils of technology". Furthermore, the case to transition to eMRs is not compelling as there is currently no compelling evidence on error reduction nor a reduction in the cost of error, with a corresponding lack of evidence for significant improvements in productivity. An insight was shared where a hospital that was recently constructed to comply with the highest level of eMR application compared the benefit of implementing eMR against the paper based benchmark. It was determined that the return on investment was very low given the large costs of implementation and driving the technology throughout the hospital, with no obviously identifiable material patient benefit or cost benefit. Nevertheless, the fact that technology exists, albeit with an unclear value proposition, does indicate the potential for disruption in the service model in the future.

Radiology is an example where the potential for a computer-assisted diagnosis is real and enabled by algorithms that allow interpretation of a series of images. Pathology is another example of digital disruption whereby assays have become automated and the need for human capital is reduced. In both instances, technology has enabled these services to be delivered at scale and remotely, realising efficiencies and cost savings as a result.

On the contrary, investment may be considered necessary because of a need to present the business of healthcare provision as technologically advanced—crucial for an industry with progress through scientific and technological pursuit at its heart. The DaVinci Robot used in prostate surgery is a prime example of a decision to invest even when the business case fails. A capital investment of $3 million upfront and consumable cost of $4500–$5000 per case is very difficult to justify when generally, reimbursement for an open procedure and robotically assisted procedure is effectively the same yet conventional methods require a much lower level of upfront capital investment.

The human interface of healthcare cannot be digitised away en masse, although opportunities may exist to increase efficiencies in components of the value chain. Areas where a digital interface already exists and is fundamental to the activity performed will be exposed to digital disruption with the impact to business delivery models limited by the extent to which human involvement is required for the delivery of care.

4.4 Economic Models of Healthcare

Healthcare is a patient-centric industry at heart which has been greatly assisted by advances in technology. Such advances have paved the path towards more personalised care but with this specificity comes more niche models that drive up unit cost per offering.

Healthcare investment in technology tends to occur in silos, while technology payoffs often occur outside of silos. Furthermore, productivity gains through technology and digitization are not always enjoyed by the stakeholders making the investment. In the case of the DaVinci Robot, whilst the hospital makes the investment in the absence of incentive from a reimbursement perspective, it can be argued that a social return on this investment is realised through quicker return to work for patients. Additionally, an investment of this type may extend the working life of surgeons/urologists because of a reduction in ergonomic challenges of surgery. The lack of consistent and reliable measurement of this type of return means that business cases involving aggregate returns are hard to quantify. In this way, benefits of investment in technology are diffuse, difficult to track and therefore unconvincing.

This could help to explain why the fundamentals of hospital operating models have not radically changed as a result of digital disruption. Despite various long-term trends such as a reduction in the average length of stay (through improvements to anaesthesia and surgical techniques), an increase in the volume of surgeries, and a change in case payments from daily basis 20 years ago to episodic payments today, there has not been an example of radical disruption to the operating model as enabled by technology alone. Whilst the transfer of information is faster and the potential for duplication of services and wastage can be reduced, this has not changed the requisite elements of the care delivery.

Apart from substantiating evidence-based care decisions, data have allowed negotiations to flow at a level beyond rhetoric. Care providers need to have systems and people focused on understanding their own data to support the business case when negotiating care payments. Therefore, whilst technological gains have manifested mainly as efficiencies that drive an increase in volume, and a consequential and often modest increase in productivity, data captured by enabling technology are also used to shape reimbursement with an encroaching transition to outcomes based payment rather than traditional fee-for-service methods.

In the short-term, real disruption is likely to follow price signals rather than any technology change in itself. Rather than having new technology or roles developed which fundamentally alter business models by making roles or treatment settings less central to the process, disruption is more likely to immediately converge on areas of the industry where price signaling is wrong such that the market will take care of itself. At this point, price referencing can play a disruptive role because technology allows access to prices beyond geographical boundaries.

Pricing should reflect cost and the appropriate utilisation of assets: The cost of administering chemotherapy is one example where reference pricing could disrupt business models across markets. In Australia the price hovers around $350 per episode delivered in a clinic ($100 cost of drug, leaving $250 for administration and nursing costs), whilst the same treatment provided in the United States could be up to five times this amount. This contrast provides an example of the cost benefits of centralising care by pricing in line with true costs.

The way healthcare is funded both fundamentally and indirectly influences the way it is delivered. For example, aside from volume based transactions encouraging business operations at scale, healthcare providers might assess investment opportunities according to traditional investment metrics such as return on investment (ROI) and opportunity costs. For example, a decision to not invest in an eMR system may be made on the basis that for a certain hurdle rate, an alternative project (such as the purchase of another hospital) with a higher ROI exists, rendering the eMR project unattractive. This is despite dominant views that encourage investment in technology as the chief method for realising efficiency and improved models of care.

5 Conclusion

Insights gleaned from key thought leaders in For-Profit, Advisory and Academic sectors suggest that whilst digital technology is implicitly involved and will play a major role in healthcare disruption, it might not necessarily serve to be the conclusive source of disruption to the underlying architecture of the healthcare industry. The disruption will impact stakeholder expectations, the organisation of activities, utilisation of resources, and economic models of healthcare delivery.

Technological advances will overhaul the way some components of healthcare are delivered, realising cost savings and efficiencies through scale such as radiology and pathology services for example. The ubiquitous requirement of healthcare in the community, labour intensive resource constraints, implicit high risk in healthcare delivery, and the corollary need for broad regulation collectively serve to protect against fundamental change.

The data that are generated, captured and analysed through digitisation in healthcare will contribute to altering the composition and organisation of critical activities in the healthcare value chain. The ability to provide more granularity and clarity to all stakeholders through this data will change expectations across the value chain, and this will fundamentally alter the conversation between providers, payers, policy makers and patients in the process. The result could deliver a more liberalised market exposed to natural regulation in supply and demand efficiencies rather than the perverse incentives created by conventional fee-for-service models.

Despite the above, one of the most difficult challenges for developers and providers of digitised services lies in how these may be effectively monetised. Unfortunately, many practices in the digital space, such as free and freemium offers, have influenced the relationship consumers have with digital technology, particularly their willingness to pay. Many users implicitly, and more often explicitly, demand the benefits of digitisation without consideration. While the provision of such services has been good for companies to differentiate themselves and gain market share, it has come at the cost of profitability. It may follow that after an initial wave of offerings, the transformation to digitisation will slow considerably due to reduced economic incentives.

Digitisation will both influence and enable industry-wide change however, the ultimate disrupter will be the change to the sociopolitical contract that underpins the healthcare system, and this is driven by the need to move from volume driven fee-for-service models to more efficient, evidence-based methods of payment based on outcomes. Digitisation will drive transformations in existing models of therapeutic care and associated business structures. This will provide the impetus for innovation, creation of new revenue streams and cost structures that will ultimately shape healthcare delivery to meet the needs of individuals and redefined measures of value.

Acknowledgments The authors would like to thank Chris Rex, Evan Rawstron and Professor Bruce Dowton for their contributions. Carl Runde also provided valuable comments.

References

Christensen, C. M., Grossman, J. H., & Hwang, J. (2009). *The innovator's prescription: A disruptive solution for healthcare*. New York: McGraw-Hill.

Clifford, L. (2008). How do your data grow? *Nature, 455*(7209), 28.

Feldman, B., Martin, E., & Skotnes, T. (2012). *Big data in healthcare: Hype and hope*. Accessed May 22, 2016, from http://www.west-info.eu/files/big-data-in-healthcare.pdf

Groves, P., Kayyali, B., Knott, D., & Van Kuiken, S. (2013). *The big data revolution in healthcare: Accelerating value and innovation.* New York: McKinsey & Company.
Healthit. (2014). *What is Telehealth? How does Telehealth differ from Telemedicine?* Accessed January 4, 2016, from https://www.healthit.gov/providers-professionals/faqs/whattelehealth-how-telehealth-different-telemedicine
Hwang, J., & Christensen, C. M. (2007). Disruptive innovation in health care delivery: A framework for business-model innovation. *Health Affairs, 27*(5), 1329–1335.
Shaw, G. (2013). *Data analytics: Actionable information to improve healthcare.* Accessed May 22, 2016, from http://www.fiercehealthit.com/offer/dataanalytics?source=library
Wi-Fi Alliance. (2016). *Wi-Fi connects providers with patients across a variety of environments.* Accessed January 7, 2016, from http://www.wi-fi.org/discover-wi-fi/healthcare

Guy Ford is a professor at the University of Sydney Business School and Director of the University of Sydney MBA program. Guy is formerly of the Macquarie Graduate School of Management, where he held the roles of Deputy Dean and Interim Dean. Prior to academia Guy worked in the Treasury Management Division of the Commonwealth Bank of Australia.

Mark Compton is the Chief Executive Officer of St Luke's Care, a company which owns and operates businesses in private hospitals, aged care and home care. Mike is an Adjunct Professor at the Macquarie Graduate School of Management, and serves as a non-executive director on the board of Macquarie University Hospital. Mark is also Chairman and Non-Executive Director of Sonic Healthcare Limited, a global medical diagnostics and healthcare organisation.

Graham Millett is a Lecturer at Macquarie University's Graduate School of Management and teaches in a range of postgraduate courses including Health Leadership, Strategic Management, and New Enterprise Management. Graham holds a Bachelor of Arts degree majoring in Economics, a Diploma of Education, and a Master of Business Administration having been awarded the Allan Knott medal for outstanding academic achievement. He is currently undertaking research into the growth of the Australian healthcare industry. Graham's academic career is complemented by extensive private sector experience across a range of industries.

Alex Tzortzis has worked in the Australian healthcare industry since 1995. In 2003, Alexandra graduated from the University of Sydney with a Bachelor of Pharmacy and since that time, has had exposure to diverse roles within pharmacy at both a state and federal level, and within community pharmacy in Australia and the United Kingdom. During her career Alexandra has taught in a clinical setting as well as in tertiary education. Alexandra has a Master of Business Administration from the Macquarie Graduate School of Management.

The Opportunities Offered by Digitizing Clinical Pathways

Sören Eichhorst, Karl Liese, Stefan Moder, and Manuel Möller

Abstract

Across numerous industries and sectors, digitization is a fundamental change process. In the healthcare sector it is already affecting how hospitals operate, and will continue to do so in the future. It can add value by facilitating communication and documentation, supporting the automation of processes and providing new opportunities—for example in regard to better patient aftercare. Numerous digital solutions are already available—however, not many of these are actually established in daily clinical practice, mainly as a result of certain key challenges, like the complexity of medical and technical processes, limited funding and the fact that digitization requires change within the entire organization. Nevertheless, experience from extensive work with clinical practitioners shows that these challenges can be overcome and that digitization can improve both the quality and efficiency of care—ultimately resulting in a positive impact on hospitals' financial performance.

S. Eichhorst (✉) • K. Liese
McKinsey & Co., Christophstraße 17, 50670 Cologne, Germany
e-mail: soeren_eichhorst@mckinsey.com; karl_liese@mckinsey.com

S. Moder
McKinsey & Co., Sophienstraße 26, 80333 Munich, Germany
e-mail: stefan_moder@mckinsey.com

M. Möller
McKinsey & Co., Taunustor 2, 60311 Frankfurt, Germany
e-mail: manuel_moeller@mckinsey.com

M.A. Pfannstiel, C. Rasche (eds.), *Service Business Model Innovation in Healthcare and Hospital Management*, DOI 10.1007/978-3-319-46412-1_5

1 Digitization Changes the Way Hospitals Operate

Digitization involves fundamental changes for companies, public institutions, and for society as a whole. Whereas in the past technology has been applied in order to make processes and procedures more efficient and effective in regard to individual steps, digitization is leading to a fundamental, human-driven change in the entire process architecture—digital communication channels, automated work flows, and data access are integrated end-to-end across entire processes.

Although digitization is already well advanced in many sectors—e.g. in retail and financial institutions—some sectors are only at the beginning of this development. This includes healthcare—particularly the inpatient sector. Since the "classic" levers for improving quality and efficiency, such as process optimization and selective use of IT, have been exhausted in many hospitals in recent years, it is clear that digitization is going to be one of the most important means of improving quality and efficiency in the future.

In 2012 already one-third of approximately 200 hospitals surveyed in Germany indicated that they used a fully functioning digital system for managing patient records across all departments (Hübner et al. 2012). This could be a good starting point by acting as a central access point for all patient medical information. This opens up possibilities for hospital digitization.

1.1 For the Sake of the Patient: The Opportunities Produced by Digitizing Clinical Pathways

Digitization generates value in patient care by combining four levers:

1. Digital interaction and communication—the use of new devices (e.g. smartphones, tablets) to improve communication, provide information, and interact with doctors and nursing staff, and also with patients themselves.
2. Digital offerings and services—the use of special digital offerings, such as "wearables" (e.g. wearable computerized systems to detect biological signals) in patient aftercare and apps to support the treatment of chronic diseases in the field.
3. Automated end-to-end processes—the optimization (from the patient's perspective or as regards the final treatment objective) of end-to-end processes, using extensive process automation and integrated views of individual steps.
4. Advanced analytics and prediction—the integration of intelligent algorithms in processes, e.g. the use of historical data and up-to-date real-time information (such as weather data) to better predict anticipated patient flows.

The comprehensive application of these four levers can result in sustained changes in patient care and patient experiences, especially in regard to inpatient facilities. To give one example, it would be feasible that, following the initial anamnesis and diagnostics, the subsequent planning of the inpatient (and

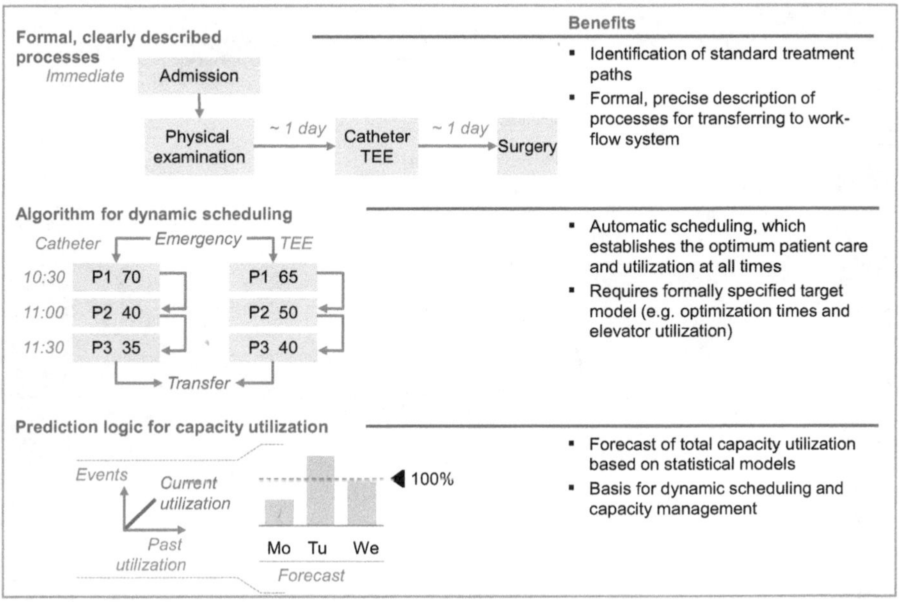

Fig. 1 Automated planning of inpatient stay. Source: Eichhorst et al. (2015)

outpatient) treatment pathway will be fully automated, and will dynamically respond to possible changes in context (e.g. the need for surgery as a result of an emergency) based on intelligent algorithms (see Fig. 1). However, due to the lack of digitized processes in the majority of hospitals and the difficulties to link different systems together this still remains a future scenario.

The active notifying of patients via mobile devices, as well as managing patients using such devices, also offers significant quality and efficiency potential. So too does the use of mobile devices to implement "open" processes—from data inputting by patients and providing patients with regular information about their treatment, to seeking their feedback on treatment processes in the hospital (see Fig. 2 for an example).

1.2 Challenges and Success Factors for the Implementation of Digitization

With the opportunities described above, it is a fair question to ask why digitization of clinical pathways is still in its infancy. We would like to give an overview of the key challenges we have identified in the course of our work with providers and other players in the healthcare sector across the globe, and how to potentially turn these challenges into success factors.

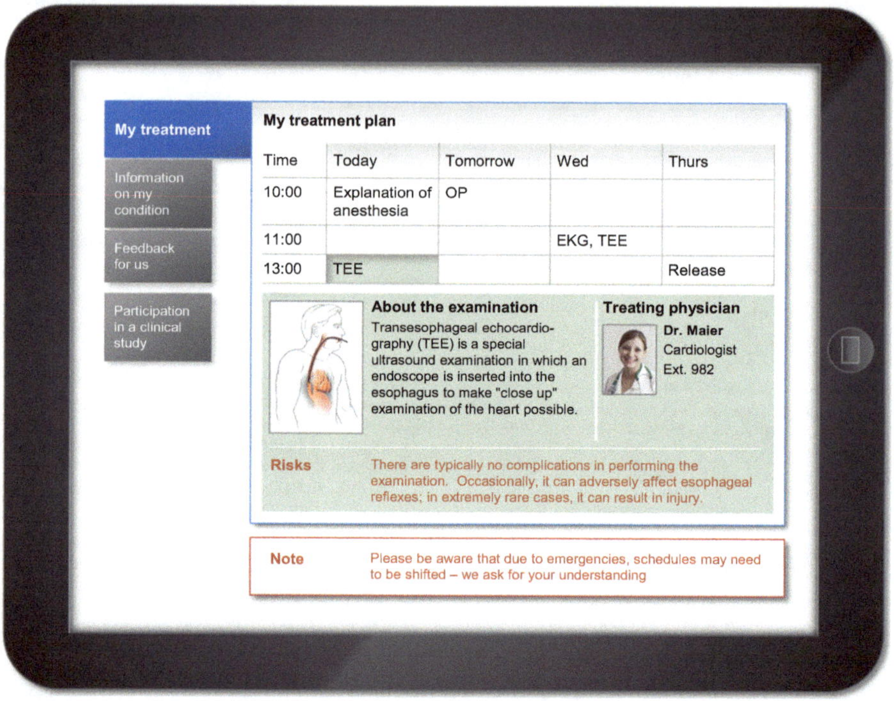

Fig. 2 Involving the patient as an active player in the treatment process. Source: Eichhorst et al. (2015)

The inherent complexity of medical interventions Owing to the sheer complexity of medical treatment routines, the main challenge for digitization projects is where to start. Digitizing an entire hospital, with all of its clinical procedures, would require a huge investment and would be a very long project, capturing key resources for many months before the first result could be seen. Thus, we recommend starting with a single clinical pathway such as, for example, transcatheter aortic valve implantation (TAVI), as described below. TAVI makes a good example because it is a well-defined clinical pathway with growing importance and a reasonable set of variances.

Learning along the way The digitization project relating to this first clinical pathway should be used to build up skills in the organization for digitization projects, while carefully avoiding tying up clinical resources. The pilot project will provide vital information about integrating the software systems, and will help build up the capabilities of medical staff, administrative personnel, and IT, which can then be used in the subsequent roll-out stages. After the first pathway is digitized, the approach can be adapted and scaled up to other pathways.

Digitization affects the entire organization Because digitization can only realize its full benefits by covering clinical pathways from start to end, all stakeholders in the hospital will be affected and will need to contribute to the project. This includes management, medical experts, IT, finance, etc. This means all of the relevant stakeholders need to be involved in the project design and need to make available sufficient resources to contribute during the implementation.

The technical complexity of legacy systems Modern hospitals typically still have a highly fragmented IT landscape. Even today, processes are partially paper-based, which poses significant hurdles for digitization projects. The key success factor for digitization is to interface with the existing systems; however, these systems are often produced by different vendors and are only loosely connected to each other—think, for example, of the financial reporting system, the system managing electronic health records and the IT system used by the cardiology team. Whenever possible, existing middleware solutions connecting existing hospital systems should be used, instead of building new interfaces.

Limited investment funds Hospitals often lack the budget required for large IT projects. The lack of money for a "big-time" platform overhaul project results in a fragmented IT system landscape, with only the most urgent problems patched up, using isolated or loosely connected solutions. In the mid-term, digitization can help reduce operating cost significantly; however, in the short term, we suggest tightly restricting the involvement of internal staff scope and, in the initial pilot phase, using only external consultants and software developers. The pilot can be used to build relevant capabilities for internal staff and the developed solution can then be scaled up to other clinical processes by the hospital staff themselves, at a later point in time.

Tapping into ambulatory data A large part of the diagnostic information and patient history is created outside the hospital, in the ambulatory system. Health systems are still struggling to develop and enact regulatory structures to standardize this information and to create interfaces for information exchange. However, there are good examples of progress in creating a common information standard across inpatient and outpatient care in some big health systems, like the UK's National Health Service and the system in Germany (where an eHealth bill was passed in late 2015). Instead of a hospital building its own interface to ambulatory care systems, we suggest relying on data transferred via these officially regulated interfaces.

Full benefits can be reached only with digitization across multiple hospitals Digitization can only produce its full value if it is not isolated but rather takes place across multiple hospitals. Today, the transfer of patients and related patient records is still cumbersome (if it happens at all). Digitization is creating large efficiencies by both simplifying the process of patient health record exchange as well as opening the door for end-to-end clinical pathway orchestration across multiple medical specialty departments.

Summarizing these success factors it becomes obvious that successful digitization is a process that requires full commitment of a broad variety of stakeholders—from physicians to IT and across all layers of the organization. Ideally this commitment is not only present in one hospital but across several hospitals or even care networks to also cover the outpatient sector. Failing at achieving the cooperation of all stakeholders will—in the best case—lead to running a successful pilot that will end up being a onetime project that cannot be replicated elsewhere.

1.3 Think Big: Types of Solutions to be Considered

A broad variety of digital solutions are available, which can be classified in various ways, e.g. on the type of device used or the type of computing involved. We have chosen a pragmatic framework that places digital solutions into five different categories, by reference to the type of process they focus on:

- Patient-centered solutions: processes by which healthcare providers and patients collect and use patient-specific data
- Telemedicine: processes focusing on consultations between patient and physician at different locations—leveraging communication technology
- Hospital operations: the optimization of operational processes in hospitals
- Predictive modeling: processes that aim to predict patient-specific risk profiles and care pathways
- Care coordination: processes for managing the coordination of care across sectors and providers

Table 1 provides a more detailed overview of the different categories and examples of solutions. This overview focuses on processes and procedures around the patient and patient care. (Of course, there are various processes that take place as part of the administrative and support activities of a hospital (for example, finance, HR, and procurement) and these can also be digitized. However, the digitization of these activities is not specific to the healthcare sector—they can be found in other industries as well—and thus this does not fall within the scope of this chapter.

The maturity of the tools mentioned in Table 1 differs—telemedicine is already used by many health insurance companies and providers (at least in pilots), whereas really well-engineered interactive care pathway solutions are neither well established in the market nor broadly implemented in real-life care settings. The second important consideration, looking at this overview, is the fact that different healthcare systems and care setups are not equally suitable for the solutions listed above. Care coordination tools, for instance, require an environment that allows the linking of inpatient and outpatient sectors.

Table 1 Overview of solutions for digitizing care processes in hospitals

Category	Solution	Description and examples
Patient-centered solutions	Remote monitoring	• Tracking of various health parameters (weight, blood pressure, blood sugar, etc.) via devices/wearables • Monitoring of health data by medical staff or device
	Medical adherence	• Reminder to take drugs on time (e.g. via short messages or through an app)
	Smart medication list	• Electronic drug prescription system • Automated check for potential drug interactions and contraindications (based on patient health record)
	Interactive care pathway	• Standardized interactive treatment plan according to international guidelines (e.g. provided through a tablet) • Suggesting specific lab tests, procedures and a therapy regimen according to patient information and diagnoses • "One-click" documentation via a portable device
	Patient education	• Device-based solutions that provide comprehensive disease-specific information and guidance for a healthier lifestyle
	Patient services	• Services facilitating and improving the hospital stay: e.g. ordering food, TV entertainment, information about upcoming procedures or timetables with appointment reminders and directions to the location of treatment.
Tele-medicine	Teleconsultation and Telediagnostics	• Physicians in hospital/practice/a telemed center can undertake consultations with patients at their homes • Allows triage of patients and early recognition of changes in health status (especially when combined with remote monitoring)
Hospital operations	E-booking and reminder tools	• Online scheduling of appointments • Appointment reminder service, e.g. via text messages, email, automated call
	Tracking solutions	• Sensors on hospital goods or patient beds allowing tracking of location of goods and/or patients • Different technologies available, e.g. radio frequency identification, GPS, Bluetooth
	Remote expert consultation	• Remote conferencing system allowing exchange of patient information and involvement of additional experts to discuss cases • Already used for tumor- and other specialist boards
	E-rostering	• Software that calculates the best roster for staff • Timesheets created automatically
	Patient flow management	• Electronic whiteboards and desktop applications, for monitoring patient flow and bed availability in real-time • Specific solutions available for emergency room (ER) and operating room management
	Triage system	• Prioritization regarding severity of cases in order to provide patient with adequate level of care • Typically ER-based but also available for other consultation settings
	Drug barcoding	• Scanning of barcoded drugs and codes on patient wristbands to ensure correct drug administration

(continued)

Table 1 (continued)

Category	Solution	Description and examples
Predictive modeling	Predictive analytics using health data	• Software using predicitve algorithms to determine the patient-specific risk of, for example, hospital admission • Health data collected by various personal mobile health (mHealth) solutions • "Regular" health data can also be used as a data source
Care coordination	Coordination of care across sectors	• Software allowing coordination of general practitioner and specialist appointments, procedures and medication • Central storage platform for comprehensive health records

Source: Own illustration (2016)

It is clear from this brief overview that in order to successfully digitize a treatment pathway the healthcare environment, the targeted process for digitization and the actual provider setting all need to be evaluated carefully.

2 Case Study: Digitization of the TAVI Procedure

To showcase the opportunities of digitization we present here a case study of one particular treatment path: the TAVI procedure, to which end-to-end digitization was applied. The TAVI procedure is a modern and minimally invasive alternative to open heart surgery for patients that require a replacement of their aortic valve. A constricted aortic valve (aortic stenosis) is the most frequent valve disorder in elderly patients and causes symptoms like dyspnea and syncope. Without treatment, it results in heart failure.

The classic procedure for treating aortic stenosis, which is currently the method of choice, is to perform a surgical intervention, which requires opening the chest. This is a well-known intervention and is performed frequently by a large number of cardiac surgeons. It is reasonably safe.

In comparison, TAVI, which can also be used to treat the condition, is significantly more expensive and is therefore applied in a fraction of the cases. Historically, TAVI was originally applied if the patient was deemed too unstable, such that it was thought that there was a risk they would not survive the classic surgical intervention. Nowadays, however, TAVI is being used more and more for patients with moderate surgical risk.

Many health systems have established clearly defined criteria that are checked by a group of medical experts (a "heart team", consisting of surgeons and

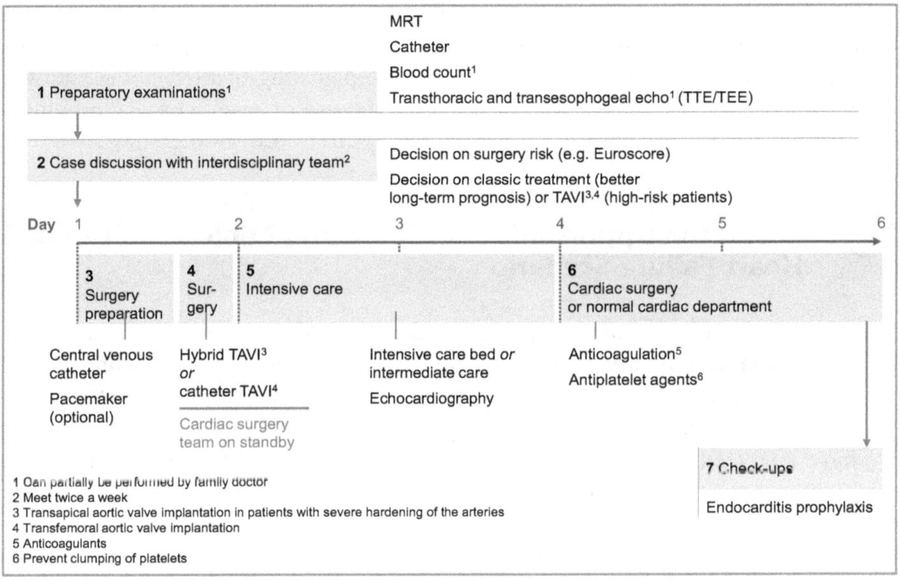

Fig. 3 High-level overview of the TAVI procedure. Source: Eichhorst et al. (2015)

cardiologists) before the decision to apply TAVI is taken. This decision is taken on the basis of diagnostic tests that start prior to hospitalization, complemented by further tests in the hospital.

From our discussions with a number of physicians, we found that TAVI is a suitable starting case for digitization as it involves a range of clinical functions but can be limited to a manageable number of process variants (Fig. 3).

End-to-end digitization of TAVI leads to the following operational improvements:

- As a result of the complete transparency that digitization allows for regarding the availability of critical resources (medical specialists, operating rooms, intensive care beds, and so on), patients are only requested to attend hospital for pre-operation when treatment can actually be carried out. Critical resources can be utilized evenly, reducing load peaks and idle times.
- The patient-centric data model allows the relevant data to be summarized for patients, allows them to move autonomously through the hospital, and to carry out typical tasks such as meal selection or finding their way to the next treatment area independently.
- At the same time, data is generated for the electronic patient records, providing information for further process optimization in the medium term and for better demand forecasting.

The TAVI case example nicely illustrates that digitization has benefits for many different stakeholders—mainly healthcare professionals but also the patient. Besides facilitating the care process for all participants digitization of the pathway helps to drive efficiency and thus to optimize the use of resources. By providing data for further process optimization it even helps to improve outcomes.

3 Sizing the Opportunities of Digitizing Clinical Pathways: A Heart Failure Scenario

The TAVI procedure is a distinct process and as such offers a very good example of how hospitals can approach digitization. However, from a healthcare system perspective it is also of interest to understand how the digitization of processes in hospitals can impact the treatment and control of widespread diseases. To this end we have analyzed the opportunities created by digitizing processes related to the inpatient treatment of patients with heart failure. 2 % of adults worldwide suffer from heart failure, which is among the leading causes of hospitalization in developed countries (it accounts for around 400,000 hospital admissions each year in Germany).

Against this backdrop we have assessed the opportunities of digitization in regard to the clinical pathway of patients with this chronic disease and have developed an approach for quantifying the impact of digitization. Although this assessment focuses on the inpatient part of the treatment only it is nevertheless important to keep in mind that digitization can provide value along the entire disease pathway—from prevention and diagnosis to outpatient treatment, and from early recognition of exacerbations to follow-up care after hospital discharge. Various solutions already exist in these areas. It is important to remember that the true value of digitization can only be captured by successfully linking care sectors—especially for patient-centered solutions and telemedicine.

Our assessment of the opportunities of digitization in regard to heart failure clinical pathways was based on a hypothetical 500-bed hospital in Germany with about 650 heart failure inpatient cases per year. First, the entire list of solutions mapped in Table 1 was screened with regards to their applicability to the care scenario. Subsequently, 10 solutions were then selected for further analysis (see Table 2). The potential impacts of each solution on parameters like average length of stay (ALOS) or readmission were defined based on literature research, case examples and expert interviews.

The applicability of case examples documented in a different setup or even another healthcare system must be evaluated carefully. Several factors, like the current standard care pathway, ALOS, follow-up in the outpatient setting or simply availability of data—to name just a few—heavily impact patient care and thus also impact the potential effect of digitizing processes.

Digitization can have a huge impact on the quality of care patients receive and on the ultimate outcome of the patient treatment, e.g. by increasing adherence to guidelines in regard to the treatment or improving patient safety due to drug

Table 2 Solutions considered for impact calculation in cases of heart failure

Selected solutions	Impact (examples)
Interactive care pathway	Reduction of ALOS through treatment that adheres to guidelines and through clear prioritization regarding use of required diagnostic procedures
E-prescription	Reduction of medication mistakes, which reduces ALOS
Remote monitoring	Early detection of, for example, exacerbations helps to reduce readmission rates or reduce ALOS by initiating treatment earlier
Telemedicine	Improved follow-up care helps to reduce ALOS (earlier discharge) and readmissions
E-booking and reminder tools	Optimized use of consultation hours drives efficiency and thereby reduces labor cost
Triage system	Improved allocation of patients to required care setting can reduce ALOS and labor cost
E-rostering	Optimized rostering allows for best use of staff and thereby helps to reduce labor cost
Tracking solution	Reduction of spend on replacing lost goods
Patient flow management	Minimized waiting times impacts ALOS and labor cost per patient stay
Patient services	Opportunity to drive additional revenues through, for example, marketing and entertainment offerings

Source: Own illustration (2016)

prescription software. Nevertheless, the focus of this analysis was on determining the financial implications of digitization in hospitals. For this reason the impact of each solution on the care pathway was translated into a specific monetary impact on the hospital profit and loss (P&L) statement. In addition, the investment costs were estimated using the sources mentioned above (literature research, case examples, etc.). To ensure the assessment was realistic, a corrective factor was included that reflects the fact that not all hospitals will be able to achieve 100 % of the effect achieved in an ideal case example, and that some potential will not be captured due to suboptimal implementation.

It is important to understand that this translation into financial impact is highly specific to the German healthcare and reimbursement system and thus cannot be transferred to a different healthcare system without any adaptation.

4 Revenues, Costs and Profit: The Impact Assessment of Digitization

Figure 4 outlines the approach that was taken to calculate the effects of the impacts set out in Table 2 on a hospital's P&L statement. In order to estimate the actual impact several assumptions had to be made. The key assumption on the revenue side is that days saved in terms of ALOS or readmissions could be filled with new cases. On the cost side of the calculation, the initial investment in the solution, staff training, and ongoing maintenance costs were all taken into account. However,

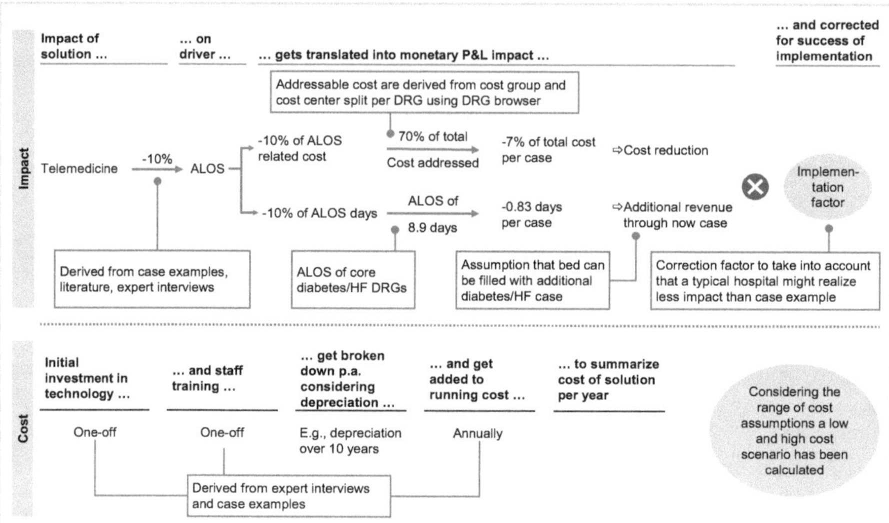

Fig. 4 Approach to translating digitization into P&L effect. Source: Own illustration (2016)

additional cost that might occur due to necessary process optimization as a prerequisite before implementing any digital solutions or support through external vendors during implementation have not been taken into account as they heavily depend on the individual local setup.

Based on the approach set out above, the impact of each solution on revenue and cost per case was calculated in order to finally determine the overall impact on profit. The baseline assumption was that all of the solutions mentioned in Table 2 are being implemented in the hypothetical hospital. Overlapping effects between solutions were considered and were corrected throughout the assessment. As mentioned above, a correction factor was included to adjust the results for the fact that not all hospitals would be able to run the implementation as successfully as described in the case examples that were used to quantify the effects.

As shown in Fig. 5, digitization can result in cost reduction and can thereby have a significant influence on the overall profit for a certain patient population. In order to specify the overall impact of digitizing the care pathway for heart failure patients the investment cost and the ramp-up of the effects mentioned above over time have to be considered. In order to reduce the degree of uncertainty, four scenarios combining different investment setups ("high investment" versus "low investment"—mainly depending on the infrastructure already available) and implementation setups ("100 % of value capture" versus "70 % of value capture" compared to case example) were assessed in these calculations. Figure 6 shows the range of impact by depicting the two most extreme scenarios:

- Scenario 1: High investment cost and low value capture (70 %)
- Scenario 4: Low investment and maximum value capture (100 %)

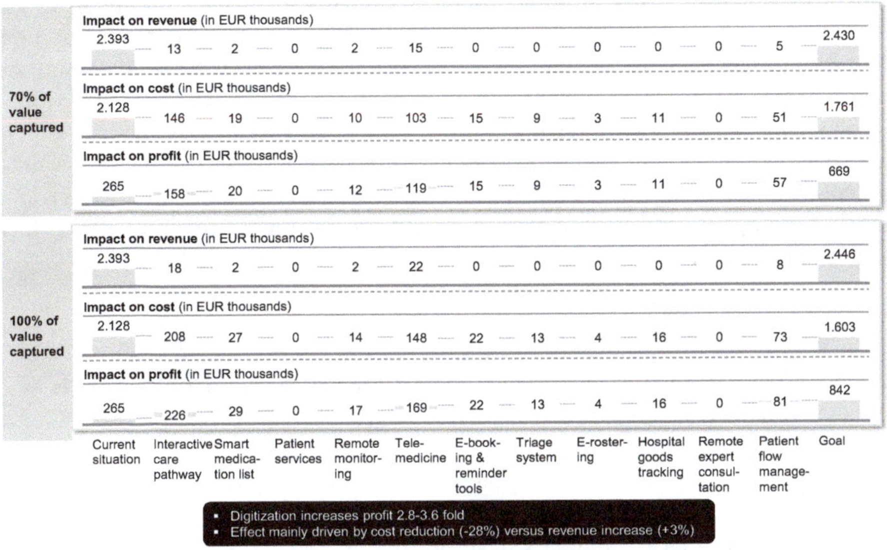

Fig. 5 Summarized impact on revenue, cost and profit of digitizing the heart failure inpatient care pathway (not including investment cost). Source: Own illustration (2016)

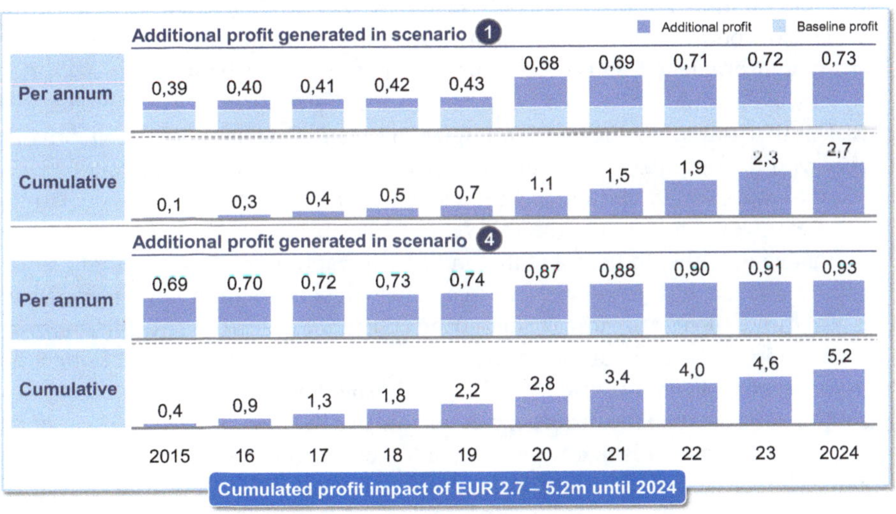

Fig. 6 Ramp-up of effect over a 10-year period of digitizing the heart failure pathway. Source: Own illustration (2016)

In addition to the baseline profit generated in these cases (which will differ significantly between hospitals, depending on the efficiency and effectiveness of their actual care pathway), Fig. 6 shows the cumulated additional profit attributable to digitization calculated based on the approach outlined above. Over a 10-year period digitization results in an additional profit of 2.7–5.2 million euros in our example for the heart failure patient population. A broader implementation of digital solutions addressing more patients can unlock an even larger potential, of course. Although these numbers need to be re-evaluated carefully for individual hospitals, as a result of all of the uncertainties mentioned above, they still show that investing in digitization is important—not only because modern healthcare systems are tending to move in this direction regardless and because digitization can improve the quality of care, but also because it can have a positive mid-term effect on a hospital's P&L.

5 Conclusion: A Perspective for Digitization in Hospitals—The Way Forward

In most healthcare systems the digitization of hospitals is a process that is still in the early stages of development. Several hurdles exist but there are ways to overcome these barriers and case examples have already shown the benefits of digitizing processes in patient care. The current healthcare environment is a challenging one for hospitals in regard to quality and efficiency. The introduction of accountable care organizations in the US and the shift to quality-based reimbursement in European countries are fundamentally changing the reimbursement structures for providers on both sides of the Atlantic. Keeping in mind that digitization can address both efficiency and effectiveness, it is time to be bold and to take this step. However, in doing so it is important to see digitization as a comprehensive approach that starts long before the implementation of actual digital solutions. It begins with the optimization of the underlying processes, and thus patient care, in hospitals—since only optimal processes will enable providers to successfully digitize pathways and capture the full value of digitization.

In this vein, it should be noted that in order to capture the value of digitization from a healthcare system perspective two developments are of crucial importance: one is to further drive the current attempts to standardize electronic health information and to improve IT interoperability. Only then will it be possible to bridge the barriers between different systems within one hospital, within a provider network—and ultimately between the different care sectors in a healthcare system. The second important development is to advance technologies that pre-sort and pre-analyze the health information data generated by digital solutions. Healthcare professionals will not be able to actively review the vast amount of data that will be generated by digitization, e.g. through patient wearables, through diagnostic devices applied by healthcare professionals, the data generated by insurance companies, etc. This information therefore needs to be processed automatically in order to detect abnormalities or patterns that can then be used by healthcare professionals to help the patient. Transforming meaningless data into helpful information to improve patient care is a key basic prerequisite for a successful digital future in the healthcare sector.

References

Eichhorst, S., Hehner, S., Liese, K., Niedermann, F., & Möller, M. (2015). *The digital patient in inpatient care – Opportunities and possible implementations*. McKinsey & Company Healthcare.

Hübner, U., Liebe, J.-D., Egbert, N., & Frey, A. (2012). IT Report Gesundheitswesen, Schwerpunkt IT im Krankenhaus, Befragung der bundesdeutschen Krankenhäuser, Schriftenreihe des Niedersächsischen Ministeriums für Wirtschaft, Arbeit und Verkehr, Hannover.

Sören Eichhorst, MD, PhD, is a board-certified physician in internal medicine with a postdoctoral lecturer qualification. Sören is a partner with McKinsey and director of the McKinsey Hospital Institute. He co-chairs McKinsey's European Healthcare Practice, leads the DACH hospital practice and is managing director of Orphoz GmbH & Co. KG, a McKinsey subsidiary that focuses on hospital implementation.

Karl Liese, MD, PhD, MBA, is a partner with McKinsey, co-chairs the European Healthcare Practice and leads the Western European and German payor practice. Karl is a physician specialized in experimental cardiology.

Stefan Moder, MD, is a project manager with the McKinsey Hospital Institute and McKinsey's Healthcare Practice. He specializes in strategic and organizational topics in healthcare.

Manuel Möller is a senior project manager and specializes in topics at the intersection between healthcare and IT.

A New Perspective of Product-Service Business Models for Customized Manufacturing in Healthcare

Golboo Pourabdollahian and Giacomo Copani

Abstract

The notable increase of average life expectancy, especially in developed countries, has resulted in a dramatic increase of aging population within the past decade. As a consequence, a better healthcare system is required to serve this aging population both in terms of healthcare service and medical products in order to provide them a better quality of life. To this end, customized medical products which are designed based on individual requirements of each patient have a considerable impact on the treatment process and quality of life. The emerging innovative manufacturing technologies facilitate development and production of customized medical products. Thanks to the new technologies such as additive manufacturing, it is even possible to produce the customized medical products efficiently in the hospitals in patients proximity, which would transform the role of the hospital from a user to a producer of the medical products. In the other words, the hospital would extend its core business from a healthcare service provider to a healthcare product manufacturer and service provider. Accordingly, a new business model is required to facilitate and support such a shift by focusing on both product and service perspectives and hence taking into account an integrated product service system approach. This chapter discusses innovative product-service business models based on customized manufacturing of medical products exploiting the potential of innovative technologies and the exchange of innovative products-services between the hospital (as the manufacturer) and the machinery producers (as the supplier). A structured business model design approach is presented, enabling the generation of different alternatives through different configurations of business model building blocks. Each alternative differs from another in terms of level of

G. Pourabdollahian (✉) • G. Copani
National Research Council of Italy (CNR), Institute of Industrial Technologies and Automation (ITIA), Via Corti 12, Milan 20133, Italy
e-mail: Golboo.pourabdollahian@itia.cnr.it; giacomo.copani@itia.cnr.it

M.A. Pfannstiel, C. Rasche (eds.), *Service Business Model Innovation in Healthcare and Hospital Management*, DOI 10.1007/978-3-319-46412-1_6

servitization and intensity of the relationship between customer and supplier. Eventually the best-fit business model can be generated and implemented by the hospital, based on the potential benefits and challenges that each alternative entails. The latter aspect will be also covered in the chapter through having a deeper look on pros and cons of each business model alternative.

1 Introduction

Aging population has been recognized as a global phenomenon around the world. While the rate of aging population is growing globally, still the more economically developed countries move at an accelerated pace compared to less economically developed countries. As a consequence of life expectancy, the population of people aged 60 or above reached to 700 million in 2006 and it's expected to surpass 2 billion by 2050 (WHO 2014a, b; Global AgeWatch 2016). The growing trend of aging population impose further pressure on healthcare systems to provide satisfactory health service to a higher number of elderly people in order to increase their quality of life. This includes not only the quality of medical services offered to aging population but also the quality of medical devices and the production of new advanced products and materials for healthcare. Rapid technological improvement in recent years enabled healthcare service providers to deliver customized services to patients based on their individual needs. An important part of personalized services related to usage of personalized medical devices such as personalized prosthesis, stents, organs, etc. Thanks to individualized characteristics and features of these devices that have been designed based on every patient's needs and biometric characteristics, application of customized medical devices results in a better function and consequently a better quality of life for patients. Moreover it can save cost for healthcare providers due to faster recovery and shorter follow post-surgery follow-ups.

The emerging innovative manufacturing technologies facilitate development and enables the production of customized medical products. Thanks to new technologies such as additive technologies (3D printing) and micro-manufacturing technologies (micro-injection moulding, micro-machining, etc.) fabrication of personalized medical devices has become a faster and more efficient process. Moreover, thanks to the small dimensions of these equipment (i.e. Desktop 3D printers), production can take place in close proximity to customers, inside or in proximity of hospitals, through establishment of micro-factories. Accordingly, the role of hospitals will be changed from an end-users of medical products and devices that they need to provide services to patients, to producers and users of personalized medical devices in their healthcare service processes. In the other words, the hospital would extend its core business from a healthcare service provider to a healthcare product manufacturer and service provider. Accordingly, a new business model is required to facilitate and support such a shift by focusing on both product and service perspectives and hence taking into account an integrated product-service system approach.

The evolution of the concept of product service systems (PSS) in recent years, has opened up new opportunities for manufacturing firms to apply it as a viable strategy and design new business models to exploit the potential of product service systems. In such a circumstances, manufacturers can deal with trends such as economic volatility, globalization, customers demands for differentiated and individualized products and increasing awareness of sustainability.

Considering the above mentioned issues, product service systems can act as a beneficial strategy for producers of medical devices and hospitals in order to deploy new technologies for fabrication of personalized medical devices. This chapter discusses innovative product-service business models for customized manufacturing of medical products exploiting the potential of innovative technologies and the exchange of innovative products-services between the hospital (as the manufacturer of medical products) and the machinery producers (as the supplier). Derived from previous research in the manufacturing sector, a structured business model design approach is presented, enabling the generation of different alternatives through different configurations of business model building blocks. Each alternative differs from another in terms of level of servitization and intensity of the relationship between customer and supplier. Eventually the best-fit business model can be generated and implemented by the hospital, based on the potential benefits and challenges that each alternative entails. The latter aspect will be also covered in the chapter through having a deeper look on pros and cons of each business model alternative.

2 State-of-the-Art

Within the last decades the concept of customization and personalization have been widely discussed in litearture. However customized manufacturing in healthcare has been in the center of attention in the recent years. When it comes to integartion of the concept with product-service system, the existing studies become even more scarce and difficult to find. In this section we present the results of an extensive review of litreature in order to understand the as-is situation of customized manufacturing in healthcare as well as product-servcie systems from a busiess model perspective. Eventually we try to underline the existing gap to link thes two concepts.

2.1 Customized Manufacturing of Healthcare Devices

In recent years the entire medical field has started to pay significant attention to personalization. Standard therapies and treatments are moving to a more tailored approach, based on single patient needs and anatomical/biological characteristics. The initiative of such a shift is not only the fact that a personalized medical device (either being an implant or an entire organ) has a great impact on improvement of a patient's quality of life, but also the rapid growth of emerging technologies such as additive manufacturing and micro-manufacturing. These technologies can be identified as the main enablers in order to realize the customized manufacturing of medical devices. Accordingly, a number of studies have been conducted in recent years to investigate the topic from different perspectives. While many studies investigate the manufacturing process of customized medical devices, there are very few studies that put a spotlight on the topic from the managerial and business perspective. However, most research efforts are common in one point: they are mainly focusing on additive manufacturing and 3D-printing as the enabler for production of personalized medical devices. In this section we will have a closer look in the existing body of literature to investigate the status quo of customized manufacturing of medical devices.

In most cases, design and development of a medical device is done through a research route, which includes several studies in order to arrive a generic solution. Such a route results in development of reliable processes in order to manufacture standards, which are applicable to as many patients as possible. Whereas such a standard process ensures an acceptable degree of safety and satisfaction to both patients and surgeons, it entails specific challenges for the stakeholders, too. For the manufacturer of medical devices it is challenging to deal with risk of compliance, cost and time of new product development and supply chain instability. For the surgeons and hospitals, the challenge is related to the lack of practice with the customized model prior to the operation, unfamiliarity with device, and the increased bargaining owner of the OEM as the entity who controls the technology. For patients, the challenge is mainly related with the low level of "patient-fitting" of the device, which can result in extended and more expensive post-surgery care and a less desired quality of life (Gibson and Srinath 2015).

Several studies have been focused on design and manufacturing processes of customized medical devices. Melgoza et al. developed an integrated tool for the design of a cardiac stent that meets the personalized needs of the patient through combination of several methods such as attribute listing and quality function deployment (QFD) (Melgoza et al. 2012). Jin et al. tried to have a closer look on the production of orthopaedic prosthesis by comparing the traditional and additive manufacturing process. The study concludes that despite of the benefits of customized orthopaedic prosthesis such as better fit and better operation result, there also challenges to be overcome from clinical, technological and financial points of view (Jin et al. 2015). On the other hand, Jin et al. have analysed the role of adaptive process planning for rapid prototyping of biomedical models (Jin et al. 2013). These models are mainly used by surgeons prior to the operation in order to figure out the precise location for the implant and the exact location of defect in the patient's body (Kruth et al. 2007). Since these models are highly customized based on the complex geometric characterizes of the patient, rapid prototyping and specially additive manufacturing can facilitate the timely and efficient production of models considering their mold-less process (Bourell et al. 2009; Sun and Lal 2002). In this regard Jin et al. focused on improvement of process planning for manufacturing and rapid prototyping of these models through four steps of process planning namely orientation determination, structure determination, slicing, and tool path generation (Jin et al. 2013). Lohfeld et al. combined both perspectives of design and manufacturing of customized implants within their study of engineering-assisted surgery. To this end, they have covered a broader scope through development of a route to digitize design and manufacturing of a customized implant. The route includes transfer of CT data, design of the implant, structural analysis of the implant, manufacturing and quality control (Lohfeld et al. 2007).

Despite of the several existing studies in terms of manufacturing and design of customized medical devices mostly through applying additive manufacturing, there are very few papers investigating the business and managerial sides of the topic. Indeed, the very few existing studies in this regard have been conducted recently and mainly from an economic perspective. Whereas Weller et al. have studied the economic implications of 3D printing in general and defined four patterns for markets of additive manufacturing (Weller et al. 2015), there are other studies which are more focused on evaluation of cost structure and develop cost models for additive manufacturing (Hopkinson and Dickens 2003; Ruffo et al. 2006; Ingole et al. 2009). Moreover, Schroder et al. have proposed a business model aiming at cost evaluation of additive manufacturing, which thus only covers the financial and economic perspective. The model identifies all the cost-relevant activities, sub-processes and main processes in order to define several cost functions. Eventually the model can be used as a decision tool to assess the cost structure of different additive manufacturing technologies and choose the most proper one (Lindemann et al. 2012). Among the very few studies, one study conducted by Zdravkovic et al. investigates manufacturing of customized medical devices from a business model perspective with a specific focus on value chain. The authors emphasize on the fact that interoperability can be seen as a significant driver for efficient manufacturing of customized medical devices since the customization process is not a single-stakeholder process but a multi-actor process including suppliers, surgeons and patients. To this end they developed a semantic interoperability framework to overcome the high complexity of the supply chain planning and execution in customized orthopedic implants manufacturing (Schröder et al. 2015).

2.2 Product-Service Systems from a Business Model Perspective

Product-Service systems have been widely discussed in literature in the past decade. This section aims at investigating the tpic in litearture first from a business model perspective and then through focusing apecifically on business models for healthcare.

2.2.1 PSS Business Models

From the early definition of the product service system (PSS) as "a marketable set of products and services capable of jointly fulfilling a user's need" (Zdravkovic et al. 2012), the concept of PSS has gained a lot of attention and evolved within time by authors who looked at it from different perspectives. In 2002, Mont revised the definition of PSS by considering other impact factors and also the potential effects of PSS paradigm. He defines a product service system (PSS) as "a system of products, services, supporting networks and infrastructures that are designed to be competitive, satisfy customer needs and have a lower environmental impact than traditional business models" (Goedkoop et al. 1999). Along with evolution of the definition of product service system has evolved during time, different studies have been focused on the topic from different points of view. While some studies have investigated the potential social and environmental impacts of PSS and thus regard it as a driver for sustainability (Mont 2002; Brezet et al. 2001), there are other studies that analyze the phenomenon from a business perspective pointing out PSS as an innovative strategy (James et al. 2001; Manzini and Vezzoli 2003). In general it is widely accepted that implementing a PSS business model brings benefits to both producer and customer through higher quality and higher level of customization, reduction of energy and resource consumption, increase of product life-cycle and job creation (Tukker and Tischner 2006; Aurich et al. 2006; Velamuri et al. 2011).

Regarding the strategic perspective of PSS, several authors conducted studies to explore the concept from a business model perspective. However, since the term "business model" itself implies ambiguity, the body of literature investigates the concept of PSS business models from different perspectives and according to the specific definition of business model that each study embraces. Moreover, despite of the potential discussed benefits of product-service systems, there are very limited studies focusing on how to implement a PSS business model (Baines et al. 2007; Velamuri et al. 2011). One of the leading early studies in this regard was conducted by Tukker, in which the author proposed three different types of PSS business models considering only the type of value proposition dimension. The three main business models defined by Tukker are: product-oriented, use-oriented and result-oriented PSS where each business model contains different economic and sustainability characteristics (Meier et al. 2010). Although still there is not a widely accepted definition for the term "business model" the studies that have in recent years have proposed more structured and clear proposal for definition and structure of a business model (Tukker 2004). There are recent studies in terms of PSS business model which takes into account a business model as a tool to create and capture value through a set of activities and operation within value chain. According to Gaiardelli et al. there are four main elements that a PSS business model entails. These elements are: value proposition which is a bundle of product and services, infrastructure and network, the relationship capital between parties, and the sustainability (Osterwalder and Pigneur 2010). Some other studies have been focused on the potential impacts of a PSS business model. Marques et al. developed a methodology for product-service system development. The proposed methodology facilitates the understanding of the process to be used in design of product-service systems, as well as the required organizational changes and eventually the integration of the concept with the business model (Gaiardelli et al. 2014). Kindstrom targets the challenge of companies in terms of shifting towards a service oriented business models and identified the key aspects of a service-based business model that need to be considered by companies. These key elements are value proposition, revenue mechanisms, value chain, value network, competitive strategy, and target market (Marques et al. 2013). Barquet et al. took a further step toward development of a structure for a PSS business model. Taking the business model canvas developed by Osterwalder and Pigneur as a reference structure, the authors defined a tailored version of business model canvas for product service systems. They also made an empirical analysis by implementing the developed business model in real case studies (Kindstrom 2010).

2.2.2 PSS and Business Models for Healthcare

Healthcare is one of the most rapid-evolving sectors. In recent years, rapid technological improvements in manufacturing sector has opened up many new perspectives in manufacturing of medical devices. On the other hand, healthcare service providers are facing several trends such as personalization, aging population, e-healthcare and patient-oriented healthcare which push them to move towards development and implementation of very flexible business models in order to be able to adapt with existing trends in the market. However, such a shift is more delicate for healthcare service providers since it can directly impact the lives of people. Moreover, in most of the countries government is a major stakeholder in healthcare system which has a regulatory role.Such a circumstance necessitates a careful development and implementation of the business model to benefit all the stakeholders and to be compliant with regulations. Nevertheless, despite of the importance of the topic, there are very few relevant studies in the literature to investigate the issue. In fact, most of the existing studies are focused on a specific part of a business model such as financial structure or supply chain management. The studies get even scarcer when integrating the topic of healthcare and product service systems. In this section, we describe a couple of existing studies in this regard.

In 2014, Nelson and Sen conducted a research to investigate the business rules management in healthcare. To this end they proposed a framework in order to facilitate the evolution of business processes and practices quickly and efficiently (Barquet et al. 2013). Bukh and Nielsen investigated the financial perspective of an healthcare business model by focusing on how financial analysis can reflect the strategy of a health care organization and which elements, from such a strategy perspective, can be perceived as constituting blocks of a healthcare organization's business model (Nelson and Sen 2014). Other scholars have focused on the topic from a supply chain perspective. There are also other studies that looked at topic from supply chain management perspective trying to identify driving factors on healthcare business model performance management (Bukh and Nielsen 2011; Chen et al. 2013). Lehoux et al. conducted a research to explore the mutual impacts of technology design and the business model for healthcare. They suggest that there are a number of business model elements that can facilitate the link between technology design and value creation in healthcare. To this end they identified these business model elements as: key characteristics, value proposition, value chain, value capture, value network, transition between value offer and value capture (Dobrzykowski et al. 2014). In a similar study, Van Liburg and van Gemert-Pijnen focused on defining of innovative business models for sustainable e-healthcare applications. According to their model, such a business model consists of nine main elements namely partner network, core capability, value configuration, Value proposition, CRM, distribution channels, target customers, revenue model, cost structure (Lehoux et al. 2014).

While the existing body of literature in terms of healthcare business model is still small and divergent, the topic is even far less investigated when it comes to creating links with the concept of product-service systems. In fact, studies that try to integrate the principles of PSS in healthcare management in order to develop innovative forms of business model are missing or are extremely rare. Indeed, the very few existing studies in this regard are more focused on the role of service in healthcare management rather than taking into account the whole concept of product-service systems. Rani et al. conducted one of these studies by investigating maintenance management strategies in healthcare facilities. Through several surveys and interviews, the authors identified the main types of maintenance strategies which are applied in healthcare structure and relevant satisfaction of the end-user for each strategy (van Limburg and van Gemert-Pijnen 2010). Another contribution made by Chen et al. to underline the systematic service innovations in e-Healthcare. Through considering the systemic nature of e-Healthcare, the authors developed a conceptual framework followed by empirical analysis of four case studies in order to unveil the key elements of business concepts for innovative e-healthcare services (Rani et al. 2015). In a recent work, Yip et al. studied the topic by extending the perspective to a product-service rather than a solely service. Through a comprehensive study, they developed a novel characterization approach to define the characteristics of product-service systems in healthcare industry (Chen et al. 2014).

2.2.3 Gap Identification

Analysis of the state-of-the-art and the relevant existing studies in literature unveils several gaps and shortcomings. In the case of customized manufacturing for healthcare devices, much attention has been paid to additive manufacturing technologies and specifically 3D printing. In addition a major part of these studies investigate the role of additive manufacturing in personalized manufacturing of medical devices only from a technical perspective without taking into account managerial and business perspectives. Indeed the very few studies that target the topic from business point of view focus on business applications of additive manufacturing and market analysis. Accordingly, there is also a lack of studies in terms of proper business models that can be deployed while implementing additive manufacturing technologies and 3D printing technique to fabricate medical devices based on the individualized needs of the patients. The gap becomes larger when it comes to investigation the role of the hospitals in manufacturing of individualized medical devices. Almost entire studies perceive hospital only as the end-user of the medical devices and thus they draw a clear line between manufacturer and user of the personalized medical devices without investigating the potential room for integration and move towards a product-service system based business model. Going through literature of the product-service system unveils the similar gap as well. While there are some studies in terms of PSS business models, very low attention has been paid to apply the concept in healthcare sector. The gap gets clearer and notables when it comes to extend the practices of PSS to increase integration between hospitals and manufacturers of customized medical devices.

To this end, this paper aims at start covering this gap by proposing innovative PSS-oriented business models in order to support manufacturing of personalized medical devices. The new business models facilitate the role change of the hospital from a solely consumer to a more active partner in manufacturing.

3 Moving Towards a Product-Service Business Model for Personalized Manufacturing in Healthcare

Analysis of the body of the literature and the identified gaps in previous section indicate the need of development for an innovative product-service oriented business model in order to deploy the new emerging technologies and to integrated them with concept of product-service system to bring advantages to patients and other stakeholders including hospitals, and manufacturers. However, prior to develop such a model, it is essential to identify the stakeholders involved in fabrication and utilization of personalized medical devices and analyze their interaction. To this end, we will start this section by presenting a preliminary stakeholder analysis to identify and map the current stakeholders as well as their interactions. This provides the required basis to understand the organizational framework that will be involved later in the proposed business model. Thereafter, the structure of the business model will be defined along with definition of building blocks and elements of the model. As a further step, we will describe how the proposed model can be used to generate different configurations of business model addressing different scenarios. Finally, we will have a closer look on potential benefits and challenges that each configuration might entail.

3.1 Preliminary Stakeholder Analysis

Stakeholder analysis is an essential part of developing a business model. The concept of stakeholders was first introduced in 1963 by Stanford Research Institute as "those groups without whose support the organization would cease to exist" (Yip et al. 2015). In 1984 Freeman improved the definition by describing stakeholders as "any group or individual who can affect or is affected by the achievement of the firm's objective". Accordingly he extended the concept by including not only the actors that affect the company, but also those who are affected by the company. This necessitates a bidirectional relationship between stakeholders and company

(Freeman and Reed 1983). In the case of personalized medical devices, there are different stakeholders who impact or are impacted by manufacturing and implementation of these devices including:

- Patient: The patient can be considered as one of the main stakeholders who plays the role of a customer for a personalized medical device. The benefit of the patient, as a stakeholder, is extremely high considering that he is the final user of the personalized device and that the whole process (manufacturing of device and healthcare service) affects directly on the quality of patient's life.
- Hospital: As a key player and a major stakeholder, hospitals can have different role sin fabrication of personalized medical devices. The role of the hospital might vary from a solely user of customized device to a more active player in terms of design and manufacturing of such device.
- Surgeon: Surgeons can be considered as technical operators in the process of delivery of medical devices to patients. Due to their primary role in healthcare and to their competences, they can be widely involved during the design process of devices through identification of patient's requirements. In other scenarios where hospital is more involved in design and production, surgeon can be also involved in testing phase of individualized anatomical models prototypes. Eventually they also benefit from a better result of their surgery thanks to the personalized devices and implants.
- Manufacturer: As the supplier of customized medical device, manufacturer plays a critical role. Considering limited of companies operating in the field of fabrication of personalized medical devices, manufacturers are considered as critical players whose function has a notable impact on other stakeholder as well.
- National Healthcare system (NHS): The healthcare system is a financial provider and a funding source to hospitals. Although National Healthcare System of a country is not directly involved during design, production and implementation of an individualized medical device, it is impacted by the result of the process, both in terms of patient's satisfaction and quality and cost of final product. Finally, the NHS has also a regulatory role which impacts on all other stakeholders.

Fabrication and usage of customized medical products require interactions among all the above mentioned stakeholders. However, structure of such interaction is different depending of the type of business models and role of each stakeholder. Figure 1 shows interaction of stakeholders in current business model for production and implementation of personalized medical devices.

As it can be seen in Fig. 1, the process of design, manufacturing and implementation of personalized medical device in the current existing business model is a timely process involving several stakeholders and requires a complicated information flow among the stakeholders. The process starts with patient going to the hospital. While the medical visit is arranged and done, surgeon should identify the individual characteristics of patient to design the personalized device and transfer required data to sales department of the hospital to issue the relevant order. Thereafter, hospital issues a request to the manufacturer and the

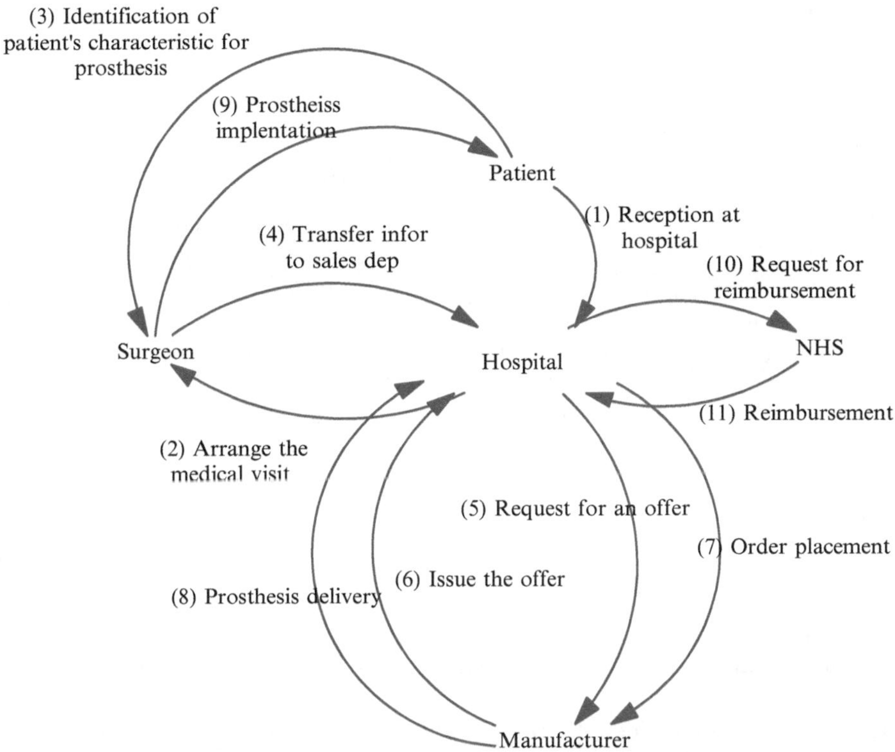

Fig. 1 Stakeholders interaction in state-of-the-art manufacturing and usage of personalized medical devices. Source: Author's own compilation (2016)

manufacturer provides an offer to the hospital. Upon finalizing the offer investigation by hospital, it places the order to the producer and at this point fabrication of personalized product starts. While the final product is ready, it will be shipped to the hospital and implemented by surgeon for the patient. Meanwhile hospital follows up its interaction with National Healthcare provider to request for the reimbursement of the relative cost. While the current business model requires a time-consuming and complicate interactions among different actors which incurs further cost to the process, a new business model can reduce and optimize these interactions through shaping a new relationship between hospital and manufacturer and consequently involving hospital in fabrication process thanks to the services provided by manufacturer. Figure 2 illustrates stakeholders interactions in the new business model.

The new PSS-oriented business model increases the integration between manufacturer and hospital by moving production to the hospital or to proximity of the hospital and establishing a new relationship between producer and hospital through demanding and offering of product-service systems. Therefore while the first phase of the process is the same as the current business model (Patient admission in the

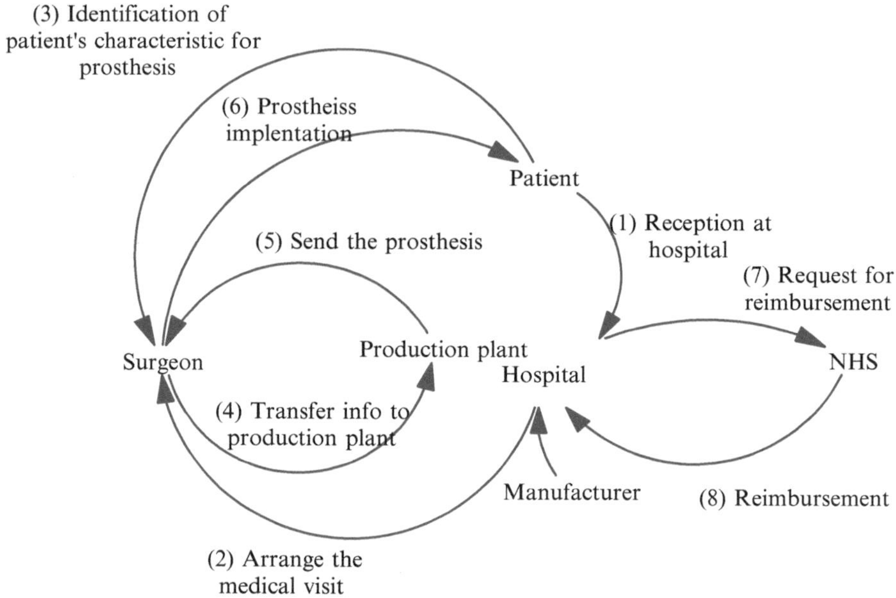

Fig. 2 Stakeholders interaction in an innovative PSS-oriented business model for fabrication and usage of personalized medical devices. Source: Author's own compilation (2016)

hospital, surgeon visit, identification of individual characteristics of the patient), the rest of the process differs in terms of interaction, time and cost. In the new business model, surgeon transfers the acquired data to the production plant located inside or in proximity of hospital. Fabrication is carried out with collaboration of manufacture and hospital and the final product will be delivered to surgeon. The final phase of the process is the same as the current business model where the surgeon implements the device. However, fewer numbers of interactions, less complicated process of information transfer and a higher integration level between actors, can result in a faster and more efficient fabrication and usage process.

3.2 Development of Business Model Structure

The results of stakeholder analysis presented in previous section clarify an overall image and a big picture of existing key stakeholders and their interaction. It also suggests how an innovative product-service oriented business model can facilitate and optimize the manufacturing process of personalized medical devices. Nevertheless, in order to design and implement such a business model, the first step would be definition of the business model structure which describes the boundaries of the business model as well as areas which are going to be investigated more in detail during development and design of the business model. Since the main focus of this study is on manufacturing of personalized medical devices, the new business model

Characteristic Features		Options			
Ownership	during phase of use	Equipment producer	Leasing Bank	Operating Joint Venture	Customer
	after phase of use	Equipment producer		Customer	
Operating Personnel	Manufacturing	Equipment producer	Operating Joint Venture	Customer	
	Maintanance	Equipment producer	Operating Joint Venture	Customer	
Location of operation		Equipment producers establishment	Establishment „fence to fence" to the customer	Customers establishment	
Single/multi customer operation		In parallel operation for multi customers		Operation for a single customer	
Payment		Pay on production	Pay for availability	fixed rate	Pay for equipment

Fig. 3 Morphological box as a framework to describe new business concepts. Source: Lay et al. (2009)

is designed focusing on defining a new structure and a closer integration between hospital and machinery equipment supplier aiming at transforming the role of hospital as a solely customer of the individualized medical devices to a producer. Consequently from now on we will refer to machinery producer as "manufacturer" and hospital as "customer". In order to design the structure of such business model, we took into account the morphological box proposed by Lay et al. as a reference structure Lay et al. (2009). This is mainly due to the fact that the morphological box is developed specifically for manufacturing sector focusing on the relationship between machinery producers and customer. Hence, it can be considered as a proper starting point and reference to design the structure of business model for personalized fabrication in healthcare. Figure 3 depicts the above mentioned morphological box.

Although the proposed model by Lay et al. covers major aspects of customer-manufacturer relationship in the field of manufacturing, some modifications were required in order to make it aligned within the context of product-service system focusing on the role of hospital and machinery supplier. To this end, the proposed structure of PSS-oriented business model for personalized fabrication in healthcare is illustrated in Fig. 4.

As it can be seen in Fig. 4, the proposed model consists of a set of building blocks shown as characteristic features which define the main aspects and points of decision to be set. Moreover a number of options are defined for each characteristic feature. These options describe the potential alternatives that can be selected to configure the business model. Obviously selection of different options results in configuration of different business models where each configuration refers to the strategy to be followed up by the customer and supplier. The first building block refers to location of production which refers to the physical place where production of personalized medical devices takes place. This can be internal (i.e. in a laboratory inside of hospital), external (the current situation, i.e. supplier's site) or fence-to-fence (i.e. a production site in proximity of hospital). "Operation personnel"

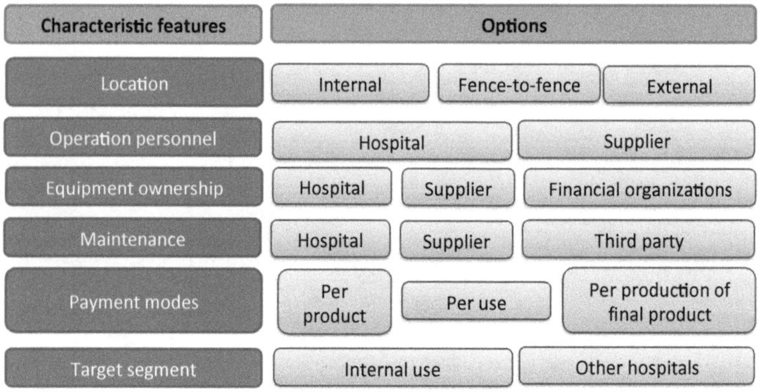

Fig. 4 Proposed structure for PSS-oriented business model for personalized fabrication of medical devices. Source: Lay et al. (2009)

describes the allocation of workforce for production. The operation responsibility can be allocated either to specialized personnel trained by hospital or to expert personnel of the supplier. "Equipment ownership" clarifies the property right to use the manufacturing equipment and machinery. In this case, machinery can be purchased and owned by hospital, or owned by supplier and leased to hospital, or owned by an external financial organization. The block of "maintenance" describes the responsible party to carry out the maintenance of the equipment which can change from hospital to supplier or to a third party who provides the maintenance service to the hospital. "Payment mode" defines if the payment is made in a traditional way for utilized, or based on the acquired usage service and function service. Finally "target segment" clarifies that if the fabricated devices are only for internal use or aimed to be sold to other customers too and generating potential source of revenue for the hospital.

3.3 Configurations of PSS Business Model for Personalized Fabrication of Medical Devices

The proposed structure in Sect. 3.2 is a starting point to generate different configurations of business model. Selection of a different option for each building block of business model results in generation of business models which not only differ in terms of options but also in terms of the agreement between supplier and hospital and thus the level of servitization. This is mainly due to the fact that PSS is generally focused on the role of agreement and integration level between producer and customer in order to better manage the life cycle of customer solution (Pourabdollahian and Copani 2014). Tukker defines three main categories of product service systems: (1) product-oriented services where the main value proposition is based on selling the product through some additional services; (2) use-oriented services where the value proposition is based on the usage of the product and thus the ownership of the product is not transferred to the customer; (3) result-oriented services where the value proposition is based on the performance agreed by customer and supplier regardless the exchange of physical products (Meier et al. 2010). Each category entails a specific agreement between user and supplier and thus a different level of servitization. In this section, we introduce four different configurations of business model where each of them presents different characteristics, different type of agreement between manufacturer and supplier and different level of servitization.

3.3.1 Product-Oriented Business Model: Manufacturing Hospital Buys Physical Product and Additional Services

In this section we present two configurations of product-oriented business model. In both scenarios hospital buys production machinery from supplier wit additional services. However the type and level of services in two scenarios are different.

- Type A: In this scenario the hospital as the final manufacturer of the personalized medical devices purchases the manufacturing machinery such as additive manufacturing equipment and micro-manufacturing equipment from supplier and considers as the owner of the equipment. Production lab is either located inside or in proximity of hospital in order to benefit from a smooth interaction between surgeons and lab operators and shorter delivery time. Hospital will be responsible for running the equipment employing its own operators. The only interaction between supplier and hospital will be in terns of maintenance where the supplier is responsible for maintenance of the equipment. This indicates that hospital buys product and an additional service from the supplier and thus puts this configuration in the category of product-oriented business mode. Accordingly payment will be based on the product purchased and the additional service. Hospital can use the produced devices for both internal use and also to sell to other hospitals and end-users (Durugbo and Riedel 2013). Figure 5 shows the configuration of this business model.

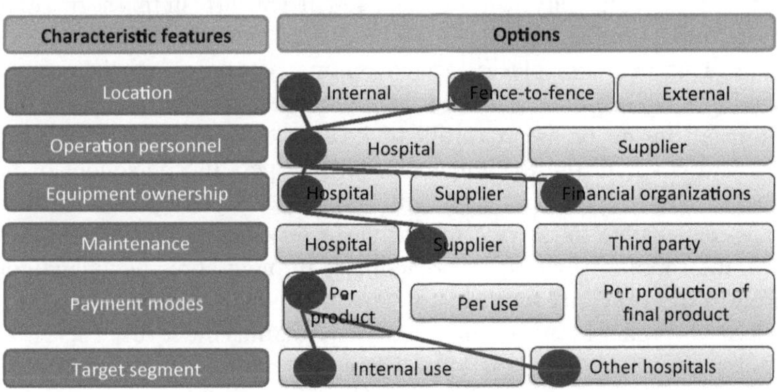

Fig. 5 Product-oriented business model type A. Source: Durugbo and Riedel (2013)

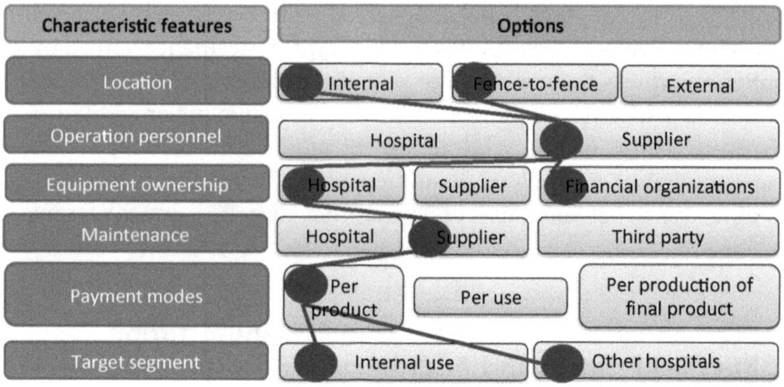

Fig. 6 Product-oriented business model type B. Source: Durugbo and Riedel (2013)

- Type B: In this scenario hospital acquires production equipment from supplier and installs them in production lab inside or in proximity of hospital. Like previous configuration, hospital acquires the additional maintenance service as well, thus supplier is responsible for maintenance of equipment. However, hospital acquires another additional service which is equipment running. Therefore supplier personnel are responsible for production of personalized medical devices as the expert human resource to run the machinery. In this regard degree of servitization in this scenario is higher than previous scenario as well as integration between producer and supplier. Payment mode is based on pay per product and additional services and the target segment can be both internal and external. Figure 6 depicts the configuration of this type of business model.

3.3.2 Use-Oriented Business Model: Manufacturing Hospital Pays per Use of Machinery

The use-oriented configuration is developed on the basis of purchasing the usage of a product rather than the physical product itself. Therefore, in this scenario hospital does not acquire production machinery and thus supplier retains ownership of equipment. This can take place through renting or leasing mechanisms. In this configuration hospital rents or leases the equipment in order to install them in a production lab inside or in proximity of hospital. While the ownership has not transferred to hospital, the equipment is run by operating personnel of hospital. Consequently supplier doesn't have any role in terms of operation. Meanwhile supplier is responsible to provide maintenance services to the hospital. Manufacturer pays the supplier per usage of machinery through agreements and contracts. Compared to the previous scenarios, degree of integration between supplier and manufacturer is higher in the use-oriented scenario, thus the level of servitization is higher since there is no transaction of physical products (Durugbo and Riedel 2013). Figure 7 shows this configuration of business model.

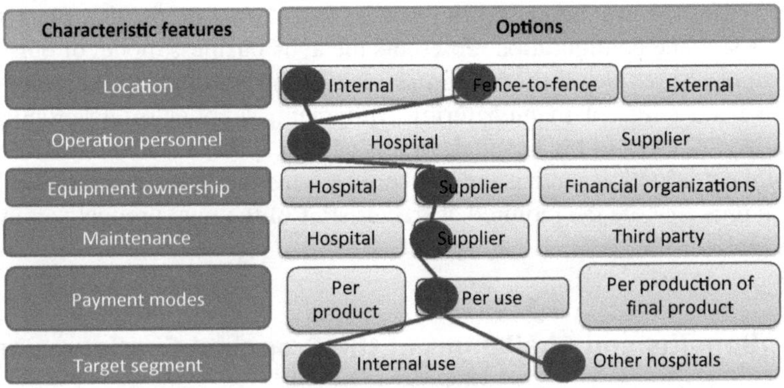

Fig. 7 Use-oriented business model configuration. Source: Durugbo and Riedel (2013)

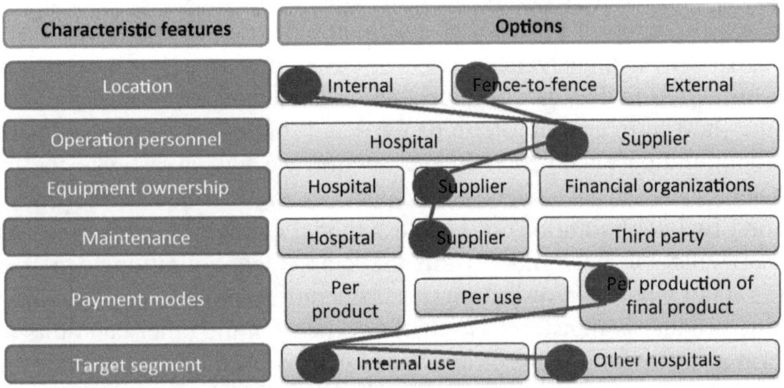

Fig. 8 Result-oriented business model configuration. Source: Durugbo and Riedel (2013)

3.3.3 Result-Oriented Business Model: Manufacturing Hospital Pays per the Final Performance

Within the result-oriented configuration, hospital takes a step forward toward more collaboration and integration with supplier. While the fabrication place remains inside or in proximity of hospital and production takes place under supervision of hospital, it is supplier who is responsible for running the production. While supplier owns the equipment and should provide additional maintenance services to the manufacturer, it is also responsible for running of production machinery through using its own expert operators. Thus hospital provides the physical place for production and supplier is responsible to use its own machinery and personnel to produce the personalized devices. As a result, hospital pays per production of final product. Sine hospital is considered as the final manufacturer of the devices, the target market can be both internal and external (Durugbo and Riedel 2013). Figure 8 illustrates this configuration.

In the case that production takes place in an external production plant such as supplier's site, the configuration represents the as-is business model of outsourcing where supplier provides a production service to the hospital. In the other words, having a wide range of manufacturing equipment, supplier offers production of personalized devices to the hospital. In this case hospital is only considered as the buyer of the production service and final product and the interaction level is limited to design phase where the required characteristics of the final product is transferred to the supplier.

3.4 Benefits and Challenges of the Proposed Configurations

All the configurations of PSS-oriented business models developed in the previous sections are designed to realize fabrication of customized medical devices. However, they differ from each other from many perspectives such as level of servitization, integration of supplier and manufacturer, financial and operational structure, level of responsiveness, level of autonomy, etc. Hence selection of the best-fit configuration does not only depend on the strategy of the manufacturer but also on the short-term and long-term benefits and challenges that a specific business model configuration encompass. In this section we will investigate the potential benefits and challenges of each business model configuration described in Sect. 3.3.

The first two configurations of business model configuration (Type A and B of product-oriented business model) are the closest configuration to a traditional business model where a physical product is acquired by the customer and ownership of the product is transferred to the customer. On the other hand this business model brings out an innovative proposal which transforms the role of a hospital to a manufacturer of personalized medical devices rather than only a user of these devices. Such a radical change in the structure of business model can results in potential benefits such as shorter delivery lead-time, a very high integration and smooth interaction between surgeons as providers of the product characteristics data and production plant. Such an effective information sharing might lead to a production process very close to the real-time process. Moreover it can intensify the brand reputation of the hospital as the user of new technologies to produce medical devices and create new sources of revenue for the hospital. While in Type A, hospital enjoys from a full autonomy, in Type B it should compromise its autonomy upon using of supplier operating personnel. In any case a product-oriented business model requires a deviation of the hospital core business which might be a source of problem. Hospitals are always considered as providers of healthcare service, and adding another business much different from its core business might be challenging to manage for a hospital. Hospitals have neither manufacturing vocation nor culture. Therefore they should setup and manage an internal factory, which will represent "a new business in the business". Another challenging issue would be the certification of the final product and production processes. According to the EU regulations, every medical device and product needs to respect the relevant medical device directive and be certified by EU notified bodies (Pourabdollahian and

Copani 2015). In addition hospital needs to make a high initial investment in order to purchase the machinery equipment and also for upgrading them. Acquiring of machinery will also limit the degree of customization can be offered to produce medical devices since only a limited number of machines can be purchased and thus the production lab do not have a large fleet of machinery. Considering the need to upgrade the equipment, distraction from core business and training personnel (in the case of Type A) a product-oriented business model might incur additional cost to the hospital.

The use-oriented configuration does not imply purchasing of machinery but using them through agreements and contracts. Therefore while still hospital enjoys the benefits of in proximity production such as shorter delivery time and higher interaction for design and manufacturing of the final product, it does not need to make a high initial investment to acquire machinery and to upgrade them. Moreover, leasing of the manufacturing equipment can be a source of tax deduction and hence cost saving for the hospital. In addition such a business model necessitates a closer integration and collaboration between producer and customer. Since ownership of equipment is not transferred to customer and supplier is responsible for maintenance, it is likely that through a better maintenance and a better professional usage of the machinery the supplier tries to prolong life-cycle of equipment and thus it has a positive impact on sustainability level as well. In addition the level of flexibility to use diverse machinery is higher since hospital can make new agreements and contracts to use more recent technologies without any need for a high initial investment. Nevertheless, hospital cannot enjoy the same level of autonomy as the previous configuration and certification will still stay a challenging issue for the hospital. Moreover, a continuous personnel training is a source of additional cost.

The final configuration of result oriented business model, suggests the lowest distraction of core business to the hospital. While machinery is owned by supplier and operation is run by supplier personnel, hospital is only responsible to provide a production plant and supervise the whole operation process as the owner of the final product. This can be a potential advantage since it lets hospital to focus on its core business to provide healthcare service to patients and avoid dedication of extra resources to a business in which is not a competent player. However, the level of autonomy is very low compared to the previous scenarios. Similar to previous configuration, no need for initial investment is a potential benefit and the possibility to use a large fleet of machines is an extra advantage to increase flexibility and production capacity. This can make hospital more flexible and responsive to differentiated demands. Moreover, a better management of equipment during its lifecycle can be a major driver to enhance sustainability and minimize environmental impacts.

4 Conclusion

The notable increase of average life expectancy, especially in developed countries, has resulted in a dramatic increase of aging population within the past decade. As a consequence, a better healthcare system is required to serve this aging population both in terms of healthcare service and medical products in order to provide them a better quality of life. To this end, customized medical products which are designed based on individual requirements of each patient have a considerable impact on the treatment process and quality of life. The emerging innovative manufacturing technologies facilitate development and production of customized medical products. Thanks to the new technologies such as additive manufacturing, it is even possible to produce the customized medical products efficiently in the hospitals in patient's proximity, which would transform the role of the hospital from a user to a producer of the medical products. In the other words, the hospital would extend its core business from a healthcare service provider to a healthcare product manufacturer and service provider. Accordingly, a new business model is required to facilitate and support such a shift by focusing on both product and service perspectives and hence taking into account an integrated product-service system approach.

In this chapter we introduced innovative product-service business models based on customized manufacturing of medical products exploiting the potential of innovative technologies and the exchange of innovative products-services between the hospital (as the manufacturer) and the machinery producers (as the supplier). A structured business model design approach was presented, enabling generation of different alternatives through different configurations of business model building blocks. Each alternative differs from another in terms of options, agreement between supplier and hospital and thus the level of Eventually the best-fit business model can be generated and implemented based on the potential benefits and challenges that each alternative entails and have been defined in Sect. 3.4 of this chapter.

Despite of the potential benefits of such a business model, it has it own limitation as well. First of all, the proposed model is a theoretical model. It requires further analysis, particularly a detailed economic assessment, to select the best-fit configuration. This study provides the first towards introduction of an innovative PSS-oriented business model for personalized production of medical devices on a qualitative base. Future studies are required to follow the concept not only from qualitative perspective but also quantitative one.

References

Aurich, J. C., Fuchs, C., & Wagenknecht, C. (2006). Life cycle oriented design of technical product-service systems. *Journal of Cleaner Production, 14*(17), 1480–1494.

Baines, T. S., Lightfoot, H. W., Evans, S., Neely, A., Greenough, R., Peppard, J., et al. (2007). State-of-the-art in product-service systems. Proceedings of the Institution of Mechanical Engineers, Part B. *Journal of Engineering Manufacture, 221*, 1543–1552.

Barquet, A. P. B., de Oliviera, M. G., Amigo, C. R., Cuhna, V. P., & Rozenfeld, H. (2013). Employing the business model concept to support the adoption of product–service systems (PSS). *Industrial Marketing Management, 42*, 693–704.

Bourell, D. L., Leu, M. C., & Rosen, D. W. (2009). *Roadmap for additive manufacturing – Identifying the future of freeform processing*. Austin, TX: The University of Texas.

Brezet, J. C., Bijma, A. S., Ehrenfeld, J., & Silvester, S. (2001). *The design of ecoefficient services*. Delft, Netherlands: TU Delft for the Dutch Ministry of Environment.

Bukh, P. N., & Nielsen, C. (2011). Understanding the health care business model: The financial analysts' point of view. *Journal of Health Care Finance, 37*(2), 8–26.

Chen, D. Q., Preston, D. S., & Xia, W. (2013). Enhancing hospital supply chain performance: A relational view and empirical test. *Journal of Operations Management, 31*, 391–408.

Chen, S. H., Wen, P. C., & Yang, C. K. (2014). Business concepts of systemic service innovations in e-Healthcare. *Technovation, 34*(9), 513–524.

Dobrzykowski, D., Deilami, V. S., Hong, P., & Kim, S. C. (2014). A structured analysis of operations and supply chain management research in healthcare (1982–2011). *International Journal of Production Economics, 147*, 514–530.

Durugbo, C., & Riedel, J. C. K. H. (2013). Readiness assessment of collaborative networked organisations for integrated product and service delivery. *International Journal of Production Research, 51*(2), 598–613.

Freeman, R. E., & Reed, D. L. (1983). Stockholders and stakeholders: A new perspective on corporate governance. *California Management Review, 25*(3), 88–106.

Gaiardelli, P., Resta, B., Martinez, V., Pinto, R., & Albores, P. (2014). A classification model for product-service offerings. *Journal of Cleaner Production, 66*, 507–519.

Gibson, I., & Srinath, A. (2015). Simplifying medical additive manufacturing: Making the surgeon the designer. *Procedia Technology, 20*, 237–242.

Global AgeWatch. (2016). *Help age International*. Accessed April 30, 2016, from http://www.helpage.org

Goedkoop, M. J., van Halen, J. G., te Riele, H., & Rommens, P. J. M. (1999). *Product service systems, ecological and economic basics*. The Hague, Netherlands: Ministry of Environment.

Hopkinson, N., & Dickens, P. M. (2003). Analysis of rapid manufacturing – Using layer manufacturing processes for production. Proceedings of the Institution of Mechanical Engineers, Part C. *Journal of Mechanical Engineering Science, 217*, C1:31–39.

Ingole, D. S., Kuthe, A. M., Thakare, S. B., & Talankar, A. S. (2009). Rapid prototyping – A technology transfer approach for development of rapid tooling. *Rapid Prototyping Journal, 15*(4), 280–290.

James, P., Slob, A., & Nijhuis, L. (2001). Environmental and social well being in the new economy. In *Sustainable services e an innovation workbook*. Bradford: University of Bradford.

Jin, G. Q., Li, W. D., & Gao, L. (2013). An adaptive process planning approach of rapid prototyping and manufacturing. *Robotics and Computer-Integrated Manufacturing, 29*, 23–38.

Jin, Y., Plott, J., Chen, R., Wensman, J., & Shih, A. (2015). Additive manufacturing of custom orthoses and prostheses – A review. *Procedia CIRP, 36*, 199–204.

Kindstrom, D. (2010). Towards a service-based business model – Key aspects for future competitive advantage. *European Management Journal, 28*, 479–490.

Kruth, J. P., Levy, G., Klocke, F., & Childs, T. H. C. (2007). Consolidation phenomena in laser and powder-bed based layered manufacturing. *CIRP Annals, 56*(2), 730–759.

Lay, G., Schroeter, M., & Biege, S. (2009). Service-based business concepts: A typology for business-to-business markets. *European Management Journal, 27*(6), 442–455.

Lehoux, P., Daudelin, G., Williams-Jones, B., Denis, J. L., & Longo, C. (2014). How do business model and health technology design influence each other? Insights from a longitudinal case study of three academic spin-offs. *Research Policy, 43*, 1025–1038.

Lindemann, C., Jahnke, U., Moi, M., & Koch, R. (2012, August 6–8). *Analyzing product lifecycle costs for a better understanding of cost drivers in additive manufacturing* (pp. 177–188). Proceedings of the 2012 Solid Freeform Fabrication Symposium, Austin, TX.

Lohfeld, S., McHugh, P., Serban, D., Boyle, D., O'Donnell, G., & Peckitt, N. (2007). Engineering Assisted SurgeryTM: A route for digital design and manufacturing of customised maxillofacial implants. *Journal of Materials Processing Technology, 183*, 333–338.

Manzini, E., & Vezzoli, C. (2003). A strategic design approach to develop sustainable product service systems: Examples taken from the 'environmentally friendly innovation' Italian prize. *Journal of Cleaner Production, 11*(8), 851–857.

Marques, P., Cuhna, P. F., Valente, F., & Leitao, A. (2013). A methodology for product-service systems development. *Procedia CIRP, 7*, 371–376.

Meier, H., Roy, R., & Seliger, G. (2010). Industrial product-service systems – IPS2. *CIRP Annals – Manufacturing Technology, 59*, 607–627.

Melgoza, E. L., Serenio, L., Rosell, A., & Ciurana, J. (2012). An integrated parameterized tool for designing a customized tracheal stent. *Computer-Aided Design, 44*, 1173–1181.

Mont, O. (2002). Clarifying the concept of product service systems. *Journal of Cleaner Production, 10*(3), 237–245.

Nelson, M. R., & Sen, R. (2014). Business rules management in healthcare: A lifecycle approach. *Decision Support Systems, 57*, 387–394.

Osterwalder, A., & Pigneur, Y. (2010). *Businessmodel generation: A handbook for visionaries, game changers, and challengers*. Hoboken, NJ: Wiley.

Pourabdollahian, G., & Copani, G. (2014). Proposal of an innovative business model for customized production in healthcare. *Modern Economy, 5*(13), 1147–1160.

Pourabdollahian, G., & Copani, G. (2015). Development of a PSS-oriented business model for customised production in healthcare. *Procedia CIRP, 30*, 492–497.

Rani, N. A., Baharum, M. R., Akbar, A. R. N., & Nawawi, A. H. (2015). Perception of maintenance management strategy on healthcare facilities. *Procedia- Social and Behaviorial Sciences, 170*, 272–281.

Ruffo, M., Tuck, C., & Hague R. J. M. (2006). Cost estimation for rapid manufacturing – Laser sintering production for low to medium volumes. Proceedings of the Institution of Mechanical Engineers, Part B. *Journal of Engineering Manufacture,* 1417–1427.

Schröder, M., Falk, B., & Schmitt, R. (2015). Evaluation of cost structures of additive manufacturing processes using a new business model. *Procedia CIRP, 30*, 311–316.

Sun, W., & Lal, P. (2002). Recent development on computer aided tissue engineering — A review. *Computer Methods and Programs in Biomedicine, 67*(2), 85–103.

Tukker, A. (2004). Eight types of product-service system: Eight ways to sustainability? *Business Strategy and the Environment, 13*(4), 246–260.

Tukker, A., & Tischner, U. (2006). Product-services as a research field: Past, present and future. Reflections from a decade of research. *Journal of Cleaner Production, 14*(17), 1552–1556.

van Limburg, A. H. M., & van Gemert-Pijnen, J. (2010, February 10–15). *Towards innovative business modeling for sustainable eHealth applications*. 2010 Second International Conference on eHealth, Telemedicine, and Social Medicine, St. Maarten, Nethelands Antilles.

Velamuri, V. K., Neyer, A. K., & Möslein, K. M. (2011). Hybrid value creation: A systematic review of an evolving research area. *Journal für Betriebswirtschaft, 61*, 3–35.

Weller, C., Kleer, R., & Piller, F. T. (2015). Economic implications of 3D printing: Market structure models in light of additive manufacturing revisited. *International Journal of Production Economics, 164*, 43–56.

WHO. (2014a). *UN Human Development Report 2005*. United Nations Development Programme, World Health Organization (WHO), New York.

WHO. (2014b). *WHO life expectancy*. WHO. Retrieved April 10, 2016.

Yip, M. H., Phaal, R., & Probert, D. R. (2015). Characterising product-service systems in the healthcare industry. *Technology in Society, 43*, 129–143.

Zdravkovic, M., Trajanovic, M., Stojkovic, M., Mišic, D., & Vitkovic, N. (2012). A case of using the Semantic Interoperability Framework for custom orthopedic implants manufacturing. *Annual Reviews in Control, 36*, 318–326.

Golboo Pourabdollahian is a post-doc research fellow at the Institute of Industrial Technologies and Automation (ITIA) of the Italian National Research Council (CNR). She received her PhD from politecnico di Milano in Management, Economics and Industrial Engineering. Her research activities and interests are on business models, personalization and mass customization, product-service systems, and sustainability. She is engaged in different projects in both European and National levels.

Giacomo Copani is the head of "Manufacturing Business Models" research at the Institute of Industrial Technologies and Automation (ITIA) of the Italian National Research Council (CNR). He is research assistant at Politecnico di Milano in the area of Industrial Marketing. His research activity is on manufacturing business models, industrial services, manufacturing sustainability and technology roadmapping, with specific focus in the industrial goods sector. He is engaged in European and National research projects, and in supporting manufacturing research and innovation policy definition at National and European level.

Patient Driven Service Delivery Models in Mental Health Care

Patricia E. Alafaireet and Howard Houghton

Abstract

Current service delivery models for mental health care (especially inpatient mental health care) frequently result in patient noncompliance and repeated admissions. This chapter addresses both the noncompliance and recidivism issues by exploring patient driven service model creation. Using socio-ethnographic tools such as concept mapping, patient led focus groups, and patient populated advisory groups, service delivery models which are more acceptable to patients, lower in cost, and higher in quality can be developed. These are characterized by a greater level of individualization to specific patient needs than is currently allowed by service calls used. Service delivery models developed under these protocols leverage community resources and non-traditional sources of patient support to create patient approved service delivery where costs, resources, and responsibilities are controlled through a distributed model. The chapter aims at creating a vision of future mental health care that is free of many of the barriers which now impede patient adherence, cost controlled services, and delivery of high quality care. The objectives of this chapter are to demonstrate such ethnographic approaches in a manner that can be used by both novice learners and those more experienced. Hands on examples in a case study are included in the chapter.

P.E. Alafaireet, PhD, MHA (✉)
University of Missouri, 734 CS&E Building, Columbia, MO 65212, USA
e-mail: alafaireetp@health.missouri.edu

H. Houghton
Department of Psychiatry, University of Missouri, #3 Hospital Drive, Columbia, MO 65212, USA
e-mail: Houghtonh@health.missouri.edu

M.A. Pfannstiel, C. Rasche (eds.), *Service Business Model Innovation in Healthcare and Hospital Management*, DOI 10.1007/978-3-319-46412-1_7

1 Framing the Issue-Understanding the Mental Healthcare Delivery Arena

Due to the inherent symptomology and social stigma associated with mental health issues, many of the strategies used in the provision of psychiatric care, including the service model under which care is provided, have been developed through research that did not involve a high level of patient input. This reticence continues, despite evidence that the lack of research into mental health service delivery models, leading to lack of effective models, leaves the world's population with a heavy disease burden, and leaves many of the world's citizens with both decreased quality of life and length of life. Whiteford and colleagues noted, in their 2010 report, that, globally, data show a significant and substantial healthcare burden from mental health illnesses, substance abuse, and disease of a neurologic nature (Whiteford et al. 2015). Their data demonstrated that these three diseases accounted for 10.4 % of global disability-adjusted life years (DALYs), 28.5 % of global years lived with disability (YLDs) and 2.3 % of global years lost to premature mortality (YLLs) (Whiteford et al. 2015). Mental health illnesses accounted for the greatest contribution to these findings (Whiteford et al. 2015).

Reporting in 2015, Walker and colleagues conducted a meta-analysis of 203 articles, representing 29 countries (distributed across six continents), examining excess mortality and disease burden in individuals experiencing mental health diseases (Walker et al. 2015). Their results outlined that 135 of the 203 studies showed excess mortality for individuals experiencing mental health disease, and that the median years of potential life lost in that population was 10 years (Walker et al. 2015). Walker and colleagues also noted that approximately eight million deaths per year, or 14.3 % of deaths worldwide, are attributable to mental health disease (Walker et al. 2015). In a departure from their historical focus on non-communicable diseases such as cardiovascular disease, Type 2 diabetes mellitus, cancer and chronic respiratory diseases, the World Health Organization (WHO) and the US based Centers for Disease Control and Prevention (CDC) have recently increased their focus on mental health diagnoses as a function related to high prevalence and contribution to global disease (O'Neil et al. 2015). The recently released WHO Global Action Plan (2013–2020) includes mental health disease prevention and control targets, while the CDC has plans to integrate mental health promotion and the prevention and management of mental health disease in its future efforts (O'Neil et al. 2015).

Suicide, a complication of a mental health disease, in both adults and children, is the tenth leading cause of death in the US (SAMHSA 2015; US HHS 1999; US Veteran's Administration 2012). Ninety percent of children who commit suicide have a mental health diagnosis (SAMHSA 2015; US HHS 1999). Unsurprisingly, employment can also be impacted by mental health disease (Greenberg et al. 2015). Dismuke and Egede reported that individuals suffering from depression have a reduction of $1,914 annually in personal income (Dismuke and Egede 2015). In the US, significant mental health diseases cause lost wages for hundreds, and $193.2 billion annually (Insel 2008). Greenberg reported that up to 50 % of the total costs of mental health disease can be attributed to lost wages and other workplace costs (Greenberg et al. 2015). Mental health disease also affects young individuals not in the workforce by impacting their attendance at, and completion of, primary education, despite special education services (Aron et al. 2007). Thirty-seven percent of primary and secondary students suffering with mental health diseases drop out of school, accounting for the highest rate for any group with a disability (Aron et al. 2007). In the US, it is estimated that 26 % of adults living in homeless shelters have a serious mental health issue, often comorbid with substance abuse (US HUD 2011).

Criminal justice in the penal system in the US is also significantly impacted, as 20 % of adult prisoners in local and state institutions have mental health diagnoses that may predispose these individuals to commit criminal offenses, and often re-offenses (James et al. 2006; Nelson et al. 2015). Despite significant financial expenditures and increasing focus on mental health services delivery, the US healthcare system appears to be less effective than desired in terms of care delivery and outcomes for citizens with mental health disease (Nat'l Institute of Mental Health 2008, 2015). Recently, the US government reported that, for individuals with a diagnosis of some form of mental health disease, 41 % received services in the previous year and for those with a diagnosis of severe mental health disease, only 63 % received services (Nat'l Institute of Mental Health 2015). Only 51 % of children between the ages of 8 and 15 years with a diagnosis of a mental health disease received services in the previous year (Nat'l Institute of Mental Health 2007, 2015). In addition to the overall low rates of intervention, Kessler comments that the initiation of care for individuals with a mental health disease is often characterized by a long delay between diagnosis and the delivery of care and management, which only complicates both care and outcome (Kessler et al. 2005).

Because so much of the cost created by mental health disease occurs outside the parameters of traditional service delivery modes, it is especially important that new, more effective, service delivery models be developed. Many of these models will necessarily need to reflect delivery modes and delivery sites that help assure access to care.

2 Importance of Service Delivery Model in Assuring Access to Care

Service delivery models often underpin access to care, or the lack thereof. Traditional service delivery models, including those that are focused on inpatient hospital care and ambulatory clinic visits that occur in a traditional medical setting, have often fallen short, both in terms of assuring access to the sheer number of individuals needing care and in the ability to provide care to members of minority groups and members of cultures outside the mainstream. In the US, for example, because African Americans tend to rely on family, religious, and social communities for emotional support, and Latinos are twice as likely to seek treatment for mental disorders from nontraditional settings, such as clergy, an approach to care that can be delivered through a respected member of a faith or cultural community may be more effective in addressing health concerns (Illness 2004a, b; Weinrich et al. 1998; Rankins et al. 2009; Byrne et al. 2012; Savoca et al. 2013). These kinds of community-centered approaches are especially needed, because not much has changed, health-wise, for those populations in the US, especially for African-American and Hispanic males, over the last 2–3 generations.

The top causes of excess deaths among African Americans and Hispanics in 2013 are almost identical to those reported in 1985, with the addition of HIV/AIDS (CDC 2014). This may be, perhaps, because men's choices around health and healthcare, including mental health care, seem to be very much rooted in the male ideology, including machismo, and in the case of older males, the nature of work (Wilkins 2008). A history of misdiagnosis, inadequate treatment, and lack of cultural understanding make such disparities worse. These disparities further create a situation where access to care is restricted. Sources of community-level care may not be effective because of such barriers as underfunding, poor service design, lack of insurance, and lack of health literacy (Smith 2008; Forrest and Leeds 2007). Service delivery models that focus on lifestyle changes, especially in older populations, may be particularly effective (Clark et al. 2012). Service delivery approaches that focus on reducing barriers to socially and culturally acceptable mental health care through methods that aim to produce a reduction in social marginalization through health skills development and social marketing have proven to be effective in reducing behavioral risk associated with mental health, and in creating an important sense of social connectedness (Victor et al. 2009). There may also be protective factors that can be exploited in the delivery of mental-health services, such as ethnic pride, that have not been traditionally included in service delivery models (Enriquez et al. 2012; Tol et al. 2013).

Changes to service delivery models have been occurring. For example, inpatient treatment for mental health disease and substance abuse has been transitioning from care delivered primarily in private, urban, and government facilities to care delivered at the community level through community hospitals, which often allows patients to be treated closer to their home (Weil 2015). However, changes to reimbursement and shifting rural population patterns have resulted in the number of community hospitals with dedicated psychiatric care units declining by 18 % from 1990 to 2008 (Weil 2015). Overall, more care is being delivered via outpatient programs, in programs designed to address more effectively socioeconomic, community, and judicial and legal components associated with individuals suffering from mental health disease (Abracen et al. 2016; Lin and Lee 2008; Kubiak et al. 2015; Compton et al. 2016; Comartin et al. 2015; Edgely 2014; Lowder et al. 2016).

Because of the costs associated with interventions and management of individuals who have both mental health disease and significant criminal and legal histories, mental health courts have been developed in an effort to leverage an intense, team-based community service delivery model aimed at decreasing hospitalizations, arrest and re-arrest, and incarcerations (Abracen et al. 2016; Lin and Lee 2008; Kubiak et al. 2015; Compton et al. 2006, 2016; Comartin et al. 2015;

Edgely 2014; Lowder et al. 2016). However, researchers focused on the mental health courts approach all state that the ideal target population that could most benefit from the courts use is not well-defined, and as with many new approaches and strategies which are expensive and have limited availability, they argue for more controlled trials to determine not only those individuals who might most benefit, but also on more exactly where the societal level benefits may occur through better coordination of care, community-level integration of patients, decreased costs of care, and decreased rates of judicial court recidivism and/or re-incarceration (Abracen et al. 2016; Lin and Lee 2008; Kubiak et al. 2015; Compton et al. 2006, 2016; Comartin et al. 2015; Edgely 2014; Lowder et al. 2016). Similar types of success and benefits have been noted for individuals with mental health disease where telemedicine in psychiatry programs have been utilized (Adler et al. 2014; Fortney et al. 2015; Gellis et al. 2014). There, also, is a need for better ways to determine which individual patients might benefit from this approach, as well as a need to understand better what could underpin further refinement in these service delivery models (Comartin et al. 2015; Edgely 2014; Lowder et al. 2016).

Much research is needed to determine fully the effects and efficacy of these changing service delivery models. Given the acute nature of the problem of delivering mental health services to all those who need them, it is helpful to consider developing service delivery models that effectively address treatment, non-adherent visits, and recidivism in patient care, as these are problems where large amounts of health care dollars are spent with little effect. Effectively addressing treatment non-adherent visits and recidivism through patient-centered service delivery models holds promise, to both increase the quality of care and reduce the cost of care, including opportunity cost born primarily by the patient. Developing service delivery models around stated patient needs, via an entry process controlled by patients, and where actual service delivery models are evaluated and validated by patients is a strategy whereby patient commitment to the care process, including their own self-care, may be increased.

3 Understanding the Utility of Treatment Non-adherent Visits and Recidivism to Inpatient Care as Markers of Improved Patient-Centric Service Delivery Models

Treatment non-inherent visits, also known as "no-shows" or "did not keep appointment" visits are, by their very nature, indicators of an ineffective service delivery model, as they are a primary indicator of a service delivery model that renders patients either unable or unwilling to meet at a prescribed time with a provider as part of their care. Treatment non-adherent visits create, in the ambulatory environment, a vicious cycle, which, in turn, creates lower reimbursement (through decreased physician and provider productivity), increased overall costs for subsequent care (which is frequently delivered in emergency departments), decreased quality of care, and often, a worsening disease state for the patient

(Misdrahi et al. 2002; Compton et al. 2006, 2016). These increased costs and reductions in care quality often continue until arrested by either extreme morbidity or mortality for the patient (Luppa et al. 2007). Although much research has been carried out around treatment non-adherent visits, especially the prediction of treatment non-adherent visits, investigation into patient-centric factors has primarily been limited to specific demographic characteristics of groups of patients (Bean et al. 1995; Cashman et al. 2004; Dove et al. 1981; Izard et al. 2005; Kruse et al. 2002; Mallard et al. 2004). This mindset that specific patient demographics somehow equals patient centeredness has limited exploration into patient-centered service delivery models, because it contributed to the general thought that non-adherence to visits is an intractable problem not solvable by the development of alternative service delivery models.

Likewise, recidivism is a complex issue requiring service delivery models that are created with patients, approved by patients, and fully participatory by patients. A recidivist, in this case, is an individual with a mental health disease who requires in-patient psychiatric care re-admission at frequent, unpredicted intervals that are typically earlier than planned, generally within less than 30 days from the date of the most recent hospital discharge (Elixhauser and Steiner 2010; Byrne et al. 2010, 2012). Many individuals with a mental health disease have a significant propensity for recidivism (AHRQ 2010; Lowder et al. 2016). High rates of recidivism among this patient population are well identified, but are poorly understood and managed (AHRQ 2010). The specific cohort of patients with mental health disease, and their potential for recidivism, have not been easy to define. While research has shown that associations are present in the available data, and are assumed to be causing recidivism, there is no mechanism based on that data that supports the development of service delivery models that are truly patient centric. Definition and collection of the key variables, both individual and/or the combinations of variables, that cause recidivism, would facilitate earlier intervention, delivery of alternate therapies, and improved service delivery, but knowing what data to collect, and finding reliable sources for those data, have proven to be a non-trivial task.

4 Capturing Useful Data for Patient-Centric Service Delivery Model Development

Developing parameters for data collection in metal health is complex and subject to barriers that are functions of care regulation, legal regulation, and societal stigma associated with mental health illness. There is surprisingly little research focused on approaching the development of data needed to create service delivery models from a patient's perspective. Many studies look at some aspect of the archipelago data needed to support such model development. For example, they may look at a particular selection of specific patient demographics, or at such treatment factors as length of stay, but very few have looked at the development of service delivery models in the context of a complex situation defined through multiple domains, including sociodemographic factors, treatment factors, payment sources, legal issues, criminal justice characteristics, ethnicity, family history, social factors, employment/living arrangements, substance abuse status, level of involvement with social or caseworker, access to support groups, access to outpatient psychological care, type of counseling available, drug therapy, adherence to treatment and follow-up, medical cost for patients, and nonmedical cost for patients (Beck et al. 2011; Bobo et al. 2004; Boden et al. 2011; Bowersox et al. 2012; Brems et al. 2004; Browne et al. 2004; Burns et al. 2007; Byrne et al. 2010, 2012; Callaly et al. 2010; Castillo and Alarid 2011; Castro and Elkis 2007; Clements et al. 2006; de Castro et al. 2010; Dermatis et al. 2006; Desai et al. 2005; Farabee and Shen 2004; Farren and McElroy 2010; Fontana and Rosenheck 2010; Goldbeck et al. 2012; Hartford et al. 2007; Hassan and Lage 2009; Heggestad et al. 2011; Irmiter et al. 2007; Jaeger et al. 2012; Kane 2006; Kim et al. 2011; Kolbasovsky et al. 2007a, b; Kolbasovsky 2009; Lin and Lee 2008; Machado et al. 2012; Madi et al. 2007; Martinez and Burt 2006; McNiel and Binder 2007; MHA 2012; Miller 2012; Min et al. 2007; Moore et al. 2012; Olfson et al. 2010; Ostman 2004; Pasic et al. 2005; Patel et al. 2005; Raven et al. 2011; Reynolds et al. 2004; Roick et al. 2004; Romelsjo et al. 2005; Rosenheck et al. 2011; Rummel-Kluge et al. 2006; Sajatovic et al. 2004; Schmutte et al. 2010; Sharifi et al. 2012; Sledge et al. 2011). It has also been suggested that early and late readmission to care may differentially influence these etiological factors, with later readmission to care resulting in more drastic influence (Schmutte et al. 2010).

Data collected in much of previous research may also be biased as a function of the researchers' focus on either patients\demographics or on providing support for a particular treatment approach, rather than a focus on the type of holistic data collection needed to understand the set of patient circumstances that should drive the development of and selection of an appropriate service delivery model. Patients, themselves, may be fully able to indicate that their needs are not being met with current service delivery, and may even be able to articulate the desire for a different model, but may be unable to describe the etiology of the mis-match between their needs and the needs that can be fulfilled with a particular service delivery model. Patients may also be unable to articulate potential solutions in the form of preferred service delivery strategies. Psychiatrists and psychiatric nurses who routinely note that some subsets of mental health patients return to inpatient care much more frequently than other patients, even patients within the same general disorder category with similar demographics, are often unable to articulate a service model that might lead to improved outcomes. Mental health care providers are often focused on prescribed treatment to the exclusion of societal or other factors that may prove useful in improved service delivery, partially because their access to information is confined mostly to medical and care documentation.

Data collection, under these circumstances, is understandably complex, and much of the data may exhibit significant levels of interrelatedness. In fact, this interrelatedness may hold the key to using data from multiple sources as a means of developing new service delivery models. Additional client data may also be needed, especially since a principal barrier comes from patients' perceptions about their situation and their care. Any exclusion of patients from the data collection process brings into question the validity of any results; therefore, systematic, rigorous, patient-centered data collection efforts are needed to support service delivery model interventions. Sources for data collection also must be expanded. Given the significant level of overlap between the population of individuals with mental health illnesses and the population of individuals within the criminal justice system, it is probably essential that data be collected from the criminal justice and penal system (Castillo and Alarid 2011; McNiel and Binder 2007; NAMI 2004). Other data will need to be collected from community-level sources, such as data from 12-step intervention programs, counseling services, employment records, military service records, and a whole plethora of other sources used. Specific data must also be retrieved from sources that encompass health promotion and management, financing and core treatment, consumer and family empowerment, and community integration.

Spiritual competencies, although not commonly included in data collection around mental health service delivery, may prove helpful in collecting the right types of data to help establish improved models. Spiritual competencies lie at the intersection of faith (which includes a great deal more than denominational religion), community, and family. Spiritual competencies include an individual's ability to manage complexity, exercise control, acknowledge the unseen, use perception to modify behavior, develop attachments to others, and use outside forces to guide behavior. Assessments may be the source of such data. These assessments might include assessment of well-being, leisure activities, and solitary activities undertaken, assessment of decision-making capabilities, assessment of problem definition abilities, assessment of ability to set boundaries, form friendships and other relationships, and the assessment of an individual's ability to assess previous life experience in terms of effect on present behavior.

5 A Case in Point

In an effort to establish a patient centric process by which service delivery models can be developed, a group of researchers at the University of Missouri School of Medicine focused on collecting as many potential data elements as possible. Potential data elements were collected via an intensive literature review process, focus groups with resident physicians, and expert guidance from an experienced psychiatrist. The literature review process, which included literature from the domains associated with medicine, legal affairs, social service, anthropology, nursing, and healthcare administration, resulted in the capture of 586 potentially useful data elements from over 600 books and articles. These potential data elements were then classified into nine domains (demographic, economic, criminal, diagnosis, cultural, legal, treatment, living arrangement, and prescription drugs) through a process that utilized eight reviewers/raters. Reviewers/raters were a multi-disciplinary group that included students, informatics faculty and staff, and

Table 1 Data elements (domains and sub-domains)

Domains	Subdomains	Number of data elements
Demographic Domain (D1)	Gender, Age, Immigration, Relationships, Community-Related Drivers, Education, and Health-Related Drivers	16
Economic Domain (D2)	Health Insurance, Income Level, Employment Status, Treatment Payment Methods, and Other Economic Related Resources	47
Cultural Domain (D3)	Region, Religion, Customs, and Family, Individual, Organization Culture, and Community	52
Criminal Domain (D4)	Sexual Crime, Criminal History, Participation In Criminal Prevention Program, Criminal Behavior, Number Of Criminal Offenses, and Type of Criminal Offenses	34
Diagnosis Domain (D5)	Type Of Mental Disease, Symptom Screening Tool Scores, Comorbid Conditions, Substance Abuse Disorders, and Uncategorized	177
Legal Domain (D6)	Court Related, Driving Related, Family-Related Drivers, Criminal Arrests-Related Drivers, Substance Abuse-Related Drivers, and Legal Issues Related To Violence	53
Treatment Domain (D7)	Hospital Stay Characteristics, Pre-Hospitalization Characteristics, Post Care, Post Outpatient Treatment, Counseling Behavior, Pharmacotherapy Treatment, Readmission Drivers, Criminal Justice, Clinical Assessment Tools, and Other Treatment	135
Living Arrangement Domain (D8)	Family-Related Issues Causing Housing Issues, Housing Type, Community Issues Related To Housing Access, Employment Problem Causing Restricted Access To Stable Housing, Relationship Issues Related To Housing Issues, and Location-Related Housing Issues	36
Prescription Drug Domain (D9)	Antipsychotics, Antidepressants, Mood Stabilizers, and Other Uncategorized Prescription Drugs	36

Table created by Alafaireet, Houghton and Bouras

psychiatrists. Each data element was considered classified at the point when there was 100 % inter reviewer/rater agreement. A summary table (Table 1) is provided above.

Given the complex inter-related nature of these data elements, interpreting data appears nearly impossible due to the high rate of hidden variables and confounders. Data in hand, the next step lay in exploring the relationship among domains, the relationship between domains and the data elements, and the relationships among the data elements themselves, with an eye to creating a process that leveraged patient input into service delivery.

5.1 Exploring Data

In the ideal situation, researchers felt that data exploration should lead to interventions, including new service delivery models that took into consideration the diverse needs and circumstances of people with mental health disease (NIMH 2008). In fact, the ideal service model design should identify and define the complementary impact of each mental health data element and the synergy among them that creates the undesired mental health outcome, as well as defining those data elements whose co-action leads to an appropriate delivery of service within the context of patient acceptance. Two tools were used to explore the data: concept mapping and graph analysis.

5.2 Application of Concept Mapping

Using the data elements and domains captured in Table 1, researchers applied concept mapping as a tool to organize and present the knowledge and concepts associated with those data elements and domains, as well as relationships that could exist between those concepts (Novak and Cañas 2008; Paul 1967). This provided a strong, multifaceted strategy that could be used to view a patient's situation or set of circumstances as a whole, rather than a piecewise measure of the effect of an individual patient's situational characteristics. This strategy also reflects the overall complexity inherent in mental health treatment, where the need to evaluate success is complicated when it is based on patient outcomes, which are, in turn, complexly related to process, especially process changes (Paul 1967). Paul argues that measuring outcomes cannot be accurately achieved without defining, in advance, the outcome variables, and that, in the complex world of mental health treatment, there may be any number of latent variables that may indirectly confound the measurement of the outcome variables (Paul 1967). Paul also suggests that, during the process of study design, researchers need to question all aspects of the situation, including the treatment prescribed to the patient, the person who is providing the treatment, and whether the treatment is most effective for this particular patient with this specific mental illness, and in the life circumstances and situation faced by the patient (Paul 1967). Researchers used concept mapping to assist in delineating multi-levels that impact at the individual patient level. This allowed researchers to identify certain constellations of data elements that could potentially interrupt the recidivist cycle.

Researchers at the University of Missouri used concept mapping to represent the extensive set of data elements (at the major domain level) by allowing individuals to visualize clearly the type of relationships to expect between drivers, as well as to visualize causal and simple elements that exist between different data elements. Please see Fig. 1.

Researchers also explored the data by applying concept mapping as a means to target interventions designed to interrupt the recidivist cycle most effectively. Figure 2 illustrates an application of concept mapping to a recidivism case

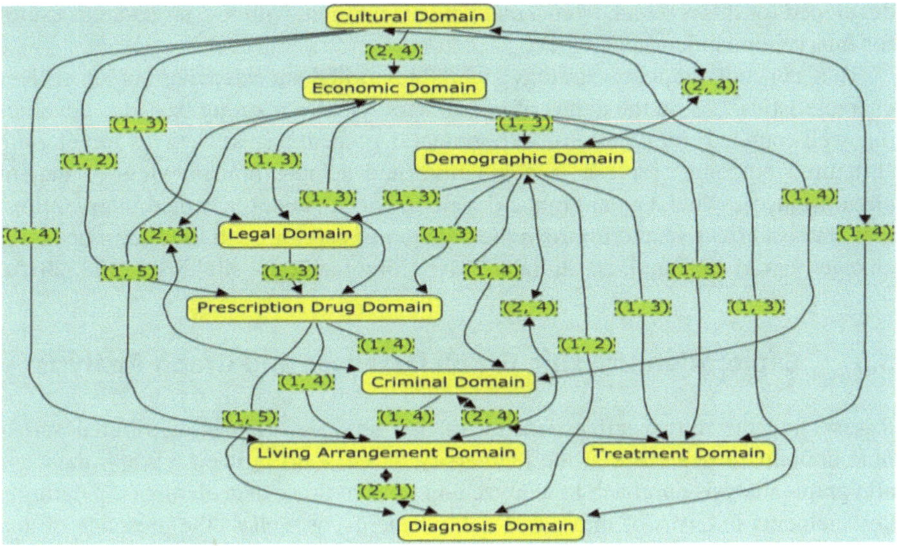

Fig. 1 High level CM summary of mental health drivers. Note: The number in parenthesis shows the type of association and the effect size of the association that can exist between domains. The type of the association is one in case of bi-directional relationship, and two for bi-directional relationship. The effects size, or the expected size of the relationship, ranges between one and five, where one refers to a weak relationship and five refers to a strong relationship. Source: Figure created by Alafaireet et al. (2015)

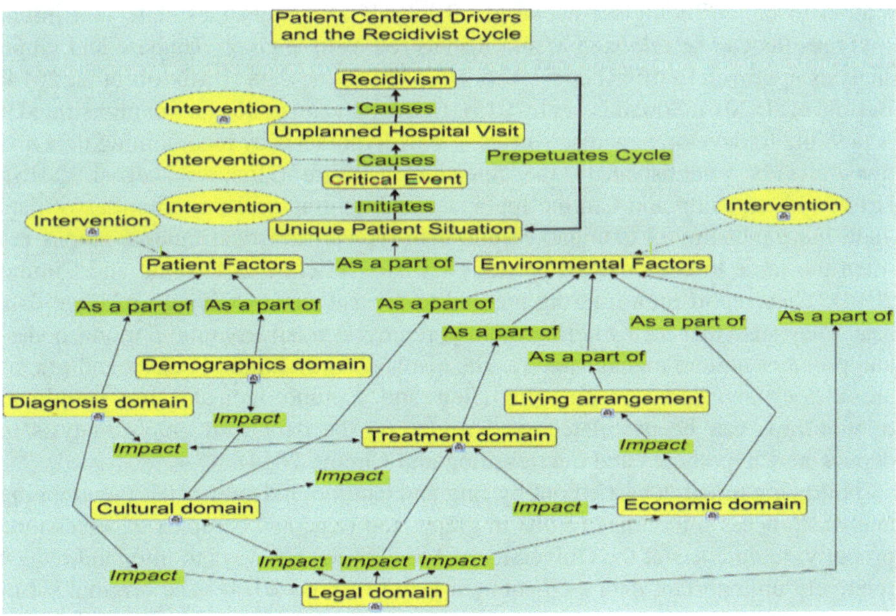

Fig. 2 Patient drivers (data elements). Source: Figure created by Alafaireet et al. (2015)

developed for this research from a real patient situation, with five target areas useful for interventions identified.

This concept mapping strategy, while requiring an extensive set of patient characteristics, has, in the hands of researchers, yielded a strong basis for developing well-founded interventions, experimental procedures, as well as developing structured outcomes for use in evaluation, and a more holistic view of patient circumstances, which can aid in the development of patient-accepted interventions that are cost effective and improve the delivery of care through long-term behavior change (van Manen et al. 2012; Saha 2010; Corcoran 2005; Alafaireet et al. 2015).

5.3 Exploration Utilizing Graph Database and Graph Analysis

Re-utilizing the retrospective data set of 586 unique variables distributed across nine domains, researchers at the University of Missouri utilized a graph database and graph analysis approach to analyze and present those data elements in defining key elements in terms of individual data elements, as well as the presence of and relationship among interrelated elements. The graphing analysis approach has a significant, and evolving, role as an approach for future healthcare research. Brinkrolf, et al., for example, report on the successful use of VANESA and its application to life-science database information as an approach that offers increased understanding of the overall context of the data (Brinkrolf et al. 2014). VANESA is a software application that allows for modeling, reconstruction, and analysis of biological networks with resultant presentation of graphic and relationship information to define biological networks. Brinkrolf and colleagues state that initial study results can be relooked at and reanalyzed using a graph database and graph analysis approach to offer better overall context to the data (Brinkrolf et al. 2014; Bertola et al. 2014; Soulakis et al. 2015). Hristovski and colleagues demonstrated it is possible to develop new discoveries or new hypothesis by recombining data and facts already established in the relevant literature (Hristovski et al. 2015). Hristovski, and Jing and Cimino report that while graphical presentations of data yield more meaningful data and results than typical statistical figures, graphs are often too large to comprehend properly (Hristovski et al. 2015; Jing and Cimino 2014). They report on a filtering method to present summary views of large data sets. They state that their filtering method removes 'relatively unimportant' nodes, and provides a more manageable results display. As the filtered results and graphs are clearer and more meaningful, Jing and Cimino indicate that additional relationships can be postulated with rerunning the data with graph analysis to deduce new hypotheses and queries (Jing and Cimino 2014).

Following research carried out by Jing and Cimino, indicating that the graphing analysis process sometimes results in graphs too large and complex to understand properly, researchers at the University of Missouri sought ways to filter and reduce relatively unimportant data elements (Jing and Cimino 2014). The original set of data was reduced to a total of 231 data elements categorized into eight domains (demographics, case management, veteran status, alcohol/substance abuse,

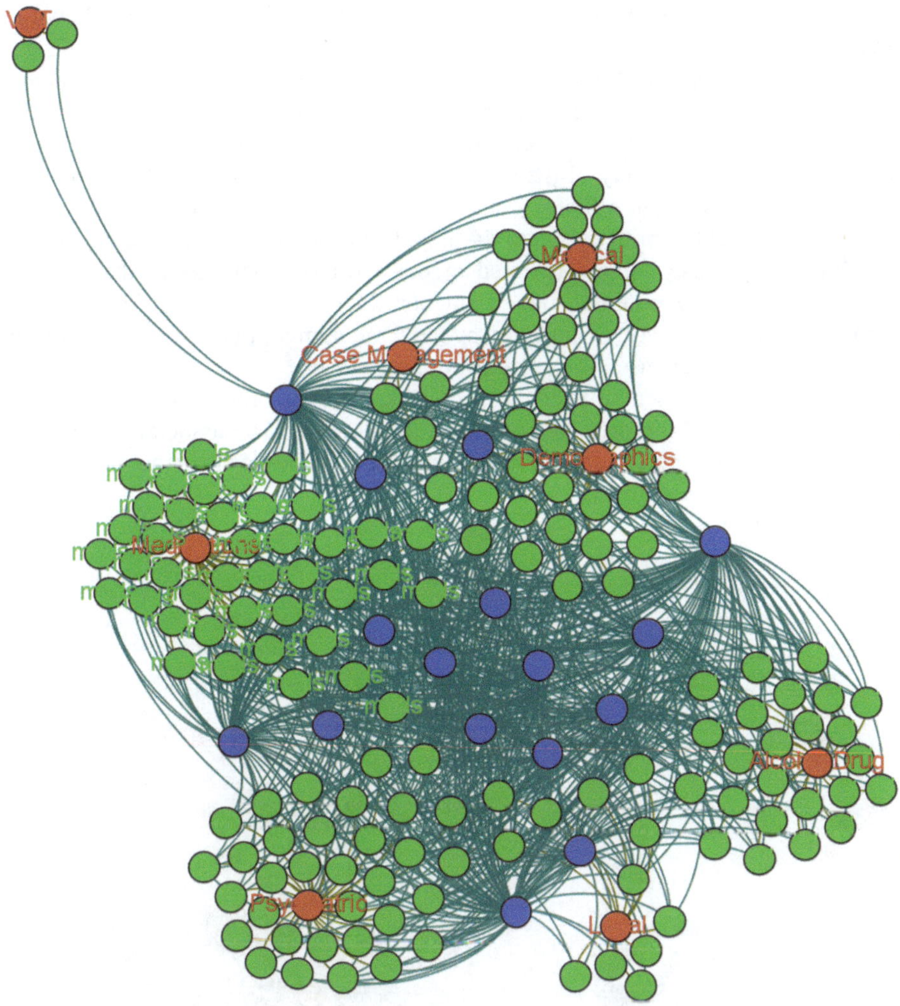

Fig. 3 Relationship among subjects (*blue*), domains (*red*), and variables (*green*)

medications, legal/criminal justice history, medical diagnoses and history, and psychiatric diagnosis and history) through a process carried out by a subject matter expert. The variable reduction process was based on the probability that the data element was predictive of, or causative for, recidivism, as well as the likelihood that the data would be present or readily available within the retrospective collection of data from various sources, including an electronic health record, census data, data obtained from the Missouri County Level Study, and from similar sources in three counties of Iowa, Case Net of Missouri and the Public Access to Court Electronic Records (PACER) system. Initial results (Shown in Fig. 3) show the relationship between the study subjects represented in blue, domains shown in red, and the data elements within that domain, which were present for the study subjects shown in green.

The data elements within each domain are clustered around the domain name. Data elements that had no presence or association for any of the subjects were not included in the graph. The connections between the data elements in the study subjects include how many of the subjects share this particular data element. For example, in the Veteran's Status domain (seen in the approximately 11 o'clock position in the diagram above) had 44 associated data elements. In contrast, the Alcohol/Drug Abuse domain (located in the 4 o'clock position in the diagram above), included 27 potential data elements; 25 of those elements were found among the study subjects, as indicated by the large number of connections between the data elements (green) and the study subjects (blue).

The researchers then utilized a Force Atlas 2 Algorithm (FA2) to create a network analysis of the data elements that could actually be associated with, and were shown to be predictive of, recidivism. Please see Fig. 4. This tool generates a

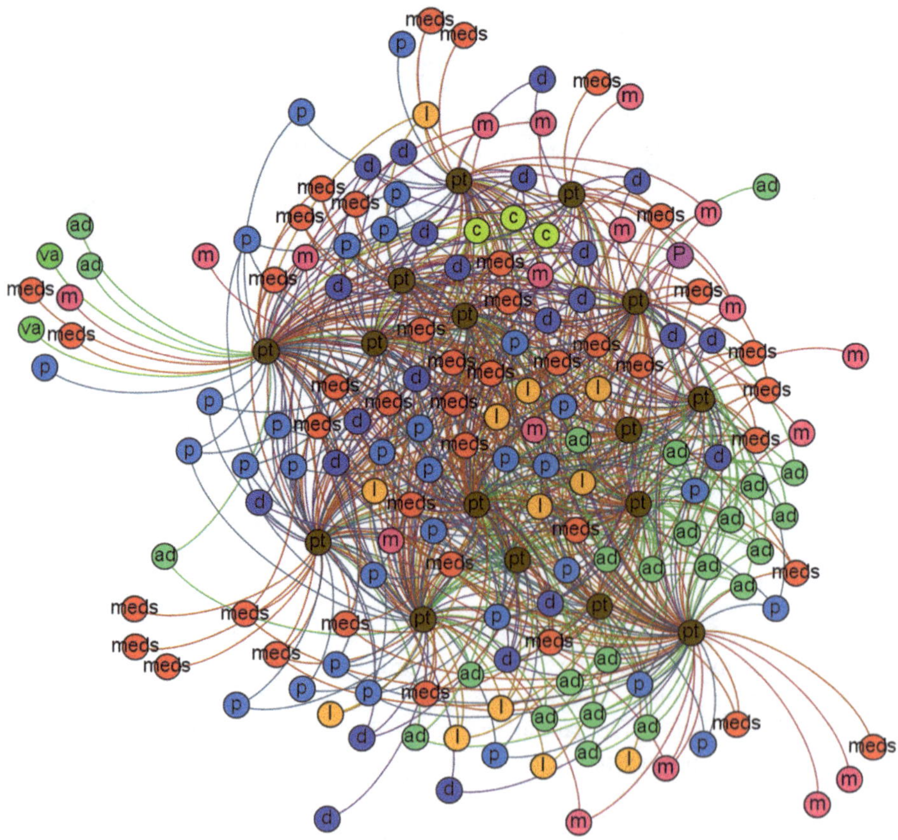

Fig. 4 Network graph demonstrating that Psychiatric Diagnoses and History, Medications, Legal/Criminal Justice History, and Alcohol/Substance Abuse domains are associated with recidivism in mental health disease. Source: Figure created by Adam Bouras and Mark Lareau (2016)

graph creation of both repulsive and attractive forces between the nodes that either do not share a common edge or do share a common edge. This creates a balanced state through which relationships can be determined.

Figure 4 represents subjects in brown and data elements in a range of colors as follows (Psychiatric Diagnoses and History (represented in blue—and labeled P), Medications (in Red—and labeled meds), Legal/Criminal Justice History (in Orange—and labeled l), and Alcohol/Substance Abuse (in Green—and labeled as ad). Domains are not shown. The variables of Psychiatric Diagnoses and History (represented by Blue—and labeled P), in the diagram visually represents how these data elements are associated with recidivism in mental health disease (evidenced by the number of connections and concentration and proximity drawn between these data elements and the study subjects.

5.4 Direct Patient Input into Generating and Evaluating Patient Centric Interventions

Exploring data centered on recidivism to inpatient mental health care in ways that enable patients to understand that data are clearly a partial step in the process of creating a patient-centric service delivery model. In order to incorporate patient input, patient approval, and patient control into that service delivery model process, researchers at the University of Missouri have developed a process that integrates patients at all junctures in the service delivery model design process. The process involves utilizing past and present patients (defined as individuals who have firsthand knowledge of the patient care process in the patient role) as co-producers and co researchers. The selection of co-researchers includes the recruitment and training of focus group coordinators, who are patients. The selection of patients as focus group coordinators has been determined to be imperative to obtaining patient perspectives in the development of care, including service delivery models (Brems et al. 2004; Clements et al. 2006; Greenall 2006).

Given the importance of communication skills and interpersonal skills as critical attributes of an effective focus group coordinator, University of Missouri researchers expect to recruit these coordinators through a process based on recommendations obtained from both physicians/practitioners and patients. In order to protect patients during the recruitment process, recommended patients would only be known to the investigative team until, upon contact, the patient agrees to participate and express permission for the patient to participate is obtained from the clinician involved in their care. Clinician, most likely psychiatrist, approval is a necessary part of ensuring that participation in focus groups and other investigatory activities will not adversely affect the patient's care or create an untenable situation for the patient. Training of these coordinators is planned to be adapted from Hancock's work (Hancock et al. 2012). Training would be, by necessity, created through a series of exercises and rentable tests that could be completed by the coordinators to increase their skills around focus group coordination and fundamentals of clinical research without impinging upon either care or their other life activities. Training processes should incorporate a continuous feedback loop from the coordinators to those that are designing the training to allow for annotation or supplementation of the material, as necessary. This will allow continuous improvement in the program for future patients who choose to become focus group coordinators. Incentivizing these focus group coordinators has also been taken under discussion. It is the plan of the University of Missouri researchers to employ these individuals as temporary part-time workers, although if a particular coordinator's main likelihood is adversely affected by the strategy, the coordinator could be rewarded for their efforts through some kind of meaningful incentive, such as utility bill credit.

Once the patient focus group coordinators have been identified and trained, a random sample of current patients and current clinical staff, including physicians, who are not otherwise participating in the research, will be contacted and recruited as focus group members. Researchers at the University of Missouri expect that numerous recruitment efforts will be necessary to recruit an adequate number of focus group participants. Focus group members, whose role is that of the patient, will be included in focus groups only upon the approval of the physician associated with their care, in order to avoid any adverse situations for the patient that may not be patient identifiable. Focus group participants are planned to be randomly assigned to respective focus groups, which are then responsible for discussion around the issues of recidivism and service delivery models that can address that issue. Much of the information will be solicited through open-ended research questions asked as part of the focus groups, where input into patient preferences and insight into patient circumstances will be consolidated into reports suitable for use by the researchers. The goal of the focus groups will be to obtain comprehensive patient perspectives on the data elements that are associated with the proposed interventions, including service delivery models that are developed. Using the data developed through concept mapping and graph analysis, as well as other data, a set of scenarios that are considered to be more prevalent in the mental health inpatient service population will be developed, and members of the focus groups will be asked about potential interventions for those scenarios. Any differences identified between what patients engaged in the focus groups and other entities who are delivering care to the patients will be reconciled by the research team based on feasibility, expert judgment, and all previous information collected for the study. Potential interventions would then be evaluated by the patient focus groups before finally being crafted into an intervention by the investigational team, and the intervention will be subject to approval by the same focus groups. For example, focus groups could consider the scenario where some patients are lost to follow-up because of the distance to their mental health provider, their ability to afford care, or the availability of treatment for their condition. Service delivery models designed to assist in this particular scenario might include providing patients with transportation to their appointments, providing additional social services within the community, or perhaps by hiring additional care coordination staff. The precise solution would then be evaluated by the patient and clinician focus groups before finally being crafted into prospective service delivery model interventions by the investigational team. Researchers plan to operationalize the updated service delivery models by creating and maintaining a long-term advisory group composed of both patients experiencing mental health disease and of diverse stakeholders who will continue to monitor the formulation of training, creation of job descriptions, and recruitment methodologies, and protect the rights of these patients. Incorporating stakeholders from healthcare, the justice system, payers, and community resource agencies creates an intervention development approach that is replicable outside of the inpatient setting, and can be sustainable.

6 Lessons Learned Around Developing Patient-Centric Service Delivery Models

Studies, such as those carried out at the University of Missouri, suggest that incorporating a patient-centered approach to developing service delivery models for improved mental health care delivery could be based on a combination of large sets of data, data exploration tools that focus on the interrelatedness of the data elements, and a service delivery model development process that is managed by patients themselves. While perhaps not being completely personalized care, service delivery models developed with a heavy focus on socio-clinical patient needs hold promise as mechanisms to increase the quality of care delivered to patients, increase the number of patients that have access to care, and decrease the cost of care, including costs typically borne by patients. Moving forward, healthcare organizations and researchers should focus on ways to combine and normalize data elements from a variety of sources that represent the socio-clinical needs of the patient in a way that successfully incorporates patient's perspectives. To be effective, service delivery models need to be developed in ways that support patient satisfaction with the care they are receiving and patient cooperation with care. To do so, patients must all be involved in the generation of the data elements required to determine both intervention points and causation of failure to receive care appropriately, but they must also be involved in the generation, critique, and planning of the use of these new service delivery models. This strategy could make future service delivery models an integral part of a health care delivery system where treatment and other kinds of care are more likely to be adopted by patients. Without including patients directly in the service delivery model creation process, it is impossible to assess both the needs of the patients and the tolerability of a specific service delivery model to patients adequately (Brems et al. 2004). This increased adoption rate is also an important factor in maximizing the use of what is a fairly limited resource of outpatient mental health professionals in inpatient mental health care. As interventions, these patient centered service delivery models may also improve equity in the provision of mental health care. Given the role of patient acceptance in medication compliance among those suffering from mental health disease, service delivery that is more acceptable to patients may increase medication adherence and substantively reduce the need for inpatient mental health care (Beck et al. 2011; Boden et al. 2011; Farabee and Shen 2004; Jaeger et al. 2012; Kane 2006; Weiden et al. 2004; Lieberman et al. 2005).

7 Conclusions

While the patient-centered methodological approach to the development of service delivery models intrinsically overcomes many of the traditional barriers to the development of such models, there will always be barriers. Given the large set of data elements required to do such an analysis, it may be difficult for some institutions to utilize a similar process because they lack the appropriate staffing, the appropriate financing, and, in some cases, appropriate access to a patient population. In the case where data collection is incomplete or inadequate, it is possible to introduce a significant level of bias into results. Service models delivered under those conditions could be flawed, because they fail to represent the patient population adequately. Even with well-developed service delivery models, there may be significant barriers to implementation within a specific healthcare organization, depending on the organizational structure and that organization's cultural capability to address, at least on a limited basis, customizable care for patients. For example, if a patient-generated, patient-approved, highly rated service delivery model included atypical appointment times or locations for outpatient psychiatrists, the health care organization might find itself in significant conflict with those same psychiatrists. Furthermore, the very organizational structure of a health care system could significantly limit the utilization of patient-centric service delivery models. Beyond just the strictly organizational structure, institutionally specific factors, such as vectors related to business culture, could also prove to be barriers. For example, psychiatrists and the mental health care providers may see patient-centric service delivery models as an interference with their traditional authority and timing. On the other side of the issue, patients themselves may see, without adequate education regarding the necessity to create patient-centric models, as something that negatively affects their confidence in the ability of psychiatrists and other providers to provide adequate care. The development process for patient-centric service delivery models could also be biased towards favoring larger healthcare organizations, given the larger amounts of resources likely available in those organizations.

Despite these potential barriers, provision of patient-centric service delivery models that have been initiated by patients, developed with input by patients, and evaluated as to acceptability by patients, hold promise to improve the quality of care, access to care, and reduce costs to deliver care borne by payers, healthcare providers, and the patients themselves.

Healthcare organizations seeking to improve the delivery of mental-health services through the utilization of patient-centric service delivery models should consider developing such models with patient input that is structured into every aspect of the development process. They should also consider developing new service models from data elements that are prospective as opposed retrospective. Since it is particularly difficult to obtain all of the data elements from a single data source because multiple data sources may still be lacking specific data elements, it may be necessary to specifically collect, prospectively, certain data elements. It may also be necessary to consider, operationally, how some of the data could be collected and entered. Given the relatedness of socio-clinical data, it may also be difficult to ensure that each data element is mutually exclusive with any other. The effectiveness of such a patient-centered service delivery model development project may also be significantly enhanced if appropriate education around the issues and reasons for such service model development has been provided to all stakeholders within the health care organization and also patients. Most likely, the healthcare industry, as a whole, will also need to see that these sorts of projects are repeatedly replicated, and that the results are transparently available to all interested parties.

References

Abracen, J., Gallo, A., Looman, J., & Goodwill, A. (2016). Individual community-based treatment of offenders with mental illness: Relationship to recidivism. *Journal of Interpersonal Violence, 31*(10), 1842–1858.

Adler, G., Pritchett, L. R., Kauth, M. R., & Nadorff, D. (2014). A pilot project to improve access to telepsychotherapy at rural clinics. *Telemedicine Journal and E-Health, 20*(1), 83–85.

Agency for Healthcare Research and Quality. (2010). National Healthcare Disparities Report 2010. Retrieved November 28, 2015, from http://www.ahrq.gov/research/findings/nhqrdr/nhdr10/index.html

Alafaireet, P., Bouras, A., Houghton, H. L., Lavoie, B. J., Lavoie, J. P., Cressman, B., et al. (2015). Applying concept mapping to solving in-patient mental health recidivism. *Missouri Medicine, 112*(1), 63–66.

Aron, L., Honberg, R., Duckworth, K., Kimball, A., Edgar, E., Carolla, B., et al. (2007). *Grading the states 2009: A report on America's health care system for adults with serious mental illness*. Arlington, VA: National Alliance on Mental Illness.

Bean, A. G., & Talaga, J. (1995). Predicting appointment breaking. *Journal of Health Care Marketing, 15*(1), 29–34.

Beck, E. M., Cavelti, M., Wirtz, M., Kossowsky, J., & Vauth, R. (2011). How do socio-demographic and clinical factors interact with adherence attitude profiles in schizophrenia? A cluster-analytical approach. *Psychiatry Research, 187*(1–2), 55–61.

Bertola, L., Mota, N. B., Copelli, M., Rivero, T., Diniz, B. S., Romano-Silva, M. A., et al. (2014). Graph analysis of verbal fluency test discriminate between patients with Alzheimer's disease, mild cognitive impairment and normal elderly controls. *Frontiers in Aging Neuroscience, 6*, 185.

Bobo, W. V., Hoge, C. W., Messina, M. A., Pavlovcic, F., Levandowski, D., & Grieger, T. (2004). Characteristics of repeat users of an inpatient psychiatry service at a large military tertiary care hospital. *Military Medicine, 169*(8), 648–653.

Boden, R., Brandt, L., Kieler, H., Andersen, M., & Reutfors, J. (2011). Early non-adherence to medication and other risk factors for rehospitalization in schizophrenia and schizoaffective disorder. *Schizophrenia Research, 133*(1–3), 36–41.

Bowersox, N. W., Saunders, S. M., & Berger, B. D. (2012). Predictors of rehospitalization in high-utilizing patients in the VA psychiatric medical system. *Psychiatric Quarterly, 83*(1), 53–64.

Brems, C., Johnson, M. E., Corey, S., Podunovich, A., & Burns, R. (2004). Consumer perspectives on services needed to prevent psychiatric hospitalization. *Administration and Policy in Mental Health, 32*(1), 57–61.

Brinkrolf, C., Janowski, S. J., Kormeier, B., Lewinski, M., Hippe, K., Borck, D., et al. (2014). VANESA—a software application for the visualization and analysis of networks in system biology applications. *Journal of Integrative Bioinformatics, 11*(2), 239.

Browne, G., Courtney, M., & Meehan, T. (2004). Type of housing predicts rate of readmission to hospital but not length of stay in people with schizophrenia on the Gold Coast in Queensland. *Australian Health Review, 27*(1), 65–72.

Burns, T., Catty, J., Becker, T., Drake, R. E., Fioritti, A., Knapp, M., et al. (2007). The effectiveness of supported employment for people with severe mental illness: A randomised controlled trial. *Lancet, 370*(9593), 1146–1152.

Byrne, S. L., Hooke, G. R., Newnham, E. A., & Page, A. C. (2012). The effects of progress monitoring on subsequent readmission to psychiatric care: A six-month follow-up. *Journal of Affective Disorders, 137*(1–3), 113–116.

Byrne, S. L., Hooke, G. R., & Page, A. C. (2010). Readmission: A useful indicator of the quality of inpatient psychiatric care. *Journal of Affective Disorders, 126*(1–2), 206–213.

Callaly, T., Hyland, M., Trauer, T., Dodd, S., & Berk, M. (2010). Readmission to an acute psychiatric unit within 28 days of discharge: Identifying those at risk. *Australian Health Review, 34*(3), 282–285.

Cashman, S. B., Savageau, J. A., Lemay, C. A., & Ferguson, W. (2004). Patient health status and appointment keeping in an urban community health center. *Journal of Health Care for the Poor and Underserved, 15*(3), 474–488.

Castillo, E. D., & Alarid, L. F. (2011). Factors associated with recidivism among offenders with mental illness. *International Journal of Offender Therapy and Comparative Criminology, 55* (1), 98–117.

Castro, A. P., & Elkis, H. (2007). Rehospitalization rates of patients with schizophrenia discharged on haloperidol, risperidone or clozapine. *Revista Brasileira de Psiquiatria, 29*(3), 207–212.

Centers for Disease Control FastStats Life Stages and Populations. (2014). Retrieved May 12, 2014, from http://www.cdc.gov/nchs/fastats/life-stages-and-populations.htm

Clark, F., Jackson, J., Carlson, M., Chou, C. P., Cherry, B. J., Jordan-Marsh, M., et al. (2012). Effectiveness of a lifestyle intervention in promoting the well-being of independently living older people: Results of the well elderly 2 randomised controlled trial. *Journal of Epidemiology & Community Health, 66*(9), 782–790.

Clements, K. M., Murphy, J. M., Eisen, S. V., & Normand, S. L. (2006). Comparison of self-report and clinician-rated measures of psychiatric symptoms and functioning in predicting 1-year hospital readmission. *Administration and Policy In Mental Health, 33*(5), 568–577.

Comartin, E., Kubiak, S. P., Ray, B., Tillander, E., & Hanna, J. (2015). Short- and long-term outcomes of mental health court participants by psychiatric diagnosis. *Psychiatric Services, 66* (9), 923–999.

Compton, M. T., Rudisch, B. E., Craw, J., Thompson, T., & Owens, D. A. (2006). Predictors of missed first appointments at community mental health centers after psychiatric hospitalization. *Psychiatric Services, 57*(4), 531–537.

Compton, M. T., Kelley, M. E., Pope, A., Smith, K., Broussard, B., Reed, T. A., et al. (2016). Opening doors to recovery: Recidivism and recovery among persons with serious mental illnesses and repeated hospitalizations. *Psychiatric Services, 67*(2), 169–175.

Corcoran, K. (2005). The Oregon mental health referral checklists: Concept mapping the mental health needs of youth in the juvenile justice system. *Brief Treatment and Crisis Intervention, 5* (1), 9–18.

de Castro, S. A., Furegato, A. R., & Santos, J. L. (2010). Sociodemographic and clinical characteristics of psychiatric re-hospitalizations. *Revista Latino-Americana de Enfermagem, 18*(4), 800–808.

Dermatis, H., Galanter, M., Trujillo, M., Rahman-Dujarric, C., Ramaglia, K., & LaGressa, D. (2006). Evaluation of a model for the treatment of combined mental illness and substance abuse: The Bellevue model for peer-led treatment in systems change. *Journal of Addictive Diseases, 25*(3), 69–78.

Desai, R. A., Dausey, D. J., & Rosenheck, R. A. (2005). Mental health service delivery and suicide risk: The role of individual patient and facility factors. *American Journal of Psychiatry, 162*(2), 311–318.

Dismuke, C. E., & Egede, L. E. (2015). The impact of cognitive, social and physical limitations on income in community dwelling adults with chronic medical and mental disorders. *Global Journal of Health Science, 7*(5), 183–195.

Dove, H. G., & Schneider, K. C. (1981). The usefulness of patients' individual characteristics in predicting no-shows in outpatient clinics. *Medical Care, 19*(7), 734–740.

Edgely, M. (2014). Why do mental health courts work? A confluence of treatment, support and adroit judicial supervision. *International Journal of Law and Psychiatry, 37*(6), 572–580.

Elixhauser, A., & Steiner, C. (2010). Readmissions to U.S. hospitals by diagnosis. AHRQ Statistical Brief #153. In AHRQ (Ed.), *Healthcare cost and utilization project (HCUP)* (Vol. #153). Retrieved April 2013, from http://www.hcup-us.ahrq.gov/reports/statbriefs/sb153.pdf

Enriquez, M., Kelly, P. J., Cheng, A. L., Hunter, J., & Mendez, E. (2012). An intervention to address interpersonal violence among low-income midwestern Hispanic-American teens. *Journal of Immigrant and Minority Health, 14*(2), 292–299.

Farabee, D., & Shen, H. (2004). Antipsychotic medication adherence, cocaine use, and recidivism among a parolee sample. *Behavioral Sciences & the Law, 22*(4), 467–476.

Farren, C. K., & McElroy, S. (2010). Predictive factors for relapse after an integrated inpatient treatment programme for unipolar depressed and bipolar alcoholics. *Alcohol and Alcoholism, 45*(6), 527–533.

Fontana, A., & Rosenheck, R. (2010). War zone veterans returning to treatment: Effects of social functioning and psychopathology. *Journal of Nervous and Mental Disease, 198*(10), 699–707.

Forrest, K. Y., & Leeds, M. J. (2007). Prevalence and associated factors of overweight among Mexican-American adolescents. *Journal of the American Dietetic Association, 107*(10), 1797–1800.

Fortney, J. C., Pyne, J. M., Kimbrell, T. A., Hudson, T. J., Robinson, D. E., Schneider, R., et al. (2015). Telemedicine-based collaborative care for posttraumatic stress disorder: A randomized clinical trial. *JAMA Psychiatry, 72*(1), 58–67.

Gellis, Z. D., Kenaley, B. L., & Ten Have, T. (2014). Integrated telehealth care for chronic illness and depression in geriatric home care patients: The Integrated Telehealth Education and Activation of Mood (I-TEAM) study. *Journal of American Geriatrics Society, 62*(5), 889–895.

Goldbeck, R., Asif, M., Sanderson, M., & Farquharson, C. (2012). Alcohol and drug misuse, risk of re-admission to a general hospital and psychiatric contact. *Scottish Medical Journal, 57*(1), 60.

Greenall, P. (2006). The barriers to patient-driven treatment in mental health: Why patients may choose to follow their own path. *International Journal of Health Care Quality Assurance Incorporating Leadership in Health Services, 19*(1), xi–xxv.

Greenberg, P. E., Fournier, A. A., Sisitsky, T., Pike, C. T., & Kessler, R. C. (2015). The economic burden of adults with major depressive disorder in the United States (2005 and 2010). *Journal of Clinical Psychiatry, 76*(2), 155–162.

Hancock, N., Bundy, A., Tamsett, S., & McMahon, M. (2012). Participation of mental health consumers in research: Training addressed and reliability assessed. *Australian Occupational Therapy Journal, 59*(3), 218–224.

Hartford, K., Carey, R., & Mendonca, J. (2007). Pretrial court diversion of people with mental illness. *Journal of Behavioral Health Services and Research, 34*(2), 198–205.

Hassan, M., & Lage, M. J. (2009). Risk of rehospitalization among bipolar disorder patients who are nonadherent to antipsychotic therapy after hospital discharge. *American Journal of Health-System Pharmacy, 66*(4), 358–365.

Heggestad, T., Lilleeng, S. E., & Ruud, T. (2011). Patterns of mental health care utilization: Distribution of services and its predictability from routine data. *Social Psychiatry and Psychiatric Epidemiology, 46*(12), 1275–1282.

Hristovski, D., Kastrin, A., Dinevski, D., & Rindflesch, T. C. (2015). Constructing a graph database for semantic literature-based discovery. *Studies in Health Technology and Informatics, 216*, 1094.

Illness, NAMI. (2004). *African American community mental health fact sheet.* Accessed April 30, 2016, from http://www.nami.org/Content/ContentGroups/MIO/Fact_Sheets1/AA_MH_Disparities_04.pdf

Illness, NAMI. (2004). *Latino community mental health fact sheet.* Accessed May 27, 2014, from http://www.nami.org/Content/NavigationMenu/Find_Support/Multicultural_Support/Annual_Minority_Mental_Healthcare_Symposia/Latino_MH06.pdf

Insel, T. R. (2008). Assessing the economic costs of serious mental illness. *The American Journal of Psychiatry, 165*(6), 663–665.

Irmiter, C., McCarthy, J. F., Barry, K. L., Soliman, S., & Blow, F. C. (2007). Reinstitutionalization following psychiatric discharge among VA patients with serious mental illness: a national longitudinal study. *Psychiatric Quarterly, 78*(4), 279–286.

Izard, T. (2005). Managing the habitual no-show patient. *Family Practice Management, 12*(2), 65–66.

Jaeger, S., Pfiffner, C., Weiser, P., Kilian, R., Becker, T., Längle, G., et al. (2012). Adherence styles of schizophrenia patients identified by a latent class analysis of the Medication Adherence Rating Scale (MARS): A six-month follow-up study. *Psychiatry Research, 200*(2–3), 83–88.

James, D. J., Glaze, L. E., & United States. (2006). *Mental health problems of prison and jail inmates* (Bureau of Justice Statistics, special report, 12 p). Washington, DC: U.S. Dept. of Justice, Office of Justice Programs, Bureau of Justice Statistics.

Jing, X., & Cimino, J. J. (2014). A complementary graphical method for reducing and analyzing large data sets. Case studies demonstrating thresholds setting and selection. *Methods of Information in Medicine, 53*(3), 173–185.

Kane, J. M. (2006). Review of treatments that can ameliorate nonadherence in patients with schizophrenia. *Journal of Clinical Psychiatry, 67*(Suppl 5), 9–14.

Kessler, R. C., Chiu, W. T., Demler, O., Merikangas, K. R., & Walters, E. E. (2005). Prevalence, severity, and comorbidity of 12-month DSM-IV disorders in the national comorbidity survey replication. *Archives of General Psychiatry, 62*(6), 617–627.

Kim, H. M., Pfeiffer, P., Ganoczy, D., & Valenstein, M. (2011). Intensity of outpatient monitoring after discharge and psychiatric rehospitalization of veterans with depression. *Psychiatric Services, 62*(11), 1346–1352.

Kolbasovsky, A. (2009). Reducing 30-day inpatient psychiatric recidivism and associated costs through intensive case management. *Professional Case Management, 14*(2), 96–105.

Kolbasovsky, A., Reich, L., Futterman, R., & Meyerkopf, N. (2007a). Reducing the number of emergency department visits and costs associated with anxiety: A randomized controlled study. *American Journal of Managed Care, 13*(2), 95–102.

Kolbasovsky, A., Reich, L., & Futterman, R. (2007b). Predicting future hospital utilization for mental health conditions. *Journal of Behavioral Health Services and Research, 34*(1), 34–42.

Kruse, G. R., & Rohland, B. M. (2002). Factors associated with attendance at a first appointment after discharge from a psychiatric hospital. *Psychiatric Services, 53*(4), 473–476.

Kubiak, S., Roddy, J., Comartin, E., & Tillander, E. (2015). Cost analysis of long-term outcomes of an urban mental health court. *Evaluation and Program Planning, 52*, 96–106.

Lieberman, J. A., Stroup, T. S., McEvoy, J. P., Swartz, M. S., Rosenheck, R. A., Perkins, D. O., et al. (2005). Effectiveness of antipsychotic drugs in patients with chronic schizophrenia. *The New England Journal of Medicine, 353*(12), 1209–1223.

Lin, H. C., & Lee, H. C. (2008). The association between timely outpatient visits and the likelihood of re-hospitalization for schizophrenia patients. *American Journal of Orthopsychiatry, 78*(4), 494–497.

Lowder, E. M., Desmarais, S. L., & Baucom D. J. (2016). Recidivism following mental health court exit: Between and within-group comparisons. *Law and Human Behavior, 40*, 118–127.

Luppa, M., Heinrich, S., Angermeyer, M. C., König, H. H., & Riedel-Heller, S. G. (2007). Cost-of-illness studies of depression: A systematic review. *Journal of Affective Disorders, 98*(1–2), 29–43.

Machado, V., Leonidas, C., Santos, M. A., & Souza, J. (2012). Psychiatric readmission: An integrative review of the literature. *International Nursing Review, 59*(4), 447–457.

Madi, N., Zhao, H., & Li, J. F. (2007). Hospital readmissions for patients with mental illness in Canada. *Healthcare Quarterly, 10*(2), 30–32.

Martinez, T. E., & Burt, M. R. (2006). Impact of permanent supportive housing on the use of acute care health services by homeless adults. *Psychiatric Services, 57*(7), 992–999.

McNiel, D. E., & Binder, R. L. (2007). Effectiveness of a mental health court in reducing criminal recidivism and violence. *The American Journal of Psychiatry, 164*(9), 1395–1403.

MHA. (2012). *Elimination of state-operated acute psychiatric inpatient and emergency services in missouri*. Jefferson City, MO: Missouri Hospital Association.

Misdrahi, D., Llorca, P. M., Lançon, C., & Bayle, F. J. (2002). Compliance in schizophrenia: Predictive factors, therapeutical considerations and research implications. *Encephale, 28*(3 Pt 1), 266–272.

Mallard, S. D., Leakeas, T., Duncan, W. J., Fleenor, M. E., & Sinsky, R. J. (2004). Same-day scheduling in a public health clinic: A pilot study. *Journal of Public Health Management and Practice, 10*(2), 148–155.

Miller, J. E. (2012). *Reclaiming lost decades: The role of state behavioral health agencies in accelerating the integration of behavioral healthcare and primary care to improve the health of people with serious mental illness*. Alexandria, VA: National Association of State Mental Health Program Directors.

Min, S. Y., Whitecraft, J., Rothbard, A. B., & Salzer, M. S. (2007). Peer support for persons with co-occurring disorders and community tenure: A survival analysis. *Psychiatric Rehabilitation Journal, 30*(3), 207–213.

Moore, G., Hepworth, G., Weiland, T., Manias, E., Gerdtz, M. F., Kelaher, M., et al. (2012). Prospective validation of a predictive model that identifies homeless people at risk of re-presentation to the emergency department. *Australasian Emergency Nursing Journal, 15*(1), 2–13.

NAMI. (2004). *Spending money in all the wrong places: Jails and prisons*. Arlington, VA: NAMI Policy Research Institute.

National Center for Mental Health and Juvenile Justice. (2007). *Blueprint for change: A comprehensive model for the identification and treatment of youth with mental health needs in contact with the juvenile justice system*. Accessed November 28, 2015, from http://www.ncmhjj.com/wp-content/uploads/2013/07/2007_Blueprint-for-Change-Full-Report.pdf

National Institute of Mental Health. (2015). *Use of mental health services and treatment among children*. Accessed November 28, 2015, from http://www.nimh.nih.gov/health/statistics/prevalence/use-of-mental-health-services-and-treatment-among-children.shtml

Nelson, S. E., Belkin, K., LaPlante, D. A., Bosworth, L., & Shaffer, H. J. (2015). A prospective study of psychiatric comorbidity and recidivism among repeat DUI offenders. *Archives of Scientific Psychology, 3*(1), 8–17.

NIMH. (2008). *The National Institute of Mental Health strategic plan*. Bethesda, MD: National Institute of Mental Health.

Novak, J. D., & Cañas, A. J. (2008). *The theory underlying concept maps and how to construct and use them*. Florida Institute for Human and Machine Cognition, Pensacola, FL. http://cmap.ihmc.us/Publications/ResearchPapers/TheoryCmaps/TheoryUnderlyingConceptMaps.htm

O'Neil, A., Jacka, F. N., Quirk, S. E., Cocker, F., Taylor, C. B., Oldenburg, B., et al. (2015). A shared framework for the common mental disorders and non-communicable disease: Key considerations for disease prevention and control. *BMC Psychiatry, 15*, 15.

Olfson, M., Marcus, S. C., & Doshi, J. A. (2010). Continuity of care after inpatient discharge of patients with schizophrenia in the Medicaid program: A retrospective longitudinal cohort analysis. *Journal of Clinical Psychiatry, 71*(7), 831–838.

Ostman, M. (2004). Family burden and participation in care: differences between relatives of patients admitted to psychiatric care for the first time and relatives of re-admitted patients. *Journal of Psychiatric and Mental Health Nursing, 11*(5), 608–613.

Pasic, J., Russo, J., & Roy-Byrne, P. (2005). High utilizers of psychiatric emergency services. *Psychiatric Services, 56*(6), 678–684.

Patel, N. C., Crismon, M. L., & Pondrom, M. (2005). Rehospitalization rates of patients with bipolar disorder discharged on a mood stabilizer versus a mood stabilizer plus an atypical or typical antipsychotic. *Journal of Behavioral Health Services and Research, 32*(4), 438–445.

Paul, G. L. (1967). Strategy of outcome research in psychotherapy. *Journal of Consulting Psychology, 31*(2), 109–118.

Rankins, J., Nathan, T., & Ralston, P. (2009). Integrating nutrition education into a faith-based prostate screening program: A strategy for reaching African American men. *Journal of Nutrition Education and Behavior, 41*(1), 71–72.

Raven, M. C., Doran, K. M., Kostrowski, S., Gillespie, C. C., & Elbel, B. D. (2011). An intervention to improve care and reduce costs for high-risk patients with frequent hospital admissions: A pilot study. *BMC Health Services Research, 11*, 270.

Reynolds, W., Lauder, W., Sharkey, S., Maciver, S., Veitch, T., & Cameron, D. (2004). The effects of a transitional discharge model for psychiatric patients. *Journal of Psychiatric and Mental Health Nursing, 11*(1), 82–88.

Roick, C., Heider, D., Kilian, R., Matschinger, H., Toumi, M., & Angermeyer, M. C. (2004). Factors contributing to frequent use of psychiatric inpatient services by schizophrenia patients. *Social Psychiatry and Psychiatric Epidemiology, 39*(9), 744–751.

Romelsjo, A., Palmstierna, T., Hansagi, H., & Leifman, A. (2005). Length of outpatient addiction treatment and risk of rehospitalization. *Journal of Substance Abuse Treatment, 28*(3), 291–296.

Rosenheck, R. A., Krystal, J. H., Lew, R., Barnett, P. G., Thwin, S. S., Fiore, L., et al. (2011). Challenges in the design and conduct of controlled clinical effectiveness trials in schizophrenia. *Clinical Trials, 8*(2), 196–204.

Rummel-Kluge, C., Pitschel-Walz, G., Bauml, J., & Kissling, W. (2006). Psychoeducation in schizophrenia–results of a survey of all psychiatric institutions in Germany, Austria, and Switzerland. *Schizophrenia Bulletin, 32*(4), 765–775.

Saha, G. K. (2010). Understanding mental sicknesses through a concept map. *Global Journal of Computer Science and Technology, 10*(4), 36–38.

Sajatovic, M., Davies, M., & Hrouda, D. R. (2004). Enhancement of treatment adherence among patients with bipolar disorder. *Psychiatric Services, 55*(3), 264–269.

SAMHSA. (2015). *U.S.A. suicide: 2013 official final data*. Substance Abuse and Mental Health Services Administration (SAMHSA). Accessed November 28, 2015, from http://www.suicidology.org/Portals/14/docs/Resources/FactSheets/2013datapgsv2alt.pdf

Savoca, M., Oakley, M., Austin, A., Wideman, L., Martinek, T., & Carter, K. (2013). Heart of hypertension project: Development of a community-based prevention program for young African American men. *Progress in Community Health Partnerships, 7*(2), 163–169.

Schmutte, T., Dunn, C. L., & Sledge, W. H. (2010). Predicting time to readmission in patients with recent histories of recurrent psychiatric hospitalization: A matched-control survival analysis. *Journal of Nervous and Mental Disease, 198*(12), 860–863.

Sharifi, V., Tehranidoost, M., Yunesian, M., Amini, H., Mohammadi, M., & Jalali, R. M. (2012). Effectiveness of a low-intensity home-based aftercare for patients with severe mental disorders: A 12-month randomized controlled study. *Community Mental Health Journal, 48*(6), 766–770.

Sledge, W. H., Lawless, M., Sells, D., Wieland, M., O'Connell, M. J., & Davidson, L. (2011). Effectiveness of peer support in reducing readmissions of persons with multiple psychiatric hospitalizations. *Psychiatric Services, 62*(5), 541–544.

Smith, A. L. (2008). Health policy and the coloring of an American male crisis: A perspective on community-based health services. *American Journal of Public Health, 98*(9 Suppl), S158–S161. PMID: 18687603 (Reprinted from *American Journal of Public Health, 93*(5), 749–752, 2003).

Soulakis, N. D., Carson, M. B., Lee, Y. J., Schneider, D. H., Skeehan, C. T., & Scholtens, D. M. (2015). Visualizing collaborative electronic health record usage for hospitalized patients with heart failure. *Journal of the American Medical Informatics Association, 22*(2), 299–311.

Suicide Data Report. (2012). *U.S. Department of Veteran Affairs mental health services suicide prevention program.* Accessed November 28, 2015, from http://www.va.gov/opa/docs/Suicide-Data-Report-2012-final.pdf

Tol, W. A., Song, S., & Jordans, M. J. (2013). Annual research review: Resilience and mental health in children and adolescents living in areas of armed conflict – a systematic review of findings in low- and middle-income countries. *Journal of Child Psychology & Psychiatry & Allied Disciplines, 54*(4), 445–460.

U.S. Department of Health and Human Services. (1999). *Mental health: A report of the surgeon general.* Accessed November 28, 2015, from http://profiles.nlm.nih.gov/ps/access/NNBBJC.pdf

U.S. Department of Housing and Urban Development. Office of Community Planning and Development. (2011). *The 2010 annual homeless assessment report to congress.* Retrieved November 28, 2015, from https://www.hudexchange.info/resources/documents/2010HomelessAssessmentReport.pdf

van Manen, J. G., Kamphuis, J. H., Goossensen, A., Timman, R., Busschbach, J. J., & Verheul, R. (2012). In search of patient characteristics that may guide empirically based treatment selection for personality disorder patients-a concept map approach. *Journal of Personality Disorders, 26*(4), 481–497.

Victor, R. G., Ravenell, J. E., Freeman, A., Bhat, D. G., Storm, J. S., Shafig, M., et al. (2009). A barber-based intervention for hypertension in African American men: Design of a group randomized trial. *American Heart Journal, 157*(1), 30–36.

Walker, E. R., McGee, R. E., & Druss, B. G. (2015). Mortality in mental disorders and global disease burden implications: A systematic review and meta-analysis. *JAMA Psychiatry, 72*(4), 334–341.

Weiden, P. J., Kozma, C., Grogg, A., & Locklear, J. (2004). Partial compliance and risk of rehospitalization among California Medicaid patients with schizophrenia. *Psychiatric Services, 55*(8), 886–891.

Weil, T. P. (2015). Insufficient dollars and qualified personnel to meet United States mental health needs. *The Journal of Nervous and Mental Disease, 203*(4), 233–240.

Weinrich, S., Holdford, D., Boyd, M., Creanga, D., Cover, K., Johnson, A., et al. (1998). Prostate cancer education in African American churches. *Public Health Nursing, 15*(3), 188–195.

Whiteford, H. A., Ferrari, A. J., Degenhardt, L., Feigin, V., & Vos, T. (2015). The global burden of mental, neurological and substance use disorders: An analysis from the Global Burden of Disease Study 2010. *PLoS ONE, 10*(2), e0116820.

Wilkins, D., Payne, S., Granville, G., & Branney, P. (2008). *The gender and access to health services study: Final report.* London: HMSO.

Patricia E. Alafaireet is a broad background in biomedical informatics, health information technology, in the delivery of healthcare, especially in rural environments. Her current research interests focus on the use of big data in predictive modeling, GUI aesthetics for physician use in the application of informatics tools to day-to-day clinical operations with a focus on mental health care. She is involved in the formulation of national level policy and standards development for usability and physician supplied data. Dr. Alafaireet is an assistant professor at the University of Missouri and is also the Dir. of applied health informatics working with HMI Group consulting.

Howard Houghton is a practicing psychiatrist and is an associate professor of clinical psychiatry at the University of Missouri. His research interests focus on treatment noncompliance and recidivism prevention in mental health care as well as innovative treatments and pharmaceuticals.

Essential Characteristics of Service Business Model Innovation in Healthcare: A Case-Study Approach

Brenda Gleason and Jennifer Bohn

Abstract

Like any business, healthcare organizations must evolve to stay competitive. Specifically, in the new healthcare environment, a firm's essential focus on the customer must expand from thinking solely of the patient to considering other healthcare providers as customers. Healthcare organizations that have succeeded in creating service business model innovation in the new world of accountable care, integrated delivery, shared-savings and value-based approaches have certain characteristics in common. In these contexts, a health organization must trust its partners more than ever before. In the old paradigm, a healthcare organization "partnered" through referrals, but there were no consequences to the organization if the referred patient performed poorly. Now, and increasingly in the future, a healthcare organization must be concerned about the quality of care a patient receives from other providers in accountable care organizations or other parts of the integrated network. Innovation that leads to improved performance requires focusing on the role of cooperation and trust in changing both processes and resources required to deliver value to customers. Organizations that were formerly competitors may become partners through service business model innovation. What does it take to create trust and cooperation between former competitors who are now internal customers? The chapter will present four case studies illustrating trust, cooperation and leadership as essential components of successful service business model innovation in healthcare. Examples will be provided that clearly show how to build trust and cooperation with other healthcare providers in clinical expertise, financial management, care coordination and patient satisfaction through strong leadership and management.

B. Gleason (✉) • J. Bohn
1881 N. Nash Street, Suite 909, Arlington, VA 22209, USA
e-mail: brenda.gleason@m2hcc.com; jennifer.bohn@m2hcc.com

M.A. Pfannstiel, C. Rasche (eds.), *Service Business Model Innovation in Healthcare and Hospital Management*, DOI 10.1007/978-3-319-46412-1_8

1 The Evolving U.S. Healthcare System

As a share of the U.S. economy, healthcare costs have grown significantly for several decades. In 2014, total spending for healthcare in the U.S. reached $3.0 trillion, nearly $10,000 per person. (Martin et al. 2016) Further, healthcare spending in the U.S. is heavily concentrated in small sub-groups of the population. In 2012, just 1 % of individuals accounted for 23 % of spending; 5 % of individuals account for 50 % of spending; the top 10 % of individuals account for 66 % of spending. Not surprisingly then, the bottom 50 % of spenders account for only 2.7 % of total U.S. healthcare spending (Cohen 2014). Certain medical conditions are particularly expensive, the top five most costly being: cardiovascular disease, trauma, cancer, mental disorders and asthma (Cohen 2014).

Accordingly, healthcare organizations need to focus innovation efforts on the 5 % of patients who account for half of healthcare spending. Thomas Robertson, the Executive Vice President of Member Relations and Insights for the University HealthSystem Consortium, an alliance of nonprofit academic medical centers and their affiliated hospitals, wrote in an opinion piece for Academic Medicine in 2015:

> "Seemingly lost in the race to manage everything everywhere is the recognition that a very small subset of very sick patients account for the vast majority of health care spending. Any programs, prospective payment systems, or policies designed to curb health care spending must focus on improving the efficiency of complex episodes of care delivered to the sickest subset of the population. Whether a population is defined as a company, a county, or a country, the overwhelming majority of its health care spending comes from a small minority of the individuals, and the bulk of that spending is associated with either largely unavoidable and unpredictable single events or complex episodes of care. Achieving an economically sustainable health care system will require more efficient and effective delivery of those complex episodes of care." (Robertson and Lofgren 2015)

The goal of delivering more efficient and effective care to patients is not new. For several decades, hospitals and physicians have entered into various integration models in an effort to reduce costs and improve patient care. Models have ranged from a traditional staff relationship, whereby physicians and other licensed providers are given clinical privileges and serve as hospital medical staff, direct physician employment by hospitals (in states where such a model is permitted), centers of excellence, and joint ventures, to name a few. Healthcare reform however, especially since the passage of the Patient Protection and Affordable Care Act (ACA) in 2010, is driving hospitals and physicians to improve their relationships and be more innovative in the ways they work together to deliver patient care. Specifically, in the new healthcare environment, a firm's essential focus on the customer must expand from thinking solely of the patient, to considering other healthcare providers as customers, as well. Healthcare organizations must now create service business model innovation in the new world of accountable care, integrated delivery, shared-savings and value-based approaches.

2 Accountable Care

In March 2011, the Centers for Medicare & Medicaid Services (CMS), an agency within the U.S. Department of Health and Human Services (HHS), proposed rules creating accountable care organizations (ACOs) in Medicare (Medicare is the federal health insurance program for people who are 65 or older, certain younger people with disabilities, and people with End-Stage Renal Disease (permanent kidney failure requiring dialysis or a transplant, sometimes called ESRD).). CMS defined an ACO as follows:

> "An ACO refers to a group of providers and suppliers of services (e.g., hospitals, physicians, and others involved in patient care) that will work together to coordinate care for the patients they serve in Original Medicare. The goal of an ACO is to deliver seamless, high-quality care for Medicare beneficiaries, instead of the fragmented care that often results from different providers receiving different, disconnected payments. The ACO would be a patient-centered organization where the patient and providers are partners in care decisions." (CMS 2011)

ACOs have several core features. First, ACOs are integrated and can provide or manage a continuum of care via a delivery system or network of providers. Second, an ACO is sizable. That is, it is of sufficient size to support comprehensive performance measurement. Third, it is capable of planning prospectively both budgetary and resource needs. Fourth, it participates in patient assignment where a payer assigns patients to the ACO. Fifth, an ACO commits to share savings generated from the integrated delivery of services through either a one-sided (upside only) or two-sided (upside and downside) risk model. (Bertko 2009) The last feature, commitment to share in savings, is a key differentiator between ACOs and integrated delivery systems. An ACO typically comes together in order to participate in a specific payer's program, for example, the Medicare Pioneer ACO Model, Medicare Shared Savings Program (MSSP) or the Medicare Next Generation ACO Model. Another key difference between ACOs and integrated delivery systems is that ACOs have patients assigned to them. While patients can opt out of participation in most ACOs, there is rarely a mechanism for a patient to actively choose an ACO.

3 Integrated Delivery

The concept of integrated healthcare delivery is not new. In 1933, in response to data that U.S. healthcare costs were consuming 4 % of the gross domestic product (GDP)—it consumed 17.5 % in 2014—the Committee on the Costs of Medical Care recommended integrated delivery of healthcare stating:

> "Medical service should be more largely furnished by groups of physicians and related practitioners, so organized as to maintain high standards of care and to retain the personal relations between patients and physicians." (Falk et al. 1933)

Integrated Health Systems (IHS), Integrated Delivery Networks (IDN) and Integrated Delivery Systems (IDS) are different terms used to describe essentially the same healthcare delivery arrangement:

> "An IDS is an organized, coordinated, and collaborative network that: (1) links various healthcare providers, via common ownership or contract, across three domains of integration-economic, noneconomic, and clinical-to provide a coordinated, vertical continuum of services to a particular patient population or community and (2) is accountable, both clinically and fiscally, for the clinical outcomes and health status of the population or community served, and has systems in place to manage and improve them." (Enthoven 2009).

Integrated delivery systems are well-positioned to participate in health reform efforts, and it is likely that existing physician practices, hospitals and other types of healthcare providers will need to reorganize and integrate across specialties and care delivery sites in order to fully participate in the new healthcare environment, especially when it comes to payment reforms (Maeda et al. 2014).

Existing integrated delivery systems may also need to innovate. In these evolving contexts, a health organization must trust its partners more than ever before. In the old paradigm, a healthcare organization "partnered" through referrals, but there were no consequences to the organization if the referred patient performed poorly. Now, and increasingly in the future, a healthcare organization must be concerned about the quality of care a patient receives from other providers in accountable care organizations or other parts of the integrated network.

4 Shared Savings and Value-Based Approaches

Shared savings is a type of payment reform stimulated largely by healthcare system changes driven by the passage of the ACA, for example, the creation of the Medicare Shared Savings Program for ACOs that began in 2012. The concept is straightforward: "Shared savings is a payment strategy that offers incentives for provider entities to reduce health care spending for a defined patient population by offering them a percentage of any net savings realized as a result of their efforts." (Bailit and Hughes 2011) By design, shared savings models require healthcare providers to take on risk. Either the providers "risk" they will not be paid as much in the new model as they would have been if they had just been reimbursed fee-for-service (known as upside risk), or providers "risk" that they may actually be required to pay money back to the payer because they didn't save "enough" money in the time period the pilot ran (downside risk). The American Medical Association (AMA) advises its members to "start thinking about developing the ability to evaluate shared savings arrangements, since it is likely that you will be invited to participate in such arrangements in the near future." (AMA 2016)

Value-based approaches, also known as alternative payment models, are any payment mechanism that is an alternative to paying fee-for-service. The overarching goal of value-based payment is to pay for "value" instead of "volume." Value-based payments could be bonus payments tied to meeting quality measures, per member per month capitation payments for performing additional coordination services, bundled payments for episodes of care or shared savings, to name a few variations. The payer push to value is real and healthcare organizations ignore it at their peril. Medicare, the largest single payer in the country, announced in January 2015 that "30 % of Medicare payments should be tied to quality or value through alternative payment models by the end of 2016, and 50 % of payments by the end of 2018." (Burwell 2015) In March 2016, CMS announced they had met their goal 11 months early, stating, "The share of Medicare payments flowing through alternative payment models has grown from 20 percent in 2014 to 30 percent as of January 2016." (CMS 2016)

Other payers besides Medicare are also committed to increasing the use of alternative payment models. In New York—as part of an $8 billion redesign of the second largest Medicaid (Medicaid is a joint federal and state program that helps with medical costs for some people with limited income and resources.) program in the U.S.—the state committed to the federal government that 80–90 % of payments to managed care providers will use value-based payment (VBP) methodologies by 2019 (New York State 2016). Additionally, in early 2016, a consortium of provider groups, payers, purchasers and patient groups came together to create the Health Care Transformation Task Force (HCTTF). The Task Force is committing "to have 75 percent of our respective businesses operating under value-based contracts payment arrangements that focus on the Triple Aim (The Triple Aim is a concept developed by the Institute for Healthcare Improvement that healthcare systems should aim to 1) Improve the patient experience, 2) Improve the health of populations, and 3) Reduce the cost of care) by January 2020 and call on the rest of the health system to do the same." (HCTTF 2016) The Task Force includes some of the largest integrated delivery systems in the country, for example, Ascension, Dartmouth-Hitchcock, Montefiore, Providence Health and Services and Trinity Health, as well as some of the largest health insurers, including Aetna and several Blue Cross Blue Shield plans. Remarkably, not only does the Task Force call on the entire U.S. health system to employ alternative payments, they also seem to imply that integrated delivery systems are the preferred service model. "We define value-based arrangements as those which successfully incentivize and hold providers accountable for the total cost, patient experience and quality of care for a population of patients, either across an entire population over the course of a year or during a defined episode that spans multiple sites of care." (HCTTF 2016) Considering that in 2013, 95 % "of all physician office visits were covered under fee-for-service arrangements," (Zuvekas and Cohen 2016) such a transition to value-based approaches would be quite extraordinary if it were to occur.

5 Trust, Leadership and Cooperation: The Pillars of Innovation

"The move toward accountable care and the resulting clinical and financial integration of providers represents a major challenge to conventional thinking." (Pavarini et al. 2015) In the fee-for-service system, which still accounts for the majority of reimbursement, financial incentives are tied to the volume of services a provider delivers. Financial success then, depends on generating volumes high enough to cover fixed costs, which can be quite high in the case of a hospital or specialty healthcare organization such as a cancer center of excellence.

Now, and increasingly in the future, a healthcare organization must be concerned about the quality of care a patient receives from other providers in accountable care organizations or other parts of the integrated network. Innovation that leads to improved performance requires focusing on the role of cooperation and trust in changing both processes and resources required to deliver value to customers. Organizations that were formerly competitors may be turned into partners through service business model innovation. Healthcare organizations that have succeeded in innovating in the new world of accountable care, integrated delivery, shared-savings and value-based approaches have certain characteristics in common. Business model innovation requires three key skills: trust, leadership and cooperation. The following case studies highlight various ways organizations are, in Pavarini's words, "challenging conventional thinking" by using these key skills (see Table 1) to create service business model innovation in the U.S. healthcare system.

6 Case Study 1: Sutter Health and the Sutter Medical Network, An Interview with Sarah Krevans and Dr. Don Wreden

Sarah Krevans was named President and CEO of Sutter Health in January 2016 after serving in several roles at the organization starting in 1999 as senior vice president of managed care, the regional executive officer and president of the Sutter Health Sacramento Sierra region of 11 years, then the Chief Operating Officer for 4 years. Krevans took the reins from Pat Fry, who had served the not-for-profit Sutter Health network for more than 30 years, culminating in his 10 year role as

Table 1 Lessons in building trust, cooperation and leadership

Trust	Cooperation	Leadership
1. Trust takes time	1. Cooperate with other provider groups	1. Develop leaders
2. Build personal relationships	2. Cooperate across types of healthcare providers	2. Get buy-in at highest level
3. Value every part of the team	3. Cooperate with other healthcare systems	3. Be willing to lead in the marketplace

Source: Authors' analysis (2016)

President and CEO. Fry is credited with creating the Sutter Medical Network. Notably, Fry explained the transition from his leadership to Krevan's as part of the Sutter process. This case study highlights the importance of trust and leadership in healthcare service model innovation.

Don Wreden, M.D., has been Senior Vice President for Patient Experience at Sutter Health since January 2015. Dr. Wreden was president and Chief Executive Officer of Sutter Medical Group for more than a decade before being named clinical partner to Krevans. This clinical and administrative partnership, a "dyad" in Sutter lingo, is central to the organizational structure.

6.1 About Sutter Health

Sutter Health is a community-owned, not-for-profit healthcare system operating in northern California. The system has over 50,000 employees and 5000 affiliated physicians. Facilities include 24 hospitals, 34 outpatient surgery centers, 9 cancer centers, 9 neonatal intensive care units, 6 behavioral health centers, 5 acute rehabilitation centers, 5 trauma centers, and more than 4000 licensed acute care beds. Sutter had more than 11 million outpatient visits in 2014. It also runs its own health plan, Sutter Health Plus, and provides education and training to healthcare clinicians through several residency programs.

6.2 Changing Healthcare Environment Requires Innovation

In the new U.S. healthcare environment, a firm's essential focus on the customer must expand from thinking solely of the patient to considering other healthcare providers as customers. Innovation that leads to improved performance requires focusing on the role of cooperation and trust in changing both processes and resources required to deliver value to customers. For example, organizations that were formerly competitors may transition into collaborative partners through service business model innovation to achieve their common goals of improving the quality and satisfaction of care while reducing the cost of care.

Sutter Health started in just one region of California. The vision was to build a patient-driven healthcare system where patients had access to a network of physicians and services. It was built as an integrated healthcare system from the beginning, explained Krevans, not as a hospital at the center with other kinds of healthcare services as satellites to the hospital.

The process of integrating was respectful and slow. Notably, as the medical groups and independent practice associations grew, they remained their own legal entities. By California law, physicians may not practice medicine as employees of the healthcare system (California Business & Professions Code §§2052 and 2400). As a result, there was a concerted effort to find ways to collaborate in order to best serve patients.

6.3 Processes

6.3.1 Find a Way to Collaborate

Dr. Wreden was the President of the Sutter Medical Group for 12 years before becoming the Senior Vice President for Patient Experience at Sutter Health. Sutter Medical Group was one of the eight medical groups in the Sutter Health family. Sutter Health was able to accomplish the integration of the broad range of clinical services it now offers by creating a common vision of what was possible. This occurred over several years, "It was a gradual building of trust and relationships," Dr. Wreden explained, "this doesn't happen overnight." (see Fig. 1).

How was Sutter able to build the trust necessary to move from a very diverse healthcare delivery system with inconsistent patient experience to a more integrated approach? First, by finding ways to collaborate. Sutter's collaboration efforts initially focused on selecting common clinical performance standards, goals and measurement mechanisms seeking to develop new and more efficient ways of delivering coordinated, consistent, high quality healthcare. It was essential to unite around common clinical goals so the medical group partners were motivated to work together in attaining clinical goals focused on patients. The common clinical goals were driven in part by looking at the varying practice styles of healthcare practitioners across the organization in a non-threatening way. For example, by aiming to reduce clinical variation, Sutter helped clinicians focus on the goal, instead of demanding practice style changes. Some of the first initiatives in reducing clinical variation were included reducing blood stream infections and

THE SUTTER MEDICAL NETWORK PARTICIPATION STANDARDS
Setting a Uniform Bar for Performance

- Quality Pay-for-Performance (P4P)
- Online Patient Services – My Health Online Usage
- Patient Experience – Patient Satisfaction
- Patient Experience – Patient Wait Times
- Clinical Variation Reduction
- Physician Email
- Electronic Health Record (EHR)
- Utilization Management

Fig. 1 The Sutter medical network participation standards. Source: Sutter Health (2016)

assisting women with their first pregnancy. These endeavors were purposefully narrow. Those tasked with developing common clinical goals at Sutter were insulated from financial arrangements between the integrated partners and were not required to develop a growth strategy for all involved. Instead, as our interviewees described it, "we got our training wheels" by doing small, focused clinical initiatives where providers could agree on the goal and "could all understand how to work together." Finally, Sutter designed common service goals, including standards of patient access and patient satisfaction. (See Sutter Medical Network Participation Standards sidebar).

6.3.2 Embrace Strong Leadership

Another process that was fundamental to Sutter's service business model innovation success was a commitment to leadership. "We remember the healthcare market of the 1990s," said Dr. Wreden, "where hospitals were buying medical groups without a clear strategy for clinical integration. We know now that didn't work out in California." Sutter nurtured engagement of physicians in leadership roles and committed to educating and training physician leaders—which was part of a cultural evolution in the industry. Developing leaders, perhaps not surprisingly, requires a vision that embraces the importance of physician leaders. One way to encourage leadership, Krevans explained, is not to be afraid of bringing in strong leaders through growth or mergers. If a strong leader exists outside the organization, it is okay to keep that leader engaged and interested in serving the Sutter mission when they come into the organization.

Why does Sutter commit to embracing strong leaders, even if they started outside the organization then come into the Sutter family? In part because Sutter recognizes that developing leaders takes time and is hard work. This highlights a second component of the Sutter leadership value proposition, a commitment to developing leaders. One particularly innovative approach Sutter uses is to evaluate for leadership potential as part of the recruitment process. "We invest in team development," Krevans said. Sutter seeks to ensure that it is growing and recruiting the right leaders; for Sutter, a leader needs to be thinking about how to better integrate the healthcare services the organization provides in service to the needs of the patient (see Fig. 2).

Dr. Wreden expanded on the concept, saying, "We facilitated this evolution by giving true responsibility to physician leaders. We ensured they were focused on partnership, collaboration, shared accountability" and they were serving patients

Fig. 2 Create common experience. Source: Wreden interview (2016)

Create a
common experience,
common learning, and
common language.

and the organization with integrity. Sutter achieves this by creating a common experience, common learning and a common language physician leaders can use to help the entire organization achieve its vision.

6.4 The Future of Service Model Innovation in Healthcare

When asked what advice Sutter has for other healthcare organizations setting out to achieve service business model innovation, these executives had some useful observations and suggestions. First, innovation needs strong leadership, but building the culture that supports a trusting, cooperative organization "is fragile, and takes time—it can't be done in a year." These Sutter executives recognized that in today's turbulent healthcare market, organizations needing to innovate will probably have to move faster than Sutter had to when they embarked upon this journey several years ago.

Second, healthcare organizations seeking to innovate their service model would do well to recognize innovation can come from people from a variety of backgrounds, including those with non-clinical training or experience. For example, in 2015, Sutter hired Chris Waugh to be its first Chief Innovation Officer. Waugh had previously held leadership roles at IDEO, a global design firm that creates human-centered design. Sutter also relies on ethnographers, technologists, and other types of experts, to name a few, to ensure the organization is always improving at serving patients. One of the key learnings from Sutter Health's innovation experience is: "Don't just value a particular kind of leader. Respect every member of the team," according to Krevans. It is important to appreciate the skills and background of all different kinds of staff within the organization. "Innovation in the service model and true breakthroughs will come from this range of expertise," she explained.

7 Case Study 2: BJC HealthCare and the BJC Collaborative, An Interview with Sandra Van Trease

Sandra Van Trease serves as a group president for BJC HealthCare, and provides strategic leadership and direction to the BJC Collaborative. In 2012, Van Trease was appointed president of BJC HealthCare's Accountable Care Organization and leads BJC's overall efforts in Population Health. Before joining BJC in 2004, Van Trease served as the president and CEO of UNICARE, a managed healthcare company serving 1.7 million members as part of the WellPoint Health Networks Inc. family of companies, as well as serving in leadership roles at RightCHOICE Managed Care (former parent company of Blue Cross Blue Shield of Missouri and HealthLink, Inc.).

7.1 About BJC

BJC HealthCare is based in St. Louis, Missouri and includes Barnes-Jewish Hospital and St. Louis Children's Hospital. It is one of the largest nonprofit healthcare organizations in the U.S. and it is the largest provider of charity care in the state of Missouri. In 2012, Saint Luke's Health System in Kansas City, Missouri, and CoxHealth in Springfield, Missouri, as well as Memorial Health System in Springfield, Illinois, joined BJC to form The BJC Collaborative. The Collaborative has three primary focus areas:

1. Implementing clinical programs and services to improve access to and quality of healthcare for patients;
2. Lowering healthcare costs and creating additional efficiencies that will be beneficial to patients and the communities served by the member organizations; and
3. Achieving cost savings. (BJC Collaborative 2016)

Over the past few years, four more organizations joined the Collaborative including: Blessing Health System in Quincy, Illinois (2013), Southern Illinois Healthcare in Carbondale, Illinois (2013), Sarah Bush Lincoln Health System of Mattoon, Illinois (2015) and Decatur Memorial Hospital in Decatur, Illinois (2016). Collaborative members have combined annual revenues of over $9.3 billion but remain independent, serving residents of Illinois, Kansas and Missouri. The Collaborative did not change the governance or ownership structures of any of the entities involved, but instead allows the organizations to share information about best practices and reduce costs.

7.2 Changing Healthcare Environment Requires Innovation

The importance of trust and relationships is on point, especially in this kind of organization, where entities are coming together as a collaborative, explained Van Trease. For example, the senior leadership of these organizations knew each other before the Collaborative was formed. "We already knew each other, we knew each entity was high performing, we held similar values, we all recognized a need for evolution and change in the healthcare system," said Van Trease. Common values were a key component to building the Collaborative. All of the organizations are not-for-profit, all are Midwest-based and all are high-performing systems. As such, they were not looking for capital from one another. While some aspects of the work of the Collaborative centered on identifying economic improvements, the organizations' common social mission and mutual trust was foundational to developing more strategic priorities related to adapting to the changing healthcare system.

Additionally, the leaders had a history: they had gotten to know each other through other membership organizations and academic circles they had in common.

Because of their common values and trust built over time, they knew how each approached issues, and served patients, families, staff, clinicians and the community as a whole. "If we came together," explained Van Trease, "we felt comfortable we would all be of the same mind on key issues."

7.3 Processes

7.3.1 Set Priorities That Matter to Staff and Leadership

While it is clear that leadership and strong relationships drove the creation of the Collaborative, the process the Collaborative uses to determine priorities is also driven by a structure built on trust and leadership.

Van Trease explained the Collaborative uses a committee and roundtable structure, followed by whiteboard exercises to narrow projects of importance, for example, supply chain relationships, clinical asset management or uses of information systems and technology. Three broad criteria drive the process. First, the project must be relevant to the people who actually spend time doing it. Second, the project should be something the organization is willing to resource with staff and budget. Third, senior executives must be committed to the project. "It has to be important at that level," said Van Trease, "because senior leadership has the world view at their organization and can commit resources accordingly."

7.3.2 Get Results

Notably, Van Trease explained that getting results also helped to build trust, which in turn, drove improved results. After the priorities are set, and the teams start to move forward, spending time together at every level of the organization is essential. Van Trease also acknowledged the importance of setting priorities during the committee and roundtable process that are S.M.A.R.T.—the classic business management acronym for Specific, Measurable, Attainable, Relevant and Timely goals. If the goals are SMART, results can be tracked and celebrated. High-performing systems are like competitive athletes, always wanting to improve and set higher goals. Getting results makes people more likely to trust each other, and the process, creating momentum that generates further progress, explained Van Trease.

7.3.3 Communicate What Works

Celebrating and sharing successes and best practices that can be replicated is essential. At the BJC Collaborative, there is a dedicated communications roundtable that captures this information, writes it up, and then disseminates it to each local health system. In turn, the organizations who work in the Collaborative use their own communication strategies and tools to disseminate the information internally, externally or both, as each entity finds most appropriate. This approach acknowledges and maximizes the "collective benefit mindset" of the Collaborative, meaning not every entity receives the same value from each component of work at the same rate or degree. A particular best practice might be uncovered and be of disproportionate interest to some organizations, but not others. The communications roundtable design allows every best practice to be shared, even if not every best practice is immediately useful to every member of the Collaborative. "Comparing different approaches and measuring patient-specific outcomes will help us determine what works best and for whom. While BJC may have coined the phrase, each system is equally committed to "Making Medicine Better." (CoxHealth 2012)

7.4 The Future of Service Model Innovation in Healthcare

As other case studies in this chapter have highlighted, organizations in competitive markets may transition into collaborative partners through service business model innovation to achieve their common goals of improving the quality and satisfaction of care while reducing the cost of care. In the case of the BJC Collaborative, the first four systems that came together to form the Collaborative were proactively anticipating changes in the U.S. healthcare system. "We recognize that medical science and technology is advancing rapidly, making it more and more difficult for smaller healthcare organizations to keep pace. We anticipate that new payment models, such as accountable care organizations or specialty care bundles or other innovative approaches, will require higher levels of care coordination, sizable investments in information systems, and greater assumption of financial risk." (CoxHealth 2012)

8 Case Study 3: Massachusetts General Physician Organization, An Interview with Dr. Daniel Horn

Daniel M. Horn, M.D., is the Assistant Medical Director for Ambulatory Quality at the Massachusetts General Physicians Organization (MGPO). In his role, Dr. Horn leads efforts to improve the quality of care for 160,000 patients across 21 primary care practices. Dr. Horn is also a primary care physician and Unit Chief at Internal Medicine Associates, where he provides comprehensive primary care and helps with day-to-day leadership of the largest primary care practices at Massachusetts General Hospital (MGH).

8.1 About MGPO

The Massachusetts General Physicians Organization (MGPO) is a multi-specialty medical group that provides patient care, teaching and research in partnership with the Massachusetts General Hospital and in cooperation with Partners HealthCare. Partners is a not-for-profit healthcare system that was founded in 1994 by Brigham and Women's Hospital and Massachusetts General Hospital, and today consists of primary care and specialty physicians, community hospitals, a managed care organization, specialty facilities, community health centers and other health-related entities. Several of the hospitals in the Partners HealthCare system, including the Massachusetts General Hospital, are teaching affiliates of Harvard Medical School.

8.2 Changing Healthcare Environment Requires Innovation

While many of the partners within the Partners HealthCare system have been working together for more than three decades, that doesn't mean the organization, and the entities within it, have stopped trying to innovate. Dr. Horn's work is focused on the next steps in quality, especially since measuring quality is a building block for payment and delivery system reforms, such as accountable care, integrated delivery, shared-savings or value-based approaches. However, there is a difference between true quality of care and quality measures. Improving patient outcomes is likely to represent high quality of care, but how would that be measured?

At MGPO, the organization is using the current "binary fail" method of measuring quality as an opportunity to build trust. For example, most healthcare providers are in some way subject to quality measures designed for health plans called the Healthcare Effectiveness Data and Information Set (HEDIS). The HEDIS quality measure set has more than 50 measures across almost ten domains of care. Dr. Horn used the example of the HEDIS measure for controlling blood pressure to explain the problem of the "binary fail." Heart disease and stroke is the leading cause of death in the U.S., and because high blood pressure (hypertension) increases the risk for heart disease and stroke, there is no question that controlling high blood pressure is important. What is at issue, is the *way* providers are measured on the concept of "controlling".

Controlling high blood pressure, according to HEDIS, is the measurement of the percentage of patients 18–85 years of age who had a diagnosis of hypertension and whose blood pressure (BP) was adequately controlled during the measurement year, for example, by showing the patient's blood pressure was less than 140/90 mm Hg. In a clinical practice, this means the denominator is the number of patients who come into the practice in the first 6 months of the year where the clinician submitted a bill with the appropriate ICD-10 code related to an abnormal blood pressure reading without a hypertension diagnosis, and the numerator is the number of patients who come into the practice in the second 6 months of the year and have a blood pressure reading below 140/90 mm Hg. Even a non-clinical reader can quickly see various patient scenarios that would fall outside of this narrow consideration of the quality measure called controlling high blood pressure; hence, Dr. Horn's pronouncement that the HEDIS measure creates a binary fail for measuring the control of a patient's blood pressure. Building trust, then, is accomplished by rewriting the measures with an algorithm for all of your patients. MGPO developed a measure that is clinically valid and acknowledges what the clinician knows, which is that it might have taken 18 months to control a patient's blood pressure, for example (see Fig. 3).

Fig. 3 Better measures. Source: Horn interview (2016)

"Let's build better measures."

8.3 Processes

8.3.1 Create Quality Measures That Are Clinically Valid and Meaningful

Dr. Horn explained that in response to the changing healthcare environment, and in an effort to build trust with clinicians to show that their work and interest in patient care is paramount to the organization's success, MGPO addressed the gap between payer-defined measures, such as HEDIS, and clinically valid and meaningful quality measures. His team, in close cooperation with other clinicians, has helped the organization rewrite measures used internally so they would be clinically valid in the healthcare provider's point-of-view. "We have electronic health record (EHR)-based data sets to manage clinical care, so let's build better measures, then maybe build that into contracts," said Dr. Horn.

8.3.2 Change the Mentality

Thinking first about how clinicians work and why they choose to serve patients, meant changing the rhetoric and mentality around payer-driven measures. Dr. Horn explained, "We want to empower you to do this work and we want to define it in clinically meaningful terms." By doing this over the past 3 years, the system is, in a way, divorcing itself from the market-driven quality measures when it comes to thinking about true quality and patient outcomes. MGPO has rolled out its quality tool to every primary care practice at both MGH and Brigham and Women's Hospital, Partners HealthCare is also a driver in the "change the mentality" approach. Partners uses an Internal Performance Framework that was designed to evaluate the marketplace and come up with measures that could be performed well, but also "engage clinicians." The Framework drives strategy, quality and trend for the entities within Partners HealthCare, but notably, not every component of the framework is based on an external quality measure.

"We might decide we want to be better at X," said Dr. Horn, while realizing no payer is currently incentivizing care in that patient service area. "We may decide it is important to us culturally, and that clinicians serving patients find it important, so we start to collect that performance data, then benchmark against it internally to drive improvement and clinically meaningful quality changes."

8.3.3 Usable Data

Trust is also bolstered when data being used to measure quality and performance is actually usable. Clinicians are more likely to trust data with three characteristics, according to Dr. Horn. First, it must be reliable. Second, the measurement criteria being used "must represent something they believe in as a physician." Third, the data must be timely. To incentivize behavior change, showing a clinician or clinical practice information from 6 to 12 months ago is simply too old. The data should be real-time, valid and represent clinician values. In Dr. Horn's experience, showing data that has even a single mistake or two is enough to create some distrust with clinicians.

8.4 The Future of Service Model Innovation in Healthcare

MGPO has made significant progress in putting clinicians first, when it comes to measuring quality, and like Partners HealthCare, it has driven a change in mentality about how to measure performance that actually improves quality and patient outcomes instead of just meeting payer-defined metrics. As MGPO looks to the future, Dr. Horn is thinking about how to create truly accountable care, especially as accountable care organizations, integrated delivery, shared-savings and value-based approaches to healthcare delivery and payment seem to be creating measure sets focused on the provision of primary care.

As noted in the introduction to the chapter, a "very small subset of very sick patients account for the vast majority of healthcare spending." (Robertson and Lofgren 2015) At MGPO, most of the patients are taken care of by a specialist, or even a sub-specialist. "How do we share that care, engage sub-specialists and create medical neighborhoods that permeate every office visit, every touch?" wondered Dr. Horn. MGPO and Partners HealthCare have certainly driven innovation forward since 1994. The future of service model innovation at these organizations, as it has been in the past, will be driven by keeping the clinician's point-of-view clearly in focus and using that trust to continuously improve on the way high quality care is provided to patients.

9 Case Study 4: Baylor Scott & White Health, An Interview with Michael Mack, M.D.

Michael Mack, M.D., is the Medical Director of Cardiothoracic Surgery for Baylor Scott & White Health and the Chairman of The Heart Hospital Baylor Plano Research Center. Dr. Mack is on the team of physicians on the medical staff that oversees medical care provided in The Heart Valve Center of Texas in the Center for Advanced Cardiovascular Care.

9.1 About Baylor Scott & White Health

Baylor Scott & White Health (BSWH) is the largest not-for-profit healthcare system in Texas and one of the largest in the U.S. The merger of Baylor Health Care System and Scott & White Healthcare in 2013 created an organization that in 2016 has nearly $10 billion in assets, including 48 owned, operated, joint-ventured and affiliated hospitals, 140 satellite outpatient facilities, 476 specialty, sub-specialty and multi-specialty clinics, 155 primary care clinics, as well as emergency medical centers, urgent care clinics and retail pharmacies providing more than five million patient visits a year (Baylor Scott & White Health 2016).

9.2 About Cleveland Clinic

Cleveland Clinic, based in Cleveland, Ohio, has the top ranking hospital health program in the U.S.—a title it has held every year consecutively since 1994. According to U.S. News & World Report's rankings, it is one of the top hospitals in the country overall, with five programs ranked in the Top 2 nationally, nine programs in the Top 5 and ten other specialties in the Top 10. (Cleveland Clinic 2016) Not surprisingly, Cleveland Clinic is one of the most recognized brands in healthcare, and is a "destination medical center" with patients that come from all across the U.S. and around the world.

9.3 Changing Healthcare Environment Requires Innovation

In December 2014, three Baylor Scott & White Health hospitals—Baylor Jack and Jane Hamilton Heart and Vascular Hospital, Baylor University Medical Center at Dallas and The Heart Hospital Baylor Plano—were invited to join the Cleveland Clinic's National Cardiovascular Network, the first hospitals in the Southwest to be invited. These three hospitals were invited to join the network, in part, because they are some of the best in the region. The Baylor Jack and Jane Hamilton Heart and Vascular Hospital was awarded Texas's highest honor for quality and organizational performance in 2014; Baylor University Medical Center at Dallas, one of the flagship hospitals of BSWH, is the *U.S. News & World Report*'s #1 Best Hospital in the Dallas Metro area, and has the second largest heart transplant program in the country; and The Heart Hospital Baylor Plano is the largest cardiovascular specialty hospital in the U.S. ranking in the top 8 % in the U.S. in quality by The Society of Thoracic Surgeons for aortic valve replacement, coronary artery bypass surgery and aortic valve replacement with coronary artery bypass graft procedures (PR Newswire 2014).

There is no question that the Cleveland Clinic's National Cardiovascular Network is a "collaboration of the future," as Joel Allison, CEO of Baylor Scott & White Health called it. (PR Newswire 2014) The network already includes partnerships with other institutions, for example, the MedStar Heart Institute in the Washington, D.C., metro area and Northwell (formerly the North Shore-Long Island Jewish Health System) in the New York City metro area. Different in kind than the other case studies of this chapter, the BSWH collaboration with Cleveland Clinic spans geographies, but not medical specialties. Instead of cooperating in a geographic area with a broad range of healthcare provider types, this collaboration is based instead on the quality of a single medical area of focus: heart disease.

9.4 Processes

9.4.1 Trust Is Built over Time

Trust takes time, and the collaboration between BSWH and Cleveland Clinic to deliver best-in-class cardiovascular services to patients is no different. In this service model innovation the importance of trust is multifaceted. First, it took both organizations years to build the depth of trust with patients as high quality healthcare providers. "The Cleveland Clinic brand is recognized and trusted around the world as an organization that provides clinical excellence, an outstanding patient experience, and valuable medical information for patients and physicians." (Interbrand Health 2014) Similarly, the three BSWH hospitals invited to the network have been awarded for their high quality by a range of entities. Joseph Cacchione, chair, operations and strategy, Cleveland Clinic Heart & Vascular Institute, said of the Baylor hospitals, "We knew the product they are delivering there is outstanding." (Jacobson 2014)

Second, as Dr. Mack explained, the relationships between the physician leaders making the decision to consider the collaboration were long-standing and personal. "The folks at Cleveland Clinic were known to us, and us to them," Dr. Mack said. The partnership wasn't the result of "responding to a request for proposals." That being said, even such deep-seated trust was not enough to seal the deal. Joel Allison, chief executive officer of BSWH, wrote, "This invitation was extended only after a year-long, intensive due diligence process, and we are honored that our commitment to quality was recognized as being of the same high standards as the Cleveland Clinic's. Today, these three Baylor Scott & White Health hospitals are proud to be trusted to deliver the same level of care as the world-renowned Cleveland Clinic to patients right here in North Texas." (Allison 2015)

9.4.2 Leadership Takes Vision

"The idea behind the model is a vision of how the business of healthcare is going to change in the upcoming years," explained Dr. Mack; "this was an opportunity to develop a business model to best adapt to that changing paradigm of healthcare going forward." What does that paradigm look like? To BSWH and Cleveland Clinic, it is thinking less about serving a market based on geography, and thinking more about serving the entity who pays for the care, the patient or the employer, for example.

"Teamwork is the next phase of American medicine. Hospitals and medical centers are reaching out across cities, regions and state lines. We're finding new ways to combine our strengths for better patient care," said Toby Cosgrove, M.D., president and CEO of Cleveland Clinic. (Magaw 2014)

9.5 The Future of Service Model Innovation in Healthcare

Dr. Mack explained that much of the appeal of the BSWH participation in the Cleveland Clinic National Cardiovascular Network goes beyond just providing high quality care. The service business model innovation the network pushes forward is not only to provide high quality healthcare but also to provide predictability and transparency to the final purchaser—whether a patient, an employer or a payer. This model "shifts the risk from the insurer to the provider," said Dr. Mack; "we are providing a high dollar operation, and we guarantee the price and quality." In the Southwest region, BSWH can provide Cleveland Clinic level quality at a known reimbursement rate, a predictability factor that is enormously valuable to a national employer, for instance, who might have employees in the Dallas-Ft. Worth metro area in need of heart surgery.

Providing "transparency of care, transparency of quality and transparency of price," said Dr. Mack, is moving the healthcare market closer to the way other markets function. "You wouldn't go into a Best Buy [consumer electronics store] without knowledge of the product and price of the product you are considering for purchase," explained Dr. Mack. Providing transparency of care, quality and price, whether to patients, employers or other aggregators of lives, such as accountable care organizations or payers, is certainly an innovation in healthcare. But it couldn't have been created without trust, cooperation and leadership—in this case from BSWH.

10 Conclusion

Healthcare organizations that have succeeded in creating service business model innovation in the new world of accountable care, integrated delivery, shared-savings and value-based approaches have certain characteristics in common. In these contexts, a health organization must trust its partners more than ever before. This chapter presented four case studies illustrating trust, cooperation and leadership as essential components of successful service business model innovation in healthcare. The experts interviewed for the case studies highlighted several examples that clearly show how to build trust and cooperation with other healthcare providers in clinical expertise, financial management, care coordination and patient satisfaction. Their advice to other organizations embarking on service business model innovation includes the following:

- Trust takes time. Every case study presented in this chapter stressed the importance of the time needed to build trust. This means organizations either must be patient when embarking on innovative service models, or they must start the work with another organization with which they have already built a trusting relationship.
- Leadership takes vision. A commitment from top leadership on the vision for change was a suggestion from Sutter Health. Commitment from top leadership to ensure proper resourcing was part of the BJC message.
- Find a way to collaborate. BJC, MGPO and Sutter all discussed collaborating on the creation of common clinical goals and provided specific examples on processes they used.

- Build better quality measures. BJC and Sutter both discussed processes for designing meaningful projects that were clinically driven in order to improve quality. MGPO commented on the importance of leading the market away from payer-driven quality measures to measures that clinicians believe measure patient outcomes and quality.
- Change the mentality. A common theme from all four of the case studies presented, two cases, BSWH and MGPO, specifically addressed changing the mentality in a way that focused on the external marketplace.
- Get results. While results certainly matter to all of the organizations that served as case studies, BJC explained the usefulness of getting results in helping to build trust and cooperation. BSWH used results as a way to offer transparency of price and quality to healthcare purchasers.

In addition to the key skills of trust, cooperation and leadership, the four case studies presented in this chapter identified another condition necessary for service business model innovation in healthcare, that is, the need to be "clinician-forward," which we define as reflecting or elevating the mindset and experience of healthcare clinicians without being exclusive of other inputs or opinions from those not specifically trained in medicine or other healthcare professions that diagnose and treat patients. In every case, the innovation in their healthcare service business model was not just about changing processes and resources, but also about achieving meaningful improvements for patients, their families and the clinicians and staff that serve them and their communities. Trust, cooperation and leadership were not just tools the organizations used, but were in fact, the very foundation of the innovative healthcare service business models they created.

Acknowledgements Thank you to Dr. Horn (MGPO), Sarah Krevans (Sutter), Dr. Mack (BSW), Sandra Van Trease (BJC) and Dr. Wreden (Sutter) for participating in interviews in March and April, 2016, on behalf of their organizations.

References

Allison, J. (2015). *Collaborating with the nation's best to improve your heart health*. Accessed April 28, 2016, from https://www.baylorscottandwhite.com/ceo-notes/pages/collaborating-with-the-nations-best-to-improve-your-heart-health.aspx

American Medical Association. (2016). *Shared savings*. Accessed March 25, 2016, from http://www.ama-assn.org/ama/pub/advocacy/state-advocacy-arc/state-advocacy-campaigns/private-payer-reform/state-based-payment-reform/evaluating-payment-options/shared-savings.page

Bailit, M., & Hughes, C. (2011). *Key design elements of shared savings payment arrangements*. The commonwealth fund issue brief. Accessed April 28, 2016, from http://www.commonwealthfund.org/~/media/Files/Publications/Issue%20Brief/2011/Aug/1539_Bailit_key_design_elements_sharedsavings_ib_v2.pdf

Baylor Scott & White Health. (2016). *Our numbers*. Accessed March 25, 2016, from https://www.baylorscottandwhite.com/pages/our-numbers.aspx

Bertko, J. (2009). *Delivery system reform: Developing accountable care organizations*. Brookings Institution. Accessed March 25, 2016, from http://www.academyhealth.org/files/Bertko.pdf

BJC Collaborative. (2016). *About us: The BJC Collaborative*. Accessed April 28, 2016, from http://www.bjc.org/About-Us/The-BJC-Collaborative

Burwell, S. M. (2015). Setting value-based payment goals—HHS efforts to improve U.S. health care. *New England Journal of Medicine, 372*(10), 897.

Centers for Medicare & Medicaid Services. (2011). *What providers need to know: Accountable care organizations*. CMS Fact Sheet. Accessed March 25, 2016, from https://www.cms.gov/Newsroom/MediaReleaseDatabase/Fact-sheets/2011-Fact-sheets-items/2011-03-315.html

Centers for Medicare & Medicaid Services. (2016). *Better care. Smarter spending. Healthier people: Improving quality and paying for what works*. CMS Fact Sheet. Accessed March 25, 2016, from https://www.cms.gov/Newsroom/MediaReleaseDatabase/Fact-sheets/2016-Fact-sheets-items/2016-03-03-2.html

Cleveland Clinic. (2016). *U.S. news rankings*. Accessed April 28, 2016, from http://my.clevelandclinic.org/us_news_rankings

Cohen, S. (2014). *The concentration of health care expenditures and related expenses for costly medical conditions, 2012*. Statistical Brief 455. Rockville, MD: Agency for Healthcare Research and Quality. Accessed May 3, 2016, from http://meps.ahrq.gov/mepsweb/data_files/publications/st455/stat455.pdf

CoxHealth. (2012). *BJC collaborative Q & A*. Accessed April 28, 2016, from http://www.coxhealth.com/BJCCollaborativeQA

Enthoven, A. C. (2009). Integrated delivery systems: The cure for fragmentation. *American Journal of Managed Care, 15*(10 Suppl), S284–S290. Accessed March 25, 2016, from http://www.ajmc.com/journals/supplement/2009/A264_09dec_HlthPolicyCvrOne/A264_09dec_EnthovenS284to290/

Falk, I. S., Rorem, C. R., & Ring, M. D. (1933). *The costs of medical care: A summary of investigations on the economic aspects of the prevention and care of illness* (pp. 515–593). Chicago: University of Chicago Press. as cited in Crosson FJ. 21st-century health care—the case for integrated delivery systems. N Engl J Med. 361(14):1324–1325.

Health Care Transformation Task Force. (2016). *Patients, payers, providers and purchasers committed to better value now*. Accessed March 25, 2016, from http://www.hcttf.org/

Horn, D. M. (2016, April 20). Telephone interview.

Interbrand Health. (2014). *Best global brands: Cleveland Clinic*. Accessed April 28, 2016, from http://interbrandhealth.com/views/best-global-brands-cleveland-clinic-paul-matsen/

Jacobson, G. (2014). Baylor, Methodist hospital systems aligning with elite. *The Dallas Morning News*. Accessed March 25, 2016, from http://www.dallasnews.com/business/health-care/20140829-baylor-methodist-hospital-systems-aligning-with-elite.ece

Maeda, J. K. L., Lee, K., & Horberg, M. (2014). Comparative health systems research among Kaiser Permanente and other integrated delivery systems: A systematic literature review. *Permanente Journal, 18*(3), 66. Accessed March 25, 2016, from http://www.ncbi.nlm.nih.gov/pmc/articles/PMC4116268/pdf/permj18_3p0066.pdf

Magaw, T. (2014). Cleveland Clinic's heart program forms alliance with three Baylor Scott & White Health Hospitals. *Crain's Cleveland Business*. Accessed March 25, 2016, from http://www.crainscleveland.com/article/20141219/FREE/141219826/cleveland-clinics-heart-program-forms-alliance-with-three-baylor

Martin, A., Hartman, M., Benson, J., Catlin, A., & National Health Expenditure Accounts Team. (2016). National health spending in 2014: Faster growth driven by coverage expansion and prescription drug spending. *Health Affairs, 35*(1), 150–160.

New York State Department of Health Medicaid Design Team. (2016). *A path toward value based payment: Annual update June 2016: Year 2. New York State roadmap for medicaid payment reform*. Albany, NY: New York State Department of Health.

Patient Protection and Affordable Care Act, 42 U.S.C. § 18001 et seq. (2010).

Pavarini, P., McGinty, C., & Schaff, M. (2015). *The ACO handbook: A guide to accountable care organizations* (2nd ed.). Washington, DC: American Health Lawyers Association.

PR Newswire. (2014). *Baylor Scott & White Health launches alliance with America's No. 1 Heart Hospital, Cleveland Clinic*. Accessed April 28, 2016, from http://www.prnewswire.com/news-releases/baylor-scott--white-health-launches-alliance-with-americas-no-1-heart-hospital-cleveland-clinic-300012013.htm

Robertson, T., & Lofgren, R. (2015). Where population health misses the mark: Breaking the 80/20 rule. *Academic Medicine, 90*(3), 277–278.

Sutter Health. (2016). *2016 SMN dashboard: Setting a uniform bar for performance*.

Wreden, D., & Krevans, S. (2016, March 1). Telephone interview.

Zuvekas, S., & Cohen, J. (2016). Fee-for-service, while much maligned, remains the dominant payment method for physician visits. *Health Affairs, 35*(3), 411–414.

Brenda L. Gleason, President and Founder, M2 Health Care Consulting; Lecturer, George Washington University Milken Institute School of Public Health. Before founding M2 in 2005, Brenda co-ran a hedge fund in New York and was the Vice President of Healthcare Markets for Informed Decisions. From 2012 to 2014, Brenda served as adviser to the Rhode Island Health Benefits Exchange, 1 of only 14 state-based exchanges in the U.S. With M2, Brenda services a broad range of clients from across the healthcare spectrum, including several Fortune 100 companies. Brenda is co-editor of Essential Case Studies in Public Health: Putting Public Health into Practice by Jones and Bartlett Publishers. She earned an MA from Boston College and an MPH from Boston University.

Jennifer R. Bohn, is Director of Operations and Senior Consultant, M2 Health Care Consulting. Prior to joining M2 in 2013, Jennifer worked at Deloitte in several capacities. First, as a hospital consultant, Jennifer worked with multiple major hospital and academic health care systems across the U.S. to improve their operations. She subsequently managed the health policy research center for Deloitte. Jennifer joined Deloitte from the New York University Langone Medical Center where she served as a strategic and financial analyst for several years. Jennifer received an MPH from the Boston University School of Public Health and an MBA from Columbia University.

Characteristics of Service Innovation in Hospitals: A Case Study of Three Mexican Hospitals

Leonel Corona-Treviño and Constanza Márquez-Aguilar

Abstract

The aims of this chapter are: 1) to present a review of theories on service innovations, and how they could be focused on hospitals; 2) to present a methodology based on these theories in order to identify and to understand hospital innovations. This is done through interviews based on a questionnaire to detect services innovations, which are generated and adopted by hospitals; 3) to understand the role of national public health institutions and the actors involved in the service innovations in three hospitals in Mexico. The results show that there are four sources of innovations: a) Those external policies or guidelines that come from public health or federal or state regulatory institutions; b) the internal hospital initiatives of medical personnel, administrators and workers; c) the hospital's suppliers; and d) the hospital's patients, who, in the case of Mexico, scarcely participate in innovations, while they quite commonly do so abroad. Hospitals' innovativeness is correlated with the phase reached, beginning with knowledge and continuing with persuasion, decision, implementation and confirmation. The main contribution to innovations in the hospitals studied comes from the medical services. A recommendation is the involvement of the clients to improve and participate in the hospitals' innovations.

L. Corona-Treviño (✉) • C. Márquez-Aguilar
Facultad de Economía UNAM, CEPCyT, Av Universidad 3000, Mexico City 04510, Mexico
e-mail: leonel.corona.trevino@gmail.com; marconstanza@gmail.com

M.A. Pfannstiel, C. Rasche (eds.), *Service Business Model Innovation in Healthcare and Hospital Management*, DOI 10.1007/978-3-319-46412-1_9

1 Introduction

Health is one of humanity's basic needs which is defined as "...a state of complete physical, mental and social well-being and not merely the absence of disease or infirmity." (Word Health Organization 1948).

Mexico, like other developing countries, is facing a demographic transition which means that there are many young people of working age. Therefore young people demand employment opportunities and at the same time may mean the chance to generate wealth for the country as never before. However, at a later stage the State will need financial sources when elderly people become the largest part in the population pyramid.

There is also an epidemiological transition as Mexico is in the process of gradual change from infectious diseases to chronic and degenerative illnesses as one of the main causes of death (Mazón 2008), as well as the reappearance of new supposedly controlled ailments. Thus, patient attention will necessarily be longer and more expensive, so the State will require private-public financial sources to tackle these changing processes.

Along with this, Mexico's expenditure on health, in relative terms, is 6.2 % of GDP in 2013, while it was 17.1 % in the United States and 11.3 % in Germany (World Bank 2015).

Another concern regarding health is maternal mortality, which in Mexico is 38.2 for every 100,000 births in 2013, well above the UNO's "Millennium Development Goals" figure of 22 by 2015 (Sistema de Información de los Objetivos del Milenio 2013).

All of these results appear in a context where there is increasing pressure with respect to the number of users and the need for better quality in the public health system for compliance purposes (García 2014).

Considering the circumstances mentioned above and the lack of resources, innovation in services is a necessary answer to the challenges faced by the public sector and has been identified as a key step to coping with the existing problems (Akenroye and Kuenne 2015).

In Mexico, hospitals make up an important part of the organizations dedicated to the provision of public health services and they are in the process of adapting themselves to the idea of innovation as a tool to develop better hospital services.

To classify the innovation research, hospitals are considered to combine a set of constituent or core services assembled in three categories: medical, management and support (Djellal and Gallouj 2005). Moreover, innovation is not addressed as a linear process, but rather as a dynamic approach that implies that innovation is an output of interactive sequences.

The empirical research is based in three public maternity hospitals settled in the city of Toluca, Mexico state, using the adaptation of an innovativeness index (Corona 2015), based on the selection of the 10 most important innovations for each hospital in the period from 2010 to 2014. Those 10 innovations were identified and selected by the hospitals' governing bodies.

The general aim of this research is to measure the innovativeness of each hospital, identifying, as is presented here, the innovation of its core services, with respect to type, degree of novelty, origin and stages, with the purpose of establishing the contribution made to the hospital's innovation capabilities and results.

2 Literature Review

2.1 Service Innovation

Services are characterized as either being intangible (that cannot be touched), heterogeneous (it is hard to standardize them and every way they are presented can be different), inseparable (their production and consumption cannot be divided), perishable (cannot be stored) and imply an intense relation between producer and consumer (Cowell 1991; Gallouj and Weinstein 1997).

The services sector used to be considered as non-dynamic, with low capital intensity, low skilled labor and with no innovation (Bohrer and Vargas 2014). It was only a few decades ago that more importance began to be given to this sector because the share of services in the GDP is increasing and as a result of the strategic efforts made to improve them (Miles 2008).

To define service, Gadrey et al. (1995) point out that:

> To produce a service, therefore, is to organize a solution to a problem (a treatment, an operation) which does not principally involve supplying a good. It is to place a bundle of capabilities and competencies (human, technological, organizational) at the disposal of a client and to organize a solution, which may be given to varying degrees of precision.

Innovation processes in the services sector are not completely different from those of innovation processes in manufacturing. Therefore, according to Gallouj and Savona (2009) an integrative approach, as a frame of reference for analyzing innovation in services and manufacturing is the most plausible, given that the intangible component of manufactured goods takes on more relevance, as standardization of certain services activities becomes easier and cheaper. This is a convergent process (Kodama 2014).

Gallouj and Savona (2009) classify the approaches in the literature for studying service innovation as follows:

1. The technological or assimilation approach, which equates innovation in services to the adoption or use of technologies.
2. The service oriented or differentiation approach, which seeks to identify any possible particularity in the nature or organization of service innovation in order to develop a specific analytical framework.

3. Integrative or synthesizing approach that takes into account the convergence between goods and services, and tries to develop a common analytical framework, for either tangible or intangible products (Gallouj and Savona 2009).

And even when they recognize this last approach is emerging and expanding, "a proper integration should by no means overlook the specificity of services or the concern for the purely technological aspects of innovation in services." (Gallouj and Savona 2009, p. 11).

To understand this integrative approach of the innovation theory for products and services, tangible or intangible, it is relevant to review the concept of product stated by Lancaster (1966), for whom consumption is an activity in which goods, simple or combined, are entries and from them come the outputs made up of a list of characteristics. Thus, the product may be represented as a set of characteristics related to its internal structure and external properties.

Some post-Lancasterians (Belleflame et al. 1986) stated a functional vision of economic activity, according to which, a need, that is to say a function may be satisfied through the consumption of a good, a service or both, so its condition of good or service becomes redundant, as the act of consuming is the act of satisfying a need. Lancaster and post-Lancaster perspective to define the product represents a theoretical tool for the operationalization and analysis of ways of innovation.

In this manner, Gallouj and Weinstein (1997) picked up the thread of the Lancasterian concept and considered that goods and services provide a "product", and in both cases, this product can be expressed in service provided to its final consumer. Therefore, they suggested taking into account a single innovation analysis model for all products, whether they be materialized in a physical way or as services (Several authors have used this model for studying innovation in services (Gallouj and Savona 2009; Windrum and García-Goñi 2008; Bohrer and Vargas 2011). Some have even added to the user and producer competencies those of policy makers (Windrum and García-Goñi 2008).

The services provision model is represented by: ([C'], [C]) the supplier and the user or client competences vectors, respectively; [X], the technical characteristics, that is, technical ways used to achieve final characteristics which embody knowledge in tangible or intangible systems, and may or may not be expressed in technology; and the use of the characteristics vector (Y). Therefore, in this model there is no process vector (Z), as there is in other ones, because "the process lies in the heart of product" (Gallouj and Weinstein 1997, p. 543). Therefore, technical characteristics include those involving the client and those which take place without them in the production of services.

This model has been used for studying hospital services, such as the "Mapping innovation dynamics in hospitals" (Djellal and Gallouj 2005).

2.2 Types and Degrees in Services Innovation

For analyzing innovation types in the hospitals studied, the following classification is used:

1. Product: these are the new or improved services to clients.
2. Process: those are improvements or novelties in the production processes and services supply or delivery methods.
3. Marketing: new behaviors in the market, for instance, finding a new market niche, or product promotion in a new industry and its market.
4. Organizational: new methods or ways of managing in the firms' business practices. (OECD 2005).

2.3 Stages of the Innovation-Decision Process

The innovation-decision process phases, presented in a linear form, could help to analyze a real phenomenon although in it is quite complex and disperse (Farías and Almeida 2014). These stages are (Rogers 1983):

1. Knowledge: the decision-making unit is exposed to an existing innovation and understands how it works.
2. Persuasion: the decision-making unit takes a positive or negative attitude to the innovation.
3. Decision: the decision-making unit makes efforts through activities that become in the choice of either adopting or rejecting the innovation.
4. Implementation: the decision-making unit puts into practice a new idea.
5. Confirmation: someone looks for reinforcement to an innovation decision already made.

Farías and Almeida (2014, p. 385) point out that "the diffusion process (of innovation), taking into consideration each one of its stages (described above), is permeated by the organizational and individual factors that will hinder or contribute to the success and fluidity of the process and its consolidation".

2.4 Service Innovation in Hospitals

Innovation has been recognized as a key step to facing current problems with health care (Akenroye and Kuenne 2015, p. 2).

According to Djellal and Gallouj (2005), there are four approaches to research innovation in hospitals understanding them as:

1. Production functions.
2. Sets of technological and bio-pharmacological capacities.

3. Information systems
4. Service providers and healthcare system hubs

In this study, hospitals are considered complex providers of services, intensive in knowledge and in interactions with their context, considering themselves as a part of a network and then widening their innovation potential in interplay with a complex environment.

> "Healthcare innovation can be defined as the introduction of a new concept, idea, service, process, or product aimed at improving treatment, diagnosis, education, outreach, prevention and research, and with the long term goals of improving quality, safety, outcomes, efficiency and costs" (Omachonu and Einspruch 2010, p. 5)

3 Methodology

For the analyses of hospital product/service, the innovation mapping model of Djellal and Gallouj (2005) is taken as a reference that includes four types of variables:

1. Constituent services (Si): they make up the total product of the organization. In hospital institutions these are divided into: medical services (medical, paramedical, auxiliary diagnosis); support services (hotel, laundry, and catering type); and administrative or managerial services.
2. The characteristics of service or utilities achieved.
3. The competences of service providers.

The study of hospital innovation is relevant, because as Adams (2003) notes, despite the increasing attention of policy makers to health sector innovation, service innovation is a largely ignored field in healthcare research.

To identify hospital innovation two assumptions are considered: they must be implemented for the first time in the specific hospital that is being studied, and they must be working or in force.

The hospitals are at one of the innovation-decision process stages (Rogers 1983) and compared with the innovativeness index, described in the following section.

3.1 Hospital Services Innovativeness

The INDICO Index is applied to measure the innovativeness within firms. The index varies between 0 and 10 points summing up two main components: capabilities for innovation and results (output). The first component consists of Knowledge capabilities (hardware, information); Training, Personnel Certification, Education levels, R&D organization, Knowledge linkages and the Innovation decision' stage. The second includes the outputs: Innovations, Intellectual Propriety and Markets, Product's Certifications and Service Knowledge Intensity (Corona 2015).

The information is obtained by interviewing a hospital's executive personnel, based on an INDICO questionnaire oriented towards hospitals. Therefore, departing from a Service innovation questionnaire, some adaptations and adjustments were made considering hospitals innovation characteristics as in public organizations (Specific adaptations are made accordingly to the industry application—mainly goods or services—on a base innovation methodology.).

The general structure of the index is preserved, that is its two main components: capabilities and results. Nevertheless, changes in both of them were made to be consistent with the analysis of a public organization.

The members of the board of directors of each hospital were asked about the 10 most relevant innovations made during the period 2010–2014. Research about contextual information was also conducted.

4 Results

4.1 General Description of the Hospitals Studied

The hospitals referred to in this paper are maternity hospitals that is, serving pregnant women and their newborn children. They are the only three public hospitals of this sort in the city of Toluca, Mexico, namely: Hospital de Gineco-obstetricia del Instituto Materno Infantil del Estado de México (HGO), Hospital Materno Perinatal "Mónica Pretelini" del Instituto de Salud del Estado de México (HMP) y el Hospital Materno Infantil del Instituto de Seguridad Social del Estado de México y Municipios, gynecological-obstetric and neonatology sections (HMI).

4.2 Service Scope (Market)

With reference to the population attended by each hospital, HGO and HMP serve the uninsured population or people which have only "Popular insurance" access ("Popular" medical insurance which is provided by the Mexican government to people who do not have access to full social security coverage.). About 1,598,375 inhabitants of the State of Mexico are women of childbearing age and potential users of these services (INEGI 2010). On the other hand the HMI serves the population with public sector social security who work for the state and municipal governments. It has 1,198,000 users (Information obtained from the interview in HMI 2015.), although there is no precise record of women of childbearing age.

4.3 Dimensions

Hospitals dimensions can be described according to the following data (Table 1):

The number of patients attended in each type of service varies considerably, even when the number of employees is similar as in the HGO and HMI. Likewise, patient hospitalization days are not proportional to the number of beds registered (beds that generate hospital discharge). This indicates that productivity in those hospitals varies according to their organization, and as the evolutionist theory points out, even having similar technologies (and we could say similar non technological resources) results in each organization are different (Table 1).

The HMP has the highest number of personnel, even though the proportion of medical staff is smaller, 66.6 % (Table 2).

Table 1 Main services provided in public maternity hospitals in Toluca, Mexico

Service	HGO	HMP	HMI
Registered beds (They are large hospitals compared with other hospitals. For example, Mexico's National Institute of Perinatology has 179 registrable beds.)	136	89	149
Operating theater services	13,000	6466	1765
Emergencies attended	36,500	12,045	2060
Medical consultation	24,000	51,610	23,866
Hospitalization (patient days)	18,250	36,025	46,596
Employees	784	1103	721

Hospital base data 2014 (Differences between data mentioned may be the result of the existence of formal mechanisms to measure services in some hospitals, even having a biostatistics department, while other only have estimated data)

Source: Prepared by the authors based on the information provided by the hospitals governing bodies 2015

Table 2 Distribution of employees in constitutive services according to their function. Maternity hospitals in Toluca, Mexico, 2014

Types of personnel	HGO	% of the total	HMP	% of the total	HMI	% of the total
Physicians	112	14.29	204	18.50	142	19.69
Paramedics	103	13.14	48	4.35	45	6.24
Medical residents	69	8.80	46	4.17	90	12.48
Nurses	363	46.30	437	39.62	303	42.02
Office workers (management)	82	10.46	158	14.32	112	15.53
Support	55	7.02	210	19.04	29	4.02
Total	784	100.00	1103	100.00	721	100.00

Source: Based on data collected directly from author's interviews with the hospitals' governing bodies in 2015

4.4 Innovativeness Index

As already mentioned, the innovative index is made up of a scale from 0 to 10, in which 10 means the most innovative. The hospital that obtained the higher index is HMP with 6.11 points, followed by HGO with 5.88 points, and in third place the HMI with 5.56 points; the average is 5.85 points. The Indico Index is the sum of the "Results" and the "Capabilities" and in the case of the hospitals studied, "Results" contribute to the index more than "Capabilities", indicating high levels of efficiency in the three hospitals (Table 3).

A definition for classifying innovations was presented to the interviewees according to their type and degree. However, there were no innovations fully identified with client participation. Nevertheless, we could find some examples where the combination exists.

In general, in those hospitals knowledge learning based innovations (process and organization) or the adoption of processes developed in other institutions are more common. The traditional case of innovation based on technology is significant only in the HMP.

Table 3 Innovativeness index about ten more important innovations in the three maternity hospitals in Toluca, México, 2010–2014

		Results		Max	Capabilities			
Questions	Max	HGO	HMP	HMI	Max	HGO	HMP	HMI
Innovations	3.5	2.54	2.63	2.29				
Public value	2	1.80	1.80	1.52				
Users	2	1.77	2	1.74				
Service certification	1	0.33	0.33	0.29				
Knowledge intensity of services	1.5	0.58	1.24	0.75				
Capacities intensive in knowledge (means)					2	1.31	1.36	1.30
Training					1	1.00	0.36	0.82
Certification of personnel					1	0.03	0.00	0.07
Level of education					1	0.21	0.18	0.26
R&D organization					2	1.00	1.00	1.00
Links to R&D					2	0.80	0.53	0.89
Innovation process stage					1	0.40	0.80	0.20
Total	10	7.02	8.00	6.59	10	4.75	4.23	4.54
Innovativeness index: Average (R + C)/2				5.88	6.11	5.56		

Source: Based on data collected directly from author's interviews with Hospitals' governing bodies in 2015

5 Discussion

5.1 Innovation Types and Degree of Novelty

Most innovations (71 %) occurred in medical services, followed by those in management (29 %), while in support services like cleaning, catering, surveillance, there were not innovations, at least they were not mentioned amongst the 10 most important. This might be because the belief that if the medical services are predominant, then there is a 'good hospital' (Djellal and Gallouj 2005), but there is a big opportunity to improve management and support services. So far, most innovations in the health sector are oriented to clinical products and medical technologies (Akenroye and Kuenne 2015). Also the reports published are focused on medical services as referring to the three constitutive services type, it underlines that "as has already been noted, attempts to innovate within hospitals (as well as the research on innovation carried out by social scientists) tends to focus on the first group at the expense of the others. However, the other groups' potential ... (to innovate) ... is very considerable. It should not be ignored, just as we should not ignore the opportunities for innovation offered by other categories of services" Djellal and Gallouj (2005, p. 826).

In relation to innovation types, 26.7 % correspond to service-product, 30 % to organization, and 6.7 % to marketing. In practice, in the cases of service delivery and organization, it was sometimes hard to make a clear difference between product and process innovations, because the boundaries that delimit them are fuzzy. This is the case of electronic clinical records which could be linked to the concept of Co-producers—which means the process and consumption of services are provided at the same time and in the same place. Thus "the distinction between product and process works well when one is dealing with manufacturers, but may be less helpful with services (where process, product, delivery, and consumption can be heavily entangled)" (Miles 2008, p. 128).

With regard to the novelty involved in the innovations, 50 % are improvements, 33 % are radical, 13.33 % incremental, and 3.33 % are ad hoc and vary for each hospital (Table 4). Nevertheless, it is important to emphasize that:

1) Sometimes, the same innovation was implemented in more than one hospital but the governing bodies classified it differently.
2) Radical innovations are those, which affects the whole hospital system, whether or not it had been implemented in other institutions.

5.2 Sources of Innovations

The innovations at the three hospitals come from several sources. The main source is (47 %), public policies (federal and state institutions). These policies are the health authorities' regulations covering all the country's hospitals. The second

Table 4 The ten more relevant innovations (in force) according to constitutive services in Public Maternity Hospitals in Toluca, Mexico, in the period 2010–2014

HGO					HMP					HMI				
Innovation year	Name of innovation	Constituent service[a]	Type of innovation[b]	Degree of innovation[c]	Innovation year	Name of innovation	Constituent service[a]	Type of innovation[b]	Degree of innovation[c]	Innovation year	Name of innovation	Constituent service[a]	Type of innovation[b]	Degree of innovation[c]
2013	Pharmacovigilance program	M	Pc	Im	2014	Biological reproduction service	M	Pd	In	2012	Nosocomial infection prevention program	M	Pc	Im
2013	Mater Code: Obstetric emergencies networks program	M	O	Ra	2013	Tomography service	M	Pd	Im	2011	Catheter clinic implementation	M	O	In
2012	Nurses' sheet for electronic clinical report	M	Pc	Im	2013	CoolCap and RetCam (imaging for retinopathy of prematurity screening)	M	Pd	In	2010	Cesarean medical intervention attention process	M	Pc	Im
2012	Antibiotic single dose	M	Pc	Ra	2012	Breast milk bank	M	O	Ra	2013	Electronic clinical record	Ma	Pc	Ra
2011	Total parenteral nutrition system	M	Pc	Ra	2012	Catheter clinic implementation	M	Pc	Ra	2011–2012	Mater Code: Obstetric emergencies networks program	Ma	O	Im
2010	Clinic organization in the hole hospital	M	O	Im	2012	Hand washing campaign	M	M	Im	2010–2012	Promotional program of safe practices for patients	Ma	O	Im
2014	Newborn baby friendly hospital nomination	M y Ma	O	Im	2012	Safe surgery campaign	M	M	Im	2011	Federal web platform used to report results	Ma	O	Ra
2014	Electronic national vaccination card	Ma	Pd	Im	2010	Mater Code: Obstetric emergencies networks program	M	O	Im	2011	Civic endorsement incorporation	Ma	Pd	Ra

(continued)

Table 4 (continued)

HGO					HMP					HMI				
Innovation year	Name of innovation	Constituent service[a]	Type of innovation[b]	Degree of innovation[c]	Innovation year	Name of innovation	Constituent service[a]	Type of innovation[b]	Degree of innovation[c]	Innovation year	Name of innovation	Constituent service[a]	Type of innovation[b]	Degree of innovation[c]
2014	Electronic birth certificate	Ma	Pd	Im	2010	Telemedicine: telepresence and teleconsultation	M	Pd	In	2011	New committee implementation	Ma	O	Im
2010	Electronic clinical record	Ma	Pc	Ra	2011	User satisfaction improvement through a device	Ma	Pd	Ra	2011	Service subrogation	Ma	O	Ah

Source: Based on data collected directly from author's interviews with Hospitals' governing bodies in 2015
[a]Medical (M), management (Ma) and support (S)
[b]Product (Pd), Process (Pc), Organization (O), Marketing (M)
[c]Radical (Ra), Improvement (Im), Incremental (In), Recombination (Rec), Ad Hoc (AH), Formalization (Fo)

source, with similar importance (45.7 %) stem from the initiatives of each hospital's medical personnel, administrators and workers.

The third source of innovations are hospital's suppliers and patients, which are less significant (5.66 % and 1.66 %, respectively). However, the role of these two types of actors in innovation cannot be bypassed, as these service innovations are associated with an important information flow between provider and user. Several authors even define the client interface as an innovation dimension, and say "the communication between service suppliers and clients, forms a major area for service innovation" (Belleflame et al. 1986, p. 13). Undoubtedly, interaction between these actors and between suppliers and service providers generates ideas that drive the innovation process.

5.3 Innovation Users

The main beneficiaries or users of innovations are external. It should be noted that according to the Provision services model ([C'], [C], [X], [Y]), users must activate some competences in order to use services. However, the interviews in the three hospitals show that users do not participate in innovation but when some innovations have been implemented, the users have to adapt and develop competences. During this learning process the hospital personnel sometimes modify the innovation. This could be characterized as "passive client participation model of innovation" (PCMI) in the hospitals.

5.4 Components Contributing to Innovation

Different components have been related to innovation, and according to the innovativeness index, there are three broad headings: 1) technology and science: research and development, and design-engineering; 2) production tools: hardware, software, and organization; 3) delivery service: promoting strategy/means of distribution; and delivery service moment.

On one hand, in the three hospitals' innovations, some of these broad headings or components are not present. This could be explained as either they were not necessary, or because the innovation was not designed inside the hospital, but rather were adopted, even though in the cases where they might be required.

In the other hand, technology components were the most important components for carrying out innovations. Although the hospital governing bodies interviewed pointed out that innovations were not, in any of the cases, the result of R&D departments, but instead were done through non-centralized processes throughout the hospital.

With regard to production tools, virtually every hospital took advantage of this broad heading to make their innovations, with an emphasis on organization, and a lower incidence of software and hardware components.

Service delivery contributes to most innovations, with an emphasis on the moment of delivery, that is, the user-provider interface becomes relevant. Even "as a consequence of interaction between service providers and clients, one part of the innovation activities is oriented to adapting services to users' needs, what could be considered as an innovation" (Rodríguez 2010, p. 55).

5.5 Means of Delivering Innovative Services

Concerning the means of delivering services, provision of knowledge is always present. Tacit knowledge, that is to say, that constitutes routines but is not documented, represents 40 %, while codified knowledge represents 60 %. It was noted that the fact of having codified knowledge is, in many cases, due to rules issued externally at higher state levels or by the national government.

Meanwhile, information was on most occasions a medium to provide innovative service-products too, by means of its processing or logistical management that involves its collection, production, capture, transportation, filing and updating. 73 % of information used to produce innovative services is internally processed and the other 27 % is handled externally.

The use of material media for delivering innovative services is slightly lower than the other two types of media, and 64 % is concentrated on equipment and machinery, while 34 % corresponds to material inputs.

5.6 Innovativeness Index and Process Innovation Stages

Regarding the hospitals' governing bodies perception of the innovation process stage of their hospitals, it was found that HGO was at the "persuasion stage", that is they are people who make decisions in the hospital, in general, who have taken a favorable or unfavorable attitude towards innovation, based on its advantages, compatibility, complexity and observability.

The HMP was at the "implementation stage", which means that the members of the governing body think that decision makers in the hospital are making efforts to choose, adopt or reject innovation. This is the most advanced stage found, and at the same time, this institution has the highest index ranking of all three hospitals (Table 5).

Meanwhile, the HMI is at the stage of the process stage where the focus "is on knowledge", which happens when decision makers have been exposed to innovation and have understood how it works and some of its implications, but they still have a long way to go.

In relation to these stages, it is important to point out that progress in the innovation process correspond to the innovativeness index level, as can be observed in Table 5.

Table 5 Innovativeness index and the innovation process stages in Public Maternity Hospitals in Toluca, Mexico, in the period 2010–2014

Hospital	Innovativeness index	Stage: process innovation (five stages)
HMP	6.11	4 Implementation
HGO	5.88	2 Persuasion
HMI	5.56	1 Knowledge

Source: Based on data collected directly from author's interviews with Hospitals' governing bodies in 2015

5.7 Research and Development and Linkages

Although the three hospitals have departments of Research and Development they are not involved in the innovations reported. Instead, other hospitals areas carry out the innovations. R&D departments have very few employees (in two of the R&D departments is there only one person while in HMP, there are four researchers). Their main function is training (continuing education, seminars, conferences, courses, certification procedures) and disseminating information inside their hospitals.

The hospitals' innovations, are not products of a planned innovation process, but rather from random situations which are encountered and exploited (It is important to say that "innovation generation... carries efforts and results that are circumstantial many times, or (depend on) the abilities and knowledge stockpile, or (on) specific appropriation conditions..." (Jasso 2004, p. 11). Besides services innovation is more flexible, in the sense that "the service sectors are laggard innovators and—at best—passive adopters of technology form elsewhere", and see it as "the core engine of the new knowledge based economy" (Gallouj and Savona 2009, p. 3).

Concerning outside institutional linkages, two of three hospitals limit them to national institutions. However, "hospitals are increasingly opening up to their environment and are becoming agents among others in healthcare systems. This involvement in the external environment is not confined to the world of healthcare. Hospitals are tending to develop various forms of partnerships, including those with private organizations." (Djellal and Gallouj 2005, p. 824). This inter-organizational dynamic implies different agents and resources to improve innovativeness potential. It is important to highlight that "the essence of a system able to generate and develop creative ideas for the improvement or the creation of new products, services and processes, lies on a network of canals and interactions among different agents involved in the use and production of knowledge" (Torres and Jasso 2014, p. 159).

5.8 Certification, Personnel and Training

None of the three hospitals is certified under the Consejo de Salubridad General (General Health Council). However, they have other national certifications, and two of them have a state level, such as the "smoke-free hospital", which is not directly related to substantive processes.

We have to highlight that in the state of Mexico there are only ten certified hospitals, and only three in Toluca, one of which is public and two private (Consejo General de Salubridad 2015).

Moreover, the level of education and health personnel development through training and certification programs are linked to "competences concept", which comes from basic education, continuing training, experience and, interaction. They are not easily transferable and are not detachable from the individual. Competences can be developed or enhanced either by experience or professional practice, or by the formal tools of training and certification.

With respect to those people who took part in formal training and certification processes, the best-ranked hospital is HGO, which reaches 1.26 of 2 points allocated to the issuc in the innovativeness index, while the other hospitals did not even reach one point, registering their greatest weakness as a lack of certified employees.

With respect to workers education level, the highest level is in the HMP, even when its level is still far below the maximum two points in this issue. In this case, there are areas of opportunity, reducing the studies gap between medical professionals and other personnel without specialized training (It is important to remember that appropriate healthcare attention requires ... "preparing professionals, scientists and technologists who are graduate of universities and research centers. Constructing and maintaining key institutions for learning, absorption and creation of knowledge is fundamental to build long term scientific and technological capabilities in health sector" (Torres et al. 2013, p. 374).

6 Conclusions

Hospitals are a part of an institutional network not only in the health space, but also in other kinds of organizations in which many actors are involved. It is important to point out that the 30 innovations obtained through interview give evidence of these being complex institutional networks.

Measuring the innovativeness for the three hospitals—by means of the Indico index-, the output higher than the capabilities meaning a good level of efficiency to achieve them.

The values scored by the three hospitals show an opportunity for them to strengthen their capabilities, the means of service provision, the training and certification of their staff, their level of education, the organization of research and development, linkages and the stage of innovation. Innovation was concentrated in the area of medical services (71 %) above the management services (29 %) while there were none in support innovation.

It is also important to point out that in practice, and in the case of health service facilities, it was complicated in several occasions to clarify whether the innovation was process or product, since the borders between them are fuzzy.

Regarding service-product novelty, this study shows that most of them are of the of the incremental innovation type, although the structure is variable between the hospitals. Nevertheless, it is worth mentioning two aspects of the results in relation to the levels of novelty: the first is that on several occasions the same innovation has been introduced in more than one hospital. The second aspect is that radical innovations are classified when they change the system of the hospital where it is introduced. This is the creation of a new system or a new set of vectors of competencies and technical characteristics that provides the same vector of characteristics of the service.

When discussing the sources of the innovations, we should note that they represent nearly the same percentage those coming from external sources (47 %) as those originated internally (46 %). The internal innovations and the decision making stage (Table 5) give an indirect/approximate idea of the relative autonomy on this matter. So the HMP reach a better autonomy level.

Related to users, the beneficiaries of the innovations referred to are mainly external (85.7 %). However, the study proved, that the adoption of innovations needs efforts to learn who uses them or adapts them to the context in which they are applied, and that has to do with the invention or solution of problems.

Despite the fact that Science and Technology was a very active component, according to the boards of directors of the hospitals studied, none of the Research and Development offices were involved the 30 innovations identified, rather non-centralized areas and mechanisms throughout the hospitals participated. Given this situation, the innovation process of service providing organizations is considered to be more disperse, is less formal and can be promoted by fostering an innovative culture, throughout the organization as a permanent aspect of their work. The difficulty of controlling and systematizing the innovation process, viewed as a disadvantage, can also be an advantage in which all areas have a potential for innovation.

According to data collected from the interviews with the boards of directors, organizational innovations seem to become relevant due to two circumstances: 1) the scarcity of resources that imposes the need to change the way things are done, and 2) the need to adopt technology—adaptations and learning—, coming from regulations issued by a third party (at a higher external state level or by the national government).

Hospital innovating with other institutions brings to light the following facts:

1. Linkages with academic institutions is not so frequent.
2. There are important learning processes in the participating institutions, mainly through informal mechanisms; and:
3. Formal linkages are increasing because of the use of Information and Communication Technologies.

The level of formal education for the workers of the three hospitals is relatively low, since those in charge of constitutive management and support services in general have little or no specialized training. Nevertheless, in terms of index, in the case of hospital institutions, for further research we propose making new adjustments considering that not all services given by a hospital need a high level of training (MA or PhD) and that all hospitals have resident doctors who do not have postgraduate studies.

Training for hospitals gets only marginal attention, except for the training of medical residents that participate in Formal Education. This becomes evident for updating/in service training given that few people get training, and even fewer get certifications. Some of the people interviewed said that there are non-economic incentives that influence the decision to go through a certification process, and also they imply high costs.

Regarding the processes of institutional certification, no international acknowledgement was mentioned, nor any directly related to the mission of the organization. Then, certification of the substantive areas will have a high impact on services.

There is a dirсct correspondence between the stages of the innovation process and the innovativeness of the Hospital (Table 5). However, no specific way to establish a direct relationship between the two indexes is developed.

Other elements of analysis in the interview are the physical location of hospitals. Maybe it would be of relevance in the case of public hospitals, to ask this question to those who take the decisions to relocate them in one or another place. The factors considered were: 1) proximity and accessibility of resources and subcontracted services; 2) proximity and accessibility of urban services and quality of infrastructure where the hospital is located; 3) availability of specialists; 4) availability of qualified staff (non-medical); 5) R&D and educational infrastructure.

This research is limited to three maternity public hospitals in one city, consequently conclusions could not necessarily be generalized.

Future lines of research could be necessary for building a new framework to collect data on innovation in public institutions in general, and especially in public hospitals.

References

Adams, R. (2003). *Perceptions of innovations: Exploring an developing innovation classification.* PhD Thesis, School of Management, Cranfield University, Bedford.

Akenroye, T. O., & Kuenne, C. W. (2015). Key competences for promoting service innovation: What are implications for the health sector? *The Innovation Journal, 20*(1), 1–21.

Belleflame, C., Houard, J., & Michaux, B. (1986). *Innovation and research and development process analysis in service activities.* Occasional papers, No. 116, FAST, Brussels.

Bohrer, C. T., & Vargas, E. R. (2011, September 7–10). *R&D and innovation in services: Case studies in University Hospitals in Brazil and France* (Vol. 1, pp. 1–16). XXI Reser Conference Proceedings, Hamburg.

Bohrer, C., & Vargas, E. R. (2014). Can R&D be identified and measured in services? Empirical evidence from university hospitals. *Science and Public Policy, 41*(6), 793–808.

Consejo General de Salubridad. (2015). *Sistema Nacional de Certificación de Establecimientos de Atención Médica.* México: Consejo General de Salubridad, Salubridad. Accessed August 27, 2015, from http://www.csg.gob.mx

Corona, L. (2015). *Índice Índico: Innovación, Difusión y Competitividad.* México: Universidad Nacional Autónoma de México.

Cowell, D. W. (1991). *Ther marketing of services.* London: Butterworth-Heinemann.

Djellal, F., & Gallouj, F. (2005). Mapping innovation dynamics in hospitals. *Research Policy, 34* (6), 817–835.

Farías, J., & Almeida, J. (2014, September 11–13). *Technology adoption in service organizations: A framework proposal for studying ICT diffusion in healthcare and hospital services* (pp. 383–395). XXIV Reser Conference Proceedings, Helsinki.

Gadrey, J., Gallouj, F., & Weinstein, O. (1995). New modes of innovation. How services benefit industry. *International Journal of Service Industry Management, 6*(3), 4–16.

Gallouj, F., & Savona, M. (2009). Innovation in services: A review of the debate and a research agenda. *Journal of Evolutionary Economics, 2*(19), 149–172.

Gallouj, F., & Weinstein, O. (1997). Innovation in services. *Research Policy, 26*(4–5), 537–556.

García, S. S. (2014). *Prólogo. En: Seminario Futuro y Tendencias en Formación de los Recursos Humanos en Salud en México para la Cobertura Universal basada en la Atención Primaria a la Salud* (p. 48). México: Secretaría de Salud, Organización Panamericana de la Salud, Organización Mundial de la Salud.

INEGI. (2010). *Censo de Población y Vivienda 2010*. México: Instituto Nacional de Geografía y Estadística.

Jasso, S. (2004). Relevancia de la innovación y las redes institucionales. *Aportes, enero-abril, VIII* (025), 5–18.

Kodama, F. (2014). MOT in transition: From technology fusion to technology-service convergence. *Technovation, 34*(9), 505–512.

Lancaster, K. J. (1966). A new approach to consumer theory. *The Journal of Political Economy, 74* (2), 132–157.

Mazón, R. J. J. (2008). *Las transiciones demográfica y epidemiológica en México*. Accessed December 12, 2015, from http://v880.derecho.unam.mx/DUAD/boletin/pdf/TRANSICIONES_FACULTAD_DE_DERECHO.pdf

Miles, I. (2008). Patterns of innovation in service industries. *IBM Systems Journal, 47*(1), 115–128.

OECD. (2005). *Oslo Manual. The measurement of scientific and technological activities. Proposed guidelines for collecting and interpreting technological innovation data* (3rd ed.). Paris: OECD Eurostat.

Omachonu, V., & Einspruch, N. (2010). Innovation in healthcare delivery system. A conceptual framework. *The Innovation Journal: The Public Sector Innovation Journal, 15*(10), 1–20.

Rodríguez, A. (2010). *La internacionalización de los servicios intensivos en conocimiento: cooperación, innovación e implicaciones del offshoring de I+D*. Tesis doctoral ed. Universidad Carlos III de Madrid, Madrid.

Rogers, E. M. (1983). *Diffusion of innovations* (3rd ed.). New York: The Free Press.

Sistema de Información de los Objetivos del Milenio. (2013). ¿Cómo va México? Accessed December 12, 2015, from http://www.objetivosdedesarrollodelmilenio.org.mx/cgi-win/odmsql.exe/CDR,E

Torres, A., & Jasso, S. (2014). Knowledge and quality innovation in the health sector: The role of public research organisations. En: A. Y. J. C. (Ed.), *Quality innovation knowledge, theory and practices* (pp. 159–188). s.l.: Hershey, PA: IGI Global Disseminator of Knowledge Editorial.

Torres, A., Jasso, S., & Calderón, G. (2013). *Investigación científica y actividad inventiva en el sector salud en México: el caso del Instituto Mexicano del Seguro Social* (pp. 373–396). Report: Juan Manuel Corona (Coord) Desarrollo Sustentable. Enfoques, políticas, gestión y desafíos. UAM-X, México.

Windrum, P., & García-Goñi, M. (2008). A neo-Schumpeterian model of health services innovation. *Research Policy, 37*(4), 649–672.

Word Health Organization. (1948). Preamble to the Constitution of the World Health Organization as adopted by the International Health Conference, New York, 19 22 June, 1946; signed on 22 July 1946 by the representatives of 61 States. Accessed December 12, 2015, from http://www.who.int/about/definition/en/print.html

World Bank. (2015). Health expenditure, total (% of GDP). Accessed December 12, 2015, from http://data.worldbank.org/indicator/SH.XPD.TOTL.ZS

Leonel Corona-Treviño is a full time Senior Professor in the Graduate School of Economics at the National University of Mexico (UNAM). He founded, and is currently coordinator, of the Economy of Innovation Studies. He has a Ph.D. in OR from the UNAM (1975) and a Masters in Industrial Engineering from the University of Louvain (1966). He has been visiting research fellow at the SPRU, University of Sussex (1982), and at the University of Pernambuco, Brazil (1980). He has published 11 books and approximately a hundred articles and papers on subjects related to contemporary problems that arise from the interaction of Science, Technology and Society.

Constanza Márquez-Aguilar has a Bachelor degree in Political Science and Public Administration and a Master in Economics. She has worked as an advisor for ministries in several sectors such as urban development, social media and strategic projects. For over 8 years she coordinated diploma and other courses on topics such as hospital management, quality health systems, health management and leadership for public health managers, as well as prospective and strategic planning in the Public Administration Institute of the State of Mexico.

Business Model Design and Entrepreneurial Risk Evaluation for Health Service Innovations

Martin Dietrich and Florian Hilfinger

Abstract

We discuss the application of a business model-based approach for designing health service innovations and related risk evaluation. As an example we describe a horizontal backwards integration of hospitals' business models by designing an integrated preventive health service. The business model template consists of five partial models, the value proposition model, the market model, the resource model, cost model and revenue model which are discussed within the context of integrated care. By means of a decision tree analysis, we apply an economic pre-evaluation of potential net benefits of the preventive program compared to the status quo. As a hypothetical example we analyze a stroke prevention program that screens arrhythmia among risk patients and use input parameters based on public epidemiological data. To take risk evaluation into account a simulation is applied in order to demonstrate how entrepreneurial risk in terms of net benefit distributions can be assessed.

1 Introduction

In the upcoming decades demographic, epidemiologic and societal changes are going to transform health care needs and this will put enormous financial and structural pressure on many hospital organizations (Gröne and Garcia-Barbero 2001). Therefore, hospitals have to consider their roles in changing health service settings and are in need for extending their business model conceptions. While the traditional business model of hospital organizations is focused on the treatment of isolated acute illnesses, modern societies struggle with the significant increase of

M. Dietrich (✉) • F. Hilfinger
Faculty of Law and Economics, Saarland University, Campus, Building B4 1, 66123 Saarbrücken, Germany
e-mail: info@mdg.uni-saarland.de; florian.hilfinger@mdg.uni-saarland.de

M.A. Pfannstiel, C. Rasche (eds.), *Service Business Model Innovation in Healthcare and Hospital Management*, DOI 10.1007/978-3-319-46412-1_10

chronic diseases (Barnett et al. 2012). Regardless of the need for full cycle health care, many hospitals are still operating within a framework of traditional highly fragmented health care delivery. Furthermore, hospitals have to deal with a growing mismatch between the necessary integration of hospital care and the trend towards more inter and intra-professional specialization in medicine (Detsky et al. 2012).

Because of its network character integrated health care concepts can be a way to deal with the increasingly fragmented health care delivery. Integrated care models that attempt to cover the full cycle of care require business models that take into account coordinated health delivery rather than isolated treatments of medical conditions. Business models are simplified representations of the way organizations create value (Shafer et al. 2005), and can be a useful tool for managers in strategic management analyzing opportunities and risks of innovative health care services (Hwang and Christensen 2008). One way to extend the business model of inpatient hospital care is by a horizontal backwards integration (e.g. Harrigan 1986) focusing on the prevention of chronic illnesses. When supporting health, especially with respect to cost-intensive chronic diseases, the idea is to increase cost effectiveness in health care by focusing on measures that can prevent or attenuate illnesses at early stages. Hospital organizations are well advised to consider collaborations with other health care providers for delivering the preventive services and health insurers to pay for the preventive services. The idea behind such shared saving contracts is that integrated preventive programs are cost effective which constitutes the necessary condition for the program to be contracted by a health insurance in a selective contracting agreement. Unfortunately, evidence of primary prevention's cost effectiveness, for example in the case of cardiovascular disease, is currently sparse (Schwappach et al. 2007). Therefore, it is essential that a potentially new health service innovation is assessed with respect to potential health outcomes and cost effectiveness. An additional challenge is the risk that is involved in undertaking the endeavor to innovate health services. Approaches which allow for unveiling entrepreneurial risks specific to health service innovations will help decision makers identify risk factors and make more informed decisions.

In this article we will address the entrepreneurial uncertainty in the creation of new health service processes and will show how service innovations in the hospital setting can be analyzed using a business model approach. Our goal is to provide a conceptual blueprint for business model development and evaluation in the setting of health service innovations that can be used as a template for specific, real data driven health service innovation problems. After illustrating the basic concept of business models in health care, we present a simplified business model concept and discuss the application to a hospitals' business model extension. Therefore, we discuss the importance of integrated health care in general and specifically the potential integration opportunities for hospital organizations. We will point out the growing significance of preventive care programs and will describe how hospital organizations can establish new business models through backwards integration and a focus on preventive care. In an example we demonstrate how the business model concept can be transferred to the economic analysis and will calculate the expected economic benefit of a potential new preventive care service, while specifically considering epidemiological data. Applying a decision tree analysis of entrepreneurial risk from a market perspective illustrates how hospital organization can evaluate the financial viability and entrepreneurial risk of potential new business models that extend inpatient health services.

2 Theoretical Background

A business model is a simplified description of how an organization creates, delivers, and captures value (Teece 2010). Business models have become a valuable tool for managers to explore possibilities for future development (e.g. Baden-Fuller and Morgan 2010) and can be helpful for strategic considerations in health care management as well (Christensen et al. 2009). Integrated care models that attempt to cover larger parts within or full cycle of care require business models that take into account coordinated health delivery and not only the isolated treatments of acute medical conditions.

2.1 Business Models in Health Care

The use of business models is a crucial part in developing innovations (Chesbrough 2012). While there is no widely accepted definition and also many different concepts of business models, broadly speaking business models can be defined as simplified representations of the way organizations create value (Shafer et al. 2005). That is to say, business models answer the question about the nature of the business (Drucker 1954). They are "[...] a description of a value a company offers to one or several segments of customers and the architecture of the firm and its network of partners for creating, marketing and delivering this value and relationship capital [...]" (Osterwalder 2004, p. 15). Business models can help identify the necessary circumstances for a viable business concept by illustrating benefits, essential intra- and extra-organizational conditions and potential risks (Magretta 2002). Especially when taking on a market based perspective business models are a vital part of innovation management and have also been discussed as an important tool for analyzing current and new health service structures (Hwang and Christensen 2008).

Although the business model concept has gained considerable attention recently, its definition and translation into operable structures which are distinctively linked to economic analyses remain a challenge (Morris et al. 2005). Therefore, in our analysis we suggest a simplified business model with two conceptual dimensions and five interrelated partial models (Dietrich et al. 2014). The first conceptual dimension consists of the operating level and the financial level, while the second dimension can be subdivided into the organization side and the market side. The five partial models are the resource model, the cost model, the market model, the revenue model and the value proposition as the core of the business model (see Fig. 1).

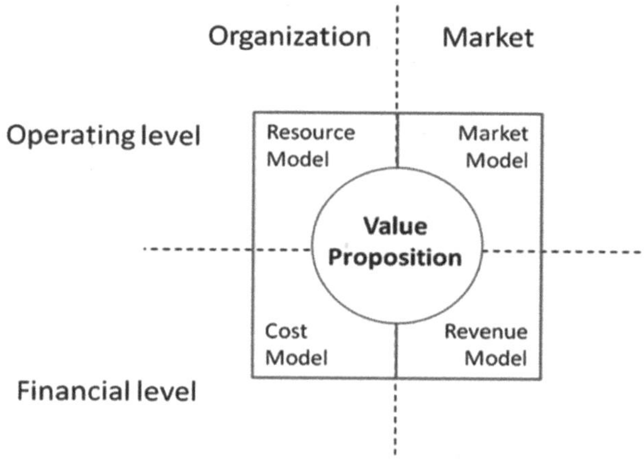

Fig. 1 Business model. Source: Dietrich et al. (2014), p. 250

On the organization side, the resource model describes what material and immaterial resources, processes, abilities and other inputs are used to create goods and services, the cost model answers the question about the associated costs. The resource model is not limited to one organization and also includes aspects of cooperation and networking activities. On the market side, the market model focuses on the needs and demands of customers as well as on larger societal or political requirements and demands, while the revenue model describes how revenue can be created when serving those needs and meeting those demands. The partial models show the necessary domains for a successful task realization on a financial and operating level. On the financial level, the cost model and the revenue model are the basis for a financially stable business model. On the operating level, the resource Model and the market Model show what value can be created and what resources can be used to do so. Effective business models not only balance the four partial models but also always keep the specific business solution for a given demand in mind. This actual value proposition is the core of the business model and not only incorporates the surrounding four partial models, but also considers the financial and operating level as well as the organization and the market side.

2.2 Integrated Health Care

In the upcoming decades the business model of inpatient hospital care will also have to include processes before and after traditional treatment of acute illnesses (Wagner et al. 2001). The reason behind this is a more and more fragmented health care delivery due to an aging society and a significant increase of chronic diseases (Barnett et al. 2012). The treatment of these chronic illnesses is already absorbing a big part of health care resources. Yet, hospital organization are often not adapting to the need for full cycle health care and rather still focus on acute medical care (Barnett et al. 2012). Furthermore, the fragmented health care delivery is also driven by the trend towards more intra-professional specialization in medicine

(Detsky et al. 2012). The mismatch between highly fragmented and complex health care delivery on one side, and an increasing need for full cycle health care on the other side, puts enormous pressure on hospital organizations. In order to avoid unnecessary costs and a lower quality of care because of inefficient use of resources, hospital organizations have to consider these epidemiologic and structural changes and find new business models for integrated health care.

The integration of fragmented health care delivery will be one of the most important tasks. In order to enable health service systems to provide full cycle health care, the goal is to integrate the delivery of health care across different providers and boundaries of health services (Gröne and Garcia-Barbero 2001). Because of the network character and the cooperation of otherwise separated service providers, integrated health care concepts are a promising approach to tackle the problem of increasingly fragmented health care delivery (Kodner and Spreeuwenberg 2002). When we analyze integrated care programs as a business model, improved health care by achieving better health outcomes at lower or reasonable costs, e.g. by avoiding unnecessary medical treatment, becomes the value proposition of such a program. In order to be favorable compared to the traditional care or status quo, the economic benefit has to be large enough to cover expenses for the integrated care program and still result in financial viability (Hildebrandt et al. 2010). It is not enough to evaluate the medical effectiveness on the operating level. It also has to be shown on the financial level, that an integrated care program can be economically sustainable. Therefore, also the financial risk has to be evaluated for new programs and it can be assumed that the lack of reliable data and appropriate methods are relevant causes for the fact that the dissemination of integrated care has not met expectations yet.

3 Business Model Extensions of Hospital Services

The concept of integrated care seems to be especially suited for providing preventive health care programs (Gröne and Garcia-Barbero 2001). Hospital organizations have the chance to take part in integrated care programs and use selective contracting arrangements to extend the business model of traditional inpatient care. As chronic diseases are increasingly drawing from health systems' resources and are claiming even larger shares in health systems' finances, hospital services have to be partially re-defined in the context of full cycle health care to be a productive and cost-efficient part of upcoming health service environments. Extending the business model of inpatient hospital services can be achieved by a horizontal backwards integration focusing on the prevention of chronic diseases. Hospitals do have specific competencies in handling acute episodes of chronic diseases and are experienced with specific causes which trigger acute treatment needs. This specific knowledge could be employed to create additional value in health care if this information is used for preventing unnecessary and cost intensive stationary treatments. But in order for integrated preventive care programs to be successful a risk evaluation based on a business model approach is needed.

To convince health care providers about the cost saving opportunities as well as the financial sustainability of a new health prevention program, hospital organizations have to be able to evaluate the business model from a market based perspective. This is to say, epidemiological data as well as patients willingness to participate has to be a key factor in the analysis.

3.1 Preventive Care and Backwards Integration

Chronic diseases are often correlated with health behavior (Glanz et al. 2008). Everyday stress, the lack of physical activity and malnutrition are assumed to be contributing factors (e.g. Bagust et al. 2002). Promoting health behavior has been shown to be a promising approach for reducing the risk of prevalent chronic conditions such as cardiovascular disease and diabetes (e.g. Tuomilehto et al. 2001). Broadly speaking, preventive health behavior can be defined as an activity that is undertaken for the purpose of preventing a chronic condition or combat a disease at an early stage (Kasl and Cobb 1966). While the goal for primary prevention is to avoid the development of new diseases, secondary prevention focuses on the early treatment of an already existing condition (Jekel et al. 1996). Tertiary prevention aims to soften the impact of an ongoing illness or injury that has lasting effects (Dekker and Sibai 2001, p. 209). The example we will later use to show a way for evaluating the financial risk of a new preventive business model for hospital organizations focuses on secondary prevention via an early diagnosis.

The basic idea of primary and secondary prevention programs is to support health, especially in respect to cost-intensive chronic diseases (Jekel et al. 1996). That means that the interventions should prevent or postpone illnesses because of the assumption that a healthier population should produce lower costs than a less healthy population (Prochaska 2008). The question is: how can hospital organization use the possibilities of preventive care programs? If hospitals want to set themselves apart in the competitive environment by offering preventive care, they have to look for effective collaborations between other health care providers and health insurers. From the perspective of the hospital organizations, the idea behind such shared saving contracts is a backwards integration focusing on preventive care treatments as a new business model. If the traditional inpatient care concepts for chronic illnesses, e.g. adjusting the blood sugar for diabetic patients or treating acute coronary syndromes, become too costly or economically less relevant, then a possible strategic reaction could be to focus on preventive measures regarding the illnesses (Cohen et al. 2008).

3.2 Evaluation of Business Model Extensions

In order to finance such a strategic shift it is necessary to use selective contracts with health insurers in integrated care models (Kodner and Spreeuwenberg 2002). Only if the costs in the preventive program are lower than the risk adjusted norm costs, a health insurance earns a surplus. Consequently, the cost savings have to be calculated and translated into revenue streams for health care providers. To do so, the integrated preventive program has to be described in a simplified business model and the cost saving potential has to be calculated from a market base perspective with respect to epidemiological data as well as the willingness of patients to participate. To illustrate how hospital organization can evaluate the financial viability of potential new business models in inpatient care, we will evaluate a fictitious new simple and low-cost diagnostic tool in a made up scenario.

Consider the following situation: In order to stay competitive a hospital organization wants to stop focusing on the acute treatment of coronary syndromes and instead provide more preventive treatment. To be able to do that the hospital organization wants to create an integrated care program with local primary care physicians and promote a new low-cost diagnostic tool that can be used to identify cardiac arrhythmia. The idea is for the primary care physicians to consult with risk group patients and use the diagnostic tool for screenings, and then for the hospitals to be able to use preventive medicine rather than having to treat acute coronary syndromes. The primary care physicians would then refer the patients to the hospital organization for the preventive treatment. To pay for the reimbursement of the physicians and the diagnostic tools there has to be a selective contract with a health insurer. For the insurer to consider this undertaking, it has to be shown that the costs of the integrated preventive program are lower than the risk adjusted norm costs. Only then the health insurance earns a surplus and it can be a win, win, win situation for them, the physicians and the hospital organization.

To evaluate the cost-benefit ratios, the prevention program first has to be described in the simplified business model we introduced earlier. The value proposition of this diagnostic tool is to prevent costly acute treatment by being able to use suitable early therapies to prevent strokes, heart failure or cardiac arrest (Mendis et al. 2011). The market model not only considers epidemiological facts about cardiac arrhythmia of specific risk groups, but also incorporates the willingness of the target group to participate. As part the resource model we analyze sensitivity and specificity. This includes the technical capabilities of the diagnostic tool, as well as obstacles such as mistakes in the application of the tool by the primary care physicians. The cost model calculates the direct costs of the treatment, costs of possible side effects and the compensation for the primary care physicians. In the revenue model we assume that the direct cost of traditional acute treatment of a stroke or a cardiac arrest can be prevented and thereby become the revenue of our business model.

On the basis of the described business model we can use decision analysis tools that are appropriate for such a calculation with an epidemiological background (Haddix et al. 2003). A simple decision tree analysis on the estimated costs with and without the use of the new diagnostic tool is a suitable option (Hertz and Thomas 1983). For the calculation probability-parameters and expected outcomes have to be modeled on every step of the process. Since even small inaccuracies in the probabilities of the relevant parameters can have a big impact on the overall result, the calculation has to include sensitivity analysis that can tell us which parameters are the most important (Saltelli et al. 2000). With this we can do simulations that show us the expected distribution of the most relevant parameters of the new business model, most importantly the cost-benefit effect.

4 Health Service Business Model Evaluation: A Simplified Example

In order to illustrate how the creation of a new health service process can be analyzed with a market based business model approach, in the following hypothetical example a hospital is assumed to plan a backwards integration of its inpatient hospital services. The goal of the service is to prevent incurring strokes for risk patients with cardiac arrhythmias by implementing a screening program that can detect arrhythmias. The risk population is defined as people older than 55 years. The screening program is assumed to be a simple test that identifies arrhythmias.

An essential part of the analysis is a decision to implement or not to implement the prevention program, which constitutes a decision problem under uncertainty. As a criterion from the business model perspective the expected economic value under the condition with or without introducing the prevention program is to be considered. Decision making under uncertainty can be analyzed by means of decision tree analyses which is used in the health service design problem at hand. As input for the decision tree analysis specific data is needed that is presented in Table 1.

Direct Costs of Stroke per Year: In the example the costs of strokes per year are calculated based on economic evaluations and epidemiologic data from Germany (Kolominsky-Rabas et al. 2006). The data is based on values for the year 2005, which means that the total direct lifetime costs per ischemic strokes (43,000 euros) need to be adjusted for an annual interest rate of 3 %. This leads to today's (2016) lifetime costs of ischemic strokes of 59,922.06 euros. Mean life expectancy after the first stroke has been shown to be 5.9 years in the same study. Based on this data annual direct costs per stroke and patient are assumed to be 9920 euros.

Each identified arrhythmia is assumed to be treated by standard therapy of anticoagulation (0.20 euros daily costs) (Arbeitskreis Pharmakotherapie der Ärztekammer Krefeld 2012) and four control examinations per year. In accordance

Table 1 Cost estimates

Direct costs	Value	Comment
Annual direct costs per stroke and patient	9920 euros	Based on estimated lifetime cost per ischemic stroke (59,522 euros)/mean life expectancy (~6 years) = 9920 euros
Annual direct treatment costs of arrhythmia (atrial fibrillation) per patient	173 euros	Estimated treatment cost by assuming standard therapy (anticoagulation, daily costs = 0.20 euros × 365 = 73 euros) and four control examinations (4 × 25 = 100) = 173 euros

Source: Author's own compilation (2016)

Table 2 Decision tree probability assumptions

Probabilities	Value
Agreement after consultation	90 %
Incidence rate arrhythmia in risk population	10 %
Test sensitivity	80 %
Test specificity	95 %
Adherence rate	80 %
Stroke incidence rate without arrhythmia, no treatment	0.05 %
Stroke incidence rate with arrhythmia, no treatment	0.15 %
Stroke incidence rate without arrhythmia, with treatment	0.06 %
Stroke incidence rate with arrhythmia, no treatment	0.07 %

Source: Author's own compilation (2016)

with fees paid for similar examinations, 25 euros per control examinations are assumed. This leads to the assumption of 173 euros direct treatment costs for arrhythmia (atrial fibrillation) per year.

To calculate the expected economic value, probabilities have to be introduced as relevant input data for the decision tree (Table 2). The first probability is taken from the arrhythmia incidence in the risk population that is assumed to be 10 % (Kip and Pfarr 2015, p. 14). Among arrhythmia patients, stroke incidence in the hypothetical example is assumed to be 15 %. Patients without arrhythmia are assumed to have a stroke incidence of 5 %. Test sensitivity of the screening program is assumed to be 80 %, i.e. the screening program would identify 80 % of arrhythmia patients correctly. Test specificity is assumed to be 95 %, i.e. 95 % of patients having no arrhythmia would be identified correctly. After having identified patients with arrhythmia, patients' adherence is assumed to be 80 %, i.e. 80 % of identified risk patients are assumed to reliably implement the physicians' therapeutic directives. When adhering to the therapeutic directives stroke incidences are assumed to be reduced from 15 % to 7 %. Finally, the calculated expected economic value of the screening program is compared to the expected economic value of the status quo that would be the decision to not introduce the program.

Basically, the value proposition of the preventive health service is the assumption that conducting a test and then treating arrhythmia patients accordingly will prevent strokes and reduce respective direct follow-up costs. The expectancy value of not introducing a preventive screening procedure then has to be compared to the expectancy value of introducing the procedure in order to decide whether or not to introduce the prevention program. For the given hypothetical example and the assumed data, the expected economic costs for not introducing the screening program (status quo) are −595.20 euros. Compared to this, the introduction of the health service program of screening shows expected economic costs of −570.77 and therefore implies an economic benefit of 24.42 euros. From this perspective this result would imply that it is favorable to engage in the screening program (Fig. 2).

Up to this point, this decision analysis has been conducted without including costs for the screening program. The results imply that there is financial scope for

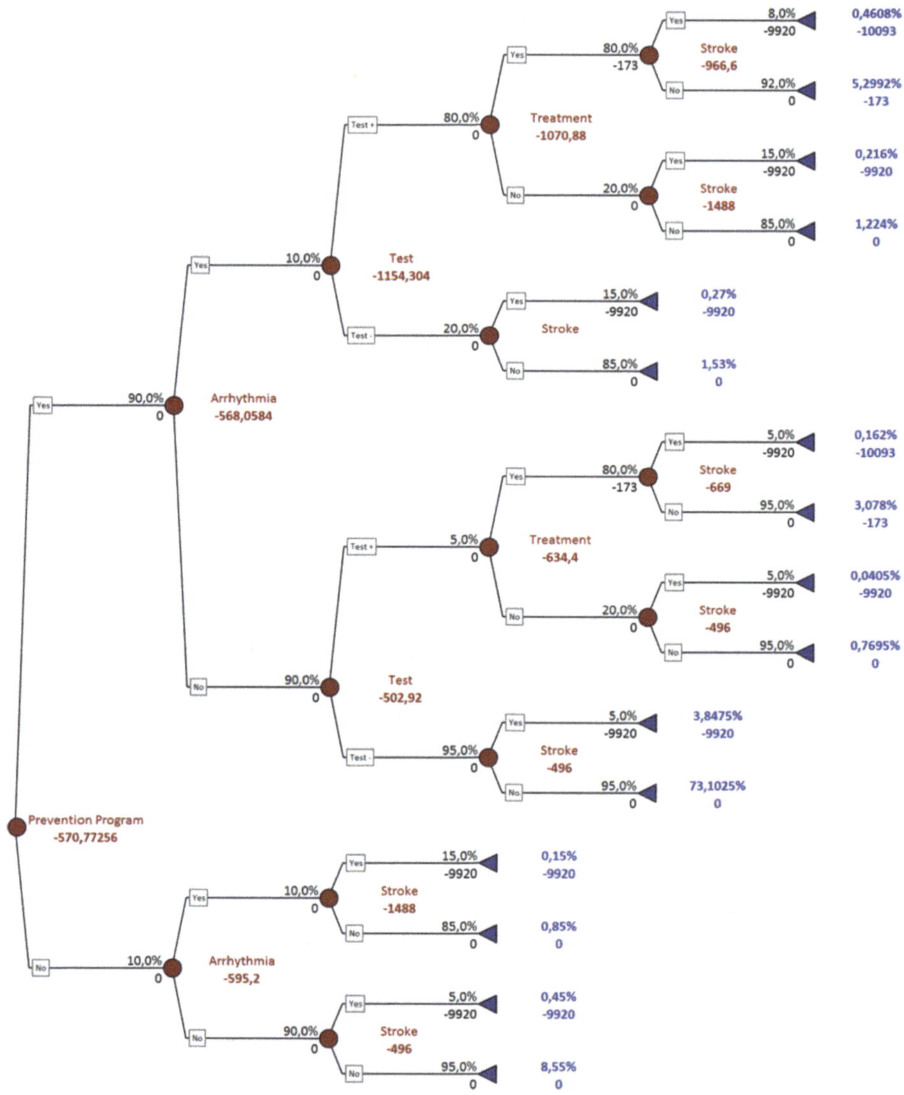

Fig. 2 Decision tree for the introduction of the prevention program. Source: Author's own conception (2016)

allowing reimbursement fees based on the generated cost savings. From a business model perspective, the question arises for the hospital up to what program costs the expected economic benefit would persist. Adding a reimbursement fee for medical consulting and conducting the test of 10 euros each would lower the economic benefit from 24.42 euros to 5.43 euros, still indicating an economic benefit for introducing the prevention program compared to the status quo. These calculations are of interest for health insurances as the reimbursing institution because both, the costs of the prevention program as well as the costs of stroke, lead to according spending. Insofar the entrepreneurial hospital can clarify expected net benefits for the reimbursing institution in terms of improved outcomes and saved costs, the likelihood of realizing a business model extension may rise substantially in negotiating reimbursement fees for the prevention service. Net benefits per capita resulting from this decision analysis are to be interpreted as a source of the hospital's potential revenues for implementing and running the prevention program. Because the analysis doesn't consider the size of the risk population and the absolute number of strokes prevented, aggregated cost savings would have to be considered in a further analytical step in which the population size would have to be factored in. The economic viability would depend on whether the population covered by the program would be large enough to cover all relevant costs of this specific intervention.

From a business model perspective, an entrepreneurial risk of introducing the prevention program exists due to uncertainties of the input parameters of the decision model. Although a decision tree as it has been used here is explicitly designed for capturing uncertainties, it is useful to consider further ambiguities in the input data. Additional sources of uncertainty are for example direct annual cost of stroke survivors and treatment costs for arrhythmia patients. For example, cost studies on direct stroke costs reveal substantial cost intervals rather than valid point estimates. One way to handle uncertainty is to conduct one- or two-way sensitivity analyses which would allow for identifying threshold values at which results are reversed. For example, assuming annual direct stroke costs in the given hypothetical example to be 8573.91 euros, everything else equal, resulted at identical economic values of both alternatives. Similarly, direct arrhythmia treatment costs of 233.31 euros in this hypothetical example would also lead to identic economic results for both alternatives.

A more informative way to illustrate entrepreneurial risk is to conduct simulation analyses by applying probability distributions on uncertain input parameters. Uncertain input parameters are, for example, direct cost or program effectivity in terms of patients' agreement to participate or adherence rates. Applying probability distributions on these variables gives us the opportunity to simulate the decision variable. Simulation on the decision variables reveals probability distributions of the net benefit so that entrepreneurial uncertainty can be captured in terms of resulting decision variable intervals and relative frequencies. To illustrate how entrepreneurial risk can be represented by decision variable simulation, in the given example direct stroke costs are varied according to a more or less arbitrarily truncated normal distribution, with $m = 9920$, $SD = 992$, truncated at the left side at 7750 euros and at the right side at 12,000 euros. Direct treatment costs of arrhythmia are modeled by a truncated normal distribution between 130 and 220 euros, $m = 173$, $SD = 17$. Patients agreement to participate in the screening program is modeled by a triangular probability distribution with $mode = 0.9$, $min = 0.7$, $max = 0.99$, adherence rate is also modeled by a truncated normal distribution, $m = 0.8$, $SD = 0.08$, left hand side truncated at 0.65, right hand side truncated at

0.98. Figure 3 depicts simulation results of the decision variable net benefit after 5000 iterations.

In this example, the expectancy value is 0.53 euros, the 90 % interval of the decision variable distribution is between −6.31 and 8.27 euros with a span of 14.58 euros. Setting the consulting reimbursement fee at 25 euros would result in a net benefit distribution as depicted in Fig. 4.

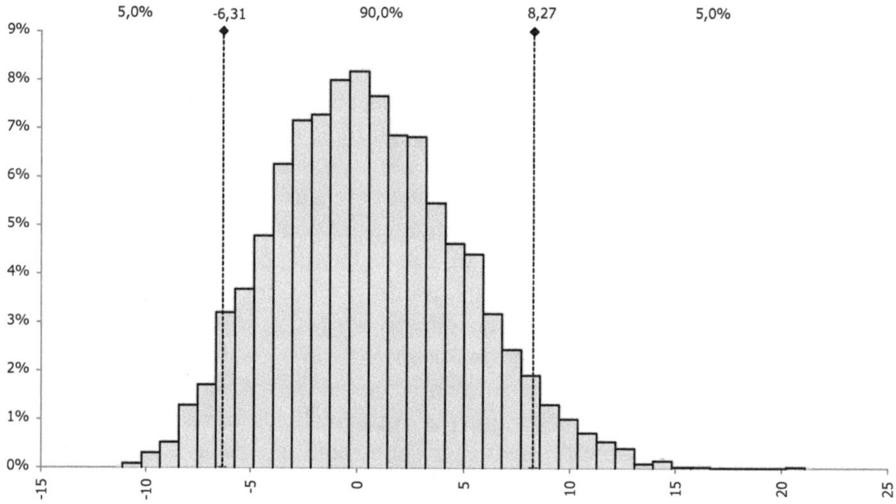

Fig. 3 Simulation result of net benefit distribution, reimbursement fee for consulting (=10 euros), estimates based on 5000 iterations. Source: Author's own conception (2016)

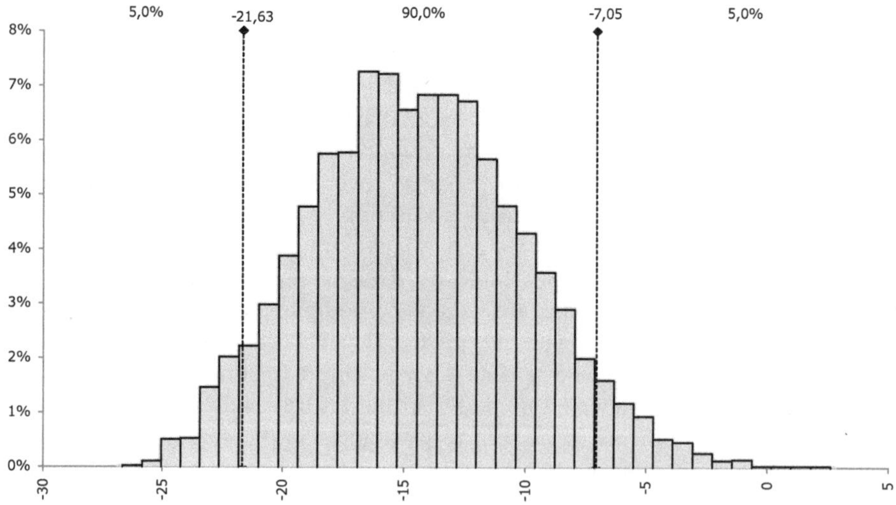

Fig. 4 Simulation result of net benefit distribution, reimbursement fee for consulting (=25 euros), estimates based on 5000 iterations. Source: Author's own conception (2016)

In this example, the expectancy net benefit value is −14.47 euros, the 90 % interval of the decision variable distribution is between −21.63 and −7.05 euros with a span of 14.57 euros indicating that for this reimbursement fee the net benefit of the screening program would not suffice to represent economic advantage. Further analyses reveal that in both settings (reimbursement fee = 10 euros or 25 euros) the most influential variable for net benefit is annual direct costs of stroke per patient (absolute regression coefficient value = 0.79, not presented here), followed by the adherence rate (absolute regression coefficient value = 0.47, not presented here). This means that the higher annual stroke costs and the higher the adherence rate, the higher the net benefit. From a qualitative perspective, these results are not surprising. But from a quantitative perspective, estimates on net benefits and the identification of entrepreneurial risk factors help the decision maker to consider the business model extension and its economic consequences more thoroughly.

In order to evaluate the cost effectiveness of the screening program, the economic net benefit does not suffice as a single criterion. Cost effectiveness means that the additional costs of the screening program have to be put in relation to the improved health outcomes. In the given example, the question would be whether the negative net benefits combined with better health outcomes in terms of strokes avoided are worth the costs. An according assessment would have to be conducted by the decision makers on the basis of further health economic evaluations and in comparison to other intervention alternatives.

5 Conclusion

Current developments in modern societies change the needs for health care due to demographic and epidemiologic changes as well as developments in the field of health care provision. These developments bear the need of hospital business models' adaption. As the business model concept is currently rather elusive we presented in this paper a simplified business model conception and suggested its application on health service innovations and related risk evaluation. Our proposed business model template comprises five partial models, the value proposition model, the market model, the resource model, cost model and revenue model.

We applied our business model conception to a horizontal backwards integration of hospitals' business models in which an integrated preventive health service was analyzed. We transferred the business model application to an economic evaluation by means of a decision tree analysis. As a decision criterion, we applied an economic pre-evaluation of potential net benefits of the preventive program compared to the status quo. As a hypothetical example we analyzed a stroke prevention program that screens arrhythmia among risk patients and used input parameters based on public available epidemiologic data. In order to assess the entrepreneurial risk of extending the hospitals' business model we applied a risk simulation to the decision tree analysis and demonstrated how to assess entrepreneurial risk in terms of net benefit distributions.

We think that our analysis helps to better understand the mechanisms by which the development and innovation of health services are to be assessed from a business model perspective. Although the parameters used in our hypothetical example were calibrated form public available data on arrhythmia and stroke epidemiology and do not represent a specific situation, our analytical approach serves as a conceptual blueprint that can be applied to data of a specific situation. The example given in this study is aimed at demonstrating how business model approaches can be applied to analyzing and appropriately designing health service innovations and how risk evaluation can be implemented. Substituting our hypothetical parameters by real input parameters in a specific study would lead to informative results which can be used for better business model innovation decisions in health care.

References

Arbeitskreis Pharmakotherapie der Ärztekammer Krefeld. (2012). *Leitfaden zur Anwendung der neuen Antikoagulantien zur Prophylaxe von Thrombosen und Schlaganfällen und Therapie bei thromboembolischen Erkrankungen*. Accessed April 30, 2016, from https://www.aekno.de/downloads/aekno/leitfaden_neue_Antikoagulantien2012-12.pdf

Baden-Fuller, C., & Morgan, M. S. (2010). Business models as models. *Long Range Planning, 43*(2), 156–171.

Bagust, A., Hopkinson, P. K., Maslove, L., & Currie, C. J. (2002). The projected health care burden of Type 2 diabetes in the UK from 2000 to 2060. *Diabetic Medicine, 19*(Suppl 4), 1–5.

Barnett, K., Mercer, S. W., Norbury, M., Watt, G., Wyke, S., & Guthrie, B. (2012). Epidemiology of multimorbidity and implications for health care, research, and medical education: A cross-sectional study. *The Lancet, 380*(9836), 37–43.

Chesbrough, H. (2012). Open innovation. Where we've been and where we're going. *Research–Technology Management, July–August*(Special Issue), 20–27.

Christensen, C. M., Grossman, J. H., & Hwang, J. (2009). *The innovator's prescription. A disruptive solution for health care*. New York: McGraw-Hill.

Cohen, J. T., Neumann, P. J., & Weinstein, M. C. (2008). Does preventive care save money? Health economics and the presidential candidates. *New England Journal of Medicine, 358*(7), 661–663.

Dekker, G., & Sibai, B. (2001). Primary, secondary, and tertiary prevention of pre-eclampsia. *The Lancet, 357*(9251), 209–215.

Detsky, A. S., Gauthier, S. R., & Fuchs, V. R. (2012). Specialization in medicine: How much is appropriate? *JAMA, 307*(5), 463–464.

Dietrich, M., Molter, N., & Znotka, M. (2014). Sustainable business models in healthcare systems. In J. Zentes & C. Scholz (Eds.), *Beyond sustainability* (pp. 245–262). Baden-Baden: Nomos.

Drucker, P. (1954). *The practice of management*. New York: Harper and Row.

Glanz, K., Rimer, B. K., & Viswanath, K. (2008). *Health behavior and health education. Theory, research and practice* (4th ed.). San Francisco: Jossey-Bass.

Gröne, O., & Garcia-Barbero, M. (2001). Integrated care. *International Journal of Integrated Care, 1*(2), 1–16.

Haddix, A. C., Teutsch, S. M., & Corso, P. S. (2003). *Prevention effectiveness: A guide to decision analysis and economic evaluation*. Oxford: Oxford University Press.

Harrigan, K. R. (1986). Matching vertical integration strategies to competitive conditions. *Strategic Management Journal, 7*(6), 535–555.

Hertz, D. B., & Thomas, H. (1983). *Risk analysis and its applications* (pp. 11–15). Chichester: Wiley.

Hildebrandt, H., Hermann, C., Knittel, R., Richter-Reichhelm, M., Siegel, A., & Witzenrath, W. (2010). Gesundes Kinzigtal integrated care: Improving population health by a shared health gain approach and a shared savings contract. *International Journal of Integrated Care, 10*(2), 1–14.

Hwang, J., & Christensen, C. M. (2008). Disruptive innovation in health care delivery: A framework for business-model innovation. *Health Affairs, 27*(5), 1329–1335.

Jekel, J. F., Katz, D. L., Elmore, J. G., & Wild, D. (1996). *Epidemiology, biostatistics and preventive medicine*. New York: Saunders.

Kasl, S. V., & Cobb, S. (1966). Health behavior, illness behavior and sick role behavior: I. Health and illness behavior. *Archives of Environmental Health: An International Journal, 12*(2), 246–266.

Kip, M., & Pfarr, L. (2015). Epidemiologie. In M. Kip, T. Schönfelder, & H. H. Bleß (Eds.), *Weißbuch Schlaganfallprävention bei Vorhofflimmern* (pp. 13–25). Stuttgart: Georg Thieme Verlag.

Kodner, D. L., & Spreeuwenberg, C. (2002). Integrated care: Meaning, logic, applications, and implications–a discussion paper. *International Journal of Integrated Care, 2*(4).

Kolominsky-Rabas, P. L., Heuschmann, P. U., Marschall, D., Emmert, M., Baltzer, N., Neundörfer, B., et al. (2006). Lifetime cost of ischemic stroke in Germany: Results and national projections from a population-based stroke registry the Erlangen stroke project. *Stroke, 37*(5), 1179–1183.

Magretta, J. (2002). Why business models matter. *Harvard Business Review, 80*(5), 86–92.

Mendis, S., Puska, P., & Norrving, B. (2011). *Global atlas on cardiovascular disease prevention and control*. Geneva: World Health Organization.

Morris, M., Schindehutte, M., & Allen, J. (2005). The entrepreneur's business model: Toward a unified perspective. *Journal of Business Research, 58*(6), 726–735.

Osterwalder, A. (2004). *The business model ontology: A proposition in a design science approach*. Dissertation 173, University of Lausanne, Lausanne.

Prochaska, J. O. (2008). Multiple health behavior research represents the future of preventive medicine. *Preventive Medicine, 46*(3), 281–285.

Saltelli, A., Chan, K., & Scott, E. M. (2000). *Sensitivity analysis* (Vol. 1). New York: Wiley.

Schwappach, D. L., Boluarte, T. A., & Suhrcke, M. (2007). The economics of primary prevention of cardiovascular disease–a systematic review of economic evaluations. *Cost Effectiveness and Resource Allocation, 5*(1), 1.

Shafer, S. M., Smith, H. J., & Linder, J. C. (2005). The power of business models. *Business Horizons, 48*(3), 199–207.

Tuomilehto, J., Lindström, J., Eriksson, J. G., Valle, T. T., Hämäläinen, H., Ilanne-Parikka, P., et al. (2001). Prevention of type 2 diabetes mellitus by changes in lifestyle among subjects with impaired glucose tolerance. *New England Journal of Medicine, 344*(18), 1343–1350.

Teece, D. J. (2010). Business models, business strategy and innovation. *Long Range Planning, 43* (2), 172–194.

Wagner, E. H., Austin, B. T., Davis, C., Hindmarsh, M., Schaefer, J., & Bonomi, A. (2001). Improving chronic illness care: Translating evidence into action. *Health Affairs, 20*(6), 64–78.

Martin Dietrich studied business administration, economics and health services management from 1994 to 1999 at Freiburg University, Germany, where he also earned his doctoral degree and his habilitation. Since 2011, Martin Dietrich is full Professor and Head of Chair in Business Administration and Health Services Management Research at Saarland University, Germany. His research and teaching focuses on understanding the nature and effects of a changing economic, societal and epidemiologic environment in health service systems on health care consumers' and providers' behavior and health service organizations' performance.

Florian Hilfinger studied business administration, economics and health services management at Freiburg University, Germany. After he received his degree in 2012, he started working as a research and teaching assistant at the Chair in Business Administration and Health Services Management at Saarland University in Germany. Since 2013 his research mainly focuses on the diffusion of innovation in the health care sector.

Guided Business Modeling and Analysis for Business Professionals

Steve Boßelmann and Tiziana Margaria

Abstract

Business modeling has become a popular tool of creativity for entrepreneurs and start-ups, as well as a common technique for promoting innovation and business re-design of established companies. As a consequence, the number of available digital tools in the form of both web-based editors and applications for mobile devices is ever increasing. But these tools lack guidance and support for specific business domains, not to mention features towards structured analysis and comparison of business models beyond basic cost and revenue estimates. This article presents an approach to design domain-specific business modeling tools that provide support for all these expedient but neglected features and supports modelers and analysts alike. The Business Model Developer (BMD) here described has been developed and applied in a German project addressing business models for Personalized Medicine. The outlook concerns the further development of a business modeling toolbox that provides design freedom in a rigorous way and supports analysis and comparison of business models.

1 Introduction

Business models are valuable instruments of communication. They provide a compact view on the key aspects of a business for the stakeholders involved, addressing corporate management and external decision-makers alike. The

S. Boßelmann (✉)
Department of Computer Science, TU Dortmund, Otto-Hahn-Str. 14, 44227 Dortmund, Germany
e-mail: steve.bosselmann@cs.tu-dortmund.de

T. Margaria (✉)
CSIS and Lero, The Irish Software Research Centre, University of Limerick, Tierney Building, Limerick V94 T9PX, Ireland
e-mail: tiziana.margaria@lero.ie

M.A. Pfannstiel, C. Rasche (eds.), *Service Business Model Innovation in Healthcare and Hospital Management*, DOI 10.1007/978-3-319-46412-1_11

motivation for creating business models reaches from sketching ideas for an innovative venture to the creation of a thorough documentation of existing business concerns. Hence the requirements towards covered aspects and the form of presentation vary, particularly in regards to the degree of detail. Tools that seek to provide effective support of the design of business models must meet these demands.

The most common tools today provide a graphical representation that surmounts a mere spreadsheet-based approach by introducing meaningful layouts. This is done by defining a graphical template by means of partitioning some kind of worksheet into categorical tiles. These are filled with model components that represent the key aspects of the considered business. The spatial arrangement of these tiles involves particular semantics. Adjacent tiles represent contiguous categories of aspects that typically are interrelated, hence facilitating the depiction of close relationships. For templates created by this means the term 'Canvas' has established, whereas the Business Model Canvas (BMC) (Osterwalder and Pigneur 2010) is the most prominent instantiation.

1.1 Business Model Canvas

The BMC is a very generic approach to business modeling. It is a conceptual template to be filled with business-related entities, referred to as "business items" throughout this article. According to the specified business items, the BMC depicts "a description of the value a company offers to one or several segments of customers and the architecture of the firm and its network of partners for creating, marketing and delivering this value and relationship capital, in order to generate profitable and sustainable revenue streams!" (Osterwalder 2004). Its basis is the Business Model Ontology (BMO) (Osterwalder 2004) that defines nine separate model segments representing semantic categories. We will refer to them as 'canvas categories' throughout this article. Reasonably arranged, they form the tile-based partition of the graphic depiction of the BMC. Each of them represents a container to hold specific business items. But the BMC only loosely restricts the kind of items to be placed inside. In particular, the restriction is merely of a descriptive nature by means of informal textual explanations or instructions to be conveyed in workshops and moderated modeling sessions. Typically, users brainstorm and create notepads with keywords to be placed on a physical sheet of paper that the BMC has been drawn or printed on, such as on a flip-chart. Because it has initially been created as a handcrafted modeling approach.

Starting with an empty canvas it remains up to the modeler to create a design that is meaningful as well as semantically correct. This circumstance might be acceptable in the context of pen-and-paper approaches, but one legitimately would expect more extensive support from a software solution. Unfortunately, today's software tools in this context do not meet this requirement. In contrast, they mean little added value compared to the pen-and-paper approach as they basically replace the action of putting notepads on a physical canvas by putting virtual notepads onto a virtual canvas.

1.2 State of the Art

Underlying a Creative Commons license (Creative Commons 2016), the BMC has undergone various adaptations by different communities. And although its design allows for the creation of business models in a pen-and-paper approach, the list of realizations in terms of web-based editors and applications for mobile devices is ever increasing. This is particularly motivated by the demand for information sharing and collaboration, which obviously is best addressed by digital solutions. However, apart from this specific benefit available editors do not unleash the full potential typically implied by integrated modeling environments. This circumstance has even been emphasized by the inventors of the BMC when formulating the need for sophisticated software-based solutions (Osterwalder and Pigneur 2012). Currently, many promising aspects are completely out of focus.

Modeling Guidance Available software-based model editors lack support for the model design process itself. Step-by-step guides that put design steps in a meaningful order are not to be found. On the contrary, these tools provide a blank canvas to start with. And the required knowledge on how to actually fill the canvas is not conveyed. Instead, comprehensive knowledge and modeling experience are usually presupposed. Practitioners try to compensate this by attending workshops and intensive training in filling the canvas. But this means initial effort and investment upfront before creating the first model. Hence, though the BMC has been conceived with brainstorming and innovation in mind there is quiet an initial hurdle to be taken, especially by inexperienced modelers like entrepreneurs.

Domain-Specificity Furthermore, there are virtually no domain-specific solutions, i.e. tools that specifically guide the creation of business models for specific types of businesses or application domains. Instead, available solutions follow a generic modeling approach based on unspecific model components. In particular, the actual components that make up the BMC are realized by means of generic notepads that hold textual snippets conceived by the user. This is not to be confused with design freedom or enabling creativity. As an example from another creative field, drawing programs support the design of common shapes and provide powerful editing tools instead of leaving the user with a freehand tool and some good advice on how to do it. This does not limit design freedom or creativity but in contrast pushes effectiveness of the model design. However, the same positive effect can be expected from domain-specific solutions in the context of business modeling.

Model Validation Although generic model components are in accordance with the initial pen-and-paper approach of the BMC, they eventually yield unstructured models. However, available model editors do not provide support for avoiding mistakes. Basically, users are free to specify anything they want, independent of aspects like completeness or correctness. We consider it a crucial feature of model editors to prevent structural defects and support the creation of meaningful models instead of solely leaving it up to the user to create models that are structurally correct or not.

Analyzability The argumentation so far addresses the design aspects of business models. But business models are not an end in itself. They represent a shared piece of information to support monitoring and decision making for both internal and external parties. However, decision making would benefit from structured model analysis and comparison, which is completely out of focus of current software solutions. This is no surprise as structured analysis requires structured models the lack of structure in today's solutions has just been outlined. On the other hand, analyzable models would mean added value for the whole business model life-cycle and therefore are absolutely desirable.

Being able to apply model validation, analysis and comparison might be a crucial factor in supporting business model innovation, in general as well as in the context of the current challenges in healthcare (Rasche et al. 2016) in particular. This article presents a simplicity-driven, structured approach to domain-specific business modeling that has been conceived to overcome the drawbacks of the software-based solutions currently available. We describe the genesis of a prototype, present intermediate results and point out ideas concerning future improvements.

2 Domain-Specific Modeling

Models in general consist of components that represent entities from the respective area of application. In terms of business models these are business-related entities to be referred to as 'business items' throughout this article. The type of these business items heavily depends on the actual application domain. As an example, business models related to hospitals address very different business items compared to models related to car manufacturing. Hence, we argue that although both models can be created with generic components, a domain-specific modeling environment significantly improves the modeling efficiency by serving the respective modeler with well-known concepts. This typically results in effective support in the creation of meaningful models.

In contrast to the very generic approach of the Business Model Canvas, our approach facilitates a domain-specific setup of the modeling environment. The definition of this setup takes place in a distinct customization step typically preceding the actual model design phase. Here different stakeholders with often entirely different disciplinary backgrounds might be involved, spanning application experts, domain experts as well as the actual modelers from the application domain. This is in accordance with the fact that business models—like models in general—represent a shared piece of information to form a common language and support discussion, reasoning and decision making (Kühne 2006). For this purpose, all stakeholders need to understand the model and its components. Hence the latter should be well-defined and selected based on the skills and knowledge of the participants in order to build a modeling language that everybody agrees on. However, these stakeholders do not necessarily have business modeling skills or broad knowledge of formal models in general. Hence, a decent amount of simplicity throughout the model life-cycle as well as in software design is key for success. But the notion of simplicity as a driving paradigm in information system development has been explicitly identified as an important research topic, yet it is still poorly understood (Floyd and Boßelmann 2013; Margaria and Steffen 2010) and not widely adopted in research (Margaria and Hinchey 2013).

The core of a domain-specific setup is the definition of building blocks that represent available model components. Providing predefined building blocks has significant advantages over approaches that merely rely on generic elements like labeled notepads. Some of them are discussed here.

Assistance and Guidance Instead of serving the user a completely blank canvas with which to begin, a library of building blocks provides valuable assistance and guidance e.g. to entrepreneurs for designing first business models. Building blocks are considered natural and intuitive in context of most software tools targeting creative tasks. As an example, modern graphics tools provide the feature of drawing basic shapes instead of leaving the user with a freehand pen and some good advice on how to do it. However, the latter case is the state-of-the-art in regards to available business modeling tools.

Discover Unused Potential As predefined building blocks represent business items that are relevant for the considered domain, they offer the modeler an incentive to discover unused potential. They facilitate the outlining of aspects that otherwise might not have been taken into account.

Shared Vocabulary Predefined building blocks serve as a shared vocabulary that participants with different professional background can agree upon in order to increase communicability and information exchange amongst them. This understanding is essential because in general models are created to point out crucial aspects to support reasoning and decision-making.

Analyzability Building models from a collection of building blocks means that the components a model can consist of are known. This makes it possible to develop analysis methods based on this knowledge that are applicable to any model built with these building blocks. We will come back to analysis aspects and discuss them in a separate section.

The building blocks are thought to be exchangeable at any time. This way, they can be adapted to the actual application domain. In order to additionally allow for the specification of different characteristics of one and the same model component we have further applied the concept of component-specific parameters. As these are out of focus for this article, we refer the interested user to the respective publication for a discussion in more detail (Boßelmann and Margaria 2014).

3 Case Study in Personalized Medicine

The presented structured approach to business modeling as well as an early instantiation by means of a software tool named Business Model Developer (BMD) has been developed in the course of the joint project Service Potentials in Personalized Medicine (DPM) (Universität Potsdam 2016), funded by the German Federal Ministry of Education and Research (BMBF). The main objective of the project was a market analysis of Personalized Medicine to identify key actors, drivers and barriers, that included the analysis of current and future business models within this specific market segment. The Business Model Developer was developed not only under consideration of the project's findings but also practically applied in interview sessions with industry experts as well as repeatedly tested and evaluated by project partners. Experiences and insights achieved this way have directly influenced further improvement of the modeling concept as well as iteratively driven the evolution of the software in an agile manner.

The prototype of the Business Model Developer that has been developed in the course of the DPM project is an Android-based App for tablets and smartphones. The following subsections comprise an overview of the project setup as well as a short description of the tool's user interface and explains how to create business models with it.

3.1 Domain-Specific Setting

In the course of the DPM project a domain-specific library of building blocks has been created containing components that are most likely for business models in the area of Personalized Medicine. The identification of suitable building blocks has been done by conducting and evaluating surveys and interviews with industry experts with a focus on diagnostic companies. The results of this evaluation have been transferred into a suitable taxonomy by applying abstraction and generalization. The interested reader is referred to (Kamprath and Halecker 2012) for further details. As an example, building blocks for the category Key Partners span rather generic items like Research Institutes, Companies and Investors as well as items that are specific for the domain of diagnostic companies, such as Biobanks, Biological Databases as well as Researching Physicians. Analogously, the building blocks for other canvas categories have been tailored towards this distinct field of application.

The building blocks have been categorized, which means the library maintains a list of building blocks for each canvas category. At model design time, this enables to only provide those building blocks that are suitable for a specific canvas category. This has multiple advantages. It creates more convenience for the modeler, provides guidance in filling the canvas and at the same time facilitates the correctness of the model. While e.g. a Research Institute might be in category Key Partners, listing it as a key activity would not be correct as it just does not represent an activity. The separation of the building blocks by category prevents structural defects of such kind.

In order to allow for design freedom and brainstorming beyond the defined framework, the user might specify custom components that do not correspond to any of the building blocks on demand. However, most of the advantages of using the building blocks do not apply on custom components, in particular the validation as well as the analyzability of the model is limited or just not given anymore. The user should be aware of this and hence is notified by the editor when using custom components.

The Business Model Developer allows for the specification of annual costs and fix costs for the components of almost all canvas categories (in fact, the only components that do not cause costs are revenue streams). Costs are specified by means of simple numerical values. The semantics of these costs depend on the respective canvas category of the respective component. As an example, the cost factors for a component of the partner network can be interpreted as the actual costs that are caused by the interaction with the respective partner.

According to the layout of the Business Model Canvas, the Business Model Developer provides a canvas category Cost Structure. This category might hold components that represent additional cost factors that can not directly be associated with a single component on the canvas. Additionally, this category shows a total sum of annual costs and fix costs that have been specified for components all over the canvas.

The canvas category Revenue Streams basically behaves the same as the category Cost Structure by means of enabling the user to create components representing revenue streams that correspond to the current business model as well as the expected value. Analogously, this category shows a total sum of the value of all revenue streams throughout the canvas.

3.2 Canvas-Based Modeling

The visualization of the workspace is based on the layout of the Business Model Canvas and adopts the arrangement of its nine canvas categories. The modeler successively enriches them with model components from the library of building blocks. This library is accessed via the context menu of a canvas category. As the Business Model Developer is an Android-based App, the context menu is shown if a canvas category is long-touched or double-tapped with a finger. It only lists building blocks that are suitable, i.e. building blocks that are allowed to be used as components for the respective category. This way, the user interface avoids the misplacement of model components in a rigorous manner. It is just not possible to create components in a canvas category it has not been specified for, nor is it possible to move existing components to the wrong category.

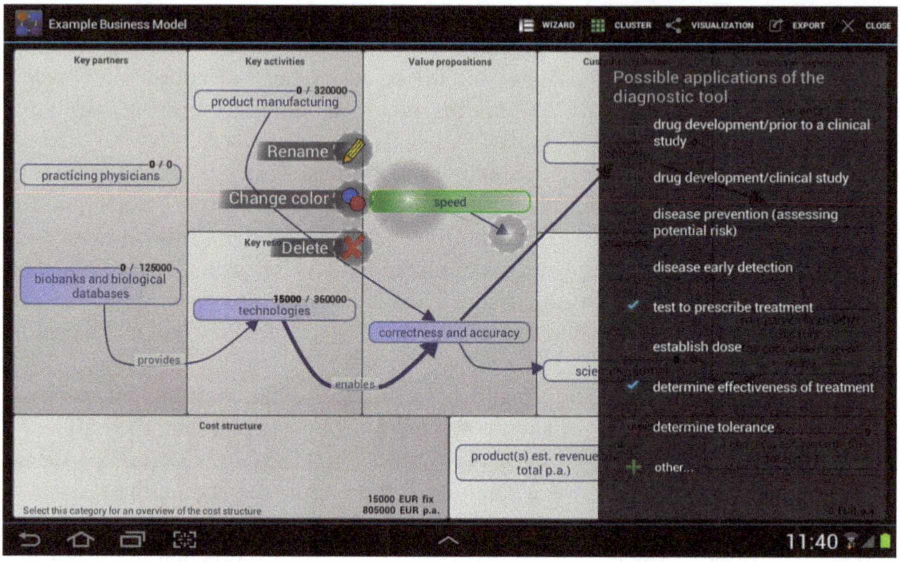

Fig. 1 Canvas-based modeling with the Business Model Developer. Source: Originally in Boßelmann and Margaria (2014)

Figure 1 shows a screenshot of the tool's user interface with a depiction of the canvas. It shows how the different canvas categories are filled with labeled rectangular nodes that represent model components. The right-hand side of the screenshot shows a canvas overlay that lists available parameters of the currently selected component (in this example, the green-colored node in the center of the canvas). This is how additional information on the component can be provided in order to realize different characteristics.

While the canvas overlay is shown whenever a node is selected, a context menu is shown if it is double-tapped or long-touched. This context menu lists additional interaction possibilities with the respective node. Besides customizing its appearance by means of renaming or changing its color, this context menu shows a starting point of an outgoing edge. By dragging the arrowhead of this dangling edge and dropping it on another node a new directed edge between source and target node is created, representing a relation between the respective components. Edges can be named via its context menu which is specifically helpful to specify the actual type of the relation. Additionally, the line of an edge can be adapted via bending points.

3.3 Wizard-Based Guidance

While the above concepts of creating business models with the Business Model Developer rely on direct interaction with the canvas, the tool provides an alternative way to design a model. In this approach the user accesses a so-called Wizard which

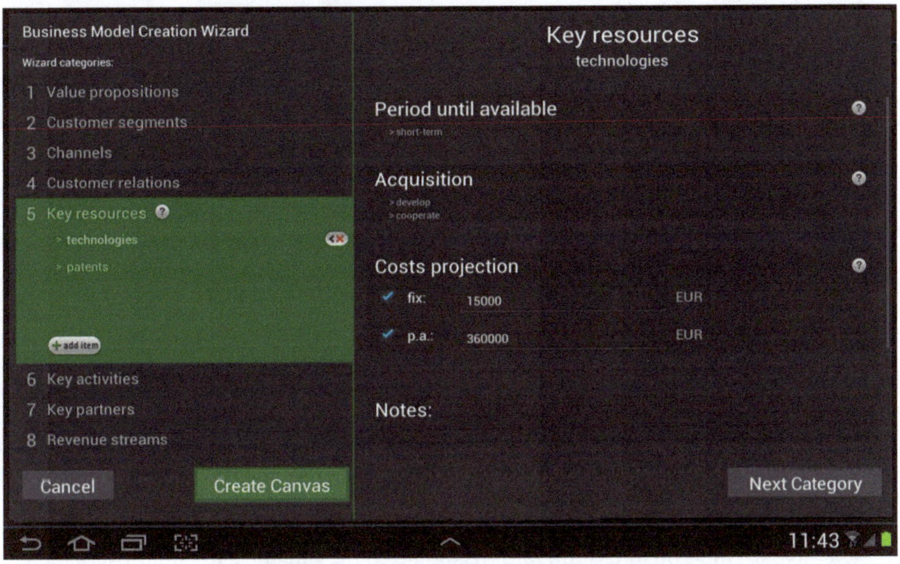

Fig. 2 Wizard-based modeling with the Business Model Developer. Source: Originally in Margaria et al. (2015)

is dialog-based, i.e. the modeler follows a structured approach similar to a questionnaire. The Wizard lists the nine categories of the canvas in a predefined order and guides the user through the necessary steps to fill them with model components. This guidance is realized by means of significant descriptions and supporting hints regarding the meaning of the different categories as well as the purpose of the various component characterizations. Figure 2 shows a screenshot of the Wizard and in particular the various hints and help texts for all structural elements to be accessed via one of the buttons labeled with a question mark '?'.

This Wizard-based approach is especially helpful for beginners as it supports the creation of first business models in a directed fashion, improving completeness while maintaining syntactical correctness. The actual graphical representation of the business model is successively created in the background based on the information the modeler provides during the interaction with the Wizard. The user can switch to the canvas view at any time, as filling some categories might as well be skipped in the Wizard and instead done directly on the canvas. However, the Wizard does not only provide initial guidance. It is intended to be used as an alternate view on the business model. Thus, the Wizard can be re-entered at any time and for any model state. That means the user can switch between these different views on demand.

3.4 Integrated Model Analysis

Models created with the Business Model Developer base on building blocks and structured component characteristics. These form the basis for the application of model analysis. In the course of the DPM project a systematic analysis technique has been developed that enables a comparison of business models (Kamprath and Halecker 2012). This analysis is based on the collected data regarding business models of diagnostic companies, accessing the same data that has been defined via the DPM-specific library of building blocks. Based on the evaluation of this data, distinct clusters have been identified that represent a partition over different instances of business models.

Based on the definition of these clusters, a calculation method of cluster membership has been developed and implemented in the Business Model Developer. This makes it possible to compare the created business model to the current state of the market in the area of Personalized Medicine. For the calculation, it is analyzed which building blocks have been used within each canvas category as well as what are the specified characteristics.

The investigated business model is assigned to the cluster with smallest distance. As the details of the cluster technique are out of focus for this article, we refer the interested user to the respective publication for a complete discussion (Kamprath and Halecker 2012). As a result, the Business Model Developer provides the modeler some descriptive information on what the result of the cluster analysis means as well as a diagram overview of derived clusters. Figure 3 shows a screenshot of the latter.

3.5 Lessons Learned

With the development and application of the Business Model Developer in the course of the DPM project we have successfully demonstrated that a structured approach to business modeling has the expected advantages, above all the immediate analyzability of the created models. With this, the tool is actually delivering useful feedback for the modeler, by which the business model becomes more than just a graphical representation.

We have also learned from interviews with industry experts that there is need for more design freedom by means of canvas customization.

4 Canvas Customization

The tailoring of the modeling environment towards a specific domain so far has focused on the model components. We have introduced the concept of building blocks and motivated their characterization. However, the layout of the canvas has not been touched. With the further development of the Business Model Developer, this is about to change as custom canvases are introduced. The current version is

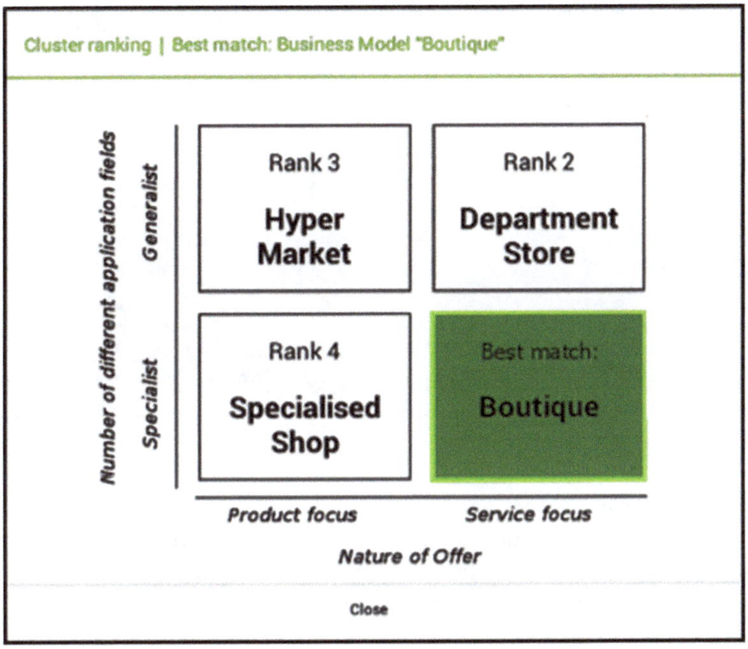

Fig. 3 Result of cluster analysis. Source: Author's own illustration (2016)

developed with the CINCO SCCE Meta Tooling Framework (Naujokat et al. 2016) that facilitates the development of domain-specific graphical modeling tools in a rigorous model-driven fashion. Following the XMDD paradigm (Extreme Model-Driven Design) (Margaria and Steffen 2012) the development process puts the domain expert (typically a non-programmer) in the center of the development process.

Building custom canvases in the context of the Business Model Developer does not only mean renaming or moving tiles but also deleting them or inventing completely new ones from scratch. The experience that we gained from applying our modeling tool in practice and evaluating the feedback is that business professionals are really interested in re-designing the canvas. One of the most recurring comments of industry experts from hands-on sessions with our tool is that the canvas would be missing a tile. On the other hand, various communities have created custom canvases for specific purposes, already. These can be separated into two groups. Some canvases are thought as an alternative to the Business Model Canvas, like the Lean Canvas (Leanstack 2016) or the Strategy Sketch (Kraaijenbrink 2016). Others are designed to be compatible with existing canvases and model parts of them in more detail. The Product Canvas (Romanpichler 2016) and Value Proposition Canvas (Business Model Generation 2016) are prominent examples.

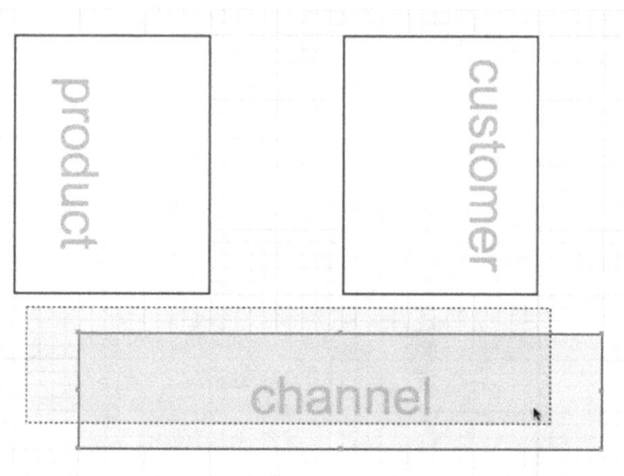

Fig. 4 Tile arrangement for a custom canvas. Source: Author's own illustration (2016)

Again, these examples are generic approaches that do not take advantage of the potential of a domain-specific canvas regarding informative value and expressiveness. In the following we describe our approach to custom canvases as the last step to complete domain-specific business models.

4.1 Tile Arrangement

The crafting skills that are needed to build a custom canvas layout are rather little sophisticated as it all comes down to painting tiles and giving them a name. The editor needs to support the creation of such shapes. In context of our tool, tiles may be rectangular or complex polygonal shapes, as well as circles or ellipses. Figure 4 shows a screenshot of a simple arrangement of tiles in the creation process of a custom canvas layout.

It is noteworthy that building a layout for a custom canvas is an activity that is not part of the actual business model design but takes place in the preceding customization phase along with the definition of building blocks to create a domain-specific setup. It is more like creating a model of a business model, which is generally referred to as meta-modeling (Kühne 2006).

4.2 Containment Rules

Having created and properly arranged the tiles of the canvas layout, there still needs to be defined what is allowed to be inside. As collections of building blocks are part of the domain-specific setup, they need to be linked to the tiles of the canvas. The editor of our tool makes this a specifically simple task as collections of building blocks can be dragged to the canvas and dropped on the respective tile. This triggers the creation of a node in the tile that represents this collection. Figure 5 shows a

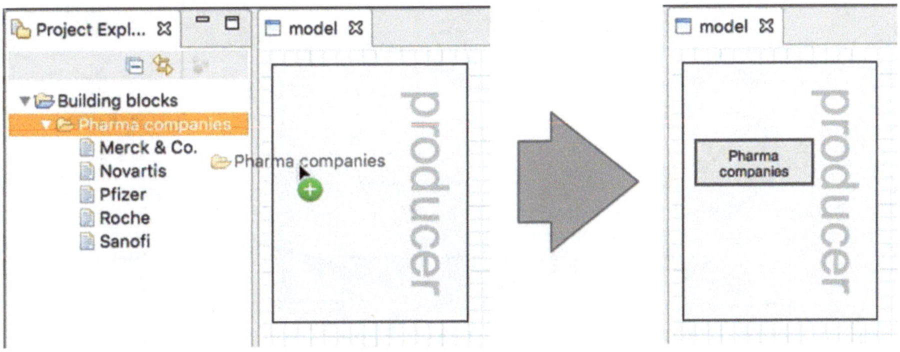

Fig. 5 Definition of containment rules. Source: Author's own illustration (2016)

screenshot with an example, in which a collection of building blocks (in this case companies) is linked to a tile labeled 'producer'. The created node can be interpreted as a containment rule, which specifies that all building blocks inside the referenced collection can be used to fill the respective tile at model design time.

Again, it is noteworthy that this specification of containment rules is not part of the actual business model design, but takes place in the preceding customization phase.

4.3 Canvas Templates

The model of a custom canvas, i.e. the arrangement of tiles with its containment rules and the respective collections of building blocks, represents a canvas template. The model editor of our tool is capable of providing a modeling environment based on the template definition. With this, users are able to create business models based on the specified template. That means the tiles of the canvas can be filled with building blocks according to the specified containment rules. This action is generally referred to as instantiation of the template.

Following this approach even sophisticated canvas layouts can be defined. Figure 6 shows a model realized with the methods of canvas customization based on polygonal shapes. Note that the editor automatically applies a suitable layout to the nodes inside tiles with polygonal shape in a smart manner.

The template-driven approach still is in accordance with the proposed structured approach to business modeling. In particular, the business models based on custom templates can be validated and analyzed in a structured manner.

4.4 Analysis Tables

Following the described approach to build custom canvases means that the tiles of the canvas as well the building blocks the model can consist of are known at any

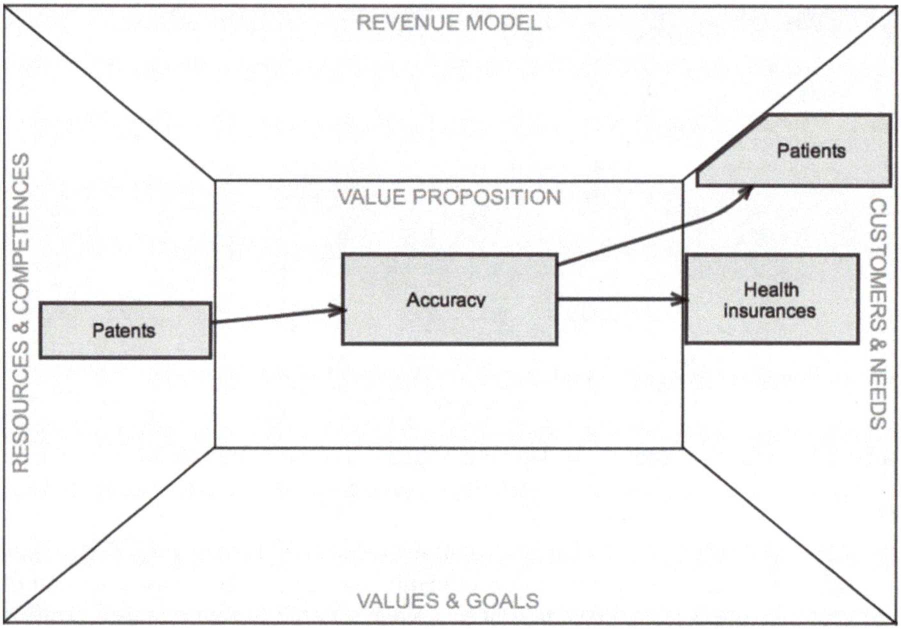

Fig. 6 Example of a custom canvas. Source: Author's own illustration (2016)

	Extended Model	Basic Model	+
Patents	YES	NO	
Focus on Patients	YES	NO	
Known Risks	3	2	
+			

Fig. 7 Analysis table. Source: Author's own illustration (2016)

time throughout the model life-cycle. Their definition in the customization phase to form a template makes it possible to apply structured model analysis on any instance of this template.

To give an example, we introduce the concept of analysis tables. Figure 7 shows a screenshot with an example of a analysis table that may be filled by the user. The column headers hold references to business models in the workspace that have been created by instantiation of the same template. Hence the building blocks used to create them are from the same collections. The row headers are to be filled with simple checks that are provided by the editor. In this example, there are two basic checks to be applied. The first is checking for the existence of a specific building block. That correlates to the question, whether a specific building block has been used in the model or not. The second check is related to quantity, as it simply counts all occurrences of a specific building block in the respective model.

The checks are listed in a palette of the editor. Note that they are generated and provided for specific tiles of the canvas. As an example, as the Business Model Canvas has a category Key Partners the editor provides an existence check called 'KeyPartnerExists'. It has a parameter that lets users specify the building block of interest. As possible values for this parameter, the editor lists all building blocks that might have been used in the Key Partners category. As an example, if the collection 'Pharma companies' depicted in Fig. 5 would have been linked to the Key Partners category of the business model, the user would be able to e.g. select Roche as the building block of interest. This relates to answering the question, whether the company Roche is in the partner network of the respective business model.

A check is integrated into the analysis table by dragging it from the palette and dropping it on a placeholder in the row header. This placeholder is depicted in Fig. 7 as a rectangular node with a dashed border. The placeholder is then replaced by a node that represents the selected check to be applied. At the same time the values for all remaining table cells in this row are calculated and updated to show the result of the check applied to the business model referenced by the header of the respective column. In case of existence checks the values would simply be 'Yes' or 'No'. If it is a quantity check the table cells show numerical values representing the amount of the building blocks that have been count.

5 Conclusion

We have presented a structured approach to domain-specific business modeling based on predefined building blocks, component characteristics and custom canvases. This approach has been motivated by the fact that structured models allow for the application of structured analysis, which enables model comparison.

We have shown the genesis of the Business Model Developer as a software-based solution to support this structured approach. The presented tool provides added value and guidance for new entrants and business professionals alike by means of facilitating correctness and completeness of the created models.

References

Boßelmann, S., & Margaria, T. (2014). Domain-specific business modeling with the business model developer. *Lecture Notes in Computer Science, 8803*(1), 545–560.

Business Model Generation. (2016). *Strategyzer*. Accessed July 7, 2016, from http://businessmodelgeneration.com/canvas/vpc

Creative Commons. (2016). *Creative commons*. Accessed July 7, 2016, from http://creativecommons.org/licenses/by-sa/3.0/

Floyd, B. D., & Boßelmann, S. (2013). ITSy – simplicity research in information and communication technology. *IEEE Computer, 46*(11), 26–32.
Kamprath, M., & Halecker, B. (2012, June 17–20). *A systematic approach for business model taxonomy – how to operationalize and compare large quantities of business models?* Proceedings of ISPIM Conferences, Barcelona, Spain.
Kraaijenbrink. (2016). *The ten elements of the strategy sketch.* Accessed July 7, 2016, from http://kraaijenbrink.com/2014/03/ten-elements-strategy-sketch
Kühne, T. (2006). Matters of (meta-) modelling. *Software and Systems Modeling, 5*(4), 369–385.
Leanstack. (2016). *Don't write a business plan, create a lean canvas instead.* Accessed July 7, 2016, from https://leanstack.com/lean-canvas
Margaria, T., Boßelmann, S., & Wickert, A. (2015). Der Business Model Developer Entwicklung eines Tools zur Erstellung und Analyse von Geschäftsmodellen. In E. Eppinger, B. Halecker, K. Hölzle, & K. Kamprath (Eds.), *Dienstleistungspotenziale und Geschäftsmodelle in der Personalisierten Medizin* (pp. 95–115). Wiesbaden: Gabler Verlag.
Margaria, T., & Hinchey, M. (2013). Simplicity in IT: The power of less. *IEEE Computer, 46*(11), 23–25.
Margaria, T., & Steffen, B. (2010). Simplicity as a driver for agile innovation. *IEEE Computer, 43*(6), 90–92.
Margaria, T., & Steffen, B. (2012). Service-orientation: Conquering complexity with XMDD. In M. Hinchey & L. Coyle (Eds.), *Titel des Sammelbandes* (pp. 217–236). Wiesbaden: Springer.
Naujokat, S., Lybecait, M., Kopetzki, D., & Steffen, B. (2016). CINCO: A simplicity-driven approach to full generation of domain-specific graphical modeling tools. (To appear in STTT.)
Osterwalder, A. (2004). The business model ontology – a proposition in a design science approach. PhD Thesis, Universite de Lausanne, Switzerland.
Osterwalder, A., & Pigneur, Y. (2010). *Business model generation.* Hoboken, NJ: Wiley.
Osterwalder, A., & Pigneur, Y. (2012). Designing business models and similar strategic objects: The contribution of IS. *Journal of the Association for Information Systems, 14*(5), 237–244.
Rasche, C., Margaria, T., & Floyd, B. (2016). Service model innovation in hospitals – beyond expert organizations. In M. A. Pfannstiel & C. Rasche (Eds.), *Service business model innovation in healthcare and hospital management.* Wiesbaden: Springer.
Romanpichler. (2016). *The product canvas.* Accessed July 7, 2016, from http://www.romanpichler.com/blog/the-product-canvas
Universität Potsdam. (2016). *Dienstleistungspotenziale in der Personalisierten Medizin.* Accessed July 7, 2016, from http://uni-potsdam.de/dpm/

Steve Boßelmann is doctoral student at the Chair of Programming Systems at the Department of Computer Science, Technical University of Dortmund with the dissertation subject "Agile Process Management". He has interest and knowledge in Model-driven Software Development, Business Modeling and Business Process Management. As a researcher he has taken part in the EU-FP7-project "ITSy—IT Simply Works" to generate a set of innovative research topics on the notion of simplicity as a driving paradigm in ICT development. In the course of the project "Service Potentials in Personalized Medicine" he has developed an innovative approach to structured domain-specific business modeling and analysis.

Tiziana Margaria is Chair of Software Engineering and Head of Department at the Dept. of Computer Science and Information Systems at the University of Limerick (Ireland). She is also a Principal Investigator of Lero, The Irish Software Research Center, where she is heads the Committee on International Relations Development. In Lero, she heads research projects on Scientific Workflow and model-driven HW/SW Cybersecurity. She received a Laurea in Electrical Engineering and a PhD degree in Computer and Systems Engineering from the Politecnico di Torino, Italy. She has broad experience in the use of formal methods for high assurance systems, in particular concerning functional verification, reliability, and compliance of complex heterogeneous systems, through major industrial projects (where she won the European IT Award in 1996, and a start-up competition in 2001) and consulting, as well as through her activities as founder and CEO of startup companies, holding two USPTO patents, one of which with NASA. She is currently Vicepresident of the European Association of Software Science and Technology (EASST), President of FMICS (the ERCIM Working Group on Formal Methods for Industrial Critical Systems), and steering committee member of ETAPS, the European joint Conferences on Theory and Practice of Software, member of the Board of EF-ICST, the European Forum on Information and Computation Science and Technology.

Modeling Directly Executable Processes for Healthcare Professionals with XMDD

Steve Boßelmann, Alexander Wickert, Anna-Lena Lamprecht, and Tiziana Margaria

Abstract

While various modeling languages emerged to express activity sequences and service interactions, current standards and best practices in workflow and process description and modeling are far away form the needs of healthcare professionals. In particular, they are too technical for direct embrace by these professionals, and mostly they just describe processes that still have to be handed over to programmers for implementation from the ground up.

In contrast, we are convinced that in terms of process modeling, a simplicity-driven and domain-specific solution best fits the need to involve business professionals in the model design phase. With eXtreme Model-Driven Design (XMDD) we present a modeling approach that focuses on comprehensible process models that are executable from the first minute and facilitate the user-driven creation and test-running of rapidly designed prototypes.

The applications discussed in this article show examples of using XMMD for clinical paths design and processes of care in the screening of diabetic retinopathy and diabetes day care, as well as patient classification, physical training, and laboratory procedures in cancer-related cachexia research.

S. Boßelmann (✉)
Department of Computer Science, TU Dortmund, Otto-Hahn-Str. 14, 44227 Dortmund, Germany
e-mail: steve.bosselmann@cs.tu-dortmund.de

A. Wickert
Institute for Computer Science, University of Potsdam, August-Bebel-Str. 89, 14482 Potsdam, Germany
e-mail: alwicker@uni-potsdam.de

A.-L. Lamprecht • T. Margaria
CSIS and Lero, The Irish Software Research Centre, University of Limerick, Tierney Building, Limerick V94 T9PX, Ireland
e-mail: anna-lena.lamprecht@lero.ie; tiziana.margaria@lero.ie

M.A. Pfannstiel, C. Rasche (eds.), *Service Business Model Innovation in Healthcare and Hospital Management*, DOI 10.1007/978-3-319-46412-1_12

1 Introduction

In healthcare, processes of care, compliance, standard operating procedures and best practices are increasingly recognized as central assets in guaranteeing quality and efficiency. While most of these processes and guidelines are described in a textual fashion, IT-mapped descriptions are being adopted as a means to "reify" the procedures in a less ambiguous and interpretation-prone fashion. This way, the formalization of the processes in description languages and models is gaining foot, and is perceived as a certainty-increasing measure for these vital descriptions.

In terms of process-driven development, various modeling languages emerged in the last decade to express activity sequences and service interactions. Today, standardized representations like the Business Process Model and Notation (BPMN) (Allweyer 2009; White and Miers 2008) and related approaches help to automate processes designed that way, leading to software systems that take on the model execution and enact it like programs. However, these languages have a number of drawbacks that particularly affect their utilization by healthcare professionals with sparse technological background. A prominent example leading to easy confusion are vast palettes of modeling components. In practice, almost always only a smaller selection of the available components is needed, and the palette should be reduced to a sufficient and smaller subset, this way limiting confusion and shortening the learning curve for participating stakeholders. Ambiguous model constructs with sometimes blurred meaning add to this lack of simplicity. And finally, the strive for standardization is often achieved via workflows built-in into vendor's proprietary tools. This impairs the creation of domain-specific solutions.

Altogether, the design and the implementation of such processes and workflows is mostly still in the hands of IT professionals and consultants, and is thus neither "owned" nor carried out by the healthcare professionals themselves.

In contrast, a simplicity-driven and domain-specific approach to process modeling best fits the needs of health care professionals, and enables them to design and compose "living" models that are readily executable. With eXtreme Model-Driven Design (XMDD) (Margaria and Steffen 2012) we present a simple modeling approach where intuitively comprehensible process models are executable from the first draft, and facilitate the user-driven creation and test running of rapid prototypes.

In this paper we briefly illustrate the concept of XMDD in Sect. 2, then we discuss applications in clinical paths design and documentation (Sect. 3.1), processes of care in the diabetic retinopathy (Sect. 3.2), and finally clinical therapies for cancer-related cachexia (Sect. 4).

2 Domain-Specific Process Modeling

Processes consist of interrelated tasks. They describe workflows that express how a team or an organization operationally achieves their goals. At the core of any process are the people and professionals who enact it by means of carrying out each single task in their everyday work. Describing these tasks requires a certain understanding of the procedure to follow as well as regulations and constraints that apply. In the context of healthcare, the procedures concern how physicians, nurses and administration interact, and the constraints concern for example precedences, required competences or the knowledge of the best practices in the profession.

Due to the various alternatives and exceptions that can accompany even the simplest treatments, the knowledge required in the profession is continuously increasing and capturing the logic of a process has become a crucial aspect in managing procedure-related issues. Due to this inherent complexity, it is necessary to involve the professionals that best understand the respective domain, which typically are non-IT experts. If these professionals are to take a lead in the design and evolution of workflows, the technology to model, deploy and evolve processes must be accessible in an intuitive manner. Hence simplicity is considered a key regarding both the modeling environment as well as the process models themselves. However, while we propose the notion of simplicity to be a driving paradigm in information system development it is yet poorly understood and remains an actual research topic (Margaria et al. 2011; Margaria and Steffen 2010, 2011; Merten and Steffen 2013).

2.1 XMDD

Simplicity for the model design and validation by subject matter experts like healthcare professionals is achieved in the XMDD (eXtreme Model-Driven Design) (Margaria and Steffen 2012) software development paradigm by focusing on processes that comprise both tasks to be enacted by people (activities) and by software applications (services). In the context of process modeling, the XMDD paradigm enables users, even on their own, to rapidly create domain-specific processes that are immediately executable. That means the user is provided with a software prototype that supports enactment of tasks according to the created process models from the very beginning. This tremendously eases the user experience, and also eases validation and evolution of the process models: it all happens by directly manipulating the 'one thing' so central to the One-Thing Approach (OTA) (Margaria and Steffen 2009), through adequate views tailored to the competences of the involved stakeholders.

2.2 One-Thing Process Design in the jABC

The reference implementation of the XMDD paradigm and the One-Thing Approach is jABC (Java Application Building Center) (Steffen et al. 2007). It facilitates the rigorous use of user-level models and their evolution and adaptation throughout the process and software life-cycle.

Figure 1 gives a snapshot of the jABC in action: Users create a process model by arranging pre-defined building blocks from a library displayed in the upper left of the window. They are integrated into the model in a drag-and-drop fashion and

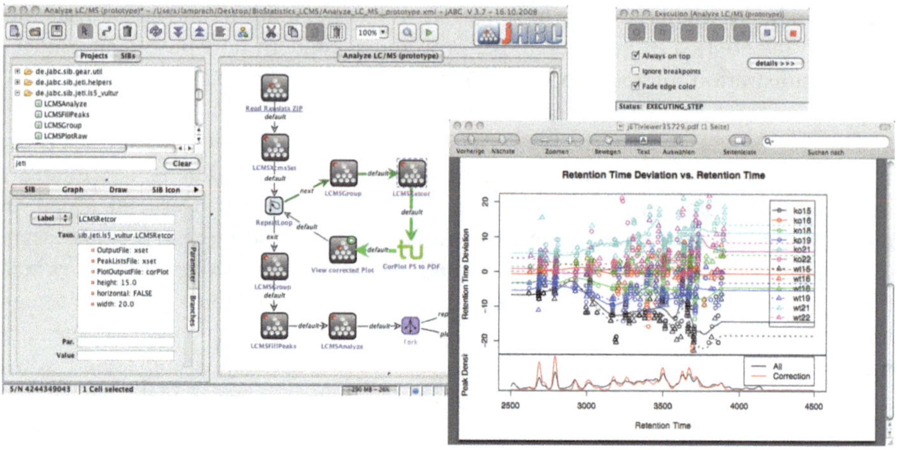

Fig. 1 LC/MS data analysis process modeling and execution with the jABC framework. Source: Author's own illustration (2016)

connected with each other through labeled edges. The graph structure created this way represents the actual process, that is, the sequences of tasks to be done as well as decisions to be taken.

As in the XMDD paradigm the modeling elements are things and actions from the user's domain, users work all the time with familiar terminology and concepts. This way, the jABC facilitates the design of process models directly at the user's level of expertise. As all these process elements are inherently executable, these process models are everything needed to create a running software application. In particular, no programming is required at any time in the design phase.

2.3 Library of Building Blocks

The jABC modeling environment provides pre-defined building blocks called Service-Independent Building Blocks (SIBs) that represent the domain entities as services. A service might be anything that can be performed by a piece of software, e.g. simple calculations, sending e-mail, or complex things like booking a flight. They might need input to execute correctly (like the address of the recipient of an e-mail), and produce output as a result of execution (like a confirmation that the message has been sent).

The process models in jABC are built by connecting SIBs from the library of building blocks. They represent the different steps of the modeled process, and the direction of the connecting arrows expresses the sequence in which the steps have to be performed. Process models contain a dedicated start node and might contain one or more end nodes at which they terminate. Technically, the jABC process models are graph structures, and are amenable to corresponding mathematical analyses and validation.

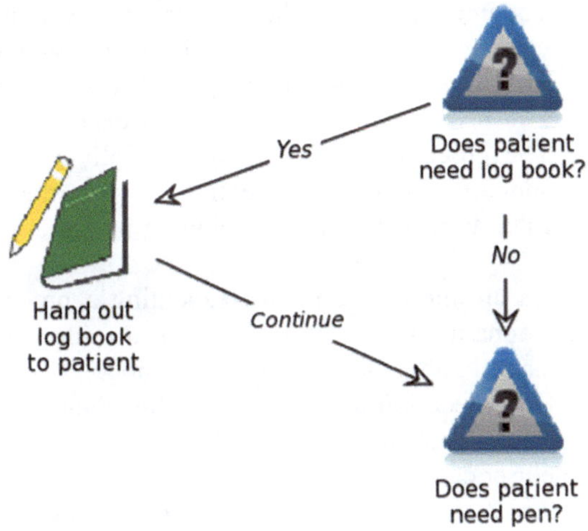

Fig. 2 Modeling decision points in jABC. Source: Author's own illustration (2016)

Each SIB comes with its own icon, but SIB-icons may be changed to something more specific and intuitive or meaningful to the specific context. This allows further expressiveness for the users, adapting the modeling environment to the respective application domain and create a unique user experience.

As shown in Fig. 2, to model decision points according to the outcome of execution, SIBs can have multiple outgoing branches. As an example, a simple yes-or-no decision SIB will have two outgoing branches labeled Yes and No, respectively.

2.4 Model Reuse and Hierarchical Models

To help organize large processes meaningfully, process models can be included as process SIBs in other models, creating hierarchical model structures. This is done in a drag-and-drop fashion analogous to the handling of standard SIBs, and its icon can be changed as well, to better visually express the respective model task.

This concept of easy model reuse avoids repetitive work at model design time. From another perspective, the building blocks available for modeling can be extended by the respective user. This enables building rich domain libraries and complex process models from smaller user-defined components.

2.5 Process Execution

Process models in the context of jABC are executable from the very first minute, provided that the following conditions are satisfied:

- The integrated SIBs themselves are executable. In practice it is also possible to use non-executable SIBs as placeholders for executable SIBs not yet available. This way, the structure of a process can be defined using the placeholders, that in a subsequent time are replaced by executable SIBs.
- The process models are syntactically correct. The editor tool of the jABC supports the user in creating correct models by applying model validation rules at design time or forbidding incorrect model constructs.

As an alternative to just executing a process model, the jABC provides the functionality to *trace* it. That means, the execution starts and progresses as described above but pauses at each node.

The execution path that led to this point is highlighted in the model to provide valuable feedback to the user, facilitating the validation of the intended behavior. The user can manually trigger the further execution to proceed with the next node. Figure 3 shows an example of tracing a process model with the taken path highlighted in green color.

The following sections provide an overview on some case studies regarding the proposed process modeling approach in a healthcare-related setting.

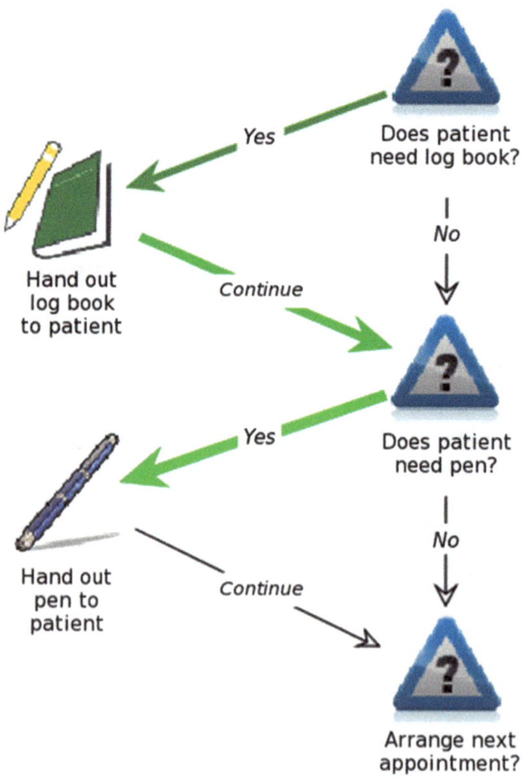

Fig. 3 Tracing a process model in jABC. Source: Author's own illustration (2016)

3 Case Studies in Diabetes Care

Since 2013, 382 million people have been diagnosed with diabetes worldwide, that is 8.3 % of the adult population, with equal rates in both women and men. Up to 90 % of these people are affected by Type 2 diabetes. In Italy, for example, the percentage of population affected by diabetes is about 5 %, with an increasing trend.

The World Health Organization (WHO) projections foresee a doubling of diabetic cases in Europe by 2025, as a result of the rising of the risk factors as ageing population, sedentary lifestyle and unhealthy eating habits.

Usually diabetic patients are subject to regular monitoring, with screenings every few months. These processes are addressed in the case study of Sect. 3.1.

Retinopathy is the vascular complication that can lead to blindness. Mostly it requires a strict and correct glycemic control and it is highly specific for both types of diabetes. These processes are addressed in the case study of Sect. 3.2.

3.1 Polyclinical Workflows of a Diabetes Day-Care Clinic

In this case study, first reported in Margaria et al. (2013) we applied XMDD-based process modeling to systematically examine workflows of a day-care clinic that treats diabetes mellitus patients. The case study has focused on polyclinical workflows as amongst the processes of the clinic they were best structured and had a high repetition rate. They cover a patient's sequential pass through three discrete operational stages of the clinic, which are the outpatient reception, patient care and medical examination.

The actual on-site workflows had already been identified in employee surveys and documented by means of tabular activity catalogues prior to our study. Based on these tables, workflow models in terms of Event-driven Process Chains (EPCs) (van der Aalst 1999) were created. Figure 4 shows an example of a complete model. The clinic management had already used the ARIS (Scheer 1998) toolset based on EPC models in previous projects and decided to stick with this approach in order to preserve consistency in the modeling technology. In our work, we applied the XMDD-based approach to the EPC solution, designing executable process models in jABC equivalent to the EPC-based models. The goal was to provide a fair comparison of ARIS and jABC models based on the same workflows. We did not engage therefore in process redesign or optimization, even when the jABC representation uncovered potential that was difficult to spot in the EPCs.

Our evaluation focused on simplicity in the design phase as well as readability of the models by means of the typical users, i.e. the healthcare professionals carrying out the workflow tasks.

Model Representation Figure 5 shows the ARIS model and the jABC model representing the task sequence depicted in Fig. 4. At first sight, the jABC model looks significantly more compact: it needs only four SIBs to express the same workflow for which the EPC syntax requires 14 node elements. This superior

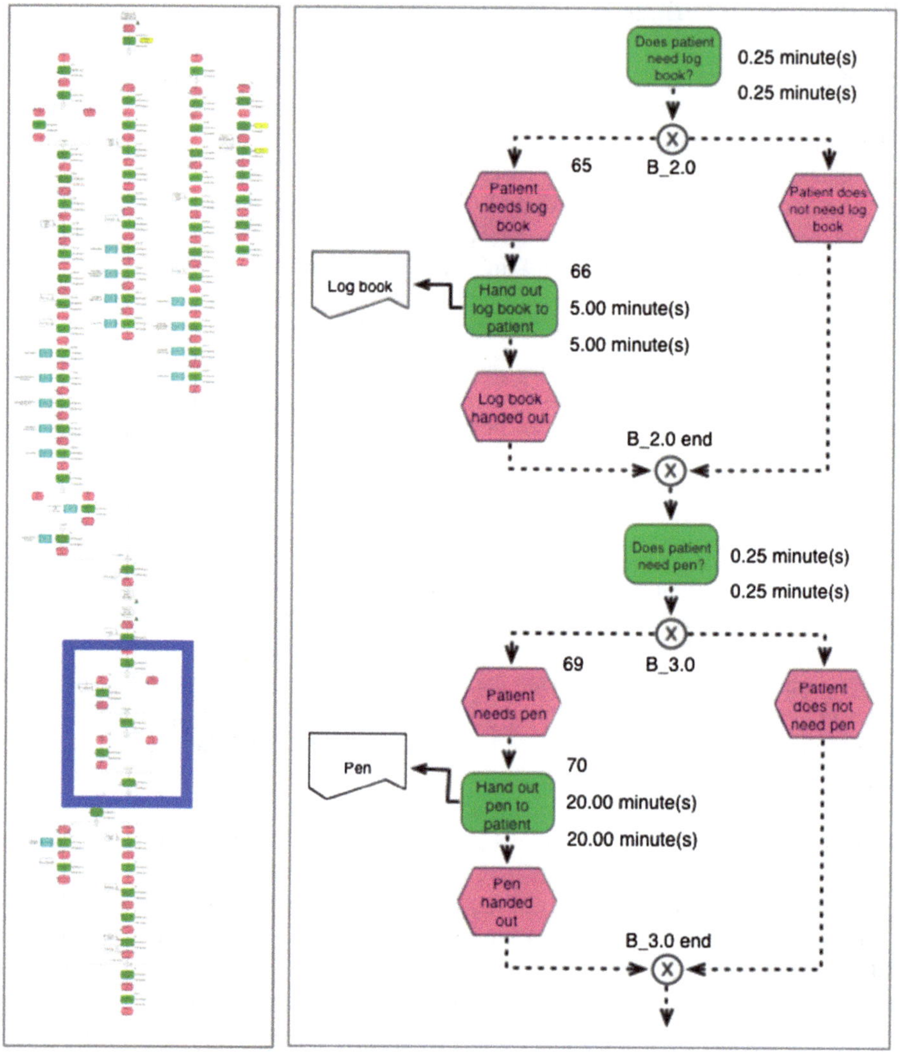

Fig. 4 EPC model representing the complete patient care workflow (*left*) and a detailed view of the bordered area (*right*). Source: Originally in Margaria et al. (2013)

compactness mainly results from the use of labeled edges in jABC instead of EPC's verbose modeling style of decision points, based on logical connectors and separate event nodes. Accordingly, the jABC models were significantly smaller: 619 nodes in ARIS vs. 187 nodes in jABC, i.e. the ARIS models were over three times as large.

Model Simulation The goal of the EPC modelling was to identify total execution times of patient visits based on assumed durations of the single tasks and the number of available professionals. As a second result, we could show that the

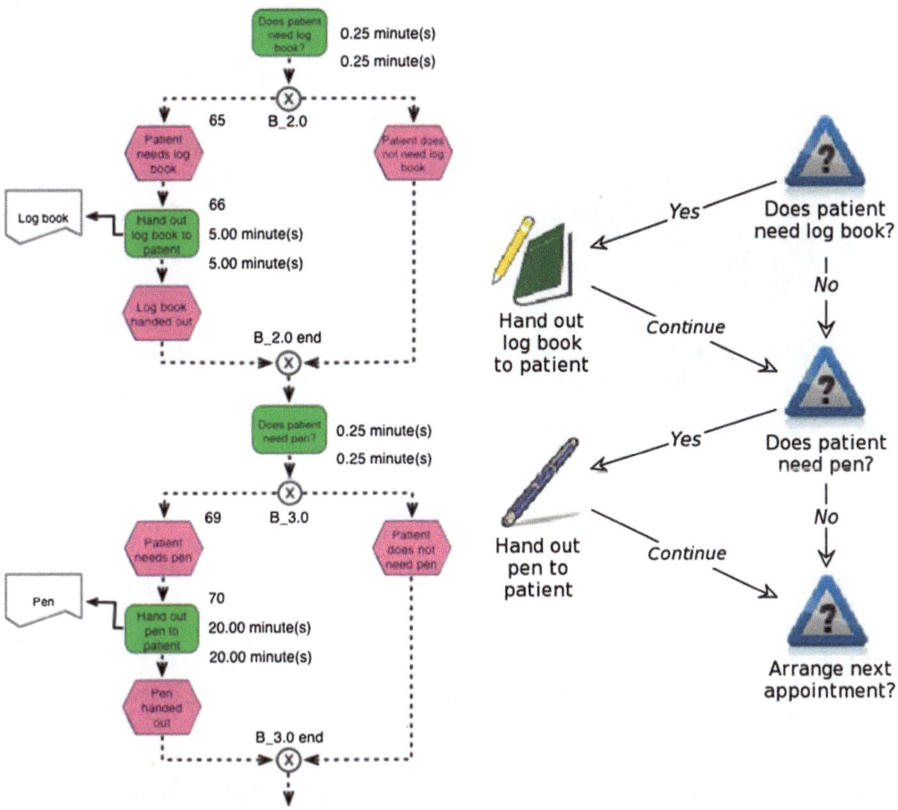

Fig. 5 Comparison of modeled decision points: ARIS model (*left*) vs. jABC model (*right*). Source: Originally in Margaria et al. (2013)

rapid creation of prototypes from the jABC models supported the immediate execution and hence validation of process models. For execution we used a simple task management system that is part of the jABC framework. With this, tasks can be allocated to a specific user or user role, identified by its name, and be managed in separate role-specific task lists for the administration assistants, nurses and doctors. The system is started on process execution and accessible from other computers in the local network. For process modeling, we used a specific TaskSIB that creates tasks in that system upon execution. As soon as the current task is marked completed in the system, the process execution proceeds with the next SIB. Figure 6 shows the task management system in action, depicting the execution of the workflow shown in Fig. 5.

We showed that the model validation via execution following the XMDD-based approach with jABC is simple enough to let workflow practitioners and domain professionals design process models and execute them in a simulation environment without previous knowledge of formal representations nor of programming.

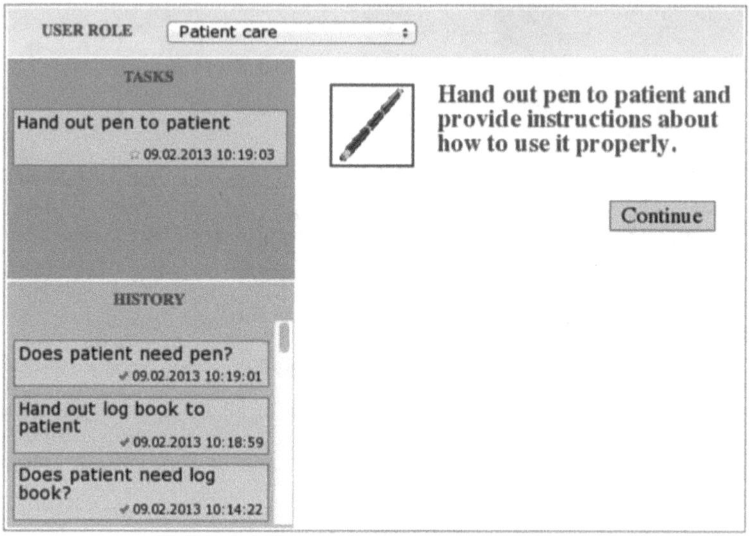

Fig. 6 Task management system with task list and history. Source: Originally in Margaria et al. (2013)

3.2 Retinopathy Screening Workflows Along a Diabetes Care Clinic

This case study was carried out by Claudio Cioè in the Fall 2015 in the Turin Diabetic Retinopathy Centre (CRD), promoted by Dr. Massimo Porta, who set it up in 1998 in Torino (Italy), in the context of a redesign and modernization of the information system currently in use for the screening.

Diabetic Retinopathy is one of the four main causes of blindness in the world and the first cause of blindness among adult patients in Italy. The Diabetic Retinopathy screening is the most effective instrument to prevent the blindness caused by this pathology, and the Diabetic Retinopathy Centres enable to accomplish this activity.

The study analyzed the national guidelines for DR screening, and went through three phases of modelling and refinement including an on-site observation and understanding phase, a preliminary model of the screening workflows in UML activity diagrams (the current standard of process modelling in model-driven software development), ending with a collection of processes in jABC. These artifacts reflect the practice in the Centre in Torino, but can also serve as a reference for best practices at a national level. The study is documented in detail in Cioè (2016), and here we summarize a few highlights with permission of the author.

The entire process landscape concerns the interplay of the four roles patient, nurse, oculist, and physician, and the data landscape includes the data models for the patient, image, and screening information systems. As an example, the top-level patient acceptance workflow is depicted in Fig. 7. There we see that the process

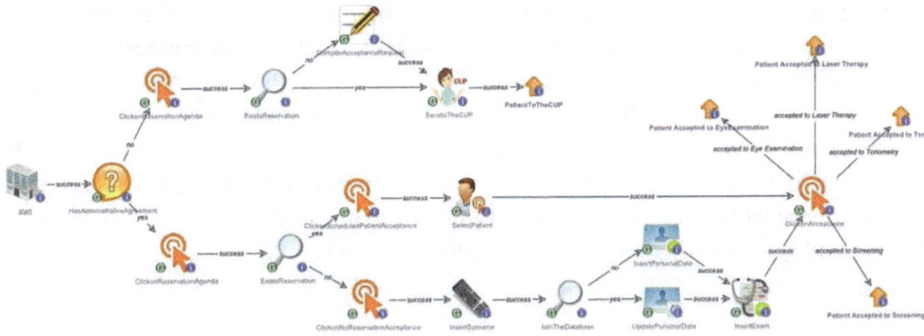

Fig. 7 Diabetes retinopathy centre—patient acceptance process in jABC. Source: Originally in Cioè (2016), with the author's permission

modeling style is consistent with the principles and practices described in the previous case study, including for instance the compact representation, the use of branches to express alternative pathways, the use of icons to suggest intuitively what happens at that step (e.g. a look-up in some list of patients with reservations, a check in an IT system, filling a form, or inputting data in an IT system). The use of hierarchy is very prominent: all the SIBs with a green dot and a G represent integrated process models, i.e. they can be opened revealing their internal models, that are in many cases themselves refined by more models.

The tidy and understandable appearance strikes the viewer: this is a top level representation of what happens globally, answering the question "how do you organize the acceptance process?". This model says what are the steps or activities and their organization, but without delving immediately in all the details. When one is interested to see how one of these steps is realized, they can open the corresponding model and see the process and the sub-steps, in a nice hierarchical organization that manages the separation of what is done from how it is done.

4 Case Study in Cancer-Related Cachexia Research

Cachexia is a complex wasting syndrome associated with a marked detrimental effect upon life quality and survival in patients with cancer, chronic obstructive pulmonary disease (COPD), chronic heart failure, AIDS, and chronic kidney disease, among other conditions. Its prevalence is of around 5–15 % in cardiac patients at end stage, rising up to 30 %, in COPD and chronic kidney disease patients, and to 80 %, in patients with advanced cancer.

In this case study, we present how domain-specific workflows can be designed by researchers and scientists that are not IT experts, this time in the context of an interdisciplinary research study led by Prof. Marilia Seelaender at the Cancer Metabolism Research Group of the University of São Paulo (Brazil). It is aimed at providing insights on the importance of detecting early signs of inflammatory changes in patients and examining the mechanisms that act in concert, inducing cachexia symptoms. A first special issue on the outcomes of this research project appeared in "Mediators of Inflammation" in 2015 (Seelaender et al. 2015).

We illustrate our approach for both kinds of processes that are most frequently found in such studies: processes that involve computations and potentially data analytics, illustrated on a small example in Sect. 4.1, and reference processes on laboratory practice, as high-level lab protocols in Sect. 4.2.

4.1 Patient Classification Workflows for Cachexia

Based on the cachexia definition of Evans et al. (2008), the researchers at the Cancer Metabolism Research Group of the University of São Paulo (Brazil) designed and refined in several iterations a spreadsheet-based tool (see Fig. 8) to classify their patients in the context of the cachexia research study. This classification is based on a multidisciplinary scoring system, where several parameters such as the weight loss and BMI of the patient, analysis of blood samples and symptoms based on patient self assessment are combined with the existing cancer diagnosis and then match a patient to one of the following groups:

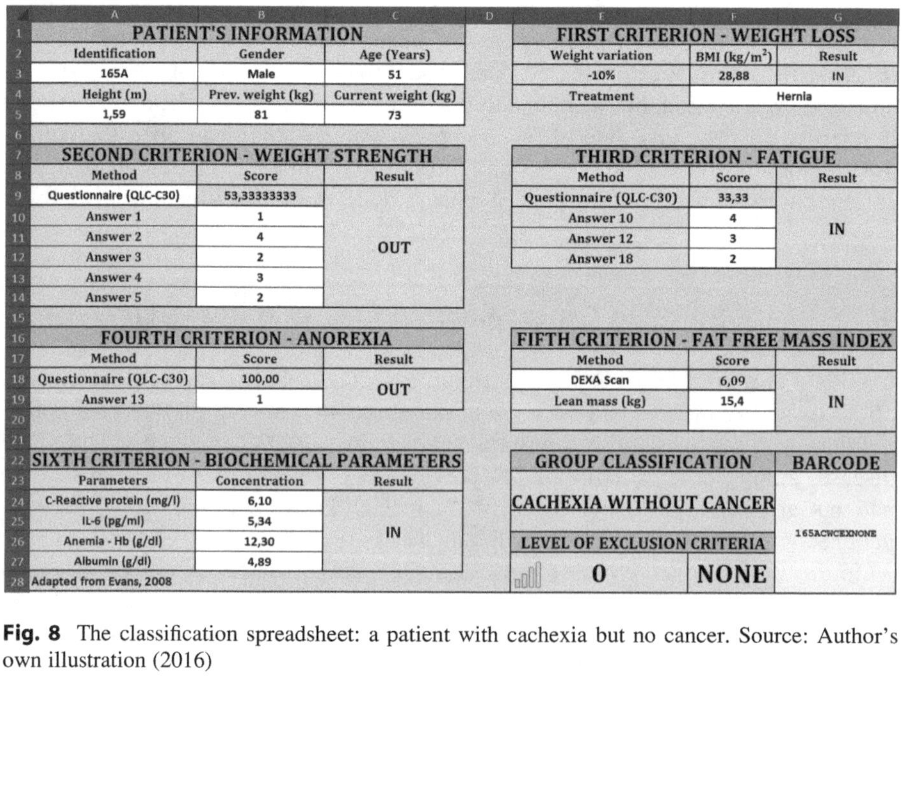

Fig. 8 The classification spreadsheet: a patient with cachexia but no cancer. Source: Author's own illustration (2016)

- Excluded By Weight
- Control
- Cancer Without Cachexia
- Cachexia Without Cancer (as in Fig. 8)
- Cancer Cachectic

The classification considers six complex criteria.

The first criterion (weight loss) computes the weight variation and BMI of the patient based on anthropometric information i.e. gender, age, height and weights. If the result of this criterion is IN, then the values match the definition of a cachectic patient, otherwise it will be OUT.

The QLQ-C30 quality-of-life questionnaire, used in international clinical trials in oncology (Aaronson et al. 1993), is used in the patient self-assessment and it is used in criteria 2–4. The measured biochemical values are considered in criteria 5 and 6.

The scoring "logic" is expressed by Excel formulas, created manually. A central disadvantage of this solution is that the formulas for each criterion and also the overall score calculation are very complex and not easy to read, understand and maintain. Figure 9 shows the formula corresponding to the second criterion.

Additionally, every data item of the patients has to be input manually, thus this tool is very error-prone, and a sheet is needed per patient.

In the case study, reported initially in Margaria et al. (2014), we combined the DyWA tool for data modelling (Neubauer et al. 2014) and the jABC to model the data management processes contained in the spreadsheet. As we use exactly the terminology of the spreadsheet, any researcher accustomed with these entities and concepts is equally able to create, understand, and ultimately work with the resulting models.

As an important side effect, these tools allow the automatic transfer of data from devices or storage to the database of DyWA, eliminating the current issue of data retrieval sheet by sheet.

Domain Modeling in DyWA To represent the domain entities, a user defines the "things" in that domain to be types. For example, the patient's anthropometric information, or the weight, height and age are types. Some types are basic, like the age to be an integer number, some others are composed types, with their attributes

```
=IF(AND(A9="Questionnaire (QLC–C30)";B10<>"";B11<>"";B12<>"";B13
    <>"";B14<>""); (1-(AVERAGE(B10:B14)-1)/3)*100; IF(AND(A9="
    Handgrip Test"; B3="Male"; B10<44;B10<>""); "POOR"; IF(AND(A9
    ="Handgrip Test"; B3="Male"; B10>44;B10<>"");"GOOD"; IF(AND(
    A9="Handgrip Test"; B3="Female"; B10<23;B10<>"");"POOR"; IF(
    AND(A9="Handgrip Test"; B3="Female"; B10>22;B10<>"");"GOOD
    ";"---")))))
```

Fig. 9 The excel formula for the score of the second criterion (cell B9). Source: Author's own illustration (2016)

also expressed in this way as types in DyWA. For example, the Patient Information is a composed type containing the anthropometric information but also the criteria score relative to this patient.

In order to manage the values for the types defined in DyWA, SIBs for the basic operations create, read, update, and delete (so called CRUD operations) are automatically generated for each of these types and provided in the jABC project to be used by the domain experts for designing processes that realize the functionality of the Excel formulas. While doing so, the DyWA domain model can still be improved and refined if there is any need.

Process Modeling in jABC Figure 10 exemplarily shows a process that calculates the Body Mass Index (BMI) of a patient. It reads the current weight and height of the patient, transforms them into the reference unit of measure (here we use the SI, thus meter and kilogram) and then calculates it stepwise following this formula:

$$BMI = \frac{weight(kg)}{height(m)^2}$$

The resulting BMI value is written to the DyWA database.

The process-oriented design shows another advantage of this realization, concerning uniform references and reusability: every unit modeled once with a "conversion factor" to meter or kilogram can be used for the input data. The conversion factor computation is a tiny process that can be shared in a large community and reused whenever it is needed. This flexibility of (data) conversions and mediations and the benefit of reuse (write-once principle) are especially helpful in international

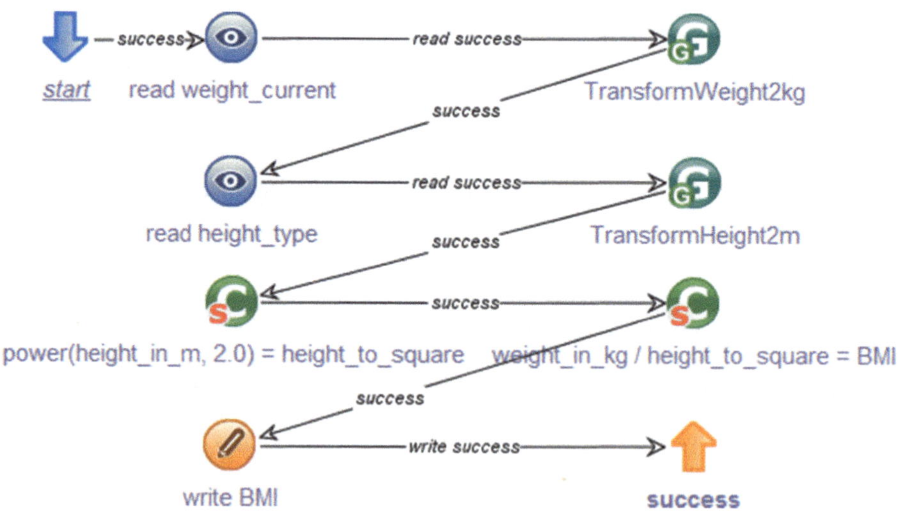

Fig. 10 The jABC process to calculate the BMI of a patient. Source: Author's own illustration (2016)

projects, with databases at different locations using different units and requiring a reliable and possibly uniform compatibility mediation.

The created process models are hierarchical and reuse a relatively large number of sub-processes. This leads to another advantage of our approach: All the threshold values used for the patient classification are set in one type. This renders anyone able to edit the threshold without touching the underlying model structure itself. In this way, the researcher can try several thresholds, e.g. to get a more accurate classification or when needing ad-hoc population segmentation.

The resulting web application can be shared and accessed worldwide. Furthermore, the framework allows the collection of anonymized data of patients in a central database repository, which also eases the work in this international project. While the processes are immediately executable and customizable, the scientific workflow itself is still open for adaptations.

4.2 Laboratory-Related Workflows in Cancer/Cachexia Research

In the course of the collaboration with the cancer/cachexia research group at the University of São Paulo, Brazil, we also collected exemplary documentation processes, which describe sample processing and raw data collection procedures in the lab and in the hospital.

These processes are carried out manually by the researchers and cannot (or at least not easily) be automated by computer software.

Figure 11 is a description of the physical training and assessment procedures that all patients taking part in the study have to follow. The physical training comprises seven weeks in total, where week "0" is a pre-training phase during which the patient is introduced to the training and his initial constitution is assessed. Weeks 1–6 require daily training on the treadmill, with additional tests performed at the end of weeks 3 and 6.

Figure 12 describes in greater detail the blood sampling procedure, which appears three times in the training protocol of Fig. 11. A nurse takes a number of blood samples from the patient, which are then processed in three different ways. The first is used for plasma analysis, and as shown in the figure it goes to centrifugation, the upper phase is kept on ice in an Eppendorf container labeled with "P", which is stored in a freezer at −80 °C until the blood profile analysis begins (described in yet another model).

For serum and lactate analysis, the Eppendorf containers are labeled with "S" and "L", respectively, and sent to a service company (RDO) for analysis.

These process models are reference processes, expressing best practices of how to do things (without embedded computations). In some sense they are only "drawings" that do not represent (automatically) executable processes, but being represented in the same formalism that we use for all other processes within the project, they are a simple and coherent means for documenting experimental procedures in an easily understandable way.

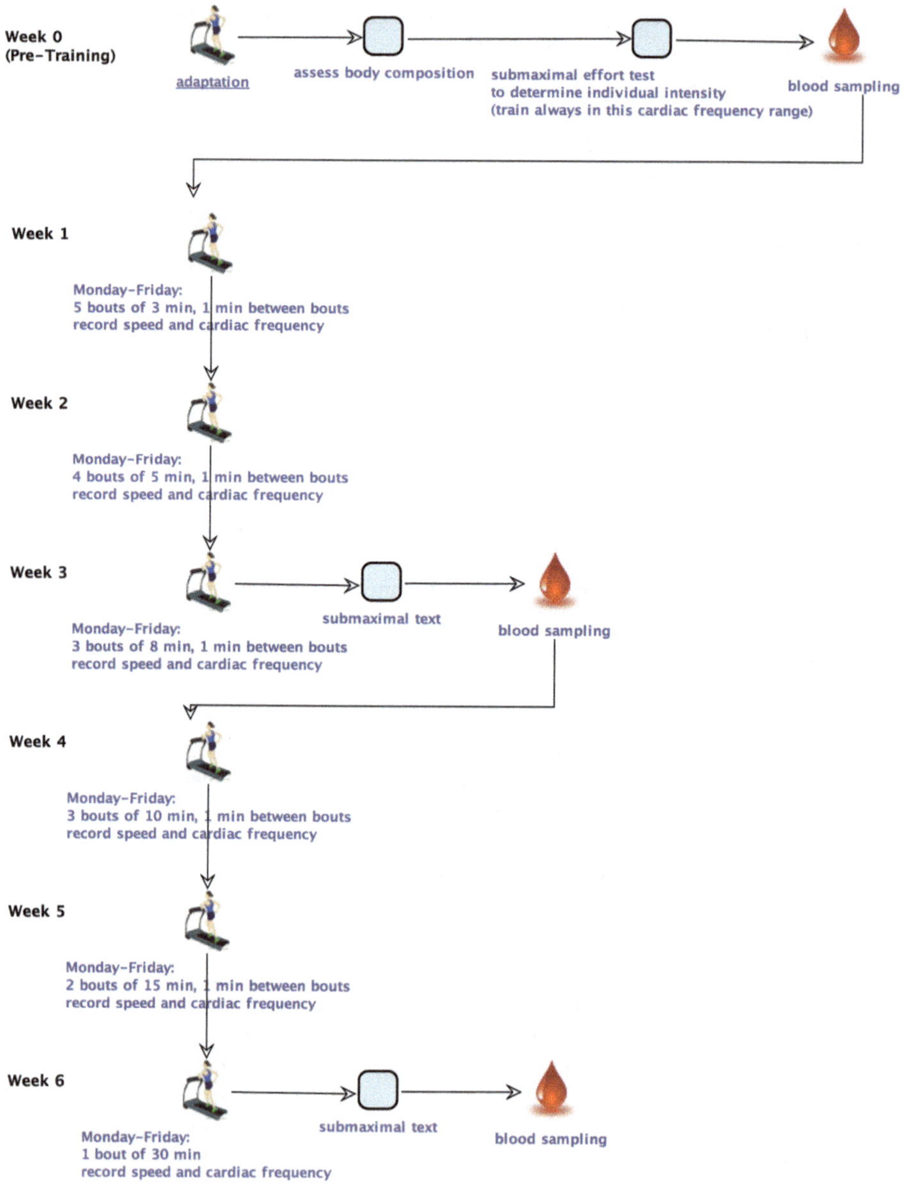

Fig. 11 Process describing patients' physical training and monitoring. Source: Author's own illustration (2016)

The recognized benefits are for documentation, for training of new personnel, for comparison with the practices in other labs, and to communicate and enforce standards of practice across different groups.

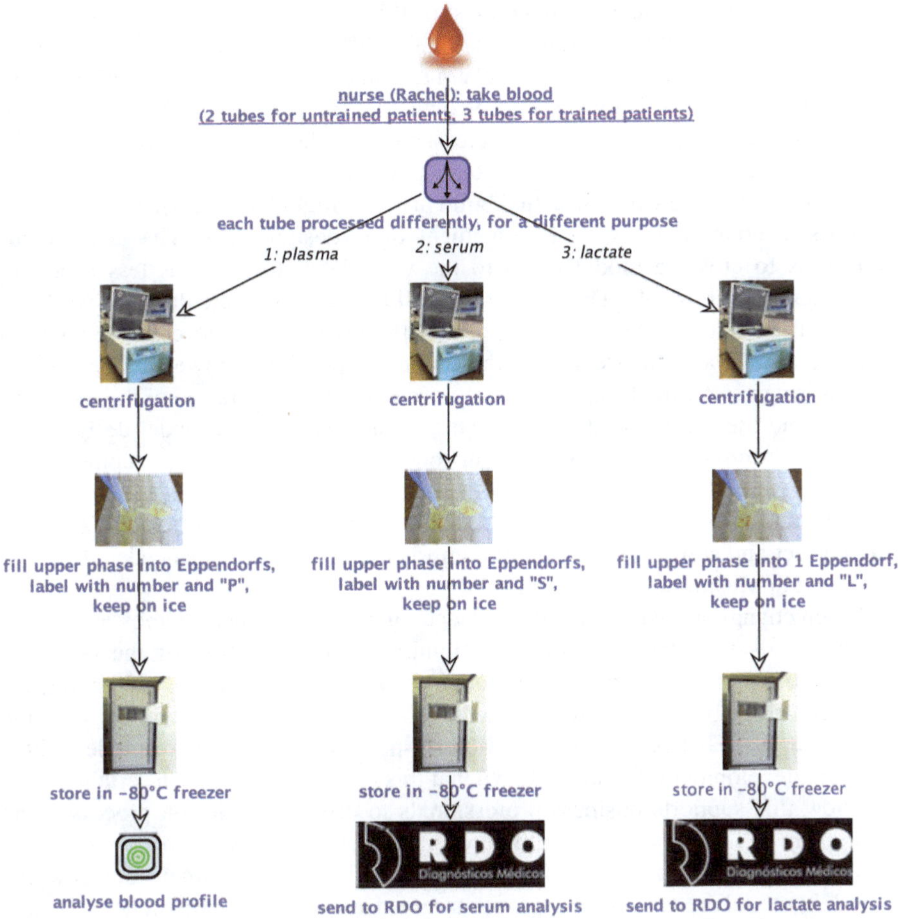

Fig. 12 Process describing the blood sample processing in the lab. Source: Author's own illustration (2016)

5 Conclusions

Business-related models are omnipresent in many of today's professional environments, including health care. They span organization charts, responsibility matrices, business process models as well as activity diagrams. While these models are meaningful by means of presenting key aspects of the modeled entity to the participating stakeholders, in practice most of these models do not go further than providing a graphical representation in terms of a drawing. However, there is a substantial difference between model drawing and the modeling of a software application, which is the difference between pure visualization versus programming.

For professionals other than IT-experts this difference sometimes is hard to recognize. This might result from the particular difference of software development compared to the classical use of models in architecture or engineering. All of these disciplines create a utilizable product as outcome. But in terms of creating physical structures like houses, bridges or vehicles a model rather serves as a blueprint to be transferred into physical reality at some point after its creation. The timespan between model design and the actual build process might be huge, spanning various analysis, evaluation as well as refinement or re-design steps. The goal in this context is to create a model down to the very detail to leave as less room for interpretation as possible. The succeeding build process is where the main work has to be carried out by professionals like construction workers to create a physical instance that is as consistent with the model as possible. However, the goal of model-driven software development is to overcome this separation of the modeling process and the actual build process. This would result in the model design itself being programming already, as program code of the target software is composed at modeling time. And deploying the software product and putting it to work might just be a question of minutes, provided that the model is sufficient, that is, structurally correct and complete in terms of comprising the components needed to weave the target application.

When changing the model and experiencing its outcome takes almost no time at all this leads to a basically different thinking and utilization of the outcome. Imagine the architect adding a few more shapes to the blueprint and having the modeled bridge built in just seconds without construction yard or any construction workers at all. That is the potential we are speaking of in terms of model-driven software development. We have shown that this is already reality to a certain degree and how this supports business professionals to effectively design processes and bring them to life in order to facilitate validation and push evolution.

With the illustrated case studies, we have sketched several dimensions in which a modern model driven design approach targeted at a direct domain modeling by the healthcare and subject matter experts themselves can provide a significant advantage of simplicity, natural intuition, and efficiency to the modeling itself, while offering "living models" that can be enacted and executed. This capability and flexibility are uncommon in today's IT system landscape, and we are confident that they can be coupled at an operation and management level within institutions and organizations with the strategic level of managing goals and ecosystems via the Business Modelling Tool described in Boßelmann and Margaria (2016) in order to deliver the 6S advocated in Rasche et al. (2016).

Acknowledgments This work was supported, in part, by Science Foundation Ireland grant 13/RC/2094 and co-funded under the European Regional Development Fund through the Southern & Eastern Regional Operational Programme to Lero—the Irish Software Research Centre (www.lero.ie). The case study on cancer-related cachexia research was partially funded by DAAD PROBRAL grant 369/12 (2011–2013).

References

Aaronson, N. K., Ahmedzai, S., Bergman, B., Bullinger, M., Cull, A., Duez, N. J., et al. (1993). The European organization for research and treatment of cancer QLQ-C30: A quality-of-life instrument for use. International clinical trials in oncology. *Journal of the National Cancer Institute, 85*(5), 365–376.

Allweyer, T. (2009). *BPMN 2.0 – Business process model and notation*. Books on Demand, Norderstedt.

Boßelmann, S., & Margaria, T. (2016). Guided business modeling and analysis for business professionals. In M. A. Pfannstiel & C. Rasche (Eds.), *Service business model innovation in healthcare and hospital management*. Wiesbaden: Springer.

Cioè, C. (2016). *Software requirements for a diabetic retinopathy centre*. Master's Thesis, Politecnico di Torino, Italy.

Evans, W., Morley, J. E., Argils, J., Bales, C., Baracos, V., Guttridge, D., et al. (2008). Cachexia: A new definition. *Clinical Nutrition, 27*(6), 793–799.

Margaria, T., Boßelmann, S., & Kujath, B. (2013). Simple modeling of executable role-based workflows: An application in the healthcare domain. *Integrated Design & Process Science, 17*(3), 25–45.

Margaria, T., Floyd, B., Lamprecht, A., Camargo, R. G., Neubauer, J., & Seelaender, M. (2014). Simple management of high assurance data in long-lived interdisciplinary healthcare research: A proposal. In T. Margaria & B. Steffen (Eds.), *Leveraging applications of formal methods, verification and validation* (Lecture notes in computer science, Vol. 8803, pp. 526–544). Berlin: Springer.

Margaria, T., Floyd, B. D., & Steffen, B. (2011). *IT simply works: Simplicity and embedded systems design* (pp. 194–199). Computer Software and Applications Conference Workshops (COMPSACW), IEEE 35th Annual.

Margaria, M., & Steffen, B. (2009). Business process modelling in the jABC: The one-thing-approach. In J. Cardoso & W. van der Aalst (Eds.), *Handbook of research on business process modeling* (pp. 1–26). Hershey, PA: IGI Global.

Margaria, T., & Steffen, B. (2010). Simplicity as a driver for agile innovation. *IEEE Computer, 43*(6), 90–92.

Margaria, T., & Steffen, B. (2011). *Special session on "Simplification through change of perspective"* (pp. 67–68). Software Engineering Workshop (SEW), 34th IEEE.

Margaria, T., & Steffen, B. (2012). Service-orientation: Conquering complexity with XMDD. In M. Hinchey & L. Coyle (Eds.), *Conquering complexity* (pp. 217–236). Wiesbaden: Springer.

Merten, M., & Steffen, B. (2013). Simplicity driven application development. *Integrated Design & Process Science, 16*(3), 9–23.

Neubauer, J., Frohme, M., Steffen, B., & Margaria, T. (2014). Prototype-driven development of web applications with DyWA. In T. Margaria & B. Steffen (Eds.), *Leveraging applications of formal methods, verification and validation* (Lecture notes in computer science, Vol. 8802, pp. 56–72). Berlin: Springer.

Rasche, C., Margaria, T., & Floyd, B. (2016). Service model innovation in hospitals – beyond expert organizations. In M. A. Pfannstiel & C. Rasche (Eds.), *Service business model innovation in healthcare and hospital management*. Wiesbaden: Springer.

Scheer, A. W. (1998). *ARIS – business process modeling* (2nd ed.). New York: Springer.

Seelaender, M., Laviano, A., Busquets, S., Pschel, G. P., Margaria, T., & Batista, M. L. (2015). Inflammation in cachexia. *Mediators of Inflammation, 2015*, 1–2. Article ID 536954.

Steffen, B., Margaria, T., Nagel, R., Jörges, S., & Kubczak, C. (2007). Model-driven development with the jABC. In E. Bin, A. Ziv, & S. Ur (Eds.), *Hardware and software, verification and testing* (Lecture notes in computer science, Vol. 4383, pp. 92–108). Berlin: Springer.

van der Aalst, W. (1999). Formalization and verification of event-driven process chains. *Information & Software Technology, 41*, 639–650.

White, S. A., & Miers, D. (2008). *BPMN modeling and reference guide*. Lighthouse Point, FL: Future Strategies Inc.

Steve Boßelmann is doctoral student at the Chair of Programming Systems at the Department of Computer Science, Technical University of Dortmund with the dissertation subject "Agile Process Management". He has interest and knowledge in Model-driven Software Development, Business Modeling and Business Process Management. As a researcher he has taken part in the EU-FP7-project "ITSy—IT Simply Works" to generate a set of innovative research topics on the notion of simplicity as a driving paradigm in ICT development. In the course of the project "Service Potentials in Personalized Medicine" he has developed an innovative approach to structured domain-specific business modeling and analysis.

Alexander Wickert holds a Diploma in Computer Science from University of Potsdam, Germany, where he is currently a PhD student at the Chair of Service and Software Engineering. He was previously part of the SHADOWS EU project on "Self-Healing Approach to Designing Complex Software Systems". His interests are in model driven development of service-oriented systems applied to healthcare and to scientific workflows, as well as in semantic models and domain specific languages.

Anna-Lena Lamprecht is a Research Fellow at Lero—The Irish Software Research Centre at the University of Limerick, Ireland, where she works on research projects on Continuous Software Development and on Software for Efficient Analysis of Complex Scientific Big Data. She has mainly worked in the areas of scientific workflows and computational science education, bringing together the work on scientific questions with modern software engineering methods. Her particular research focus is on the use of formal methods in the workflow design process, in order to provide domain-specific, semantics-based support that makes the semantic gap smaller and leverages application development to a higher level of abstraction. She obtained a Masters degree in Applied Computer Science from the University of Göttingen and a PhD (Dr. rer. nat.) from the TU Dortmund in Germany. Her doctoral dissertation with the title "User-level workflow design. A bioinformatics perspective." was published in Springer's LNCS series and received the 2013 dissertation award of the Faculty of Computer Science of the TU Dortmund. Before joining Lero, she was a research assistant (PostDoc) at the Institute for Computational Science at the University of Potsdam, Germany, where she extended her work to other scientific disciplines, in particular geoinformatics, business analytics, and medical research. She has joined the Research Data Alliance (RDA) and was called to the Advisory Board of the EMBRACE Data and Methods Ontology (EDAM). She is a member of the European Association for Software Science and Technology (EASST) and Managing Editor of its open access journal (ECEASST).

Tiziana Margaria is Chair of Software Engineering and Head of Department at the Dept. of Computer Science and Information Systems at the University of Limerick (Ireland). She is also a Principal Investigator of Lero, The Irish Software Research Center, where she is heads the Committee on International Relations Development. In Lero, she heads research projects on Scientific Workflow and model-driven HW/SW Cybersecurity. She received a Laurea in Electrical Engineering and a PhD degree in Computer and Systems Engineering from the Politecnico di Torino, Italy. She has broad experience in the use of formal methods for high assurance systems, in particular concerning functional verification, reliability, and compliance of complex heterogeneous systems, through major industrial projects (where she won the European IT Award in 1996, and a start-up competition in 2001) and consulting, as well as through her activities as founder and CEO of startup companies, holding two USPTO patents, one of which with NASA. She is currently Vicepresident of the European Association of Software Science and Technology (EASST), President of FMICS (the ERCIM Working Group on Formal Methods for Industrial Critical Systems), and steering committee member of ETAPS, the European joint Conferences on Theory and Practice of Software, member of the Board of EF-ICST, the European Forum on Information and Computation Science and Technology.

Lean Tools for Service Business Model Innovation in Healthcare

Elliott N. Weiss, Sean Jackson, Austin English, and Donald Stevenson

Abstract

In this chapter, we describe lessons learned from a number of lean process improvement projects we have implemented at the University of Virginia Health System (UVAHS). Working at multiple levels, facilities, and geographic locations has enabled us to become familiar with the organization's vast range of goals, initiatives, and needs. Lean project locations have included a remote clinic, the departments of medicine and radiology, and the advanced microscopy core facility. Other efforts have included the clinical research process; instructional support, billing and payroll processes; hiring, credentialing and onboarding processes; and high-level budgeting and planning. The chapter describes common themes and principles for successful lean transformations in health care operations. Most of these begin with a value stream analysis of a process whose value has never been evaluated across organizational or departmental (silo) boundaries or for which embracing continuous improvement as a way of life has never been seriously attempted. The emphasis is on implementation challenges.

E.N. Weiss (✉)
The Darden School, University of Virginia, Charlottesville, VA, USA
e-mail: WeissE@virginia.edu

S. Jackson
University of Virginia, Charlottesville, VA, USA
e-mail: sean.jackson@virginia.edu

A. English
RCF Associates, Charlottesville, VA, USA
e-mail: aenglish@rcfassociates.com

D. Stevenson
Gist Learning, Charlottesville, VA, USA
e-mail: don@gistlearning.com

M.A. Pfannstiel, C. Rasche (eds.), *Service Business Model Innovation in Healthcare and Hospital Management*, DOI 10.1007/978-3-319-46412-1_13

1 Lean Tools for Service Business Model Innovation in Healthcare

Lean is a systematic way to enhance value delivery, whatever form that value may take. Lean thinking frames every request for value as an opportunity to improve by teaching participants to notice wasteful action (or inaction), then carefully remove that waste, leaving the value intact. This can be achieved by anyone following three basic premises.

First, gather data to help you understand your customer's pain points, the criteria for improvement, and priorities for implementation. Second, set a standard for any means of value creation, recognizing that each standard must be protected relentlessly, not as an isolated project but as a continuous mission that involves engaging and empowering everyone in the enterprise. Third, the best way for value delivery to approach its ideal form is for changes to comprise removing waste wherever found, regardless of scale; what remains will reveal what is essential and invite a new evaluation, in a virtuous cycle of refinement.

Lean is not rocket science. One of our favorite definitions of Lean is "common sense rigorously and vigorously applied." Many of the solutions and recommendations are elegant in their simplicity. The hard part comes early, when initial implementation likely requires a shift in organizational culture toward heightened collaboration, empowerment, and cross-functional trust. Many firms attempt Lean transformations as a series of transactional improvements, but such attempts inevitably yield superficial and temporary results; for the necessary transformational change to occur, radical reforms are usually required, and some may not like it, at least at first. But once a firm survives that initial period of disruption and the individuals involved experience some quality of work-life benefit, the improved conditions, work flow, and productivity tend to speak for themselves.

Notice that the terms "manufacturing," "private sector," or "for-profit" have not been used in the above descriptions. The evolution of Lean techniques and vocabularies has historically taken place within manufacturing and the for-profit, private sector but has never been limited to it. In retrospect, yes, postwar Japanese manufacturing can be seen as uniquely fertile ground for the blossoming of such a system, but with every new application of its lessons, it becomes clear that Lean methods are universal in nature. Lean thrives on waste, and waste is everywhere—in the health care setting more than most, due in part to its uniquely dense conglomeration of technology, regulation, administration, and service delivery.

2 Lean's Early Development

After the Second World War, Toyota could not possibly have employed the mass-production techniques of Ford and General Motors, even if it wanted to. Henry Ford's assembly line model leveraged economies of scale and division of labor at the expense of choice ("any color, so long as it's black"); Alfred Sloan of GM adapted Ford's model to provide a modicum of product variety and customization.

Toyota had neither the capital to invest in such scale nor the market presence to justify it.

What Toyota did have was Taiichi Ohno, a mechanical engineer who started at the original Toyota, a spinning and weaving company, then transferred to Toyota's automotive division when the former dissolved in 1943. Within a few years following the war, Ohno was managing an engine machine shop. His means of controlling cost was not scale, which was prohibitive, but the elimination of waste, which might be anywhere. For Ohno, the idea of the loom as an autonomous machine maintained by human vigilance persisted as a metaphor in his mind, "a text book in front of my eyes." The notion of maintaining a steady flow of work through constant monitoring and improvement came naturally.

Meanwhile, Kiichiro Toyoda, son of the company's founder and initiator of its transition to automobiles, had a vision, also inspired by the automated looms, of what would eventually be known as Just-in-Time inventory management. With proceeds from his father's sale of loom patents, Toyoda presciently purchased simple and flexible manufacturing equipment, which allowed Ohno to retool frequently and experiment with small batch sizes of components. In this manner, Toyota (the firm) was able to make a variety of vehicles in relatively low numbers better matched to demand, with higher levels of quality and fewer defects. The process was inherently constructivist, that is, learned by doing, with elements adopted pragmatically from a range of sources, including American and German manufacturing. Most important, factory workers were empowered to innovate and refine as they went.

The process was not even documented until 1965, as the company sought to set up a pull system with its suppliers. A mere decade later, in the early to mid-1970s, oil prices forced a reevaluation of industry practices in the United States. This, in turn, led to the transfer of the Toyota system to the United States and to the development of a vocabulary of Lean. Ever since, Lean has increasingly been revealed—as its proponents have long understood—to be universally applicable to any enterprise in any culture.

3 Origin and Implications of Lean as a Term

The term Lean emerged in opposition to existing terms used to characterize manufacturing processes, perhaps most obviously in contrast to the "mass" in mass production. But it also emerged from a benchmarking model used by Haruo Shimada, a visiting professor at MIT during the study of the automotive industry in the 1980s (Holweg 2007). Shimada saw manufacturing on a continuum according to the manner in which it addressed risk. Western firms were deemed more "robust" or "buffered" due to the strategy of storing vast inventories and retaining redundant work forces as hedges, a figurative layer of fat taken on as insulation from any contingency, bringing with it large, unacknowledged and unnecessary costs.

In comparison, Japanese firms, considered by Shimada to be at the other end of the spectrum, were first described as "fragile," perhaps in the sense of vulnerable, then "Lean," to avoid negative connotation. Yet "fragile" bears a clue to another way of thinking about Lean, in terms of attunement, nurture, or sensitivity: a clear and prompt acknowledgment of any flaw, so that fixing it becomes more imperative. Robust, buffered operations may be insulated from shock, but volume and overreliance on insurance may obscure a sluggish indifference to detail.

To some, the term Lean may suggest austerity, but it is more about heightened awareness and energetic engagement. The irony is that a Lean operation is in no way starved—on the contrary, it retains everything it requires and only rejects what cannot nourish it anyway. A better metaphor related to nourishment might be that, as unnecessary additives and contaminants are removed, the nutritional impact of the main ingredients increases. Lean does not "make do." It allows an operation to thrive by removing distractions and returning constantly to what is most important.

4 Ohno's Categories of Waste: TIM WOOD (and U)

There are two Japanese terms and phrases associated with the diagnosis of a problem. "Going to the gemba" ("real place") suggests that no theory or metric will help so much as the detailed concrete information of direct observation, so the "gemba walk," or tour of the production space, is a routine element of Lean management.

Kaizen (literally, "change for good") can refer globally to continuous improvement efforts but frequently refers to a specific campaign or heightened investigative exercise in response to a perceived opportunity to improve. Theoretically, such scrutiny should be happening at all times, but the emergence of a defect sometimes presents an opportunity to redouble efforts and leverage momentum.

Central to Ohno's approach was the identification of muda, or wasteful activity; mura, unevenness in demand; and muri, unnecessarily difficult or complex activity, wherever it was found. Ohno arrived at seven categories of waste, since then often organized in English into the mnemonic TIM WOOD.

T = Transportation
I = Inventory
M = Motion
W = Waiting
O = Overproduction
O = Overprocessing
D = Defects

4.1 Transportation

Workflow that is neither direct nor smooth, with multiple zigzag movements or multiple material-storage locations, resulting in excess transport. In healthcare, transportation wastes are generally exacerbated by delays stemming from a centralized transportation department.

4.2 Inventory

Inventory in excess of immediate needs, sometimes indicative of a push system, where the emphasis is on keeping a resource busy, its productivity decoupled from downstream use and thus allowed to accumulate. In a production environment, inventory may be raw material, work-in-process or finished goods. Inventory is often undesirable because it (a) represents wasted labor deployed at unnecessary times; (b) hides defects, a common cause of much rework, and (c) bloats processes and lead times, inviting confusion. In health care environments, in addition to excess materials, inventory can be thought of as patients waiting for service, reports waiting to be analyzed or medical records waiting to be scanned into patient files.

4.3 Motion

Non-value-adding movement by workers. Widely dispersed material and excessive bending and reaching by the operator are examples of this type of muda. Poor work center layout and storage procedures frequently cause unnecessary operator motion, which may be either physical (looking for a hard copy of a file) or virtual (looking for a file on a computer drive). Poor room layout and rooming procedures may cause repeated minutes of wasted motion throughout a healthcare professional's day.

4.4 Waiting

Inefficient work sequence. Workers and other resources may be waiting for other workers or resources to finish a task, or work itself may be waiting for a worker or resource to become available. In healthcare environments, waiting for permission or authority tends to waste a significant amount of time.

4.5 Overprocessing

Work that adds no value to the product or service as experienced by the customer. Redundant processes and inconsistent quality standards are characteristics of processing waste, caused by such things as insufficient or unclear understanding of customer standards and poor process design. Over time, a legacy of ad hoc solutions failing to address root causes will create unnecessary, non-value adding work.

4.6 Overproduction

Producing ahead or in excess of demand. Overproduction can be recognized by variation in the workflow, excessive finished-goods inventory, and large batch sizes. It can result from an absence of procedural standards, poor forecasting, or an attempt to compensate for lengthy setup times.

4.7 Defects

Rework, scrap and returns. Excessive scrap and customer complaints are considered defects. Unsuited material and poor-quality workmanship/design are causes of this type of muda. Defects may be further characterized as "turn-backs" (defects found within the process) or "escapes" (defects found by the customer). By their nature, defects tend to be frowned upon, and in terms of reputation, escapes are regrettable, but in principle, turn-backs can and should be celebrated as opportunities for improvement. In some cases, the matter can be easily isolated and rectified; in others, the matter is systemic—even deadly—and calls for investigation.

4.8 Untapped Creativity

Frequently, a final form of waste is included for consideration: untapped creativity, or the squandering of an opportunity to enlist the imagination of those that perform the work in the solving of problems. Workers in a lean operation are given the latitude to improvise solutions as needs arise, and failing to do so can be considered a form of opportunity cost. In this vein, another of our working definitions of Lean is a continuous attempt to improve safety, quality, delivery and productivity by involving all employees in problem solving every day.

Table 1 Examples of waste in health care

Category	Health care
Transportation	Patient transport; medicine delivery
Inventory	Unnecessary supplies; patients backlogged in an emergency department
Motion	Searching for supplies; confusion over current policies and procedures
Wait	Patients waiting for doctors; clinics waiting for referral/order paperwork
Overproduction	Radiological images generated "just in case"
Overprocessing	Unnecessary tests; multiple checks
Defects	Incorrect medicines given; wrong site surgeries.
Muri (Overburden)	Ill-defined processes; understaffing
Mura (Unevenness)	Cyclical emergency room demand; uneven inpatient admission patterns; operating theater scheduling

Table 1 provides examples of the seven traditional waste categories applied to health care settings.

5 The Lean Process

Lean process improvement activities may take many forms. A widespread technique is A3 thinking, so-called because the processes are reported in a structured method using a single sheet of A3 paper, which measures 11 by 17 in. The technique was developed by Toyota and has since become standard work for reporting the results of improvement activities. The beauty of the format, particularly when compared to a multiple-slide PowerPoint deck, is that its structure encourages concision and ease of understanding. Additionally, A3 employs a version of the scientific method, something most professionals are familiar with, making adoption easier. Because the steps of the improvement process are clearly delineated, the reader knows exactly where to look for significant items. Perhaps most useful, A3 thinking provides associates with a shared problem-solving model that can be applied to proposal writing, status reporting, and almost anything else.

A3 thinking begins with the construction of a value stream map: a chart depicting existing process across multiple boundaries, carefully including multidisciplinary inputs in order to describe the existing state. Subsequently, a desired state value-stream map is also created in order to identify gaps between existing and anticipated outcomes. One metric frequently yielded by the initial value stream map is the breakdown of time spent on value-added and non-value-added activities.

The value stream map also helps identify another common source of waste in health care operations—a business structure or managerial style that perpetuates a silo mentality. Barriers put up by silo thinking hide the effects of decisions on processes, both upstream and downstream. The value stream map helps break down those silos by looking at the entire process and revealing interdependencies.

Problem-solving A3 reports usually consist of the following six elements or steps:

1. Problem Definition
   a. Why is this an important problem?
2. Current Condition
   a. What are the issues we are trying to improve?
   b. What are the metrics that indicate we have a problem?
   c. How does the current condition feel to the value stream members?
3. Goal/Target Condition
   a. What is the overarching goal?
   b. What outcomes are needed?
   c. How should the new work environment feel?
4. Analysis
   a. What is/are the root cause(s) of the problem?
   b. What else do we need to know to reach the target condition?

5. Countermeasures/Experiments/Recommendations
   (Because the map's thoroughness and accuracy will increase over the course of the process, any experimentation should be deferred until the mapping process has reached maturity.)
   a. What is/are the proposed countermeasure(s) to address each candidate root cause?
   b. What are the proposed experiments to move forward, learn, and better understand?
   c. What are the predicted results for each countermeasure?
6. Implementation and Sustainability Plan
   a. Who is responsible for what, by when?
   b. How will we maintain the gains?
   c. How will we ensure sustainable standard work?

Using the value stream as the context for problem solving keeps efforts focused, aligned, and linked to strategic imperatives. For example, leaders within a professional billing organization identified the capturing of surgical procedure charges as a process in need of improvement, but the team charged with addressing the problem grew frustrated by the complexity of the many interrelated workflows involved. Recognizing that they needed more context, the team regrouped and mapped the value stream in its entirety; this helped them identify specific "pain points" for their customers in the clinical departments, which they could then address systematically.

6 Some Health Care Lean Success Stories

We have successfully implemented Lean philosophy and A3 thinking in a number of health care settings at an academic medical center. These include:

- Value stream deployment was applied to the hiring, credentialing and onboarding process for newly hired medical staff. An improved understanding of the cross-functional, inter-departmental nature of approving new medical staff reduced the new hire process from an average of 3 months to an average of 3 weeks.
- The radiology department was able to double its monthly volume of medical imaging procedures while eliminating overtime and increasing employee satisfaction through a series of kaizen activities that emphasized the development of lean standard operating procedures, flow of patient care, and process ownership.
- A remote clinic improved its scheduling process and patient care effectiveness through better attainment of patient medical records, improved patient flow, and the development of a clinic-wide patient dismissal process using a cross functional team and A3 process improvement thinking.

- A redesigned value stream for the clinical research project approval process replaced departmental silos with a cross-functional team, decreasing response times and increasing approval percentages.
- A kaizen analysis of a surgery clinic uncovered opportunities to improve workflow, ultimately leading to reduced patient wait-times and increased patient satisfaction. Commonly observed causes for bottlenecks included multiple simultaneous initial visits, inefficient clinic layout, and inflexibility of staff roles. Using Lean principles, changes were made to improve clinic efficiency, including 1) limiting the number of initial visits during a single time block, 2) taking vitals in patient rooms to allow simultaneous review of patient charts, and 3) cross-training staff to perform multiple roles within clinic.

7 Lessons Learned

Our experience with these and other health care improvement projects has taught us the following key principles while implementing Lean within a health care setting.

1) Focus on the patient

   Our initial definition of Lean—the relentless pursuit of creating value through the strategic elimination of waste—makes it clear where all Lean projects must start: the patient. We seek to increase value for the patient through better outcomes or experiences, faster delivery, less angst and worry, or more comfort.

   Any Lean initiative in a clinical setting must begin with the patient's experience traveling through a health care delivery system that is often unnecessarily complex. To make the often ephemeral nature of services more tangible, we advise focusing first on products whose quality the patient can readily evaluate. For example, patients often visit their doctor to seek relief from physical or psychological pain or some explanation of its cause. In the latter case, the value is the diagnosis. When we conceive of the diagnosis as a product, we can ask our patients what qualities they value in a diagnosis, which might include accuracy, conclusiveness, timeliness, empathy, and empowerment. Armed with this knowledge, we can align our various processes to support the delivery of a high-quality diagnosis.

   Since the goal is continuous improvement, we need a measure upon which to improve. We must ask: what are the specific results by which we will measure those outcomes? In kaizen meetings, we try to get participants focused on the need to satisfy the patient, driving the conversation toward specific outcome and performance measures. Prioritizing the needs of the patients over those of providers or facilities taps into the main reason the majority of care givers entered the profession—a desire to help people—further motivating continuous improvement efforts.

   The challenge in healthcare, of course, is that in addition to the patient and medical providers, there are several other stakeholders involved: (1) the patients' families, friends and employers; (2) multiple levels of providers, including medical specialists and generalists, doctors, nurses and technologists; (3) payers, such as insurance companies, Medicare and Medicaid; and (4) institutional managers and administrators, including admission offices, billing departments, dining services and other ancillary services. Thus, it is difficult to use a definition of "quality" such as meeting or exceeding the customer's needs. We find it useful to separate these "customers" into three, often overlapping, groups. The groups (see Linden 1992) answer the questions: (1) Who uses? (The consumer, or patient), (2) Who pays? (The client) and (3) Who cares? (The constituent). This categorization permits us to take the point of view of the multiple stakeholders in the delivery of care. Coupled with the product focused method outlined above, we can ask specific questions about the components of value to members of the three groups.

2) Go to the gemba

Problems cannot be identified, defined and solved from the comfort of one's office. To learn the real issues, one must "go and see"—go to the gemba: the "real place," the location where value is created. Tying this to our first recommendation informs us that we must "walk in the patient's shoes" to understand his/her interaction with the health care system and understand the places where waste exists. In our successful kaizens at the remote clinics and at the surgery clinic, we did exactly this. It would have been foolish for us to hypothesize what was actually going on without some actual data, observations, and measurements and interviews with providers and patients. Lean success depends on action based on data, facts and analysis, most often a root cause analysis. This can occur only through a total understanding of what occurs at the gemba. Successful process improvement projects start with data and observations, not standards. The goal is to close the gap from a current state to a target condition, and that current state cannot be assumed or envisioned; it must be identified in person.

The action to "go and see" is often called a gemba walk. The gemba walk serves two purposes: it allows for the observation of the actual process and, perhaps more important for senior management, assists in the development of front-line providers. Gemba walks are opportunities for the management team to ask questions and to develop employees by asking appropriate questions and cultivating problem-solving skills.

3) Metrics

Any data collected at the gemba must be relevant, significant and free of misplaced precision. All waste is not created equal. The focus should be on gathering enough data about waste to describe the current state of the entire process. Better to emphasize the whole over any one part. For example, spending an inordinate amount of energy measuring the amount of time it takes for an arriving patient to be shown to the next available exam room may ignore the amount of time the patient then spends waiting in that exam room for a healthcare professional. Likewise, in the authors' experience, it is more productive to devote time and attention to waste upstream or downstream of the doctor/patient encounter. Our experience supports the efficacy of Dr. John Toussaint's

(Toussaint et al. 2010) concept of the "middle flow" (where the doctor and patient meet) and his assertion that while this "middle flow" cannot be standardized, it can be made more effective and predictable. On one gemba walk, we observed a number of rooms, assigned to individual providers, that remained vacant and unused. This ultimately resulted in a total revamp of provider scheduling and patient flow. The objective must be to measure things that matter and improve their performance, while ignoring any background noise.

4) Understand the entire value stream

Health care problems are inherently cross-functional and multi-disciplinary; they can rarely, if ever, be solved in isolation. Think of a patient who needs a body imaging procedure. Exhibit 2 depicts the steps that must be done to complete a procedure. Notice that the process is interdisciplinary; any improvement, therefore, must include stakeholders from every department involved.

If the goal of the body imaging department were to do more procedures, the initial reaction might be "we need more capacity." By looking at the entire value stream, however, we are more likely to be able to see where interactions with other parts of the health system might impact our own capacity. Thus it is essential to include representatives from all key departments in order to understand the impact of other areas upon our own performance.

Exhibit 2

The referring physician entered an order for the procedure, which then had to be reviewed and approved by a Body Imaging Department (BID) physician to ensure that the desired work could be safely performed. The procedure then often had to be pre-approved by the patient's insurance company before scheduling could occur. Once scheduled, the patient sometimes took required medications that could potentially increase the complication risk of the procedure prior to arrival in the reception area. Other pre-procedure activities also needed to take place, including issuing an ID badge and providing procedural clothing, educational information, and consent material to the patient. Once in a pre-procedure room, a physician visited the patient to obtain consent for the requested procedure, answer questions, and enter any special orders. A nurse began an IV for the patient, who was sometimes sedated or otherwise medicated in preparation for the procedure. The patient was then taken to the appropriate imaging room (if available) and then positioned as required for the procedure, which was then conducted by the attending physician and designated resident/fellow (physician in training). At this point, any special orders that had been entered for the patient required additional approvals before the procedure could begin.

After the procedure was performed and images obtained, the patient was transported to a recovery area which was staffed by a nurse. The patient, once

(continued)

recovered, was discharged, which required coordination with health system transportation and other discharge services. The image was sent for interpretation by a radiologist, either in preliminary form by a trainee or directly by the attending radiologist. This report and accompanying images were then routed to the referring physician as well as to the appropriate electronic medical record. A bill for services rendered was generated and ultimately filed (sometimes weeks later) with the insurance company and also potentially with the patient as well, generally when specific costs were not covered by the patient's insurance. The rooms utilized for the procedure were cleaned after the procedure was completed.

5) Attain top management commitment

Lean, done correctly, transforms an organization. Lean implementation is about managing change—changing the way an organization works and thinks about improving processes. Such transformational change is not possible without strong leadership and a commitment to staying the course when intermediate roadblocks loom. Additionally, the leadership team must provide a vision of where the organization needs to go and the resources to get there. Decisions must be made that reinforce the Lean journey and support people to take steps on those journeys. Ideally, the leader has a palpable enthusiasm, an appropriate sense of urgency and a commitment to investing whatever is necessary to provide a relentless focus on process improvement. This leader will not confuse effort with success.

We have found that the order of attacking problems significantly affects the sustainability of results. All too often, probably because as stated earlier the term "Lean" implies cutting fat, "Lean" efforts focus initially on cost cutting and gains in efficiency. The problem is that any gains achieved might be short-term only and result in negative connotations of layoffs and overwork. Some people equate Lean with laying people off. In most scenarios, people can be redeployed. This can have the dual result of "leaning out" your processes, and repositioning your company for growth and staffing that growth at the same time.

We find that focusing on quality and delivery first not only improves the patient and caregiver experience, but also results in long-term cost savings. Indeed, at the University of Virginia Health System, the first 2 years of the improvement experience were entitled "Be Safe," a process that no one could argue with, yet resulted in improved patient quality while preparing and training employees for a more "standard" approach to Lean. Likewise, "quick and easy" wins often show the benefits of the new system.

Is there anything that can be done without the benefit of a strong leader or leadership team? We think so, but it may be more difficult to achieve and sustain success. We have seen instances where local initiatives by informed managers yield results and then create a "pull system" where other people are interested in learning how these results occurred. For example, two of the authors of this chapter have developed personal kanban boards in order to manage projects visually. When our colleagues see these boards and we explain how they are used, they often decide: "I want one too!"

One clinic decided to get serious with continuous improvement. After reaping the benefit of their work and sharing the information with other curious individuals, multiple other clinics have now visited to learn how they too could become involved in Lean and create their own improvements. No higher leadership was involved with sharing or encouraging the other clinics' activities.

6) Develop people

Recall that one of our definitions is that Lean is a continuous attempt to improve safety, quality, delivery and productivity by involving all employees in problem solving every day. We like to say: "It's the people, stupid!" Our goal as managers is not to solve problems. Our goal is to provide resources and recruit and train the right people so that they can identify and solve the problems in a timely manner at the source of the problem. Ballé and Régnier (2007) state: "The Toyota veterans are fond of saying, lean is about "making people before making parts" or, in the wards' context, developing nurses before delivering care."

One of the best ways to convince people to take part in a Lean effort is to address the issue: "WIIFM?" ("What's in it for me?) Care givers are motivated by providing better service to their patients. Lean must be "sold" to them by assuring them that they will be able to provide better service to their patients while also offering a possibility of instilling some favorable level of sanity in their own working lives. Combining this with a shared, disciplined problem solving system, standard work for fixing things that are broken, will also improve outcomes. We must provide a system for continually improving and strive to continually improve that system.

7) Go low tech first

While it is true that, in theory at least, automating processes can reduce the impact of waste by making it "go faster," it is not a sustainable approach. Automating waste will only transform relatively tractable and inexpensive process waste into more expensive and intractable software waste, which will then be inflicted on anyone who must use the software system. Better to remove the waste first, using low-tech, lean tools, then invest in automating value-adding processes within a given value stream. Such an approach usually produces a palpable, unqualified reduction in cycle times while increasing employee morale. After all, the quality of the tools an organization provides its associates conveys unmistakably the level of respect and regard in which they are held.

8) Don't let perfect get in the way of better

A vision of perfection could conceivably spur continuous improvement but more likely will delay it. Standards of patient care are high, but so are the penalties for mistakes; a culture of "shame and blame," where mistakes are punished, will lower risk tolerance across the board. W. Edwards Deming, a key pioneer in the quality movement, reminded us how vital it is to "drive out fear," for it is fear that allows perfection to thwart improvement. The antidote to fear is respect, and with respect, everyone involved in the health care system—patients, payers, and healthcare providers alike—is more likely to embrace what is "good enough for now," recognizing that in a culture of continuous improvement, there will always be an opportunity for more.

Additionally, we have found that when a team seeks improvement through a series of many small experimental steps in rapid succession, they can afford the occasional failure and progress more quickly and effectively. We find that people are much more willing to experiment without overanalyzing the situation than they are to implement an "action plan." This may sound like semantics, but the results are positive.

The key here is that the part of our initial Lean definition that really matters is the idea of "relentless pursuit." Rather than suffer from "paralysis by analysis," the successful Lean project involves constant striving. A continual loop of "gain, sustain, repeat" will yield better patient outcomes and experiences.

8 Conclusion: Lean as Differential Diagnosis

Lean is often about a range of small enhancements that, added up, enhance operations to a surprising extent. One potential obstacle to health care workers, accustomed to focusing on big ideas or responding to urgent client needs, is that they may consider some of these examples too mundane to matter much. What they may not realize is that the tiniest removal of unnecessary activity will tend to make a process substantially more sensible, clearing away unnecessary distractions that otherwise will tend to add up to major complications. The benefits may only become obvious after the waste is removed, but to harried care givers and the patients they serve, the resulting boost in quality of care can feel like a new lease on life.

References

Ballé, M., & Régnier, A. (2007). Lean as a learning system in a hospital ward. *Leadership in Health Services, 20*(1), 33–41.

Holweg, M. (2007). The genealogy of lean production. *Journal of Operations Management, 25*, 420–437.

Linden, R. (1992). Meeting which customer's needs. *The Public Manager – The New Bureaucrat, 21*, 49–53. Winter 1992–1993.

Toussaint, J., Gerard, R. A., & Adams, E. (2010). *On the mend*. Cambridge, MA: Lean Enterprise Institute.

Elliott N. Weiss is the Oliver Wight Professor of Business Administration at the Darden School of Business at the University of Virginia. Weiss teaches in the Operations area and is the author of numerous articles in the areas of production management and operations research; he has extensive consulting experience, for both manufacturing and service companies, in the areas of production scheduling, workflow management, logistics, total productive maintenance, and lean implementation. He is the author of the book, The Lean Anthology, and over 175 cases and technical notes in the area of operations management.

Sean Jackson is the CIO of the University of Virginia School of Medicine. He joined the University of Virginia Physicians Group as its Chief Information Officer (CIO) in December 2011. In this dual role he has operational responsibility for the Information Technology function across both organizations. A Lean practitioner and Six Sigma Black Belt, Sean has more than 20 years of experience leading technology operations in complex non-profit and higher education organizations including 6 years in various technology leadership roles at Yale University and 5 years as the Director of Advanced Technologies at the Howard Hughes Medical Institute. Sean established and led the global PMO for Stanley Black and Decker where he was responsible for IT portfolio management and strategy deployment (Hoshin Kanri).

Austin English is President of RCF Associates and is an expert in implementing Lean Enterprise practices to improve operational performance. Austin's successful line operations experience is the basis of his ability to convert business theories into practical bottom-line solutions. His two decades of managing change enable him to foresee problems and assist clients in avoiding potential pitfalls. He has helped transform various organizations in multiple industries as diverse as cosmetics, health care, education, construction, aerospace and shipbuilding.

Donald Stevenson is owner and operator of Gist Learning, specializing in writing and editing of educational materials. Prominent among his clients are faculty members of the University of Virginia's Darden School of Business.

Continuous and Co-creative Business Model Creation

Seppo Kuula and Harri Haapasalo

Abstract

Digitalization is feeding globalization, breaking the industrialization-driven business, marketing, and management logics. The industrial revolution came about in order to create efficiency in scale, whereas the digital revolution is scaling creativity and creating inter-industry competition. Customer interface owners are winners in this change, where customer-oriented service design is in the key role and the value chain becomes pull-directed. The internet is accelerating the speed of everything. Product, service, and design life cycles are getting shorter. It is difficult to create a sustainable competitive advantage in a constantly changing business environment, especially with hardly-protected digital components. The durability of the business model has to be constantly compared to the changing business environment, and continuous iterative business development is required for an agile response to challenges and opportunities.

Where digitalization has returned individual customer needs to the center of value creation, replacing industrialization-driven mass production and market share, the transition towards service—dominant business logic (SDL) is accelerated. Based on SDL, in the service economy neither product nor service creates value on its own—value is co-created with the customer. Business model development is an interesting and understudied notion, especially in the value co-creative business environment where business development happens continuously with the customer. The main contribution of this paper is the framework for continuous business model development in a digitalization-driven, service-dominant, co-creative business environment, which we present

S. Kuula (✉) • H. Haapasalo
Industrial Engineering and Management, University of Oulu, P.O. Box 4610, 90014 Oulu, Finland
e-mail: Seppo.kuula@siili.com; harri.haapasalo@oulu.fi

M.A. Pfannstiel, C. Rasche (eds.), *Service Business Model Innovation in Healthcare and Hospital Management*, DOI 10.1007/978-3-319-46412-1_14

through a descriptive case study of business model innovation in the health care business.

1 Introduction

Service is the focus of economic exchange in all the developed economies, driving business and marketing thinking towards service-dominant logic (SDL) (e.g. Edvardsson et al. 2012; Grönroos and Gummerus 2014; Gummesson et al. 2010; Vargo and Lusch 2004, 2008, 2014). Based on SDL, in the service economy neither product nor service creates value on its own—value is co-created with the customer. In other words value is embedded in the value creation processes rather than provided as a service to the customer. Co-creation allows for customized services (products) while still taking advantage of economies of scale. Still, most of the business models are goods dominant, which has its roots in industrialization, as do traditional management and organizational structures (Vargo and Lusch 2014).

Digitalization is accelerating globalization and returning the customer to the center of business modeling, driving us away from the misconception of service mass-production. Digitalization offers us more opportunities to get personalized services for our individual needs and is restoring appreciation of customer interface ownership and customer encountering processes. In the digital age any business, especially any service-oriented business, can be challenged and replaced with something more user friendly, useful, and/or something cheaper. New challengers competing not only with the new embodiment of the offering and value proposition but especially with totally new business models (Kuula et al. 2015).

Digitalization has not only raised the interest of many researchers in the question of defining a "business model" but also generated new genuine interest in continuous business model development. We offer a broadened view of business model literature (e.g. Hamel 2002; Magretta 2002; Timmers 1998), exploring it from a SDL perspective and taking into account constant change and continuous business model evolution (e.g., Chesbrough 2007; Osterwalder et al. 2010).

In 1994 Drucker already saw that the theory of a business has to be tested constantly as it is only a hypothesis about things that are in constant change (markets, customers, technology). Digitalization is driving technology development fast and the third wave of industrialization is reforming markets towards service-dominant change. The so-called change model describes how a company can analyze the need and scope of the required changes in a business model. The logic of innovations needs to be understood in order to comprehend the dimensions of the required changes. (Christensen 2010; Govindarajan and Trimble 2010; Suikki et al. 2006).

In this article our aim is to broaden the view of business model literature with an SDL perspective introduced above, and to present the process of continuous business model development in service-dominant business creation through a descriptive case study of a health care business environment. We have operationalized our aim in to the following research questions:

RQ1: What kind of framework enables analysis for continuous business model development?
RQ2: What kind of business model dynamics can be seen in our case study?

The logic and methodology of this study are described in Fig. 1. First we reviewed literature to find out the acknowledged definitions and approaches behind SDL and business model creation and transformation. Subsequently we created a synthesis of the studied literature to provide a framework for understanding and steering continuous and co-creative business model development. Then we studied how to systematically utilize the created business model development framework in a practical business-to-business environment using a qualitative and descriptive single case study. Finally, we discuss and analyze the findings in relation to existing theories in order to represent a generalized solution addressing a class of problems moving conceptually from an organization-specific instance onto a more abstract level, concluding the paper with the scientific and practical contributions of the research.

Our empirical case is an innovative Finnish health care provider, Heltti Ltd. (www.heltti.fi). Heltti was founded in 2013 to redefine the occupational healthcare and wellbeing services in Finland, promoting empathy, wellbeing, and health, not just treating the diseases. They have been very active in business model development regarding the requirements coming from public authorities and the needs of their direct customers. They have renewed their offering and business model several times during their rather short existence. Therefore, we selected Heltti as a case study organization.

In our empirical study, data collection was done in two different phases between 2014 and 2016. In the first phase Heltti's offering was analyzed as a customer organization from public material. Then we had an in-depth interview for the founder and owner of Heltti. The first interview was done to connect their business model overall to a business model framework and learn about their evolution. After understanding the business model development cycles we organized more formal and detailed interviews along our theoretical framework for service-dominant

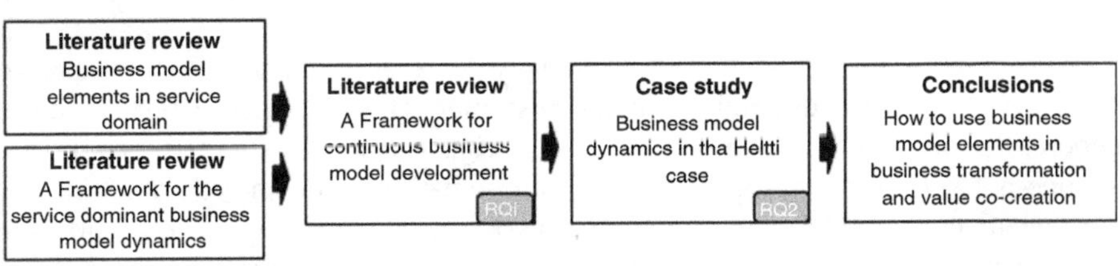

Fig. 1 The logic of this article

business model development. Analysis of all case study material was then presented on Heltti's business model development framework.

2 Business Model Elements in the Service Domain

Strategic thinking in the labile, altering business environment cannot be limited to products, services, or businesses. The firm has to be capable of envisioning the future of its industry and then going out to co-create it with its customers. The business model is a key element to consider when business logic is changing.

2.1 Literature Review: Service Dominant Logic

Service science sees service systems as the value creational configurations of people, technology, value propositions, and shared information (Maglio and Spohrer 2008). Prahalad and Ramaswamy (2000) already stated 15 years ago that value co-creation with the customer will replace the traditional goods exchange process because of the internet and collective knowledge of the available solutions. In this configuration customers are part of the enhanced network; they co-create and extract business value and are simultaneously collaborators, co-developers, and competitors. A few years later Vargo and Lusch (2004, 2008) introduced SDL through ten foundational propositions (FPs). They saw "service" as the application of competences that benefit each other (co-creation) and as the focus of economic exchange. This thinking led to a shift from operand resource exchange to operant resource exchange (e.g., competencies, knowledge, and skills). Within this logic the operant resources are the fundamental source of competitive advantage. Products are just a distribution mechanism for the service provision.

According to Vargo and Lusch (2004, 2008) SDL is based on the implication that value is defined and co-created with the consumer (FP6), where core competencies are the competitive advantages (FP1). This thinking leads to wide cross-organizational collaboration between the supplier and customer. Turning marketing logic from "making, selling, and servicing" to "listening, customizing, and co-creating" requires alignment between marketing, development, and delivery organizations. The approach is based on customers' strategic needs. The organizational foundation of SDL lies in transparent collaboration, and SDL sees all social and economic actors as resource integrators and therefore all economies as service economies.

SDL's definition states that value is always co-created by the supplier and the customer, and always determined by the customer. This definition is questioned in general (Grönroos and Gummerus 2014; Grönroos and Voima 2013) and the service-marketing-based approach sees value creation to be shared sometimes as a value in use (in SDL) but sometimes as a value in exchange, depending the maturity and relationship of organizations and actors. As the definition of "value" is not mathematically exact and value creation therefore cannot implicitly be defined,

SDL should be seen more as a service business and marketing framework than implicit theory (Vargo and Lusch 2004, 2008). Later the founding fathers of SDL have returned to further explore SDL and presented SDL as a reconceptualization of service, seen as the process wherein an actor uses its resources for the benefit of another (Vargo and Lusch 2014). Vargo and Lusch presented the original foundation points in the following four axioms:

- Axiom 1 underlined FP1: Service is the fundamental basis of exchange. Service is always exchanged for a service (operant resources).
- Axiom 2 underlined FP6: The customer is always a co-creator of the value (an interactive value creation process).
- Axiom 3 underlined FP9: All economic and social actors are resource integrators. Value creation is a network of networks.
- Axiom 4 underlined FP10: Value is always uniquely determined by the beneficiary; value is experiential and conceptual.

They also explored the core conceptualization in more detail, claiming that all actors (individuals, firms, nations) are fundamentally doing the same core activities in engaging with resource integration, exchanging service for service, and acting simultaneously as consumers and producers (Vargo and Lusch 2014). Edvardsson et al. (2012) studied resource integration and value co-creation in detail, suggesting that value is contextual and reliant on structure, which is iteratively changing itself with every instance of resource integration. Service innovation in the SDL framework is broadened to involve three different elements; the service ecosystem, the service platform, and value co-creation (Lusch and Nambisan 2015).

The study saw that a common worldview, architectural alignment, and the structural flexibility of organizations were required for co-creative service innovation. Applying SDL means that the firm is not only restricted to making value propositions but also gets opportunities to actively and directly participate in value creation with its customers. The value proposition is still required for engaging the customers but the whole value architecture—including the delivered product and/or service, the revenue model, and the organization—have to interactively deliver and co-create the proposed value. A personalized co-creation experience should suit the customer's unique desires and preferences rather than company's supply chain.

2.2 Literature Review: The Business Model

The business model concept is neither unambiguous nor commonly understood. Literature talks widely about the business model and clearly neither most business executives can describe the business model of their company (Pekuri et al. 2014), nor can most researchers agree about it and consistently present it in the literature. The term appeared in the literature for the first time in the 1970s but became more commonly used in the late 1990s, after web-based business more commonly took place as a complementary offering of forerunning IT businesses (Suikki et al. 2006).

Peter F. Drucker (1994) explored the topic for the first time in The theory of the business as "the assumptions about what a company gets paid for," connecting the business environment, mission, and core competencies. Within his article he used the phrase "the theory of the business" instead of "business model" but this can be seen as one of the earliest descriptions of the business model. Drucker also requested clarity and a rationale for enabling companywide communication about the "theory'" or the "model" of the business. We present this framework later in this study, aiming to support this communication as well as to enable testing of the required changes of the business model.

Slywotzky (1996) regards a business model as "the totality of how a company selects its customers, defines and differentiates it offerings, defines the tasks it will perform itself and those it will outsource, configures its resources, goes to market, creates utility for customers and captures profits." He also sees the need for customer-centric business design as a baseline and business model development as a never-ending interactive process.

One of the most-cited articles about business models was written by Timmers (1998), offering a framework of business models for e-commerce. He pointed out that the literature is not consistent in the usage of the term business model. Timmers (1998) described a business model as an architecture for the product, service, and information flows that includes

1. a description of the various business actors and their roles,
2. a description of the potential benefits (value) for the various business actors, and
3. a description of the sources of revenues.

The value chain's construction in e-commerce was carefully thought through as the article was written in the pretty early days of digital commerce and digitalization. Value creation and the value chain are clearly the essential parts of a business model and are therefore selected as the key elements in the business model framework presented later.

Hamel (2002) described a business model as a business concept that has been put into practice. For Hamel a business concept comprises four major components:

1. Core strategy
2. Strategic resources
3. Customer interface
4. Value network

Again, he sees core strategy as a combination of a business mission, market scope, and the elements of differentiation. Strategic resources include core competencies, assets, and processes. Hamel (2002) sees the connection between resources and strategy as the competitive factor, calling it a "configuration." This configuration is further explored as an important liaison element of the framework presented later.

Another much-cited article about business models was written by Linder and Cantrell (2000) who presented a business model as "the organization's core logic for creating value," in short, as a way for a firm to generate revenue. Linder and Cantrell (2000) outline the key elements of the business model:

1. Revenue sources (value)
2. Revenue streams (offering, value proposition)
3. Resources

All these elements are formed together to answer the question Why are we one organization? The description of the offering (the value proposition) is clearly another essential element of the business model, and the change model is further studied later in this paper.

Magretta (2002) cites Seybold et al. (2001), and Drucker (1994) in her well known HBR article Why Business Model Matter. Seybold and Lewis doom most of the web-based business models in the middle of the dot-com bubble as stories without content, and Magretta (2002) observes that the fault was not in business model thinking but in its misuse. Magretta encapsulates a business model as an answer to Peter Drucker's old question "Who is the customer and what does the customer value?" Magretta (2002) defined a business model as both the narrative part of "the story that explains how an enterprise works" and numbers that sum up how a company makes money from its activities.

Chesbrough and Rosenbloom (2002) were instructive in defining the revenue model in conjunction with the identification of the market and corresponding competition. They defined the functions of a business model as

1. value proposition,
2. market segment identification,
3. the structure of the value chain,
4. revenue generation mechanisms,
5. positioning in the value network, and
6. competitive strategy.

Johnson and Christensen (2008) presented a fresh approach for business model innovation in Reinventing Your Business Model. This article focused on the innovative business models from the past decade. The article saw a business model as consisting of four elements:

1. Customer value proposition (the customer problem it solves)
2. Profit formula (how it makes money for a firm)
3. Key resources
4. Key processes

To determine whether a firm should develop or change its business model, Johnson and Christensen (2008) advise three steps: Determine what makes your existing model successful, identify the signals treating your business model, and decide whether reinventing your model is worth the effort. Christensen (2010) also defined a type of technological shift he called disruptive technology, a shift that changes the basis of competition in an industry. This disruption has become more common in the midst of digitalization, although the term is also widely misused. When technology is seen as one of the key resources, a combination of these two approaches leads to a question about the relationship between business model development and digital disruption, which is one of the foundation points of this paper.

Al-Debei et al. (2010) defined a business model as an abstract representation of an organization. They consider a financially measured value to be one of the main dimensions of a business model, covering information related to costing, pricing methods, and revenue structure. Al-Debei et al. (2010) described a business model as "the rationale of how an organization creates, delivers, and captures value."

2.3 Business Model Elements in SDL

In a service-dominant economy neither product nor service creates value on its own—value is co-created with the customer. The value stream has to always be pull-directed as the value will be defined by the customer, and the process has to be responsive and continuously improved. In service co-creation, supplier processes are seen as a value steam while core competences are the value particles, and a suppliers' operational efficiency can be measured with value density (level of competency) and value stream density (utilization rate of value-creating actions).

In the digital age any business, especially any service-oriented business, can be challenged and replaced by something more user friendly, useful, and/or cheaper. New challengers compete not only with the new embodiment of the offering and value proposition but especially with totally new business models. To be able to constantly monitor and manage the required changes in business design, a definition of a business model must be clear, constant, and unambiguous. Based on the literature review we conclude that there are three common factors in all of the studied business model descriptions:

1. Value Creation (who the customer is and what does the customer value)
2. Revenue Stream (the offering, the value proposition, commercialization)
3. Strategic Resources (core competencies, key processes; this layer lies behind the core delivery or value for the customer and the process for delivering or encountering the value for the customer)

In Table 1 we expand the selected business model elements of a business model framework with an SDL orientation, opening each of the elements to explanatory subsections based on the above presented systematic review of the literature.

Table 1 The business model framework based on the literature review

Value creation	Revenue stream	Resources
Offering What problem do we solve? What need do we serve	Pricing model What value to customers pay for, and how much do they pay for it?	Core competences Required partners?
Value proposition How do we gain interest?	Margin model How does the customer pay? Volatile/dynamic/fixed margin model?	Processes Available technology?
Segmentation Who is the customer?	Profitability What is the cost structure per gained revenue?	Financial Required physical assets?
Co-creation How do we encounter the customer?	Sustainability Resource availability/velocity?	Information Intellectual/ access?

3 A Framework for Service-Dominant Business Model Dynamics

In 1994 Drucker already presented the idea that the theory of a business has to be tested constantly as it is only a hypothesis about things that are in constant change (markets, customers, technology) and therefore this theory should have the built-in ability to change itself. Linder and Cantrell (2000) saw the need for a "change model," which was described as the core logic for a continuously changing company to remain profitable and re-position itself when required. This change model is seen as a key element for the continuous business model renewal that is required in the changing business environment driven by digitalization.

3.1 Literature Review: Business Model Dynamics

Suikki et al. (2006) studied business models in the light of the rapidly changing digital convergence business environment. Their study is particularly interesting because digital convergence was the first form of continuous business model evolution known today as digitalization. In this research Suikki et al. (2006) selected i) the offering, ii) the value network, and the iii) revenue model of the enterprise as the key elements of the business model. The initial idea for analyzing the business model element from a company's internal perspective was to create different types of scenarios for the future state of business. The main idea was to elaborate change in one element and its affect on another. The main conclusion was that if one element changes, other elements will also most likely change, leading to business model change.

Chesbrough (2007) also presented the business model framework for assessing and altering a business model. He pointed out that even if your business model is now profitable and hard to imitate, no business model can last forever. McGrath (2011) has been studying strategy in uncertain and volatile environments and explained the recently growing interest in business model innovation with three reasons: shorter product life cycles, inter-industry competition, and disruptions from business models that offer better customer experiences. Together with disruptive "unicorns" (private firms growing to a value of over a billion dollars in a few years without significant assets but with the capability to change conventional business logic), new interest increased towards business model innovation.

McGrath (2011) underlined the need for continuous business model development in the rapidly changing market environment in which we live nowadays. She encapsulated three signs to indicate when a firm should be aware of a possible threat to their business model: fewer and smaller innovations and improvements, customers tell you when new alternatives are acceptable to them, and decreasing profitability. She strongly recommends having a process wherein alternative businesses experiment with a portfolio of opportunities. Timing and the transition process depend on the environment but at least then change is possible before the company is ruined. This thinking clearly relates to Clayton Christensen's (2010) technology S-curve theory, but applies it in another context.

The Lean approach to encountering the customer is the so-called lean startup model (Ries 2011). The iterative Build–Measure–Learn process is the core of the lean startup methodology, explaining how ideas can iteratively turn into services and products, measuring value creation from the customers' perspective, and then learning whether to save or pivot the idea. Testing value creation in the lean startup model is done through the iterative, continuous, and cross-functional minimum viable product (MVP) development process.

Girotra and Netessine (2014) described a business model as "a set of key decisions that collectively determine how a business earns its revenue, incurs its costs, and manages its risks," and saw innovations in the model as changes to those decisions. Girotra and Netessine (2014) admitted that there were challenges in creating a framework for business model innovation but they also proposed a lean startup kind of approach for testing the market and splitting the risk.

Alex Osterwalder (Osterwalder et al. 2010), father of the original business model canvas, sees a business model as a set of assumptions or hypotheses. His business model canvas is composed of the key hypothesis of firm's key resources, key activities, value proposition, customer relationships, channels, customer segments, cost structures, and revenue streams. The business model canvas describes how an organization creates and delivers value and is like a blueprint for a strategy that is to be implemented through organizational structures and processes. More than that, the value of Osterwalder's canvas lies in thousands of attempts to describe different business scenarios in thousands of workshops of business development. However, Maurya (2012) further developed Osterwalder's business model canvas with Lean thinking. He thought that the original canvas was too focused on the phase where the firm has already succeeded and created his version, called the Lean canvas. Within his canvas he replaced key partners with problem definition, key activities with solution description, customer relationships with a list of unfair advantages, and key resources with key metrics. Based on the business model canvas, a business model covers four main areas of the business: customers, the offering, infrastructure, and financial viability. In this study we reframe these as three key elements: value creation, revenue stream, and resources.

3.2 Literature Review: Innovation and Transformation

So far we have explored business model literature (finding the common elements to describe and define it at its simplest), presented SDL principles, and defined the need to use the change model approach for altering a business model based on the changing business environment, and for altering customer expectations and competition. Before combining it with SDL principles, we want to take a closer look at the definition of "innovation," which can be seen as an essential dimension in the latest business model thinking.

In 1983 Schumpeter (1983, 1912) already connected innovation to economic exchange. He defined innovation as the foundation of business improvement and the success of an organization. He defined five different types of business-related innovations; the launch of new products, the application of new methods of production or sales, opening new markets, acquiring new sources of supply, and new industry structure. All of these definitions reflect changes to the business model.

Christensen (2010) has dedicated his life to studying the sustainability of business and how this intimidates unpredictable, disruptive innovations. Christensen (2010) defined the difference between sustainable and disruptive innovation very clearly in his book The Innovator's Dilemma (Christensen 2010). Christensen focused his study on technological innovations but the same dilemma can be seen in business model innovations. Christensen's technology S-curve can be used to describe business model performance over time and even the same signs of potentially upcoming disruption are applicable to a business model, as McGrath (2011) pointed out within her studies.

Govindarajan and Trimble (2010) defined the need for the similar separation of sustainable and disruptive innovations. Whereas Christensen (2010) approached the topic from a technology standpoint, Govindarajan and Trimble studied innovation and improvements from a business perspective. They created a framework, where the company and its leaders balance the development actions between three different elements; preservation, destruction, and creation. Within this framework preservation activities are described as operational excellence and continuous improvement; creation is seen as the required innovations for long-term sustainability; and destruction activities are required to enable the change from the preserved existing business model and environment to the new model and the new competitive environment (Table 2).

Based on Christensen's, and Govindarajan and Trimble's ideas we selected optimization (preservation), transformation (sustainable innovation), and

Table 2 The elements of change for business model development

Preservation	Destruction	Creation
Existing business model	Room for transformation	Innovation
Operational excellence optimization lean efficiency	Measurement (data driven) minimizing waste	Non-linear shifts separate strategy scenarios disciplined experimentation
Processes continuous improvement	Transformation cutting underperforming business	Diversity disruption based on how an industry evolves
Accountability collaboration	Organizational learning releasing resources	Separate resources separate targets

Source: Expanded from Govindarajan and Trimble (2010)

distruption (distruptive innovation) as the measurable dimensions of business model development.

3.3 The Change Model

When a company constantly outperforms its competitors in the same industry, it is said to have a competitive advantage. The longer it lasts, the stronger it is thought to be. Porter (1985) defined two types of competitive advantage that a firm can gain: lower costs and differentiation. Differentiation is based on innovation strategy, where a firm proposes a unique value based on its offering, business model, or usability. Superior access to information is pretty rarely a competitive factor anymore, but the way in which the information is accessed is key for usability. The rapid increase in the use of mobile devices, the Internet of Things (IoT), the exponential data explosion, and unlimited scalability for services through cloud infrastructures with advanced data analytics have given unprecedented business opportunities for companies all around the world.

Digital disruption is the change that occurs when new digital technologies and business models affect the value proposition of existing goods and services. Digital disruption is a reflection of consumers' behavior. In a service-driven world it is not the companies but consumers and their behavior that lead the way. The digital age offers a new platform for liaising with customers, which is accelerating new innovations and shortening service life cycles. In industrialization, market share was the most pursued goal, but digitalization has driven customer liaison and usability to the center of the strategy process. The traditional value chain was described from resources to the customer but customer-centric thinking and SDL turn it the other way around. The starting point of the value chain is co-creation with the customer, continuing through liaison, the offering, and networks to end with the operant resources like core competences.

In the digitalized age everything is happening fast; the internet is accelerating the speed of everything. Product, service, and design life cycles are getting shorter. The same trend applies to business models. Competition is truly global and big

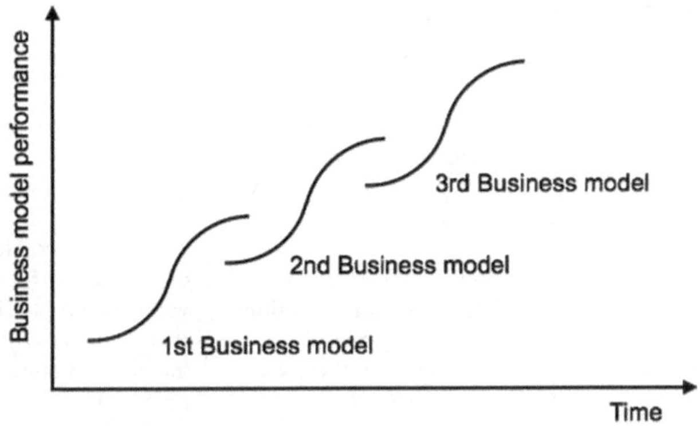

Fig. 2 Business model evolution. Source: Transformed from Christensen's (1992) Technology S-Curve

resources are not required for challenging dominant players. Christensen (1992) presented the S-Curve for technology evolution, which we suggest to be applicable also to business model evolution in a digitalization-driven service-dominant age (Fig. 2).

When the business model matures, the magnitude of its operational development slows down, and then new business model innovations challenge traditional business. A firm should always test alternative business models in order to maintain its capacity to answer to competition in the altering business environment.

4 A Framework for the Service-Dominant Business Model's Development

In the service-driven business environment, customer value is co-created with the customer and competitive edge is created progressively through a constantly improving service experience. The key ingredients for this process are listening and the very basic human feeling of empathy (the capacity to place oneself in another's shoes). The very same principles that drive design thinking reach wider recognition in a digital age, combining business, design, technology, and data. Design-driven thinking is expanding from one industry to another, offering the best tools for understanding customer needs more comprehensively.

The transformation from physical products to digital services is one the key reasons for rapid disruption. Newcomers who have limited experience of the existing products might still capture the essence of the customer need that they are able to fulfill with a simple service. Failures are basically accepted and prototyping is used for failing fast in order to be able to succeed faster. Concept design and development are done in parallel; pilot customers use the service from the early drafts up to the launched versions. The process of trial and error even continues in production. Using co-creation to create successful services is the new legacy.

Table 3 The business model development framework

	Value offering	Revenue stream	Resources
Existing	*Foundation*: What problem do we solve, what need do we serve? *Proposition*: How do we gain interest? *Segmentation*: Who is our customer, and do we have the same offering for all segments? *Encountering*: How do we liaise with the customer?	*Pricing model*: What value does the customer pay for and how much do they pay? *Margin model*: How customer pay for the value we do provide? *Profitability*: What is the cost structure (per revenue)? *Sustainability*: What is the resource reusability and velocity?	*Core competencies*: What are the operant resources? *Information*: Is there any IPR, customer (market) related, or other differentiation? *Processes*: R&D, sales, purchasing, production, outsourcing, steering? *Financial*: Capital intensive, flexible, go-to-market?
Optimization	Optimized?		
Transformation	Developed?		
Disruption	Changed?		

As noted above, based on the work of Christensen (2010), and Govindarajan and Trimble (2010) we selected optimization (preservation), transformation (sustainable innovation), and distruption (distrutive innovation) as the stages of business model development that give perspective on the required and intended change. Without these perspective development activities may be either a leap too far or for result in smaller change than anticipated (Table 3).

In the business model development framework, we combined the simplified elements of the business model in the service-dominant business environment and dimensioned the development based on the described rationale.

5 Business Model Innovation in the Health Care Business Case

In our research we used an innovative Finnish health care provider Heltti for testing the created framework. We used Heltti's services from 2014 to 2015, gaining a broad understanding of their offering and business development, but had first interviewed Heltti's founder and CEO in order to gain a deep and detailed understanding how Heltti had created its unique and competitive business model. In the interview we utilized the selected business model elements for data analysis. However, during the research period we ended up adding the change stages from innovation literature, using the improved framework to analyze the case.

5.1 The Case Company

Heltti was founded in 2013 by entrepreneurs outside the industry in order to challenge the traditional reactive and disease-treatment-oriented occupational health care model with a preventive one, returning customers' health back to the center of services. Digital collaboration tools and a customer-care-oriented pricing model were an essential part of the business idea from the very beginning. Heltti's value proposition is in the systematic and co-operative development and management of the employees' health and wellbeing, keeping employees productive at work. Approximately 65 % of health issues are handled using Heltti's digital solutions, saving working time and easing collaboration. Heltti also offers an individual wellbeing program for employees, measuring employees wellbeing status. Heltti's revenue model is based on fixed monthly fees and therefore it strongly encourages a focus on preventive healthcare services. Heltti offers three different service platforms, which may be supplemented with various additional services and welfare projects.

Heltti's resources include in-house competences in primary health care and health counseling, and coaching in wellbeing. A digital eHealth solution is a significant vehicle for value creation, which is mainly seen as a co-creative process between Heltti's specialists and customers. Heltti service platforms are designed to facilitate the co-creative sales process, always taking account of the special needs of the customer corporation. Heltti uses subcontractors for specialist and laboratory facilities, maintaining the high velocity of its resource utilization.

5.2 The Business's Development

Heltti's original differentiation idea was to renew the pricing model of occupational health care. The traditional pricing model has contradictory interests between the customer and supplier. The supplier bills the customer for transactions; appointments with a nurse, doctor, or specialist; laboratory tests; and operations. Whereas customers (companies) would like to pay for productivity and a reduction in staff absence. Heltti created a revenue model based on a monthly fee per employee and targeted its services mainly at professional service providers, where the intensity of employees' working hours has a clear and direct relation to profitability. With this original idea Heltti found a sound business model for attracting customers.

In the second business model development phase Heltti saw digital collaboration with its customers' employees as a key for maintaining profitable business. In the conventional model employees and service provider lose time by having face-to-face meetings for every question. Heltti developed an eHealth-platform, that including phone backed chat and mobile application services. Soon Heltti found out that 65 % of the questions could be handled through digital liaisons. A digital interface also enabled better use of resources; in the conventional model doctors often do nurses' work and specialists do generalists' work. Digital tools also enabled better collaboration for wellbeing services, which is an essential part of the value proposition. The company sees a significant shake-out in resource use between occupational health care (35 %), medical services (35 %), and preventive wellbeing (30 %) compared to the use of conventional service providers where 80 % of resources are used for medical services and 20 % for occupational health care. Digital tools also enable continuous data collection and analysis of wellbeing.

The third phase in Heltti's business model development was the use of collected data. Heltti extended the collection platform from its mobile application to more convenient smart wristbands. The collected data is used for predictive analysis and preventive health care. Heltti is a forerunner in enriching the medical data with wellbeing information. Heltti serves about 200 companies in Finland and is constantly collecting data and developing its business model. There still are several directions in which Heltti can develop its operations: providing service platforms, operating as a turnkey provider, and operating as a service model licensor to name just a few.

5.3 Heltti's Business Model Development Framework

Originally Heltti aimed to change the revenue model in occupational health care to align the interests of supplier, customer, and the user of services by billing a "club fee" per employee. The market response proved that the idea was right, but it was not significant enough to widely challenge the legacy business model by itself. After the launch of their service Heltti also saw that they had to be able to create additional services for club members in order to provide added value. This led to optimization in value creation as additional services were targeted towards preventive health care. Heltti's extended value proposition was well received, especially by the professional service customer segment where revenue and therefore profitability are directly driven by the presence of the workforce. This change led to optimization in resourcing and encountering, which further led to the creation of digital services for better customer collaboration. This was actually sustainable innovation and a significant competitive factor. But, just like all digital services, this was easy to copy and legacy players have been following this idea one by one. Even more significant was that digital collaboration was seen as sufficient for two-thirds to four-fifths of customer contacts. This led to a transformation in physical resourcing, requesting more time from nurses and less from doctors. This again gained Heltti competitiveness in its cost structure as a developing challenger, leading to a transformation in value creation. Heltti's business model development process, with optional upcoming development paths, is presented in the created framework below (Table 4).

Table 4 Heltti's business model development framework

	Value offering	Revenue stream	Resources
Existing	Occupational health care. – Regulatory requirement – Extended health care services Nationally specified minimum requirements for offering. The company is a customer. HR is usually a decision maker.	Transaction-based pricing. Resource-utilization-based cost structure. Low velocity and poor utilization of resources. The value provider and the customer have contradictory interests.	Nurse, general practitioner, specialist doctor, laboratory, infrastructure (processes, physical and digital). The process from nurse to general practitioner and again to specialist doctor if required.
Optimization	Preventive health care activities.	Service focus on nurse liaison.	A direct digital liaison to a health care professional.
Transformation	The decision is made by the business. Lower absenteeism, lower cost, better employer experience.	The pricing model is based on monthly fee per person. Interests in the value chain are aligned.	The remote diagnosis and treatment of patients leads to the better utilization of resources.
Disruption	Uber of occupational health care.	A resource integrator. A digital platform.	Value found in the customer experience and optimized resource utilization.

6 Discussion and Evaluation of Heltti's Case

Heltti's case reveals the natural business development path of the modern start-up in a digitized world. The case is also a good example of a company that challenges the traditional and stable business environment with a service-dominant, customer-centric business model. We can see that the business model development was done iteratively, with the company learning from every step. Heltti originally only focused on preventive healthcare, paving change with the new revenue model. Digital interaction was required for continuous collaboration, which also changed the resourcing of the customer interface and sharpened the value proposition.

This case analysis details three important aspects that reveal how SDL and digitalization are changing business model thinking. The first aspect is that business model development is a process rather than a series of separate transactions carried out by a specific function. The second related aspect is that business model development has to be iterative, systematic, and measurable. The third aspect is how the required changes are defined: how big a leap is required and which components of the business model it affects. In the study we learned how continuous and iterative business model development sharpens a firm's offering and increases its competitiveness. Co-creational collaboration with the customer makes sure that the value creation and revenue model are continuously tested and that the required resources are put to good use.

The created framework describes the steps taken by the case organization well, and even reveals options for further development. Obviously one case is not enough to prove this type of business model development is suitable or perfect for all industries but this work was done to guide business model development activities with a practical and systematic framework and to provide novel contributions for external practitioners and researchers.

7 Conclusion

In this article we created a business model development framework for continuous business development in a service-dominant business environment. Business model literature was reviewed and reflected through the SDL perspective, taking account of the continuous change in the market, and synthesis was presented as a framework. The outcome was finally tested with a real business case in the health care industry. In this study we offer a broadened view of the definition of a "business model" by including some of the latest SDL studies and change theories. Moreover, we connected these together in order to be able to explore co-creative business model development in the midst of continuously evolving and digitalization-driven change in the business environment.

The case study was conducted in the health care professional service environment between 2014 and 2016. The goal was to test the created framework for understanding the required changes in the case company's business model thoroughly. In this study we also learned the importance of change perspectives when studying the change models, and therefore we expanded the literature review to also cover some innovation theories. The case proved that the framework reflects the development path of an iterative business model development process well and ensures that all the required aspects are considered when continuous and co-creative business development is executed. The evolution of Heltti's business model development in every cycle followed the elements and stages of the framework well. It also provided a good structure for communicating about business models internally and externally.

In summary, we believe that the results of this study could help numerous organizations to understand the need for structured and continuous business model development to be an essential part of sustainable business development. Growth with the wrong business design destroys value and a stationary business model opens the door for new competition and thus weakens the firm's position in the market. We proved the usefulness of these frameworks (at least for the case organization) with our empirical results. Our aim is to get deeper into the details of this in our upcoming studies. We encourage other researchers and practitioners to apply the same frameworks and constructions in other companies in order gain more scientific evidence. This would fulfill the requirements of a semi-strong market test if the constructs were widely adopted. In addition, the case company has profitably increased sales revenue and employee headcount during the research period, which also indicates that the chosen initiative has been successful.

References

Al-Debei, M. M., Panagiotopoulos, P., Fitzgerald, G., & Elliman, T. (2010). *Rethinking the business model concept with eparticipation* (Vol. 2010, pp. 1–13). Proceedings of the tGov Workshop, London, UK.

Chesbrough, H. (2007). Business model innovation: It's not just about technology anymore. *Strategy & Leadership, 35*, 12–17. doi:10.1108/10878570710833714.

Chesbrough, H., & Rosenbloom, R. (2002). *The role of the business model in capturing value from innovation*. Oxford: Oxford University Press.

Christensen, C. M. (1992). Exploring the limits of the technology S-curve. *Production and Operations Management, 1*(4), 334–357. doi:10.1111/j.1937-5956.1992.tb00001.x.

Christensen, C. M. (2010). The innovator's dilemma 1. In *Collins business essential*. New York: Harper Business.

Drucker, P. F. (1994). The theory of the business. *Harvard Business Review, 72*(5), 95–104.

Edvardsson, B., Skålén, P., & Tronvoll, B. (2012). Service systems as a foundation for resource integration and value co-creation. In S. L. Vargo & R. F. Lusch (Eds.), *Special Issue – Toward a better understanding of the role of value in markets and marketing* (pp. 79–126). Bingley: Emerald Group Publishing Limited.

Girotra, K., & Netessine, S. (2014, July–August). 4 paths to business model innovation. *Harvard Business Review*, New York.

Govindarajan, V., & Trimble, C. (2010, July–August). Stop the innovation wars. *Harvard Business Review, 88*, 76–83.

Grönroos, C., & Gummerus, J. (2014). The service revolution and its marketing implications: Service logic vs service-dominant logic. *Managing Service Quality: An International Journal, 24*(3), 206–229. doi:10.1108/MSQ-03-2014-0042.

Grönroos, C., & Voima, P. (2013). Critical service logic: Making sense of value creation and co-creation. *Journal of the Academy of Marketing Science, 41*(2), 133–150. doi:10.1007/s11747-012-0308-3.

Gummesson, E., Lusch, R. F., & Vargo, S. L. (2010). Transitioning from service management to service-dominant logic: Observations and recommendations. *International Journal of Quality and Service Sciences, 2*(1), 8–22. doi:10.1108/17566691011026577.

Hamel, G. (2002). *Leading the revolution: How to thrive in turbulent times by making innovation a way of life*. New York: Plume Book.

Johnson, M., & Christensen, C. (2008). Reinventing your business model. *Harvard Business Review, 86*(12), 57–68.

Kuula, S., Niemi, E., & Haapasalo, H. (2015, September 10–12). Service dominant logic – how to systematize service business (RESER), Copenhagen.

Linder, J., & Cantrell, S. (2000). *Changing business models: Surveying the landscape*. Cambridge, MA: Accenture Institute for Strategic Change.

Lusch, R. F., & Nambisan, S. (2015). Service innovation: A service-dominant logic perspective. *MIS Quarterly, 39*(1), 155–175.

Maglio, P. P., & Spohrer, J. (2008). Fundamentals of service science. *Journal of the Academy of Marketing Science, 36*(1), 18–20. doi:10.1007/s11747-007-0058-9.

Magretta, J. (2002). Why business models matter. *Harvard Business Review, 2002*, 86–92.

Maurya, A. (2012). *Running lean: Iterate from plan A to a plan that works* (The lean series 2nd ed.). Sebastopol, CA: O'Reilly.

McGrath, R. (2011). When your business model is in trouble. *Harvard Business Review, 2011*, 96–98.

Osterwalder, A., Pigneur, Y., & Clark, T. (2010). *Business model generation: A handbook for visionaries, game changers, and challengers*. Hoboken, NJ: Wiley.

Pekuri, A., Suvanto, M., Haapasalo, H., & Pekuri, L. (2014). Managing value creation: The business model approach in construction. *International Journal of Business Innovation and Research, 8*(1), 36–51.

Porter, M. E. (1985). *Competitive advantage: Creating and sustaining superior performance*. New York: Free Press/Collier Macmillan.

Prahalad, C. K., & Ramaswamy, V. (2000). Co-opting customer competence. *Harvard Business Review, 78*(1), 79–90.

Ries, E. (2011). *The lean startup: How today's entrepreneurs use continuous innovation to create radically successful businesses* (1st ed.). New York: Crown Business.

Schumpeter, J. A. (1912). *The theory of economic development* (Tenth printing 2004). New Brunswick, NJ: Transaction Publishers.

Schumpeter, J. A. (1983). *The theory of economic development: An inquiry into profits, capital, credit, interest, and the business cycle* (Social science classics series). New Brunswick, NJ: Transaction Books.

Seybold, P. B., Lewis, J. M., & Marshak, R. T. (2001). *The customer revolution: How to thrive when customers are in control* (1st ed.). New York: Crown Business.

Slywotzky, A. J. (1996). *Value migration: How to think several moves ahead of the competition*. Boston: Harvard Business School Press.

Suikki, R., Goman, A.-M., & Haapasalo, H. (2006). A framework for creating business models – a challenge in convergence of high clock speed industry. *International Journal of Business Environment, 1*(2), 211–233.

Timmers, P. (1998). Business models for electronic markets. *Electronic Markets, 8*(2), 3–8.

Vargo, S. L., & Lusch, R. F. (2004). Evolving to a new dominant logic for marketing. *Journal of Marketing, 68*(1), 1–17.

Vargo, S. L., & Lusch, R. F. (2008). Service-dominant logic: Continuing the evolution. *Journal of the Academy of Marketing Science, 36*, 1–10. doi:10.1007/s11747-007-0069-6.

Vargo, S. L., & Lusch, R. F. (2014). Inversions of service-dominant logic. *Marketing Theory, 14* (3), 239–248. doi:10.1177/1470593114534339.

Seppo Kuula is an experienced business executive with versatile and multicultural background in leadership at the complex technology and professional services environment. Career is significantly focused in the value based commercialization of Professional Services, and International Sales management. Believing in lifelong learning, holding three academic degrees; M.Sc. (Ind. Eng. & Mgmt), B.Sc. (Eng.), and eMBA, conducting Doctoral research about Service Dominant Logic in Professional Services context at Oulu University. Currently serving as Chief Executive Officer with Nasdaq—listed Siili Solutions Oyj (since 2010). Nominated as the Finnish Software Entrepreneur of the Year 2014 (The Finnish Software Entrepreneurs Association) for the entrepreneurial leadership.

Harri Haapasalo has been Professor in Product Management over 15 years in the Industrial Engineering and Management at the University of Oulu. He has a Doctors degree in Technology Management and also a Master's degree in Economics and Business Administration. He has research interests in business management, product management and also in management of production processes. The list of publications covers more than 250 international scientific publications. He has been as chair and committee member in organizing numerous international conferences, and has been as a reviewer and belongs to the editorial board for several international scientific journals.

e-Health and Co-production: Critical Drivers for Chronic Diseases Management

Gabriele Palozzi, Daniele Binci, and Andrea Appolloni

Abstract

A progressively ageing population makes the healthcare management of chronic diseases (e.g. heart failure (HF), diabetes, geriatric psychosis) an extremely relevant matter for worldwide national health systems, as chronicity persists for a long time and generally cannot be permanently cured. In order to ensure the economic and social sustainability of treating such diseases, new healthcare business models, based on innovative tools and patients' participation, should be considered. The adoption of new technologies and the active involvement of patients in the therapeutic pathway might represent fundamental drivers in healthcare delivery innovation. Accordingly, empirical evidence about Chronic Diseases Management, based on new technologies, such as remote monitoring (RM) systems, shows how patients are enabled to actively take part in the follow-up process. This "co-production" approach to the service has shown a reduction in health organizations' workload for the same level of outcome (e.g. hospitalization rate reduction), suggesting new opportunities in the design of healthcare delivery systems. Moreover, within this evidence, end-users' (patients and their caregivers) collaboration, i.e. more skilled and ICT-adoption oriented, represents strong support to the medical profession, as well as to patients' satisfaction and loyalty. Drawing from these premises, this work aims at summarizing Italian empirical evidence highlighted through the case study method) of co-production and telemedicine joint implementation. Specifically, through such evidence, we aim to describe how e-Health and co-production could prove to be crucial organizational drivers in Chronic

G. Palozzi (✉) • D. Binci • A. Appolloni
Department of Management and Law, University Tor Vergata, Rome, Via Columbia, 2, 00133 Rome, Italy
e-mail: palozzi@economia.uniroma2.it; binci.daniele@gmail.com; appolloni@economia.uniroma2.it

M.A. Pfannstiel, C. Rasche (eds.), *Service Business Model Innovation in Healthcare and Hospital Management*, DOI 10.1007/978-3-319-46412-1_15

Diseases Management, both in cost reduction and in service (outcome) innovation.

1 Introduction

The dynamic environment of the healthcare sector is characterized by pressure on cost reduction, new approaches towards patients and drastic technological changes. In this scenario, in which economic crises, digitalization and new legislations are fundamental drivers, the healthcare sector should consider the adoption of innovative services in order to manage patients' diseases. Among others, chronic diseases (such as cardiovascular diseases, cancer, diabetes, respiratory failure) are crucial matters for healthcare services because they represent one of the first causes of disability, mortality and morbidity (World Health Organization 2013). These pathologies are defined as "non-communicable diseases" due to permanency, non-reversible alterations and the tendency to develop some degree of disability (World Health Organization 2013). Their importance has been highlighted also by the "Patto per la Salute 2014–16" (Pact for Health 2014–16), in which the Italian Health System promotes a multi professional and interdisciplinary model for the care of chronicity which is featured by:

- progressive deterioration;
- requests for high integration between health and social services;
- a need for the design and development of integrated facilities within the health district.

Primary prevention, early diagnosis, appropriate therapy and also patient education and empowerment become important in the life-cycle of those pathologies (both in economic terms for the health system, and quality life for the patients), in which the constant rise of complex medical devices combined with awareness of individuals will change the traditional norm of understanding and design of healthcare.

An effective "integrated management" of such chronicity, that is fundamental to precede patients' needs and to actively prevent complications, requires a cultural change based on the exploitation both of digitalization (such as telemedicine), and its impact on the innovative relationships between patients and healthcare organizations. Telemedicine, such as RM technologies, is particularly oriented to sustain such transformation, by enabling new relationships between patients and the healthcare structure, such as in the co-production perspectives, in which the patient overcomes the status of a "consumer" by becoming an active user of the health service.

In order to implement healthcare service innovation on chronic diseases, individuals should be more educated, "technologically" oriented and informed about their genetic profile, the disease they might have and the best available cares; consequently, patients can provide their personal data by themselves, so that physicians can use these ones in electronic health information standard form.

Accordingly, by adopting an empirical pilot case study, our study aims at describing the service innovation in chronicity management enabled by e-Health and co-production.

In particular, our study, as detailed later, is focused on the HF chronic disease, by considering a specific type of HF patient, defined as non-implanted (i.e. s/he has never undergone an implant of a cardiac device—such as a pacemaker, cardioverter defibrillator, loop recorder—as s/he has no other acute arrhythmia morbidity), who would be able to "co-produce" their health conditions by an innovative interaction model with the telemedicine systems.

This chapter, after the introduction related to the above-mentioned issues, follows this outline:

The second section addresses the issues of HF as a chronic disease; it will be analysed from social, economic and managerial perspectives. The third section provides insights into co-production and RM in order to better understand the type of innovation factors analysed and presented as service innovation drivers in chronicity management. The fourth section explains how these two critical ingredients are empirically exploited for remote HF management in the innovative experience of the Policlinico Casilino hospital in Rome (Policlinico Casilino); this section also provides an empirical description of the improvement of the HF patient's follow-up ("AS IS") towards the integrated tele-management healthcare pathway ("TO BE") that involves the patient's active participation.

In the last section, by also highlighting the findings, we give the conclusion and provide the strengths and limitations of the innovative service analysed.

2 The Relevance of Heart Failure as a Chronic Disease

Heart Failure is a specific chronic disease that represents one of the diseases with the worst impact on survival, quality of life and independence of patients, and then also on resource consumption. It occurs when the heart is unable to pump sufficiently to maintain blood flow to meet the body's needs (Di Lenarda et al. 2010). Signs and symptoms commonly include shortness of breath, excessive tiredness, and leg swelling.

Common causes of HF are concerned with coronary artery disease, including a previous myocardial infarction (heart attack), high blood pressure, valvular heart disease, and various cardiomyopathies.

This pathology can occur at whatever age; its symptoms are not clinically evident—in the initial phase patients are almost asymptomatic, but HF's constant evolution and the appearance of symptoms, bring patients first to have a cardiology test and then to obtain emergency room (ER) hospitalization.

Naturally the ageing population and the prognosis improvements are responsible for the epidemic incidence and prevalence rate of HF.

HF is a very serious syndrome with a well-defined evolution: the mortality rate is equal to 50 % at 5 years and increases to 80 % at 10 years; this is due to HF development in the presence of other pathologies such as ischemic heart disease, hypertension and diabetes. In Europe there are more than 15 mln HF patients, with an impact of between 2 and 3 % of people, reaching 20 % of people over 80 years old. Pharmacological and non-pharmacological therapy has reduced the overall mortality related to HF, but it still remains one of the main causes of death and hospitalization for people (Epstein et al. 2013).

The presence of chronic multi-pathologies, multiple risk factors, different drug therapies and a reduced pharmacological compliance, are clear features of HF patients all of which contribute to the design of a more complex medical case for older people (Rengo et al. 2004). In Italy more than 500 people are hospitalized due to HF every day; these data have increased by about 40 % in the last 5 years; about one in three of these patients die within 12 months (Italian Board of Health 2013).

Problems attributed to HF have an economic relevance for the worldwide National Health Systems (for example, in the US HF is responsible for 1.5 % of the yearly health expenditure, in France of 1.9 %, in the Netherlands 1.0 % (McMurray et al. 1998), especially in Italy where HF is considered to be the most expensive cardiac disease, responsible for 1.4 % of the yearly national expenditure. Because HF is associated with high levels of mortality and morbidity, with a 75 % incidence of patients over 65 years old, these conditions bring long hospitalization periods, as well as high risks of relapse after treatment caused by early readmission to hospital after discharge (Riley and Cowie 2009). Due to HF, in fact, about 25 % of patients discharged are readmitted within 30 days (Dharmarajan et al. 2013). This percentage rises to 46 % within 6 months (Hasan and Paul 2011).

As already stated, for chronic HF patients, the prognosis has significantly improved in the last 20 years, given the progress in pharmacological and non-pharmacological therapies. Despite these advances in treatment, HF patients remain at high risk rate of mortality and re-hospitalizations, especially in the early period after hospital discharge. The EuroHeart Failure survey found that within 12 weeks of discharge 24 % of patients had been readmitted and 13.5 % of patients died between admission and their 12-week follow-up (Cleland et al. 2003). In a more recent survey, the ESC-HF Pilot, the all-cause mortality rate at 1 year was 17.4 % in acute HF and 7.2 % in chronic stable HF, and 1-year hospitalization rates were 43.9 % and 31.9 %, respectively, in hospitalized acute and chronic HF patients (Maggioni et al. 2010). Moreover, costs related to HF account for 1–2 % of all healthcare expenditure, mainly the result of recurrent hospital admissions. The acute in-hospital care is responsible for up to 70 % of the annual cost of HF in developed countries (Lee et al. 2004). Prevention of decompensation and HF-related hospitalizations is important not only for the patient but also to reduce healthcare costs.

It is probable that more than half the hospitalizations can be considered as low risk; thus, as advocated by the TEMISTOCLE study (Fabbri et al. 2002), they can be considered avoidable through an alternative and appropriate management of patients.

Accordingly, HF can be considered an example of complexity; concerning the refund rate for HF diagnosis, the Diagnosis Related Group (DRG) number 127, (Italian Board of Health 2011):

- is in first place for frequency of repeated hospitalization both for absolute value and for more than three times per year;
- obtains the higher complexity index (APPRO) in comparison with any other DRG;
- is the first cause of difficult discharge from hospital; this means that more than other DRGs, HF management requests a mean duration of bed occupancy higher than the threshold expected a priori.

Effectively, DRG 127 is, in Italy, the main cause of hospitalization after natural childbirth (Italian Board of Health 2015).

Regarding the Lazio Region (the region in which the pilot case study presented in this work is implemented), a predictor study (Mureddu et al. 2012) has estimated that the prevalence of manifested HF is about 6.7 % of people. This is enough to consider HF as a socio-economically relevant problem; its treatment is aimed not only at increasing the survival rate, but also at improving patients' quality of lifestyle, their autonomy and the resource consumption. This is possible only through a new conceptualization of the healthcare approaches and services based on opportunity related to digitalization as well as patients' centrality.

The intrinsic features of this syndrome (with alternation of stationary and severe phases) brings the need for a design of a healthcare model for HF management that takes into account the different states of pathology development. Accordingly, the New York Heart Association (NYHA) defines four HF states:

A) patient at risk of HF, but without clinical evidence;
B) patient with cardiopathy, but without HF symptoms;
C) patient with HF symptoms and evident cardiopathy;
D) patient with severe HF who needs adequate and continuous care.

However, a plan for efficient HF management should:

1. early locate those patients with high risk of developing HF (A & B groups), to avoid and/or delay the development of the disease;
2. immediately include HF patient (C & D groups) in a specific therapy pathway aimed at the prevention of severe HF relapse.

This approach should drastically reduce repeated hospitalizations and patients' mortality, also reducing healthcare costs; hence it should enhance the appropriateness of the carers' and patients' quality of life.

Accordingly, co-production and telemedicine can be crucial drivers aimed at increasing the total value created in healthcare delivery for HF management, especially in relation to the above HF states.

3 Telemedicine and Co-production in Heart Failure

Telemedicine, defined as "a new healthcare delivery process, based on innovative technologies, provided when patient and professional are not physically in the same place", is a new way to take over the management of chronic patients, that allows guaranteed continuity of healthcare in far away territories and a better integration between hospital and district/patient" (Italian Board of Health, "Telemedicina – Linee di indirizzo nazionali" 2014, p. 10), can be useful to manage the reduction of HF percentages of readmissions. It can also contribute to a better service provision by allowing:

- equity in access to care;
- high quality services;
- improvement in efficacy, effectiveness and appropriateness of care;
- expenditure containment.

The Pact of Digital Health in Italy has proposed the Information System streamline project, which has allocated a specific issue to the telemedicine, recognising it as having a specific role in these areas:

- Prevention: by monitoring of vital signs;
- Diagnosis: by moving healthcare information from one place to another;
- Care: by services aimed at triage and therapeutic choice with regard to each specific patient;
- Rehabilitation: by home services provided by nurses in real time from an "e-Health" Centre.

As we describe in the following section, a specific tool of telemedicine is RM, particularly important as it enables HF patients' care, participation and adherence improvement.

3.1 Remote Monitoring Technologies: A Specific Tool for Co-production

RM goal is to detect early signs of HF decompensation, providing an opportunity for intervention before the patient requires hospitalization. It is related to the detection of some indicators of deterioration (blood pressure, weight, arrhythmia, etc.) and allows medical staff to understand patients' condition before their health level necessitates a new hospitalization. These circumstances can be a great advantage in managing HF both in terms of cost-effectiveness for the NHS and health quality levels for patients. Moreover, RM enables patients to actively participate and then co-produce the HF service.

Co-production, drawing from open innovation framework (Chesbrough 2006; Bogers and West 2012), is based on the idea of challenging the passive patient

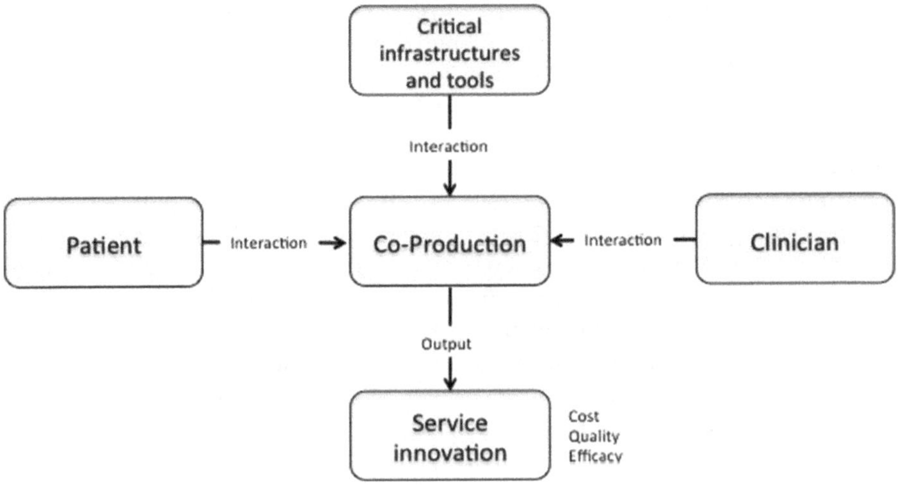

Fig. 1 A co-production framework in the healthcare service. Source: Own elaboration (2016)

approach by creating the expectation of equivalently active roles between clients (patients) and providers (healthcare infrastructure and staff) in the delivery of the service that clients will use (Cepiku and Giordano 2014; Osborne et al. 2016) (Fig. 1). Co-production is, in fact, a collaborative development between two or more stakeholders that involves knowledge inflows and outflows between complementary partners. Particularly, it is based on the establishment of partnerships between healthcare professionals and patients by overcoming the assumption that users are passive recipients of healthcare and recognises their contribution in the delivery of a service (Cahn 2000), as the relationship between clinicians and patients becomes "a meeting of two experts, where clinician has knowledge of diagnosis, treatment options and preferences, aetiology and prognosis and the client knows about the experience of illness, social circumstances, and attitudes to risks, values and personal preferences" (Realpe and Wallace 2010, p. 3). Customers that play an active role beyond the "traditional feedback approach", have the opportunity to suggest, or even develop their own services or content and collaborate with users outside the exploration of new knowledge and ideas (von Hippel 2005).

Several telemonitoring, and therefore co-production, strategies have been proposed, using regularly scheduled structured telephone interviews or more sophisticated systems, such as electronic transfer of physiological data with remote access control via external, wearable or implantable devices or implantable hemodynamic monitors. They have been assessed in retrospective and prospective clinical studies and meta-analysis with conflicting results (Sousa et al. 2014) due to the rate of adherence by patients to collaboration with their responsible hospital. Other studies have evaluated the ability of individual or combined device diagnostic data to identify patients at risk of HF decompensation and to facilitate early clinical intervention and potentially avoid hospitalization and reduce healthcare costs

(Conraads et al. 2011; Hindricks et al. 2014). In a recent multiple systematic review about the effectiveness of home telemonitoring interventions for HF patient risk, reductions in mortality and all-cause hospitalizations appear to be greater in patients who had been recently discharged ($\leq$28 days) from acute HF and that had been monitored through some non-invasive telemonitoring technologies; it seems that automated device-based telemonitoring and mobile telemonitoring were effective in reducing the risk of all-cause mortality and HF-related hospitalizations (Kitsiou et al. 2015). Another recent meta-analysis of relevant systematic reviews focuses on the comparative effectiveness of five telemedicine interventions in improving HF patient outcomes; telemonitoring as well as structured telephone support interventions were both found to be significantly better than the usual care both in reducing deaths and HF-related hospitalizations. Telemedicine interventions that involved the use of electrocardiographic (ECG) data transmission were also significantly more effective in reducing hospitalizations due to HF when compared with the usual care (Kotb et al. 2015).

Actually research is focused on the identification of the target population (we can also call it the "co-producer" population) most likely to respond to RM and to identify which parameters should be monitored, how could these parameters are monitored more efficiently and how the data obtained from monitoring should be managed by healthcare professionals.

3.2 Remote Monitoring Technologies for Implanted and Non-implanted Patients

RM, as defined by the Heart Rhythm Society, refers to "the automated transmission of data based on pre-alert related to device functionality, clinical events and clinical condition of patients" (Slotwiner et al. 2015, p. 7). This provides the possibility of rapid detection of arrhythmia events and health degeneration. All information obtained during an in-office device check-up can be obtained remotely by different kinds of sensor. In the RM process related to HF patients, two different kinds of patient are present, depending on their health and arrhythmia conditions: the implanted and the not implanted patients. Before describing in more depth the non-implanted case, which is the core of this chapter, it is worth describing the implanted case, because of the similarity of both clinical conditions and in turn their process management; it is important to consider the implanted patients' case as it can inspire, as a model, the non-implanted ones.

Implanted patients are those who have undergone the implant of an implantable cardiac device (a subcutaneous implantable sensor, such as a pacemaker, implantable cardioverter defibrillator (ICD), or loop recorder). RM has been prevalently used for this kind of patient, where devices are remotely interrogated by allowing a 100 % compliance rate from patients. For HF implanted patients, in effect, the device automatically communicates the data to the responsible hospital and the patient has just to be present in front of the transmitter during transmission (often

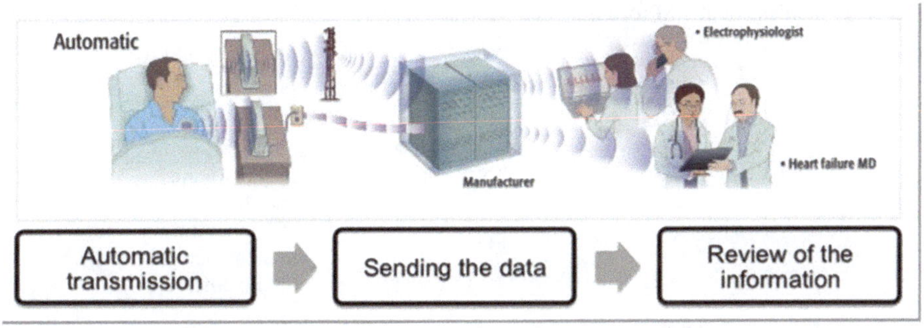

Fig. 2 Operation of an RM ICD. Source: Adapted from Slotwiner et al. (2015)

scheduled during the night), and when HF patients who have been implanted are discharged from hospital, they receive a simple explanation for the operation of their ICD; from that moment on, the remote controlled device is able to communicate easily with the web-platform of the hospital through a wireless transmitter connected to the telephone line; as shown in Fig. 2. The information detected arrives at the hospital as a common e-mail or through a cloud computing system, and this represents the starting point for the investigation of the patient's health condition. In case of need, patients are called to arrange an office visit or for further clinical checks. In this way the health state of patients is monitored at all times; this system allows the prediction and prevention of an HF relapse and the consequent readmission to hospital.

Despite the interest of the present work being related to non-implanted patients, it is worthwhile briefly citing the strengthened literature about the economic impact of RM on the management of a different but very similar population of patients in terms of health needs and communication possibilities (the implanted). This literature also supports the positive economic and managerial impacts of RM applied to HF patients, and can be considered relevant for the aim of the present work where it gives attention to the cost analysis and cost effectiveness of telemedicine employment in the arrhythmia field.

Regarding the use of RM in managing cardiac diseases and cardiac home cures, a number of studies were found that show its convenience in terms of cost savings for the same health outcome (Table 1).

3.3 Heart Failure Remote Management Studies for Non-implanted Patients

Patients who do not need implants are mainly cured by drugs therapies and periodical check-ups (non-implanted patients); they must instead actively detect their clinical parameters (with a specific tool-kit for the measurement of biomedical parameters such as ECG, weight, blood pressure, etc.) and then communicate them to the hospital. In this case patients are more autonomous (in terms of awareness

Table 1 Studies about RM for implanted patients

Authors	Year	Study type	Endpoints	Impact of RM	
				Findings	Stat value
Burri et al.	2011	SLR	RM impact on follow-ups	RM reduces costs, improves patients' care and the efficiency of the management of the healthcare system.	–
Calò et al.	2013	Prospective randomized	Assess current direct costs of 1-year ICD follow-up based on RM compared with conventional one	RM significantly reduced: The time spent by hospital staff. The costs for the hospital and pt.	$P = .03$ $P = .01$ $P = .0001$
Fauchier et al.	2005	Non-randomized. Database analysis	Calculation of expected costs of RM-related to ICD follow-up	RM reduces medical and transportation costs compared with standard ICD follow-up.	–
Guedon Moreao et al.—*ECOST Economic aspect*	2012	Randomized, prospective, multicentre	Economic impact of RM in ICD pts	RM reduced mean non-hospital costs per pt per year. RM did not significantly reduce the hospital costs per pt per year.	$P < .04$ $P = .46$ $P < .005$ $P < .05$
Kimmelstiel et al.	2004	Randomized	HF disease management	RM reduces the day hospitalization in HF management.	$P < .001$
Landolina et al.—*EVOLVO Economic aspect*	2012	Randomized prospective, multicentre	Economic impact of RM in ICD pts with HF	No significant annual cost savings for the healthcare system. Significant reduction of the annual cost for the pts and gained QALYs[a] in the RM arm.	$P = .8$ $P < .01$

(continued)

Table 1 (continued)

Authors	Year	Study type	Endpoints	Impact of RM	
				Findings	Stat value
Palozzi et al.	2014	Observational, prospective randomized	Cost analysis of direct costs of 1-year ICD follow-up based on RM compared with standard arms	RM significantly reduced: The time spent by hospital staff. The costs for the hospital and pt.	$P = .03$ $P = .01$ $P = .0001$
Raatikainen et al.	2008	Observational study	Assess whether RM offers a safe, practical, and cost-effective alternative to the in-office follow-up of pts with ICD	RM reduces costs compared with standard ICD follow-up (saving of 524 € per pt per year, 41 % of the cost of standard follow-up).	$P < .001$ $P < .001$
Tokohala et al.	2013	Randomized	Cost effectiveness of RM in HF pts	RM has the highest percentage of cost-effectiveness in the post-discharge period of HF pts in comparison with all the alternatives.	*73 % with £20,000/ QALY*

Source: Own elaboration (2016)
[a]The Quality Adjusted Life Year is a measure of disease burden; it includes both the quantity and the quality of life lived. One QALY is equal to 1 year lived in good health

both of their health condition and the severity of symptoms), and therefore more empowered (since they have to measure their vital signs themselves); this makes the patient a crucial factor in exploiting the potential of telemedicine for the prediction of their clinical condition.

Regarding this type of patient, it is important to focus on the RM of "co-production" literature related to their improvement in terms of increasing life expectancy and reducing the need for hospitalization (both the length of stay in hospital and the rate within 12 months), and related to patients' quality of life.

Most studies are concerned with home telemonitoring of HF patients' hospital readmission rates, ER visits and length of stay, or both. We highlight the findings of randomized controlled trials (RCTs) and non-randomized studies that are summarized in Table 2.

Also in these studies a cost saving was reported due to the disease e-Health management programme; in particular these savings were realized through

Table 2 Studies about RM on non-implanted patients

Authors	Year	Study type	Study size	Study design	Endpoints	Impact of RM	
						Findings	Statistical value
Benatar et al.	2003	RCT 1:1	216 HF pts	Assessment: home nurse visits vs. nurse tele-management method	Quality of life and hospital readmission	The study observed a trend towards greater improvement in quality of life in the nurse tele-management group compared with the control group. Patients in the intervention group had fewer hospital readmissions for HF, and shorter lengths of stay in hospital	$P < .01$ $P < .01$ $P < .0001$
Cleland et al.	2005	RCT 2:2:1	271 HF pts high risk of hospitalization or death	Assessment: tele-monitoring vs. nurse telephone support vs. usual care	Hospital readmission	Length of stay was 6 days less for the group with home tele-monitoring compared with the alternative. Higher mortality was observed among the pts assigned to receive usual care than among the pts assigned to receive nurse telephone services or home tele-monitoring	$P = 0.3$
Dansky et al.	2008	No RCT. 2 interv. groups ($G1 = 112$, $G2 = 127$) vs. control group (47)	284 in 10 home care agencies in the US state	Effect of tele-monitoring management of HF pts	Control of the symptoms associated with HF and mortality	G1 & G2 pts have fewer hospitalizations at 60 and 120 days [1]; 30 % of the control group had had an ER visit, compared with 24 % of G1 and 18 % of G2[2]; Mortality rate was similar between the control group G1 and G2[3]; the reduction in symptoms was more pronounced in the G1 pts, but associated with medication[1]	[1]$P = .001$ [2]$P = .01$ [3]$P = .11$ [3]$P = .47$

Del Sindaco et al.	2007	RCT	173	Assessment: combined hospital and home-based care	Verify the effectiveness of standard detailed educational programme received by pts at discharge with information on self-monitoring of BP, symptoms, weight	Incremental cost of tele-management: −$578 vs. interv. group. Total number of HF and all-cause hospital (re)admission and length of hospital stay significantly lower and shorter in interv. group	–
Esposito et al.	2008	RCT	32.930	Assessment: programme that provides primary care physician and/or cardiologist	Verify the usefulness of teaching to pts self-management skills by instructing and encouraging them to monitor their health	Incremental cost of tele-management: mean medicare expenditures −$121 significant in interv. group. No significant differences between groups in proportion of pts with hospital admission. Proportion of pts with ER visit significantly lower in interv. group	–

Source: Own elaboration (2016)

significant reduction in hospital readmissions and ER visits. Accordingly, Hebert et al. (2008) show that the costs of the disease management programme are offset by significantly less hospital costs.

The following research deserves to be highlighted and understood very well, because it is particularly suitable for the aim of our empirical research. Black et al. (2014), in the multi-centre randomized "BEAT-HF" study, conducted in California on 1437 HF patients, compared the clinical outcome of those patients that had received both intensive post-discharge education on telephone coaching and instruction on the telemonitoring equipment, with patients of a control group, monitored just by in-office visits. Patients enrolled in the intervention telemonitoring group were equipped with a transmitter, a weight scale, a blood pressure indicator and a heart rate monitor. BEAT-HF study investigators did not observe any significant effect provided by the telemonitoring on the 30 and 180 day readmission rate, or on mortality. However, patients with better adherence to monitoring (>50 % of days monitored) had a significantly lower rate of hospital readmission at 180 days ($P < 0.0001$). And mortality at 180 days was significantly lower among HF patients who completed more telephone calls with the nurses (>50 % of calls completed) and monitored their risk factors and symptoms more diligently.

This study confirms that the patient's adherence to the tele-management protocol is the determiner of success or failure of that kind of intervention. Accordingly, the study proposed in the following section aims at highlighting how it is possible to improve a patient's compliance through an improved process.

4 Telemedicine and Co-production for Non-implanted Patients: An Empirical Pilot Case Study

The results of the above mentioned literature review are coherent with NHS objectives, to decrease the cost of chronicity management as well as improve the assistance level and patients' health status. By increasing the active participation level as well as compliance with and adherence to participation on their treatment pathway provided by tele-management, patients enhance their health status, and lower their mortality and readmission rate.

However, despite much evidence on remote and tele-management of HF patients, to the best of our knowledge there is missing of empirical evidences about analysis of the follow-up pathway through a managerial perspective, oriented to the healthcare delivery process; none of the literature considers the patient as an important input of the HF healthcare process. A "co-producer" is a useful "resource" for the healthcare service sustainability, and that deserves to be the core of a framework in chronicity management based on the co-production framework (Fig. 3).

It is good that the active participation of patients means having an important support for the early recognition of HF and cardiac & arrhythmia symptoms. Such co-production can be implemented by compliance with the guidelines by patients. Given that, it is extremely important to locate those patients (based on their own

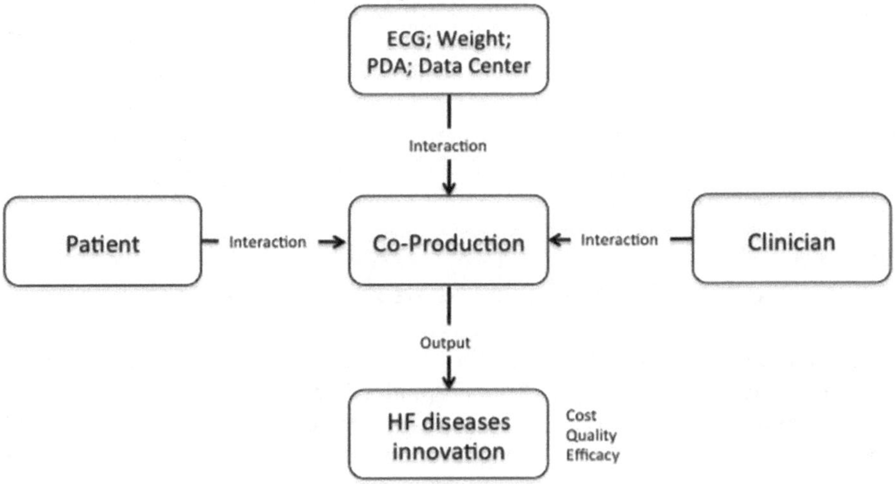

Fig. 3 Co-production for non-implanted patients. Source: Own elaboration (2016)

personal and clinical features) able to collaborate in the HF tele-management pathway; but it is just as important to implement a "co-production system" that should be easy and appropriate for the "co-production individuals".

4.1 The Overview of the Pilot Case Study Design

The Policlinico Casilino hospital in Rome has designed a new post-discharge process for HF non-implanted patients' follow-up (included in the broad "HF Project: Optimal therapy pathway" that was licensed in December 2013 by the Lazio Region Health System and began in September 2014) in which the combination of "co-production" and "e-Health" brings better chronicity management and a net cost saving in term of waste of resources.

The aim of the project is the introduction of a healthcare delivery process finalized to improve the patient's quality of life and consequently to lower the costs of the NHS. In order to describe and understand this process innovation, we adopted the case study method, a useful technique for "empirical inquiry that investigates a contemporary phenomenon within its real-life context especially when the boundaries between phenomenon and context are not clearly evident" (Yin 2014, p. 16). In order to reach information-rich key informants and critical cases we used the snowballing technique (Patton 2002), by interviewing well-situated and competent people composed of the staff of the Cardiology Department of the Policlinico Casilino. Moreover, in order to increase our understanding related to the HF process and understand the operational flowcharts, we also collected a huge quantity of information through empirical observation and internal documents as well as technical report analyses. By using Patton's (2002) sampling categories the pilot project analysed can be considered as Extreme Case Sampling: "this is information rich case because it is unusual or special in some way" (Patton 2002, p. 231). Our intention is to describe if results obtained, drawn from a sample of 50 patients (such a sample has been selected between the NYHA categories B and C), can be considered effective and, therefore, useful as a reference for this type of service. In the following section we explain our findings by analysing the AS IS and TO BE versions of the process.

4.2 The "AS IS" Pathway for Heart Failure Patients

Regarding the problems mentioned above in Sect. 2, nowadays a patient with an acute HF, after being discharged from hospital, begins an irregular pathway inside their geographic district; during the post-discharge period, the HF patient's health condition will tend to worsen. With the exception of the periodic in-office visits, without any other contact with a responsible physician of a defined organization, this patient will be destined to return to hospital again due to HF prognosis, accessing through the ER. His expectation is another long hospitalization.

This can be a general problem for the Italian NHS, especially in the case of resistance by health organizations to innovate in managing the chronicity problems, which triggers the low economic sustainability of HF management.

Without any certain and reliable information exchange between patients and the HF department responsible, it is impossible to predict a patient's health changes; if a patient feels ill, s/he can only contact a trusted doctor or a trusted clinic or can go to a First Aid centre However, very often, when a patient experiences symptoms it is too late to prevent the new hospitalization. Furthermore, given that patients go to the hospital due to shortness of breath or renal failure, very often they are hospitalized into an inappropriate department, such as Nephrology or Internal Medicine (Fig. 4).

4.3 Heart Failure Patients: A New Healthcare Service

Compared to the AS IS model of non-implanted HF patients' management (Fig. 4), the Policlinico Casilino, (an Italian public access hospital in which, under the direction of Prof. Leonardo Calò, the Cardiology Department has provided telecardiology services since 2007; this hospital in Italy assumes a considerable importance in the arrhythmia field both for the number of researches implemented by its members and for the number of patients treated) is developing an innovative project for the management of both the clinical information and then the operational processes owned by its staff. It was from the Implantable Cardioverter Defibrillator field that the telemedicine expertise of Policlinico Casilino arose (it is the top hospital in the Lazio Region for the number of Cardioverter Defibrillator implants; this means that more than 1 % of implants in Italy are provided there); its management decided that the implanting cardiologist must also perform follow-ups of

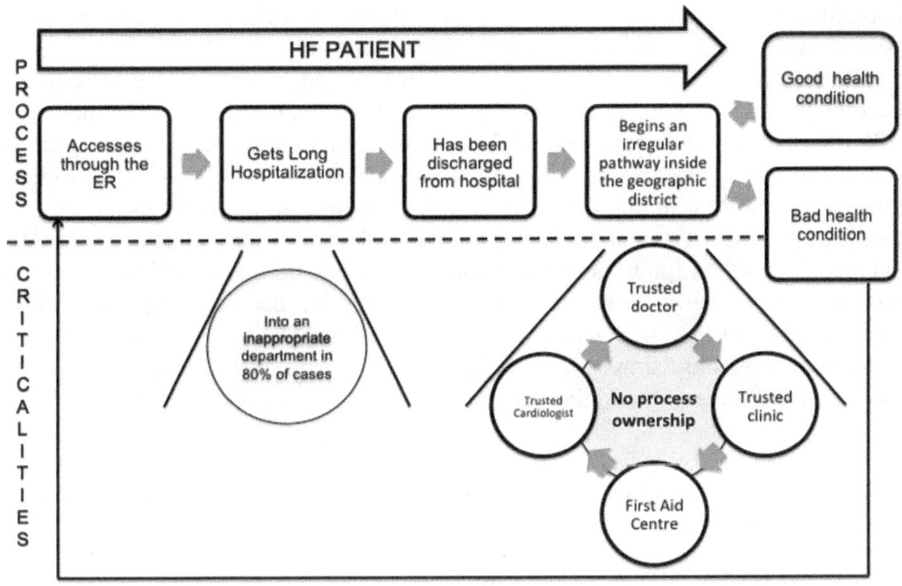

Fig. 4 Non-implanted patients: the AS IS process. Source: Own elaboration (2016)

implanted patients. A model was devised in which specialist technicians and physicians who dedicated every day to patients with an implantable device, were involved both in-office visits and in RM activities.

A specific training was designed for technicians, nurses (technical, clinical) and electrophysiology cardiologists (with clinical competences in HF) for the RM management that involves a different modality of work for HF patients. In the last 10 years this hospital has invested a lot of resources both in human capital and equipment (these efforts were introduced in 2015 in the Telemedicine HUB "*eHealth Center*", through which more than 1100 patients are actually monitored) to change the management of some arrhythmias and cardiac pathologies, in order to decrease the workload borne by staff and the whole organization in treating some kinds of diseases that need to be continually monitored.

In recent years, Policlinico Casilino has obtained important results but they deserve to be assessed by an "ongoing" follow-up. For these reasons, the challenge in which the Hospital is actually involved is to apply the remote management approach of HF patients' post-discharge period to a group of non-implanted HF patients. This is aimed at jointly demonstrating a reduction in relapse of pathology, a reduction in hospital bed occupancy and a reduction in the re-hospitalization rate, with a general reduction of cost for healthcare delivery; certainly these outcomes would bring improvement to a patient's quality of life.

As seen from the literature, the success of a tele-management approach in HF follow-up depends on the degree of patient participation. Thus, it is necessary to make the use of RM equipment managed by patients easy; in order to increase compliance with a patient's "self follow-up", the diagnostic sensors employed must be few, simple and as automated as possible.

The Cardiology Department of Policlinico Casilino, after many years' experience on cardiac markers and patterns (Calò et al. 2016), has developed a model of follow-up for the early detection of HF symptoms built on the knowledge of just a few data typologies from patients. As shown by Chaudhry et al. (2007), weight change and fluid accumulation (body impedance) in addition to the usual electrocardiogram (ECG) stream, are extraordinary indicators that forecast acute HF symptoms and then future hospitalizations. Making available just a few sensors in patients' arms means giving them the appropriate and necessary equipment that they are able to use efficiently. In the vision of the Cardiology Department of Policlinico Casilino "simple is better", in particular because a simple follow-up model means achieving a higher adherence and participation from patients.

4.4 The Implementation of the Service Innovation: The "TO BE" Model Process

Our target aims at empirically describing and analysing how Policlinico Casilino has redesigned the management of chronic disease. To do that, this study (that is a prospective, randomized, parallel group, controlled trial that will be divided into these different phases: 1-screening, 2-enrolment, 3-randomization, 4-follow-up period) considers a typology of patients that use RM equipment to participate in their follow-up. Regarding issues such as data collection, analysis and reporting, the hospital received approval from the hospital Ethics Committee and every patient has given a written informed consent. All subjects meeting the inclusion and none of the exclusion criteria are enrolled. During the enrolment, baseline data are collected in paper Case Report Forms (data include demographics, medical history, estimation of New York Heart Association (NYHA) functional class, vital signs, left ventricular ejection fraction, drug therapy, quality of life (QoL) assessment with Minnesota Living With Heart Failure Questionnaire (MLWHFQ) (Rector et al. 1987), and depression assessment with Patient Health Questionnaire (PHQ-9) (Kroenke et al. 2001)).

Subjects assigned to the RM population receive a telemedical system for ECG, and weight measurements in addition to in-person clinical visits every 3 months.

The telemedical system is based on a wireless Bluetooth system with a personal digital assistant (PDA) connected to a mobile network transmitter. Just two measuring devices are integrated into the system, one to collect electrocardiogram (ECG) measurements, and one to collect body weight with impedance indicator. Each device is equipped with a Bluetooth chip and connected to the PDA. Patients were instructed to submit daily measurements (automatic transmissions) body weight, and ECG by using the PDA. The PDA uses the mobile phone network to transmit all data in an encrypted manner to a central server where the measurements are organized and sent to the local server where the information is decrypted and uploaded in a secure website, which can be accessed by the trained health personnel dedicated to RM. Each patient is assigned to one reference nurse and a physician. The hospital organization RM model complied with the "nurse-filtered" model in which a trained technician or a nurse is responsible for patient training, remote controls, and phone contacts, for administrative activities and document filing or archiving. Dedicated RM personnel have access to the device information by logging onto a password-protected and encrypted specific website and they submit RM reports to a responsible physician in case of uncertain data interpretation or if suspected clinical data were received.

The responsible physician is then asked to make the appropriate decision, based on the interpretation of the submitted report: unscheduled follow-up visit, phone contact, wait and see, etc. A member of the telemedical staff contacts the patient or the patient's care-giver or caring physician to inform them about any events, interventions, important findings from the measurement transmissions and to communicate the necessity for changes to the patient's therapy or unscheduled follow-up visits or emergency medical services contact. The telemedical centre supports the patient's caring physician but overall responsibility for the patient's care remains with the caring physician. In such situations and in the case of symptoms, patients are also able to initiate additional transmissions of ECG stream and blood pressure measurements (manual transmissions) via the previous telephone contact of the dedicated RM personnel. In the follow-up period a programmed telephone contact between the telemedical centre and the patient will be made once a month to discuss disease status, assess any symptoms of depression, instruct the patient about dealing with emergency situations, and to solve any technical problems.

4.5 The Operative Flow Chart of the "Policlinico Casilino" eHealth Center

With an RM of ECG stream and body weight with impedance indication, it is possible to predict with high precision a patient's health status, i.e. if it is stable, or deteriorating. Before a patient's health condition worsens, a predictive model, based on patients' collaboration and the available technology, allows the medical staff to provide a doctor and nurse TRIAGE aimed at an early understanding of those patients with cardiac problems that need to be managed immediately.

This follow-up method involves two main drivers: the patient (or his/her care-giver) who effectively provides the health self-measurements and the e-Health Center that daily checks and monitors those patients enrolled in this experiment.

Resulting from our observation, "just in time" information received by the telemedicine hub allows the needy patient to be promptly managed; his/her problem can be immediately addressed by a mere telephone contact to the more appropriate clinical practice: a change in the drug therapy, an urgent in-office visit, an organized hospitalization without ER transit (Fig. 5).

According to the several interviews with the responsible members of the Cardiology Department, the HF patients' service innovation is going to produce the following:

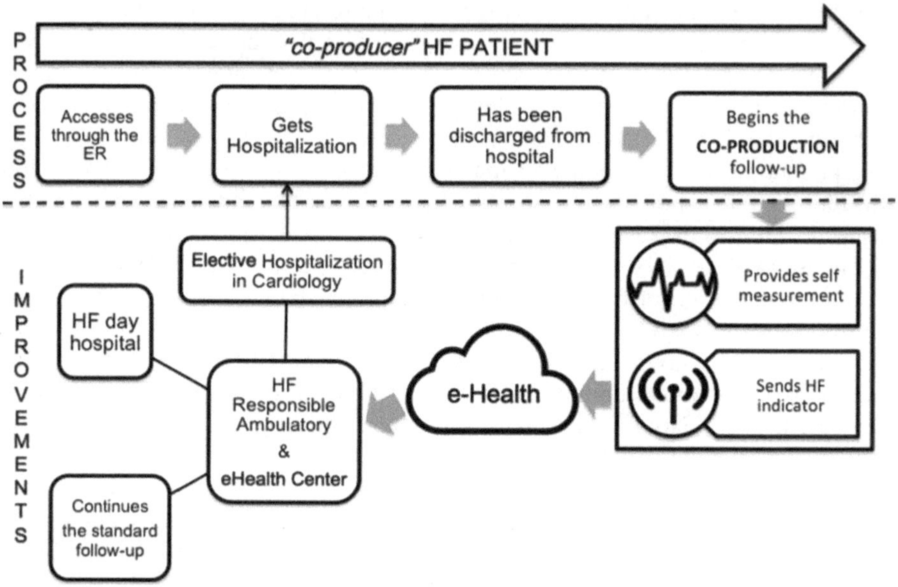

Fig. 5 Remote management of non-implanted HF patients: pilot project from Policlinico Casilino. Source: Own elaboration (2016)

- lower bed occupancy of about 30 %;
- lower rate of hospital readmission of 20 %.

An HF patient includable in this trial should not have any of the following exclusion criteria:

- Inability to provide informed consent;
- Insufficient compliance with telemonitoring or study visits;
- Impairment to use the telemonitoring equipment or appear at study visits (e.g. dementia, impaired self-determination, lacking ability to communicate);
- Age < 18 years;
- State of pregnancy or lactation;
- Unstable angina or recent (<2 months) myocardial infarction;
- Implanted cardiac assist system;
- Patients who are scheduled for or have undergone cardiac surgery in the last 90 days and those who are listed for heart transplantation;
- Planned cardiac revascularization or ICD and/or cardiac resynchronization therapy (CRT) device implantation;
- A life expectancy of <1 year;
- Use of inotropic drug therapy;
- Complex and uncorrected congenital heart disease.

4.6 The Duties of the "Co-producer" Patients

In this innovative project the non-implanted patient co-produces his/her healthcare by the self-monitoring of some vital signs. As already stated, the Cardiology Department of Policlinico Casilino decided to base the remote management model of HF patients on just two pieces of clinical information: the ECG stream and the body weight with fluid accumulation (body impedance).

For the self-measurement of these data, each patient enrolled on the trial needs three devices:

- a portable electrocardiograph with Bluetooth connection;
- a weight scale with Bluetooth connection;
- a transmitter with a mobile connection and a calling card included.

According to his follow-up protocol, with a fixed frequency (daily, weekly, monthly), each patient provides the self-measurement of the two clinical data mentioned above.

First of all the patient has to switch on the transmitter, waits for the flashing light on the device and then starts with the measurement in the following way:

1) ECG stream:
   patient switches on the portable electrocardiograph;
   in a standing position, the patient holds the device with the palms of both hands for about 30 s (the palms should be exactly on the metal plates on both sides of the device);
   device records the patient's ECG stream;
   patient, by watching the device screen, checks if his/her ECG stream has been measured correctly and then pushes the "send" key;
   now the data have been obtained by the transmitter.

2) body weight with fluid accumulation:
   patient has to be barefoot;
   in a standing position, patient gets on the weight scale for about 20 s (the soles should be exactly on the metal plates on the top of the device);
   device records the patient's weight and his/her body fluid accumulation;
   patient, by watching the device screen, checks if his weight and his body fluid accumulation have been measured correctly and then waits just few seconds for the automatic data transmission;
   now the data have been obtained by the transmitter.

Finally, the patient has just to wait for the acoustic signal from the transmitter which indicates that his/her data are sent to the telemedicine web-based platform, and are available for the eHealth Center personnel.

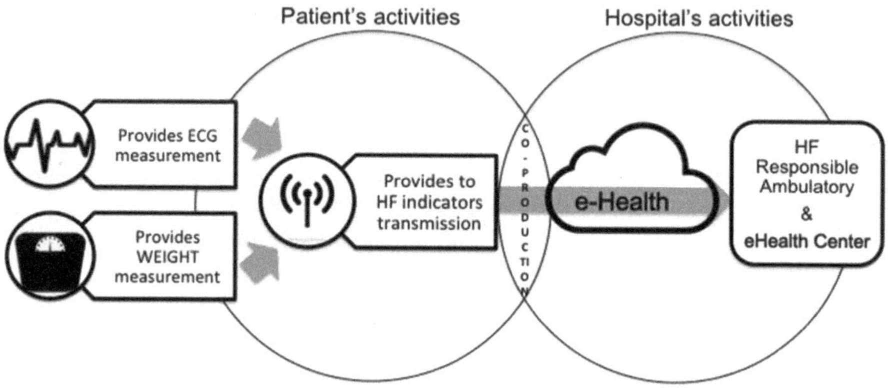

Fig. 6 The co-production steps of data processing. Source: Own elaboration (2016)

At home, by using this kind of simple transmitter, the patient can automatically send data to the eHealth Center from the devices used, with little effort and without changing his routine.

Hence, doctors have easy access to the biometric data measured by the patients and are also informed automatically by customized alarms if a scheduled transmission is missing. Figure 6 shows the steps described above.

4.7 Specific Duties of the Technicians and Doctors

As noticed by empirical observation and internal document analysis, when the clinical data provided by the patient arrive at the eHealth Center, there is an immediate check and triage service provided by the cardiology staff (technician and physician) by proceeding in accordance with the scheme included in Fig. 7.

The operational protocol implemented aims at giving priority to the transmission containing an arrhythmia event, or some other unhealthy signal that needs to be analysed immediately. There is a "semaphore light" priority code that requires a specific behaviour from the hospital staff involved in the HF management. This is the priority code:

- Green light: a transmission devoid of events and therefore requiring no intervention;
- Yellow light: a transmission with events requiring attention from the technician;
- Red light: in addition to the attention from the technician, the doctor is asked to intervene.

Now we can look at the duties for technicians and doctor.

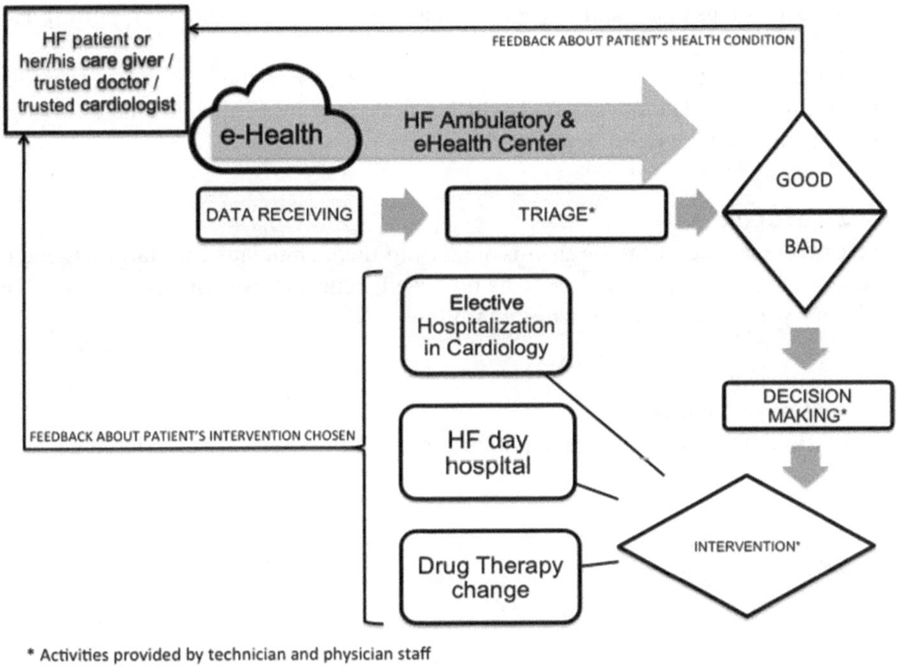

Fig. 7 An overview of the data "life-cycle". Source: Own elaboration (2016)

4.7.1 Technician

On a daily basis, the technician opens the RM system websites. Priority is given to urgent alarm-triggered transmissions or those with events.

If the transmission contains relevant events, the technician:

- Prints the event;
- Prints the most recent patient visit;
- Calls up the patient's pharmacological therapy, retrieving it from the software Cardio Management;

Opens an "Event Generated Data Sheet" in Cardio Management Software: gives event description, comments on the action taken (telephone contact with the patient, modifications to the therapy by phone, move up to office visit, false alarm; these operations are completed after contact is made with the doctor and only after the doctor has reviewed the data transmitted).

If the transmission does not contain relevant events, the technician opens a "Data Sheet" on Cardio Management Software and inserts only the data made available.

All of the patients whose transmissions were reviewed are entered onto a hardcopy log that is stamped on each page. The log functions as a report of the reviews that were carried out and is forwarded to management.

The technicians also handle telephone calls from patients who are reporting HF to the clinic.

Should any action items be left undone at the end of the day, the technician records this in the "Handover Log", which will be read by a colleague the following day when the tasks will be completed.

4.7.2 Doctor

Doctor receives the printed transmissions from the technicians for alarm-triggered cases or those that contain events to be reviewed; hence, physicians' activities in HF RM management are mainly with regard to:

- Transmission review
- Event determination
- Decision regarding calling the patient (to modify the therapy by telephone or to move up the office visit).

The technician records the doctor's actions on the "Event Generated Data Sheet".

5 Conclusion

This contribution has analysed a new approach to HF patient follow-up management drawn from the experience of the Italian hospital Policlinico Casilino. In this healthcare service innovation we have described and analysed a new HF service inspired by evidence observed in empirical as well as theoretical bases, regarding the employment of the crucial drivers, "e-Health" and "co-production", in healthcare delivery for HF disease.

The "in progress follow-up" of HF patients has shown the following findings:

- lower bed occupancy—early discharge from hospital;
- lower rate of hospital readmission;
- better quality patient experience.

This means a potential cost saving (economic as well as social) for the entire health system. It also means an improvement of quality of life for patients, as well as an improvement in the organization and management of staff workloads.

These findings can be considered very interesting, particularly if compared with the clinical outcome (the healthcare organization Policlinico Casilino has attested the comparability of the clinical outcome obtained by telemedicine to the standard care, inasmuch as the telemedicine follow-up protocol is consistent with international guidelines).

The pilot case shows how it is possible to reach some improvements in chronicity management. In fact, by changing the traditional paradigm into a new co-production scenario, the patient becomes a pro-active actor in his/her health treatment, by participating with the entire hospital staff.

In HF management in particular, the joint use of telemedicine infrastructures and patients' collaboration can be considered as a new frontier able to supply high health levels with expenditure containment. This change, both cultural and technical oriented, involves a radical transformation for hospitals, both in terms of enabling HF "co-producer" patients, and in terms of capabilities of staff to manage telemedicine equipment and infrastructure.

It is arguable, as advocated by many Authors, that telemedicine can be considered a good investment for the NHS as the cost savings it achieves can be recovered in a short time. RM, thus, can be seen as an instrument, when added to the usual cures to patients, that is able to improve the quality of life of patients affected by a chronic-degenerative disease such as HF. From the findings of the pilot case, we can assert that all patients were satisfied to be remotely monitored, because they felt themselves to be safer and were therefore more relaxed. Moreover, besides this strength, we also highlight some limitations related to such an innovation; the first is regards the cultural issues related to a new role that patients would play. It requires a change (moving from passive to active) that is not always easy for those patients who have traditional expectations in terms of healthcare services to accept. This aspect is related to professional staff as well. Furthermore, the pilot case study highlights that besides a cultural aspect there is a technological one that would involve a huge investment. This aspect also requires an investment in terms of new competences that may trigger a resistance to change process.

Despite the pilot project's findings not being generalizable, due to the sample size and the characteristics of the case study (i.e. a pilot study), we can conclude that it may be considered as a successful pilot experience that deserves to be implemented also in others health organizations.

References

Benatar, D., Bondmass, M., Ghitelman, J., & Avitall, B. (2003). Outcomes of chronic heart failure. *Archives of Internal Medicine, 163*(3), 347–352.

Black, J. T., Romano, P. S., Sadeghi, B., Auerbach, A. D., Ganiats, T. G., Greenfield, S., et al. (2014). A remote monitoring and telephone nurse coaching intervention to reduce readmissions among patients with heart failure: Study protocol for the Better Effectiveness After Transition-Heart Failure (BEAT-HF) randomized controlled trial. *Trials, 15*(1), 124.

Bogers, M., & West, J. (2012). Managing distributed innovation: Strategic utilization of open and user innovation. *Creativity and Innovation Management, 21*(1), 61–75.

Burri, H., Heidbüchel, H., Jung, W., & Brugada, P. (2011). Remote monitoring: A cost or an investment? *Europeace, 13*(2), 44–48.

Cahn, E. (2000). *No more throw away people: The co-production imperative*. Washington, DC: Essential Books.

Calò, L., Gargaro, A., De Ruvo, E., Palozzi, G., Sciarra, L., Rebecchi, M., et al. (2013). Economic impact of remote monitoring on ordinary follow-up of implantable cardioverter defibrillators as compared with conventional in-hospital visits. A single-center prospective and randomized study. *Journal of Interventional Cardiac Electrophysiology, 37*(1), 69–78.

Calò, L., Giustetto, C., Martino, A., Sciarra, L., Cerrato, N., Marziali, M., et al. (2016). A new electrocardiographic marker of sudden death in Brugada syndrome: The S-wave in lead I. *Journal of the American College of Cardiology, 67*(12), 1427–1440.

Cepiku, D., & Giordano, F. (2014). Co-production in developing countries. Insights from the Community Health Workers experiences. *Public Management Review, 16*(3), 317–340.

Chaudhry, S. I., Wang, Y., Concato, J., Gill, T. M., & Krumholz, H. M. (2007). Patterns of weight change preceding hospitalization for heart failure. *Circulation, 116*(14), 1549–1554.

Chesbrough, H. W. (2006). *Open innovation: The new imperative for creating and profiting from technology*. Boston: Harvard Business School Press.

Cleland, J. G., Louis, A. A., Rigby, A. S., Janssens, U., & Balk, A. H. (2005). Noninvasive home telemonitoring for patients with heart failure at high risk of recurrent admission and death: The Trans-European Network-Home-Care Management System (TEN-HMS) study. *Journal of the American College of Cardiology, 45*(10), 1654–1664.

Cleland, J. G., Swedberg, K., Follath, F., Komajda, M., Cohen-Solal, A., Aguilar, J. C., et al. (2003). The EuroHeart Failure survey programme—a survey on the quality of care among patients with heart failure in Europe. *European Heart Journal, 24*(5), 442–463.

Conraads, V. M., Tavazzi, L., Santini, M., Oliva, F., Gerritse, B., Yu, C. M., et al. (2011). Sensitivity and positive predictive value of implantable intrathoracic impedance monitoring as a predictor of heart failure hospitalizations: The SENSE-HF trial. *European Heart Journal, 32*, 2266–2273.

Dansky, K. H., Vasey, J., & Bowles, K. (2008). Impact of telehealth on clinical outcomes in patients with heart failure. *Clinical Nursing Research, 17*(3), 182–199.

Del Sindaco, D., Pulignano, G., Minardi, G., Apostoli, A., Guerrieri, L., Rotoloni, M., et al. (2007). Two-year outcome of a prospective, controlled study of a disease management programme for elderly patients with heart failure. *Journal of Cardiovascular Medicine, 8*(5), 324–329.

Dharmarajan, K., Hsieh, A. F., Lin, Z., Bueno, H., Ross, J. S., Horwitz, L. I., et al. (2013). Diagnoses and timing of 30-day readmissions after hospitalization for heart failure, acute myocardial infarction, or pneumonia. *JAMA, 309*(4), 355–363.

Di Lenarda, A., Tarantini, L., Cherubini, A., Pirozzi, F., Santangelo, S., Bobbo, M., et al. (2010). La prevenzione dello scompenso cardiaco. *Giornale Italiano di Cardiologia, 11*(5 Suppl 3), 81–86.

Epstein, A. E., Di Marco, J. P., Ellenbogen, K. A., Estes, N. M., Freedman, R. A., Gettes, L. S., et al. (2013). ACCF/AHA/HRS focused update incorporated into the ACCF/AHA/HRS 2008 guidelines for device-based therapy of cardiac rhythm abnormalities. A report of the American College of Cardiology Foundation/American Heart Association Task Force on practice guidelines and the Heart Rhythm Society. *Circulation, 127*(3), 283–352.

Esposito, D., Brown, R., Chen, A., Schore, J., & Shapiro, R. (2008). Impacts of a disease management program for dually eligible beneficiaries. *Health Care Financing Review, 30* (1), 27.

Fabbri, G., Ambrosio, G., Cafiero, M., Caputo, F., Lavecchia, R., & Loru, F. (2002). In-hospital outcomes of patients with heart failure by ward of admission: The TEMISTOCLE registry. *European Journal of Heart Failure Supplements, 1*, 56–57.

Fauchier, L., Sadoul, N., Kouakam, C., Briand, F., Chauvin, M., Babuty, D., et al. (2005). Potential cost savings by telemedicine-assisted long-term care of implantable cardioverter defibrillator. *Pacing and Clinical Electrophysiology, 28*(1), 225–229.

Guédon-Moreau, L., Lacroix, D., Sadoul, N., Clémenty, J., Kouakam, C., Hermida, J. S., et al. (2012). A randomized study of remote follow-up of implantable cardioverter defibrillators: Safety and efficacy report of the ECOST trial. *European Heart Journal, 34*, 605–614.

Hasan, A., & Paul, V. (2011). Telemonitoring in chronic heart failure. *European Heart Journal, 5* (32), 1457–1464.

Hebert, P. L., Sisk, J. E., Wang, J. J., Tuzzio, L., Casabianca, J. M., Chassin, M. R., et al. (2008). Cost-effectiveness of nurse-led disease management for heart failure in an ethnically diverse urban community. *Annals of Internal Medicine, 149*(8), 540–548.

Hindricks, G., Taborsky, M., Glikson, M., Heinrich, U., Schumacher, B., Katz, A., et al. (2014). Implant-based multiparameter telemonitoring of patients with heart failure (IN-TIME): A randomised controlled trial. *The Lancet, 384*(9943), 583–590.

Italian Board of Health. (2011). *Rapporto annuale sull'attività di ricovero ospedaliero - Dati SDO 2010*. Accessed April 30, 2016, from http://www.salute.gov.it/portale/temi/p2_6.jsp?lingua=italiano&id=3696&area=ricoveriOspedalieri&menu=vuoto

Italian Board of Health. (2013). *Scompenso cardiaco*. Accessed April 30, 2016, from http://www.salute.gov.it/portale/salute/p1_5.jsp?id=43&area=Malattie_cardiovascolari

Italian Board of Health. (2014a). *Patto per la salute 2014–16*. Accessed April 30, 2016, from http://www.salute.gov.it/portale/news/p3_2_1_1_1.jsp?lingua=italiano&menu=notizie&p=dalministero&id=1722

Italian Board of Health. (2014b). *Telemedicina – Linee di indirizzo nazionali*. Accessed April 30, 2016, from http://www.salute.gov.it/imgs/c_17_pubblicazioni_2129_allegato.pdf

Italian Board of Health. (2015). *Rapporto annuale sull'attività di ricovero ospedaliero - Dati SDO 2014*. Accessed April 30, 2016, from http://www.salute.gov.it/portale/temi/p2_6.jsp?lingua=italiano&id=4423&area=ricoveriOspedalieri&menu=vuoto

Kimmelstiel, C., Levine, D., Perry, K., Patel, A. R., Sadaniantz, A., Gorham, N., et al. (2004). Randomized, controlled evaluation of short – and long – term benefits of heart failure disease management within a diverse provider network. *Circulation, 110*(11), 1450–1455.

Kitsiou, S., Paré, G., & Jaana, M. (2015). Effects of home telemonitoring interventions on patients with chronic heart failure: An overview of systematic reviews. *Journal of Medical Internet Research, 17*(3), 63.

Kotb, A., Cameron, C., Hsieh, S., & Wells, G. (2015). Comparative effectiveness of different forms of telemedicine for individuals with heart failure (HF): A systematic review and network meta-analysis. *PLoS One, 10*(2), e0118681.

Kroenke, K., Spitzer, R. L., & Williams, J. B. (2001). The Phq-9. *Journal of General Internal Medicine, 16*(9), 606–613.

Landolina, M., Perego, G. B., Lunati, M., Curnis, A., Guenzati, G., Vicentini, A., et al. (2012). Remote monitoring reduces healthcare use and improves quality of care in heart failure patients with implantable defibrillators. The evolution of management strategies of heart failure patients with implantable defibrillators (EVOLVO) study. *Circulation, 125*(24), 2985–2992.

Lee, W. C., Chavez, Y. E., Baker, T., & Luce, B. R. (2004). Economic burden of heart failure: A summary of recent literature. *Heart & Lung: The Journal of Acute and Critical Care, 33*(6), 362–371.

Maggioni, A. P., Dahlström, U., Filippatos, G., Chioncel, O., Leiro, M. C., Drozdz, J., et al. (2010). EURObservational Research Programme: The Heart Failure Pilot Survey (ESC HF Pilot). *European Journal of Heart Failure, 12*(10), 1076–1084.

McMurray, J. J., Petrie, M. C., Murdoch, D. R., & Davie, A. P. (1998). Clinical epidemiology of heart failure: Public and private health burden. *European Heart Journal, 19*, 9–16.

Mureddu, G. F., Agabiti, N., Rizzello, V., Forastiere, F., Latini, R., Cesaroni, G., et al. (2012). Prevalence of preclinical and clinical heart failure in the elderly. A population based study in Central Italy. *European Journal of Heart Failure, 14*(7), 718–729.

Osborne, S. P., Radnor, Z., & Strokosch, K. (2016). Co-production and the co-creation of value in public services: A suitable case for treatment? *Public Management Review, 18*(5), 639–653.

Palozzi, G., Chirico, A., & Calò, L. (2014). Cost accounting del follow-up annuo per il controllo remoto dei defibrillatori impiantabili. *Mecosan, 90*, 71–98.

Patton, M. Q. (2002). *Qualitative evaluation and research methods*. Thousand Oaks, CA: SAGE.

Raatikainen, M. J. P., Usimaa, P., van Ginneken, M. M., Janssen, J. P., & Linnaluoto, M. (2008). Remote monitoring of implantable cardioverter defibrillator patient: A safe, time-saving, and cost-effective means for follow-up. *Europace, 10*(10), 1145–1151.

Realpe, A., & Wallace, L. M. (2010). *What is co-production?* London: The Health Foundation. Accessed May 4, 2016, from http://www.webcitation.org/6a0y0Aclb

Rector, T. S., Francis, G. S., & Cohn, J. N. (1987). Patients' self-assessment of their congestive heart failure: Part 1: Patient perceived dysfunction and its poor correlation with maximal exercise tests. *Heart Failure, 3*, 192–196.

Rengo, F., Leosco, D., Iacovoni, A., Golino, L., Borgia, F., & Senni, M. (2004). Epidemiologia clinica e fattori di rischio per scompenso cardiaco nell'anziano. *Italian Heart Journal, 5*(10), 9–16.

Riley, J. P., & Cowie, M. R. (2009). Telemonitoring in heart failure. *Heart, 95*(23), 1964–1968.

Slotwiner, D., Varma, N., Akar, J. G., Annas, G., Beardsall, M., Fogel, R. I., et al. (2015). HRS Expert Consensus Statement on remote interrogation and monitoring for cardiovascular implantable electronic devices. *Heart Rhythm, 12*(7), 69.

Sousa, C., Leite, S., Lagido, R., Ferreira, L., Cardoso, S. J., & Maciel, M. J. (2014). Telemonitoring in heart failure: A state-of-the-art review. *Revista Portuguesa de Cardiologia (English Edition), 33*(4), 229–239.

Thokala, P., Baalbaki, H., Brennan, A., Pandor, A., Stevens, J. W., Gomersall, T., et al. (2013). Telemonitoring after discharge from hospital with heart failure: Cost-effectiveness modelling of alternative service designs. *BJM Open, 3*, e003250.

von Hippel, E. (2005). *Democratizing innovation*. Cambridge, MA: The MIT Press.

World Health Organization. (2013). *Global action plan for the prevention and control of noncommunicable diseases 2013–2020*. World Health Organization (WHO). Accessed May 4, 2016, from http://apps.who.int/iris/bitstream/10665/94384/1/9789241506236_eng.pdf

Yin, K. R. (2014). *Case study research: Design and methods* (Vth ed.). London: SAGE.

Gabriele Palozzi is a Research Fellow in Management at the University of Rome "Tor Vergata"—Italy, Department of Management and Law. His studies addressed the theme of Managerial Control and Performance Management as part of Health Technology Assessment. Particularly, they regard the economic impact of telemedicine in cardiac diseases management, as support and replacement of standard in-hospital cares. Currently, he is developing a research that involves more then 1000 patients, remotely monitored by the Hospital Policlinico Casilino of Rome, that actively participate to their own follow-ups.

Daniele Binci is a Research Fellow in Management at the University of Rome "Tor Vergata"—Italy, Department of Management and Law. He received his PhD in Management from the University of Rome "Tor Vergata". His main research interests include organizational change, with a focus on leadership, climate and business process management.

Andrea Appolloni is a Research Fellow in Management at the University of Rome "Tor Vergata"—Italy, Department of Management and Law. He is currently visiting fellow at Shanghai Jiao Tong University, China. His research interests mainly lie in the fields of purchasing, supply chain management and sustainability.

FSC
www.fsc.org
MIX
Papier | Fördert gute Waldnutzung
FSC® C083411

Kolibri 360 GmbH
Ferdinand-Jühlke-Straße 7
99095 Erfurt, Deutschland
produktsicherheit@kolibri360.de